Psychoanalysis

Psychoanalysis
Its Image and Its Public

Serge Moscovici

Translated by David Macey

Edited with an Introduction by Gerard Duveen

polity

First published in French as *La psychanalyse, son image et son public* by
Serge Moscovici © Presses Universitaires de France, Paris, 1961.

This English translation © Polity Press, 2008

Polity Press
65 Bridge Street
Cambridge CB2 1UR, UK

Polity Press
350 Main Street
Malden, MA 02148, USA

ISBN: 978-07456-3268-1
ISBN: 978-07456-3269-8 (pb)

A catalogue record for this book is available from the British Library.

Typeset in 10/11.5 Palatino
by Servis Filmsetting Ltd, Manchester
Printed and bound in Great Britain by MPG Books Ltd, Bodmin, Cornwall

Every effort has been made to trace all copyright holders, but if any have been
inadvertently overlooked, the publishers will be pleased to include any
necessary credits in any subsequent reprint or edition.

Ouvrage publié avec le concours du ministère français chargé de la Culture –
Centre national du livre.

Published with the assistance of the French Ministry of Culture – National
Centre for the Book.

For further information on Polity, visit our website: www.polity.co.uk

Contents

Contents

Figures and Tables

Figures

Tables

Introduction

Gerard Duveen

1

Why read a book translated into English thirty years after its publication in French,[1] and which deals with aspects of French culture and society of the 1950s? In one sense the answer should be obvious – it is a classic work of social psychology which has had a significant effect in shaping the field of the discipline, certainly in Europe and in Latin America, and even, to a lesser degree in the anglophone world. That it has not previously been available in English might be thought to be scandalous, but, as those English-speaking psychologists who tried over the years to promote a translation discovered, the scandal was more often seen in the content of the book itself. To be sure, Moscovici has published many other accounts in English of the central themes of his theory of social representations, but in the absence of his major concrete empirical study such accounts have tended to be programmatic or abstract so that only those English-speaking readers able and willing to engage with a substantial text in French have been able to appreciate the richness and subtlety of what I have called elsewhere Moscovici's 'social-psychological imagination' (Duveen 2000). No doubt part of the sense of scandal which has hung around the work has been a reflection of this strange state of affairs in which something fundamental is claimed for the discipline of social psychology yet in the absence of an English translation of this book such a proposition has been difficult to sustain. But this is only a minor aspect of the sense of scandal. After all, other non-English psychologists have found greater acceptance in the anglophone world. Vygotsky, for instance, came to prominence on the basis of a very limited collection of his texts in English translation (and,

---

[1] This is a translation of the 2nd edition of 1976, itself a substantial revision of the original edition of 1961 (see Serge Moscovici's *Preface*). Some errors from the French edition have been corrected by the author, who has also made a few revisions to the text.

one might add, these too might be described as sharing those same qualities of appearing more often programmatic or abstract than substantial).
But to echo one of the major themes in this study of the social representations of psychoanalysis, the reception of a theory is shaped by the interest
of the audience, so that a conclusion dominates a sustained critical engage-
ment. Vygotsky's work had the happy coincidence of appearing at a time
when developmental psychology was questioning the cognitive programme of Piaget and seeking in some way to integrate social processes
into accounts of intellectual development. Rightly or wrongly Vygotsky
was called in evidence for such a shift. The scandal surrounding
Moscovici's work reflects a different conjuncture in the field of social psychology, which has drifted away from the central concerns of his work –
the transformations of knowledge as it is communicated across different
groups and parts of society, and thus also an analysis of the processes of
thought itself – towards an ever more narrowly defined experimentalism,
or a diffuse and unfocused concern with discourse. Methodologically this
study demonstrates what a critical intelligence applied to the systematic
use of survey and content analysis can achieve in constructing a viable
social psychological theory. And if the analyses in both parts of the book
frequently examine the discourses through which psychoanalysis appears
as part of the everyday world, they also remind us that discursive elements only become meaningful when they are considered in relation to the
representations and the communicative contexts which sustain them.
Against both of these growing trends from the last decades Moscovici's
book stands as a reminder of the power of social psychology to engage in
sustained inquiry of significant social phenomena and thereby to take its
place within the social sciences by expanding our understanding of these
phenomena.

In fact even when it appeared in the original French edition, the book
presented some challenging themes for the social sciences. Central to the
work is its assertion of the importance of analysing social representations
as forms of knowledge in their own right, rather than as simply degraded
or inferior forms of scientific understanding (see Moscovici's conversation
with Ivana Marková for a broader discussion of this issue, in Moscovici
2000a). As the text makes clear, the contrast was often drawn between
what was held to be the rational and logical forms of scientific thought and
the irrational and unsystematic patterns of everyday or lay thinking, a contrast which was often presented as one between science and ideology. Yet,
without abandoning the claims of science for a systematic understanding
of our world, Moscovici also insists that everyday thinking not only results
in organized structures of thought, but that these structures are significant
in so far as they are the forms through which the everyday world is constructed as a reality. There are, of course, many threads of debate around
these issues. In the context of this book we might look back to Freud's contrast of primary process with secondary process and his demonstration of

the continuing influence of unconscious processes in our conscious experience. Or, from a different perspective, to Piaget's demonstration of the way in which a capacity for logical thinking emerges from the lived experience of daily life. Both of these contributions indicate that the distinction between scientific and everyday thinking in the construction of reality is more permeable than the sharp contrast of the scientific to the ideological allows. Moscovici's perspective is focused on the ways in which knowledge circulates through society, and the ways in which each social group reconstitutes knowledge according to its own interests and concerns. We can also see in this book the role which social processes – both in the sense of intergroup processes and also in the sense of communication – play in the construction of reality, and we should recall that the first edition of the book appeared some years before Berger and Luckmann's seminal contribution (1967).

If this theme can be taken as emphasizing the *social* aspect of social psychology, the second theme I want to highlight from the book here concerns the *psychological* aspect of the discipline. Indeed, one could say that social psychology has always found itself at something of a disadvantage in the field of the social sciences precisely because of its psychological heritage. As Moscovici (1993) himself has demonstrated, there was a hostility to the claims of the psychological in the classical social sciences which preferred to consider knowledge, and even consciousness, as a wholly social product. Across a broad spectrum of authors, from the Marxists through to Durkheim, Weber and Simmel, there was a consensus on the idea that a social science worthy of the name should be free of any influences from psychology, to the point that *psychologism* became a critical term used to discredit one's opponents in any debate. And yet, as Moscovici's analyses of the work of the classical sociologists (2000b) indicated, at the same time all of them drew on psychological themes to articulate their theories. Notwithstanding this 'return of the repressed', the social sciences at the time the book appeared continued to consider the psychological as a foreign element. Indeed, as some of the analyses in Part II of the book make clear, much of this discussion was focused on responses to the work of Freud and of psychoanalysis more generally.

2

For many English-speaking readers, Part II of the book will perhaps be more surprising. As Willem Doise (1993) remarked in his comments on the reception of the theory of social representations in the Anglo-Saxon world, it was notable how little attention had been paid to this part of the book in which the content analysis of the ways in which psychoanalysis was represented in the French press allowed Moscovici to formulate a set of original hypotheses about diffusion, propagation and propaganda as distinct communicative genres. In the hypothesis he develops in Chapter 16, Moscovici links these genres to the classical social-psychological concepts of opinion, attitude and stereotype respectively. But the interest in this part of the book extends even further, since the discussion of these different communicative genres also invites some reflection on the way in which the concept of group itself is conceptualized. In contemporary social psychology the notion of group has taken on a rather homogenous form, so that all groups are considered equal in their pattern of social-psychological functioning, differing only in the set of values, ideas or attitudes they espouse. Yet the identification of these different communicative genres, and the different patterns of social-psychological functioning associated with each of them, suggests that we need to expand our understanding of the character of the group to consider also the ways in which they may also be characterized by distinctive communicative processes. In short, we need to recognize that there is an intimate relation between the values and attitudes of a group and the characteristic patterns of communication which sustain it. To do so, of course, brings with it the implication that groups are more heterogenous forms of social-psychological organization than is envisaged in contemporary theorizing.

The analyses of communicative genres in Part II of the book also bring us back to another feature of Moscovici's social-psychological imagination, the relationship between representation and influence. It is tempting to consider diffusion, propagation and propaganda as also constituting different forms of social influence. Certainly, if, as I have suggested before, the shape and form of representations is structured by the balance of influence processes operating in the communicative practices of a group at a particular time (Duveen 2000), then it would seem appropriate to consider these communicative genres as forms of social influence. Yet a word of caution is also necessary before making the link directly to Moscovici's genetic model of social influence processes (1976). The communicative genres analysed in Part II of the book emerge from the content analysis of mass media, while the genetic model of social influence stems from an analysis of face-to-face communication within a controlled experimental paradigm. While we might expect to see some continuity in the form of social influence as we move from the interpersonal to mass-mediated communication, we should also be attentive to significant differences between these contexts. In the experimental studies individuals are engaged precisely in attempts to change the thoughts or behaviour of other individuals, whereas the influence exercised through the mass media is often less immediate or more indirect. In relation to the mass media people find themselves surrounded by a flowing current of influence which sustains their affiliation with a particular group and a particular way of seeing things rather more than finding themselves exposed to a direct challenge to their point of view. We choose which magazines or newspapers we read, or which television programmes we watch, and our choices are already an expression of our affiliation with a specific social group or section of society. In this sense the contexts which frame participation in these different communicative encounters need to be examined more closely if we are to articulate a theory of social influence which can extend from the interpersonal to mass-mediated forms of communication.

3

When this study was undertaken and first published France was still living through the immediate consequences of the Second World War. As in some other European countries, the political climate in the France of the 1950s was characterized by a sharp differentiation between a mainly Catholic right wing, and a left wing which embraced a strong and powerful Communist Party. The consequences of this division appear very evidently in the content analysis of the French press in Part II of the book. For the reader today, however, it comes as something of a shock to recognize or recall (depending on their age) how powerfully this context influenced the framing of social representations of psychoanalysis. The divisions of the cold war, mirrored in the domestic political climate, dominate to an extraordinary degree. To find that psychoanalysis could become a point over which this ideological conflict could engage in a struggle is indeed surprising, almost as though it were being fought over as if it were a piece of territory to be conquered or neutralized by one side or the other. This may tell us more about the dynamics of the conflict of the cold war than it does about psychoanalytic theories of methods, but it is also informative about the dynamics of social representations themselves. And in fact France in the 1950s was an exceptionally productive context in which to investigate social representations of psychoanalysis.

   In his comments at the very end of the work Moscovici reflects on the propitious circumstances for the study, focused as it was at a time not only when psychoanalysis was becoming better known throughout French society, but where the dynamics of that society were actively shaping and framing the emerging representations of it. We have the constant impression of being in the privileged position of observing the construction of these representations in *statu nascendi*. For a genetic psychologist this is indeed a privileged position, yet all too often one which is difficult for a social psychologist to assess. Piaget could observe the development of intelligence in the crucible of its formation through infancy and childhood, while experimentalists have found ingenious ways of manipulating situations to expose the dynamics of development (we might call to mind Bartlett's studies of remembering, or other microgenetic studies). It is rare though for a psychologist engaged in the study of social phenomena to find such possibilities in front of them. Not that social phenomena are necessarily static, but that the flow of their dynamics too often has a rhythm which does not match that of psychological investigation. And indeed in the hands of other social psychologists this study too might have appeared as no more than a static snapshot of a particular moment. But Moscovici brings something else to his investigation – the eye of a *genetic* psychologist who recognizes that a moment is always a moment within a process of transformation, and who is therefore alive not only to the evident contradictions and inconsistencies in what people say or write about psychoanalysis, but also to the ways in which more subtle nuances of meaning can reveal tensions and conflicts within the structure of representations, tensions and conflicts which themselves speak to the potential transformational dynamics at work within the structure. If the idea of a relationship between communicative influences and the structure of representations is itself an insight of a genetic perspective in social psychology, it is an idea deployed to masterly effect in this study where the influences shaping the representations of psychoanalysis are revealed through the analysis of the material. If France in the 1950s was a propitious moment for this study this was in part because the forces influencing the representation of psychoanalysis were evidently very active in seeking to shape specific images of this discipline. In Moscovici this propitious moment found someone equipped and able to respond to the challenge, so that it has become also a decisive moment for the construction of a theory of social representations, and thereby also for social psychology more generally.

4

Why read a book translated into English thirty years after its publication in French? The answer to the question I began with is quite simply this: we should read this book precisely because it is in every sense of the word a contemporary contribution to social psychology. It is a classic text, but not one which ought to be consigned to the shelves of a library where it can be consulted by those with an interest in the history of the discipline, even if such scholars will surely find the book a rich source for their research. Rather, it is a text which should excite the interest of contemporary social psychologists and engage their attention. Far from being the record of past patterns of social psychological thinking, the book presents a continuing challenge to current patterns of thought in the discipline. I noted earlier that the disciplinary context of social psychology in which the English translation is appearing is different from that in which the original French edition appeared. In the 1970s, when the second French edition was published, there was much talk about the need for a genetic social psychology which could challenge the dominant functional perspectives in the discipline. This book is a part of that movement, but more than simply speaking about the need for a genetic social psychology, Moscovici through his investigation shows us the power and originality of such a perspective. It reminds us too that social psychology forms a part of the social and human sciences, but that to participate in this wider conversation it needs to be able to demonstrate its capacity for enlarging our understanding of social phenomena, of the ways in which people live and how they make sense of their situation.

One final comment. As we read this book we also see what a breadth of knowledge is necessary for the analysis of social representations – not only across the field of social psychology, but also sociology, anthropology, philosophy, epistemology, history and the history of science. Perhaps the recognition of such a breadth of knowledge might appear a daunting prospect for anyone who would seek to take up the challenge of undertaking the study of social representations. But when it comes to understanding the ways in which people make sense of their condition and their experience the divisions between academic disciplines necessarily appear somewhat arbitrary – whether we consider the expert making sense of some carefully delineated object of study, or the ways in which lay people – those insatiable amateur scientists – seek to give coherence and explanation to their worlds. This is something which was readily apparent to the great classical minds of the social sciences – think of Durkheim analysing the elementary forms of religious life, of Lévy-Bruhl examining primitive mentality, of Bartlett in his studies of remembering, or Piaget engaged in analysing the development of intelligence. It may be daunting, but such recognition may also perhaps enrich the study of social representations by reminding us that we are first and foremost concerned with phenomena of the social world whose complexity, contradictions and characteristic polyphasia mark out the distance between such phenomena and phenomena which appear only within the controlled experimental conditions of the social psychology laboratory.

Foreword

Daniel Lagache

Although it is published in the *Bibliothèque de psychanalyse*, this study of the social representation of psychoanalysis is not a psychoanalytic study, but an investigation into the social psychology and sociology of knowledge. Being a medico-psychological specialism, and a human science that opens on to the other human sciences, psychoanalysis has to a large extent penetrated what we call the 'general public' and 'the news'. It provides a golden opportunity to look at what becomes of a scientific and technical discipline when it moves from the domain of specialists into the public domain, and at how the general public sees it and models it, and how the public's image of it takes shape. These two questions govern the economy of the present work. It was possible to address the first by means of surveys and questionnaires addressed to sample populations, and to address the second by means of a detailed, if not exhaustive, analysis of the content of the French press over a determinate period. Even though the original manuscript ran to 700 pages, Moscovici's study is neither boring nor repetitive. The exposition is not burdened by the statistical apparatus, even though its quantitative accuracy leaves nothing to be desired. In order to describe some forms of the social representation of psychoanalysis, Moscovici often resorts, with both lucidity and felicity, to the construction of models. Even when he encounters tendentious positions or impassioned controversies, he never loses his main thread: the search for the truth. He thus succeeds in replacing the theoretical and abstract concept of social representation with an analysis of a real object that is both differentiated and complex, and then uses that analysis to construct a more general theoretical model. In the course of, and thanks to, his research, he elaborates a method that can be applied to other social representations such as illness, medicine, education . . . and I could go on. One of the most intriguing problems is that of the latent 'psychological models' that the members of a given society use to think about their experience and behaviour.

This problem brings us to a lacuna in Moscovici's investigations though the researcher, who has overlooked nothing, bears no responsibility for it.

It is to be regretted that the sample groups do not include a group of psychoanalysts. Psychoanalysts appear to be in a position to tell us about how their patients see psychoanalysis and what they expect of it, and about how their views change as the analysis proceeds. Some psychoanalysts were approached, but so few of them replied that it was impossible to reach any coherent conclusions. Research carried out along those lines would no doubt give a slightly different image, and it would probably be more anthropological and magical. That is because analytic investigations take us into a world of fantasies and symbols. In Western culture and at the level of Moscovici's investigations, in contrast, that backdrop is concealed or even absent, because of the dominance of the abstract, physicalist and physiological models that structure contemporary psychology. An analytic investigation often and regularly takes us in the opposite direction; obsessional patients, for example, never tire of describing the mechanical interplay of their obsessions and emotions but, sooner or later, we get beyond this and become involved in jurisdictional and secret negotiations between the figures on their stage. Abstraction is no more than the end product; intimacy is intersubjective.

Here, we encounter a related difficulty. In order to study the social representation of psychoanalysis, we must look at that representation in its own right, rather than seeing it as a technical-scientific discipline. We thus end up with a sort of composite image, and we cannot avoid asking how that image relates to the specialism with which it is concerned. This raises the question of the very nature of the latter system of reference, and it is not easy to answer that question. It is usually thought that, although the various schools of psychoanalysis have common origins and goals, there are quite pronounced differences between them when it comes to doctrine and technique. Less attention is paid to the way Freud's thought and Freudian psychoanalysis evolved, yet it is difficult to deny that this is – if only in quantitative terms and regardless of the merits of certain dissidents – of primordial importance. The history of psychoanalytic ideas demonstrates, however, that psychoanalytic thought has gone through at least three periods since its birth: during the heroic period between 1900 and 1920, it was preoccupied with unconscious fantasies, repressed sexual desires and the fearful punishments that sanctioned them; towards the end of the 1920s, its theoretical and technical preoccupations were displaced as it concentrated on the operations – 'the Ego's defence mechanisms' – whereby people attempt to defend themselves against unconscious fantasies that disturb them; in the 1930s, finally, a new interest was taken in 'object relations', or in other words interpersonal relations. The gap between psychoanalysis's theoretical preoccupations and the experience of analysis narrowed as a result. This does not mean that its history is discontinuous, as we are not talking about a revolution but about an evolution in the course of which analytic thought's centre of gravity was displaced. There is a common core to analytic anthropology. Its kernel is the notion of psychic conflict. As Freud's thought developed, it was variously explained in terms of an antagonism between the libido and the ego, between self-love and love of others, and between vitality and aggressivity. If we wish to compare the social representation of psychoanalysis with psychoanalysis 'itself', which psychoanalysis should we refer to? Moscovici refers to a conception of psychoanalysis that focuses on the concept of libido, a term designating a motor-force inherent in all the various sexual tendencies; yet Moscovici observes that the libido disappears from the social representation of psychoanalysis, rather as though, according to his interpretation, it were incompatible with social norms. It re-emerges in secondary formations such as judgements or language, and gives them a sort of erotic aura; Moscovici is obviously thinking of the Freudian model of repression and the return of the repressed. These findings, which are unexpected and therefore interesting, call for two comments.

In his attempt to elucidate how the public image of psychoanalysis distorts it, Moscovici refers to a model of psychoanalysis that focuses on the libido. If, as I maintain, the essential and constant element of analytic anthropology is indeed defensive conflict, making the libido central to psychoanalysis is in itself a distortion characteristic of certain moments or certain forms of the social representation of psychoanalysis. We can attempt to locate them in historical terms. The first point that has to be made is that centring psychoanalysis on the libido is a feature of the heroic period of psychoanalysis. Freud's discovery of the role played by sexuality in the pathogeny of the neuroses and in human existence was an intellectual shock. It gave both practice and research a systematic, even tendentious, orientation. There is nothing unusual about this: when psychoanalysts are struck by a new idea, the discovery inspires them to apply psychoanalysis to more and more domains. This is a well-known law of genetic psychology. As a child develops, any ability that has recently appeared is exploited with exuberance. The second fact that should, I think, be noted is that, despite some rare but important studies such as *La Psychanalyse des névroses et des psychoses* (Regis and Hesnard 1914), it was after the First World War that psychoanalysis penetrated France and became established there (I will speak in a moment of the second wave, which came after the Second World War). After 1920, its diffusion was restricted to intellectual circles and had scarcely any impact on the general public; at that time, its image conformed quite closely to what is sometimes called 'pan-sexualism', which, as we know, met with considerable resistance. And that image seems to me to be extraordinarily persistent and stubborn. I have encountered it many times in conversations and discussions with, for example, psychologists and sociologists. They were often well informed, thanks at least to extensive and careful reading, but had not been initiated into the non-'conventional' forms of scientific investigation, meaning, in the present case, investigations that can deal with fantasies. I have observed this so often that, even without any methodical verification, I find it difficult to regard it as fortuitous. My interlocutors are also surprised, if not sceptical or even shocked, when I tell them that sexuality does not play the central and exclusive role in psychoanalysis that they lend it. As a result, what I see as a distortion of the 'true psychoanalysis' that I am bold enough to vouch for, or in other words what I regard as something that is already a social representation, is, it seems to me, identified by Moscovici with psychoanalysis itself, or at least with a technical-scientific state of psychoanalysis. Its social representation appears to be a desexualized distortion of that state.

Which brings me to my second remark. If the social representation of psychoanalysis, as described by Moscovici, is mainly concerned with an approximate version of defensive conflict and if, as I believe, the conception of defensive conflict is indeed the constant and common core of analytic anthropology, we have to conclude that the social representation of psychoanalysis is less removed than Moscovici thinks from psychoanalytic conceptions as such. It would be over-optimistic to conclude that 'good common sense' has corrected certain excesses and 'divided the wheat from the chaff'. A more likely interpretation is based upon the fact that the public opinion surveys made by Moscovici were carried out between 1950 and 1960, or in other words during the second wave of psychoanalysis of the post-Second World War period. That wave and vogue had little in common with those of the 1920s because they were on a larger scale and because the image of psychoanalysis they conveyed was different to the more restricted wave and vogue of the 1920s: the 'new look' had more reservations about the primacy of sexuality in psychoanalysts' own representation of their discipline and the representation they transmitted, or at least in certain tendencies within psychoanalysis.

Those are some of the reflections I was inspired to make on reading Serge Moscovici's book. They appear to me to indicate that Moscovici's thought is stimulating and conducive to dialogue. Tackling the problems of the sociology of knowledge by discussing very recent events and what is sometimes a hotly contested debate is a new and brave undertaking. Moscovici tackles them with an understanding of the problems, with a sureness of touch and a writerly elegance that make him one of the 'young masters' of Francophone social psychology. It is a pleasure for a 'research supervisor' to tell the reader of his great respect for and gratitude to the man who carried out the research.

Preface to the Second Edition

The first edition of *La Psychanalyse, son image et son public* was a thesis. This second edition is, I hope, a book. In order to turn a thesis into a book, I have modified the style, the mode of exposition and the ideas, and removed certain pieces of technical and theoretical information that were of interest to only a small circle of specialists, or that have become common currency. This also corresponds, of course, to a shift in my personal and intellectual views on academic initiation rites and science. When it was published, the thesis provoked a certain unease. Psychoanalysts in particular took a dim view of my attempt to take psychoanalysis as an object of study like any other, and to situate it socially.

At the time, I was – and still am – struck by the fact that those who are in possession of a body of knowledge, scientific or otherwise, believe they have the right to study everything – and ultimately to judge anything – but think it pointless, or even pernicious, to take into account their own determinisms and the effects they produce. They are therefore reluctant to be studied in their turn, or to look into the mirror that is held up to them as a result. They regard this as an intolerable intrusion into their business and as a profanation of their knowledge – do they want it to remain sacred? – and react, depending on their temperament, either with scorn or ill temper. This is true of most scientists, and even of most Marxists. Which is why we have no sociology of science, Marxism or psychoanalysis. I have, however, noticed that attitudes have changed in the last ten years, at least where psychoanalysis and psychoanalysts are concerned, and that a more favourable view is now taken of work such as this.

The book centres on the phenomenon of social representations. Since the first edition was published, many studies, carried out both in laboratories and in the field, have been devoted to social representations. I think in particular of the work of Chombart de Lauwe, Hertzlich, Jodelet and Kaës on the one hand, and of that of Abric, Codol, Flament, Henry, Pêcheux and Poitou on the other. It allows us to arrive at a better understanding of how widespread social representations are, and of the role they play in communication and the genesis of modes of social behaviour. My own ambition was, however, broader. I wanted to use the phenomenon of social representations to redefine the problems and concepts of social psychology by emphasizing their symbolic function and their power to construct the real. The behaviourist tradition, and the fact that social psychology restricts itself to the study of individuals, small groups and informal relations, were and are obstacles in that respect. A positivist philosophy for which the only things that matter are forecasts that can be empirically verified and phenomena that can be observed directly is a further addition to the list of obstacles.

That tradition and that philosophy prevent, in my view, social psychology from developing beyond the limits that currently restrict it. When we realize this and when we dare to go beyond those limits, social representations will, I believe, find their rightful place within that science. They will also be a factor in the redefinition of the problems and concepts of philosophy that must underpin scientific work. Once again, the die has yet to be cast. On the contrary, there is still everything to play for, as is obvious from the crisis in social psychology.

This also concerns the many other fields of research that deal with literature, art, myths, ideologies and language. Trapped into outdated frames of reference, and prisoners of prejudice about the pecking order of the sciences, researchers in these fields deny themselves the resources that social psychology, in its current state, puts at their disposal. In France especially, they claim, as a result of the influence of structuralism, to be orthodox Saussureans but forget what Ferdinand de Saussure saw with such accuracy:

> Language is a system of signs that express ideas, and is therefore comparable to a system of writing, the alphabet of deaf-mutes, symbolic rites, polite formulas, military signals, etc. But it is the most important of all these systems.
>
> *A science that studies the life of signs within society* is therefore conceivable; it would be a part of social psychology and consequently of general psychology; I shall call it *semiology* (from Greek *semeion* 'sign'). Semiology would show what constitutes signs, what laws govern them. (1974: 16)

The reader does not, however, have to worry about that past, that state of science or the projects that hover around this book. Nor do I. Carrying out this research and giving it a form was an enriching experience, and I enjoyed it. All that I can hope for is that the reader enjoys it too.

Serge Moscovici

Preliminary Remarks

They say that, just before they landed in New York at the beginning of the last century, Freud remarked to Jung: 'They don't realize we're bringing them the plague.' The epidemic has been spreading ever since. Psychoanalysis, which is a science, a form of therapy and a vision of man, has indeed become of considerable importance in our culture. Its scientific character, its therapeutic value and its interpretation of psychological phenomena have been challenged for very different reasons – both philosophical and ethical or political. No one denies its impact. But we talk only about its impact on literature, art, philosophy or the human sciences. That attitude is understandable, as we are accustomed to consider theories only in terms of their influence on other theories or other intellectual activities. Because they are confined to the narrow circle of those who write and because their emergence is signalled mainly by dialogues and controversies between books and authors, theories seem to be primarily concerned with the world of *discourse*. As a result, their destiny and evolution are largely the concern of those who know: essayists, philosophers and historians of ideas.

Such an attitude, although reinforced by tradition, ignores, however, the broader implications of science, even though they represent one of its essential functions, namely transforming human lives. A science succeeds in doing so because it can make ordinary human experience revolve around new themes by giving human actions and speech new meanings and transforming them, so to speak, into a world of previously unknown relationships and events. If it succeeds, it becomes the raw material that every individual and every society uses to construct and reconstruct, after the event, their individual and social history, which is an integral part of their affective and intellectual lives. At this level, its elements work and are worked upon, go through stases, and finally merge into a mass of old raw materials and lose their individuality. A science *of* the real thus becomes a science *in* the real, an almost physical dimension of the real. At this point, its evolution becomes a matter for social psychology.

Gradually or suddenly, depending upon the country, political regime or social class in question, psychoanalysis descended from the heaven of ideas and entered into the life, thoughts, behaviour, habits and the world of the *conversations* of a great number of individuals. We see the process personified in what we imagine to be the face and characteristics of Freud, and in the details of his biography. Leaving aside the figure of the great scientist, certain words (such as complex and repression), certain particular aspects of existence (childhood and sexuality) and of mental activity (dreams and slips of the tongue) have captured the imagination and have had a profound effect on the way we view human beings. Armed with these words or relying upon this vision, most people interpret what happens to them, form an opinion of their own behaviour, or that of those close to them, and act accordingly. Certain of the categories they use to describe the qualities of a group or individual, or to interpret their motives or intentions derive from psychoanalysis, and they play an important role. Of that, there can be no doubt. They make up the hard kernel of the implicit or 'profane' theories to which we subscribe and which, in the light of so much research, determine the impressions we form of others and their attitudes in the course of our dealings with them.

The effects of these categories are probably more wide-ranging than that. If anthropological analyses are to be believed, educational practices mould the structure of the personality of members of a definite culture. A glance at the literature on pedagogy, or at the way parents' behaviour with respect to their children has changed as they try to avoid affective conflicts and to respect their individual development, reveals the diffuse influence of psychoanalytic principles. Despite warnings from many psychoanalysts, there is still a persistent belief that those principles provide the basis for a 'good education' that can teach parents what to do, and what not to do, with their children. The effects of psychoanalytically inspired parental behaviour inevitably appear in the personality structure generated by our culture.

Talk of *homo psychanalyticus* (Pontalis 1965) is a joke. But can we be sure that it is just a joke? Our language is full of expressions and phrases derived from psychoanalysis, and everyone understands them. The rhetoric of religion, politics and even economics has no qualms about using and abusing them. Comic books, films, novels and anecdotes constantly diffuse them. We have only to visit a doctor's surgery to observe the wealth of detail mothers use to describe their children's 'complexes' and 'Freudian slips'. When patients' descriptions of their state of mental or somatic health include references to 'complexes' and 'childhood traumas' of all kinds, they expect the diagnosis to be couched in the same terms. And why, for that matter, should symptoms not be distributed, combined and deciphered with the help of psychoanalytic images and psychoanalytic knowledge that have been popularized? Whatever their origins may be, these images and this knowledge always tend to be there in the background of the clinical picture. In one of his earliest papers, Freud (1893) studies the difference between organic and hysterical motor paralyses; hysterical paralysis in individuals mirrors the social schemata of the physiology and anatomy of the nervous system. The contrast between them and scientific schemata therefore influences our recognition of the illness and its therapy. If we extrapolate, it is easy to imagine how psychoanalytic notions can, especially in the domain of functional illness, fuel the proliferating symptomatology that a society needs and that it revises so frantically.

These semi-empirical observations are precious. They allow us to conclude that knowledge of psychoanalysis is, to a varying extent, refracted at the level of interpersonal relations, language, personality and, finally, symptomatology. It gives rise to a model which, once it has been assimilated, taught, communicated and shared, shapes our reality. That model regularly resurfaces in dense layers of day-to-day exchanges, intervenes in the big debates, is carried along by a powerful symbolic current, and takes over our collective consciousness. Its hold on us gives the science from which it derives the dimensions of a major social fact and grounds it in the day-to-day life of society.

It is this major social fact that I propose to study, at least in part. I am concerned with psychoanalysis because it provides me with the opportunity to do so and because of its central role in the intellectual currents of our era. Indeed, its content relates so directly to the problems that every individual or collectivity must solve that we can hope to understand those problems and the way in which they are resolved by studying its diffusion. It should not, however, be forgotten that psychoanalysis touches upon a more general problem that is, I would add, specific to modern societies. What problem? Until recently, the vocabulary and notions we needed to describe and explain ordinary experience, to predict events and behaviour and to give them a meaning derived from a language and a wisdom that regional or professional communities had accumulated over a long period. The perceptions, logical processes, practical methods and polyphony of half-imaginary, half-real beings that constituted our sense-data or rational assumptions had the same origins and proliferated within the same frame of reference. Common sense, with its innocence, its techniques, its illusions, archetypes and ruses, came first. Philosophy and science derived their most precious raw materials from it, and then distilled them in the alembic of their successive systems.

Over the last few decades, this trend has been reversed. The sciences discover and describe most of the objects, concepts, analogies and logical forms we use to face up to our economic, political or intellectual tasks. What comes, in the long term, to look like immediate sense-data or a product of our reasoning is in fact a by-product of scientific research that has been reworked. This state of affairs is irreversible. It corresponds to a practical imperative. Why? Because we can no longer hope to grasp much of the knowledge that concerns us. It is assumed that competent groups or individuals will obtain it for us or supply us with it. Increasingly, it is through the intermediary of other people that we are familiarized with theories and phenomena, and we cannot verify them on the basis of individual experience. The bloated mass of indirect knowledge and indirect realities extends far beyond the shrivelled mass of direct knowledge and direct realities, and it is spreading in every direction. Under these conditions, we think and see by proxy. We interpret social and natural phenomena that we cannot observe, and we observe phenomena that can, we are told – by others, of course – be interpreted. The process of elaborating a coherent vision of our actions and situation on the basis of derivative elements of such diverse origins is psychological and socially decisive. We constantly find ourselves in the position of a patient who, after having consulted a number of different specialists, who each examined one part of his body and identified a localized problem, after having looked at the X-rays, and after having read the abstract laboratory results, has been left alone to make the final diagnosis and prognosis that will tell him how things stand. In our society, the question of how we succeed in shaping our concrete conception of the material, psychical and cultural processes that will allow us to understand, communicate or act, is defined by the change we have just described. The emergence of a new common sense, which is now bound up with science, is in other words one of our society's essential theoretical and practical concerns.

The phenomenon of scientific penetration and the social change it represents reveal many prejudices. When we analyse them closely and get beyond the layers of prejudice, we form the impression that the knowledge that circulates from one group to another has been debased, and become convinced that most people are incapable of receiving it or using it properly. We are reminded ad nauseam of the distortions and simplifications it has undergone. If we have any doubts about this, we compare the popular version of a law or notion with the specialist version in order to pass unfavourable judgement on the former. The comparison is reassuring because it demonstrates to those who need to be convinced that a science shared is a science debased. But it is based upon a confused view of the goals of science.

When scientists carry out experiments, they are in fact trying to discover a mechanism, a substance, a law or an unknown phenomenon. Ordinary people take an interest because they are encouraged to do so by scientists, because their environment or habits are affected, or because they feel a need to keep themselves informed in case they have to rely on science. Someone with a heart condition will, for example, read up on developments in cardiac surgery, and someone living in a city will read up on air pollution and food contamination because they are worried about those issues. As they do so, they both learn, each in their own way, to handle scientific knowledge outside its context, and become imbued with the intellectual style and content it represents. Because of the political choices it implies and the fears it inspires, the atomic bomb has taught most of us an awful lot about physics. The sudden emergence of a previously unknown science or technology always has a similar impact. Our relationship with the real, our hierarchy of values and the relative importance of various behaviours are all perturbed. Norms change too: what was permissible becomes taboo, what was irrevocable becomes revocable, and vice versa. The germ theory of illness institutionalized hygiene. The rites of cleanliness, sterilization and isolation, and the advice to avoid contact with certain people, objects and animals emerged in the wake of the drugs that cured the effects of rabies, tuberculosis, venereal disease and so on. Vaccination acquired the force of law, and disinfectants the authority of rules. And gradually, we all assimilated these rites and prescriptions, imposed them on others and became, so to speak, our own doctors, armed with our own medical science.

Psychoanalysis obeys the same logic. As its therapeutic principles come to be better understood, and as we assimilate and discuss its concepts, more and more individuals begin to undertake a wild self-analysis and to analyse others. It has become permissible, or even advisable, to talk about sexuality, conflicts with parents and this or that neurosis. Few people enter the analyst's consulting room in a state of innocence and, because they have read so much about psychoanalysis, know almost as much as he does. Many psychoanalysts find this disturbing. When the patient and the therapist have the same notions, the same vision of the causes and purpose of the analysis, what is their real relationship and what is the outcome attributable to? Is the analyst's action effective because it is based upon a specific body of knowledge, or because it is based upon the collective belief that he or she embodies, rather like a priest or shaman?

There is a danger that the gap between communications determined by the transference neurosis and ritualized communication between members of a group celebrating – even if it is on a couch and at set times – the shared values of health, happiness and truth will grow narrower, or that the distinction between a therapeutic relationship and a magical one will become blurred. Paradoxically, the talking cure, which was developed by Freud as a way of getting out of the blind alley of individual suggestion, might be transformed, thanks to its diffusion, into a sort of social suggestion, whilst the analyst's interpretations might become society's figures of rhetoric. Pontalis believes that this tendency will become more pronounced,

> particularly as more than one contemporary patient has learned – this is one of the effects of the dissemination of 'knowledge' – to tell their story and even to perceive themselves in terms of an analytic conception that is often worthy of an expert. When we are trapped in this mirage, how can we tell where the

suggestion comes from? Who is whose mirror: the analyst or the patient? (1965: 34)

When, in the course of an analysis, new forms of resistance and interpretation emerge from an understanding of psychoanalysis rather than from ignorance about it, inferences made on the basis of both psychoanalysis and its social *doppelgänger* cannot but have an effect on both the theory and the technique, and the way they evolve.

As we can see, the propagation of a science is creative. We will fail to see this if we limit the discussion to talk of simplification, distortion, diffusion and so on. The qualifiers and ideas associated with those terms miss the essential feature of a phenomenon specific to our culture, namely the *socialization* of whole disciplines and not, as we go on claiming, the *vulgarization* of parts of them. If we adopt that view, we underestimate the differences between scientific and non-scientific, the impoverishment of initial propositions, the displacement of meaning, and science's point of application. We can see what is happening: a different type of knowledge is taking shape in a specific social context. It is adapted to different needs and obeys other criteria. It is not reproducing the knowledge deposited in science, and which should remain there; it is reworking what it finds there, as it wishes and with the means to hand. It is part of a subtle homeostasis, of the chain of operations through which scientific discoveries transform their environment and are themselves transformed as they move through it, and through which they generate the preconditions for their own realization and renewal. And they do so against the backdrop of a decisive historical change in the way our common sense is generated. It is no longer generated by the contagion of ideas or the diffusion of atoms of science or information, but by the process whereby they are socialized.

I have dwelt at some length on two ideas. Psychoanalysis is a cultural event which, now that it is no longer confined to the limited circle of the sciences, affects the whole of society. At the same time we are witnessing the birth of a new common sense which cannot be understood in terms of the vulgarization, diffusion or distortion of science. Sociology and history could make an essential contribution to the analysis of this event and this phenomenon. Social psychology can, by studying social representations and social communication, grasp its essential features. At this point, it seems to be essential to clarify both concepts.

The term 'social representation' was originally coined by Durkheim. He used it to try to define the specificity of social, as opposed to individual, thought. In his view, an individual representation is a purely mental problem that is irreducible to the cerebral activity that makes it possible; similarly, a collective representation is not reducible to the sum total of the representations of the individuals who make up a society. It is in fact one sign that the social has primacy over the individual, that the social extends beyond the individual on all sides. For Durkeim (1982: 41–2), the task of social psychology is to determine 'how social representations are attracted to or exclude one another, amalgamate with or are distinguishable from each other'. Social psychology has yet to do this, and that is a pity.

As we begin this study, we find that the notion needs to be more clearly defined. All representations consist of socialized figures and expressions. At the same time, social representations organize images and language because they identify and symbolize acts and situations that are, or will become, common to us all. If we consider it in the passive mode, we can grasp a representation because it is a reflection, within an individual or collective consciousness, of an object or a bundle of ideas that exists outside that consciousness. We are fascinated by the analogy with a photograph that has been taken and is lodged in the brain, and the representation's sharpness is therefore compared with an image's degree of optical definition. In that sense, we often refer to a representation (image) of space, the city, our wives and children, of science, of scientists, etc. We should, truth to tell, consider representations in the active mode. Their role is to shape something that is given from the outside, as individuals and groups deal with objects, acts and situations that are constructed in and by countless social interactions. They are certainly reproductions. But these reproductions imply the reorganization of structures, the remodelling of elements and a real reconstruction of the given within the context of the values, notions and rules with which it is now caught up. Besides, the external given is never complete or univocal; the mental activity that is trying to capture it has a lot of room for manoeuvre. Language exploits this fact so as to define it, draw it into the flow of its associations and project it into its own space, which is symbolic. That is why a representation speaks and demonstrates, communicates and expresses. Ultimately, representations produce and determine behaviour because they define both the stimuli that surround and provoke us, and the meaning of our responses to them. To cut a long story short, a social representation is *a particular modality of knowledge, and its function is to shape inter-individual behaviours and communication.*

To go back to the problem of how science penetrates society. The transition from the level of science to that of social representations implies a discontinuity, a leap from one world of thought and action to another and not a continuity, give or take a few variations. We deplore this break because we see it as an abdication of responsibility, or as a loosening of the hold of logic or reason. This noble attitude is, however, too unilateral and limited. It fails to recognize that, on the contrary, this break is a necessary precondition if any physical, biological, psychological or other knowledge is to enter society's laboratory, where all forms of knowledge acquire a new epistemological status in the shape of social representations.

I stress the specificity of social representations because I would not like to see them being reduced, as they were in the past, to mere simulacra or scraps of intellectual waste that have nothing to do with creative human behaviour. On the contrary, part of their function is to constitute reality. They constitute the only reality we experience, and the reality in which most of us move. A social representation is therefore in turn the sign of a socially valorized object, and its double. Psychoanalysis, for example, acts as a model that organizes the corresponding realities. The picture of phenomena and events that it projects on to collective life bears the mark of its intellectual grid, but it is still both different and original. There is a reason for this discrepancy: a representation is always as much a representation of someone as a representation of something. The respective functions of social groups reflect this. Catholics and Communists adopt and combine those psychoanalytic concepts – or, in other circumstances, concepts from physics or biology – that are consonant with their vision of God or history, or with their political attitudes of the moment. The map of social relations and interests can, at any given moment, be read through images, data and languages. 'Representing' does not just mean selecting and completing an objectively determined being by introducing a little extra subjectivity. 'Representing' means going beyond that stage, and constructing a doctrine that facilitates the task of detecting, predicting and anticipating that being's actions (Jaspers 1922).

Shaping representations does not mean freezing the shadow cast on societies by an experiment or by knowledge that comes to us from elsewhere; it means bringing them to life in two ways, First, by relating them to a system of values, notions and practices that enables individuals to orient themselves within the social and material environment, and to master it. Second, by furnishing members of a community with a medium of exchange and a code that allows them to name and classify clearly the various parts of their world and their individual or collective history. To describe someone as 'having a complex' or 'being repressed' is tantamount to associating psychoanalytic notions with the habitual ways in which we categorize what people do or say, justify our own behaviour with respect to that person, or, at other times, anticipate what they will do or say, or how they will behave. Indeed, it is tantamount to 'seeing' the effects a psychological mechanism has on them, to 'reconstructing' different scenarios about how they relate to their mother, father and brothers, rather as though we had witnessed these things. Taking account of this constant function of the real and of thought, of the scientific and the non-scientific, we are forced to conclude that a social representation is an organized *corpus* of knowledge and one of the psychical activities that allow human beings to make physical and social reality intelligible, to insert themselves into groups or day-to-day relations of exchange and to free the powers of their imagination.

As Diderot remarked in a letter to Necker, 'Opinion, this mobile entity whose force for good or evil we all know is at its origin nothing but the effect of a small number of men who speak after thinking.' The circulation of opinions and theories certainly does have this effect, and there is no reason to dwell on it. To a large extent, it is their circulation that makes the sciences social, and societies scientific. That is why it was essential to study communications, with reference to psychoanalysis of course. Yet one remark is called for here. The diffusion of knowledge has all too often been described as a top-down 'dissemination', or as a process whereby the ignorant masses 'copy' an informed elite. We come closer to the truth if we see it as an *exchange* that leads to a qualitative change in both the import and the content of experiences and theories. These modifications are determined by the media (newspapers, radio, conversation and so on) and by the social organization of those who communicate (churches, parties, etc.) Communication is never reducible to the transmission of the original messages, or to the transfer of data that remains unchanged. Communication differentiates, translates and combines, just as groups invent, differentiate between or interpret the social objects or representations of other groups. The rigid and basically authoritarian style characteristic of scientific exchanges is subject to variations, and changes from one node in the communications network to the next. Collective norms and symbols provide the necessary filtering of data and styles. Words change their meaning, usage and the frequency of usage change, the grammar of the rules changes and contents acquire new forms. In the communication process, we can follow the traces of the genesis of social images and vocabularies, their marriage with the dominant rules and values before becoming a *definite* language or a form of social speech. A form of speech that is meant to be listened to, exchanged and fixed in the prose of the world.

Was it appropriate to take psychoanalysis as the starting point for a study of social representations of and social communications about a science? I asked myself that question when I began this study, and I have often been asked it since. Many people refuse to describe psychoanalysis as a science: its theories can be neither verified nor refuted, its method is not experimental and there is little hope that it will one day take a quantitative form. Anyone with a close knowledge of Freud's work knows how his doctrine varies, and knows how difficult it is to grasp the conceptual unity of psychoanalysis, or the hierarchy of its concepts and the way they relate to one another. I saw no reason to dwell on these themes. They have never seemed to me to be decisive. Most epistemological decrees are negative: they tell us in peremptory fashion what is not scientific, but they are less confident when it comes to telling us what science is. If we look more closely, we find that they are always preferentially directed at particular philosophies or sciences: Auguste Comte's veto is directed at atomic theory, whilst Karl Popper's strictures, which, in the absence of anything better, are talked about so much, are directed at psychoanalysis and Marxism, and so on. What is more, these decrees have long been shown to be inapplicable. Just try to apply Popper's strictures to the theory of natural selection or to ethology, and you will find that they should share the same fate as Freud's theories, rather than Einstein's.

When, in a word, we declare one thing to be a science, and another a non-science, we are invoking the criteria of proof and rigour and not those of discovery or fecundity. According to the latter criteria, psychoanalysis has amply justified its status. As it happens, I had no reason to be so demanding: the sciences cover such a range and are sufficiently diverse as to justify its inclusion on social and epistemological grounds alone. Why not other sciences and social theories, notably anthropology, economics or Marxism? I could have studied them, just as I could have studied the biological or physical sciences. Especially now that the respective values and structure of sciences and ideologies are being challenged so relentlessly. Exploring concrete mechanisms and structures would be stimulating and would have a practical effect. If, instead, we cite the canonical texts over and over again, borrow a pinch of psychoanalysis from here, a cupful of linguistics from there – just enough to freshen up a tired rhetoric – we give the impression that we can understand and analyse the ideological phenomenon, when we are in fact merely restating the obvious and failing to analyse anything.

But I leave to others the task of painting the rather surprising picture of this desperate flight from the concrete and the particular, of the ceremonial which accompanies it, and the explanation of its causes. I am still convinced that psychoanalysis was a prime object for a study of this kind. It would have been more difficult to begin by studying the socialization of, for example, a theory in physics, mainly because my goal was to *open up a field of research*. I have exploited that possibility, but I have also placed draconian limitations on the generality of the results obtained. I hope that, even under these conditions, they are still of some use.

Although everyone agrees that they are important, social representations and ideologies are not usually the object of sustained empirical studies. Until such time as the appropriate methodology comes into being, a study of a population of *individuals* and a content analysis of a 'population' of *documents* are the techniques best suited to their scientific examination. The techniques are sufficiently simple and flexible to produce valid findings about the particular points that concern us here.

1 Populations interviewed

The survey I undertook was a survey of sample populations. It was initially intended to be a survey of a *representative* sample of the entire population of Paris. I quickly realized that that would have been a mistake in that only certain social categories would have been represented in sufficient numbers, whilst others (intellectuals, students) would have been practically absent. In order to get around this problem, I formed six groups:

- A *representative population* (RP) made up of the representative sample of the population of Paris, as seen in any opinion poll.
- A *middle-class population* (MC) made up of people in industry, artisans, office workers and housewives. Given that it was so heterogeneous in terms of levels of education and socio-economic levels, I divided this population into two sub-groups (MCA and MCB). Sub-group A included respondents with a higher level of education and from higher socio-economic levels, whilst the respondents in sub-group B had a lower level of education and were from lower socio-economic levels. The overlap between the two criteria means that this sub-division was not always strictly observed.
- A *professional population* (PP) including teachers, doctors, lawyers, technicians and priests.
- A *working-class population* (WP). The group included workers from all categories, including unskilled workers, skilled workers, foremen and so on.
- A *student population* (SP). Students from the University of Paris.
- A *population of pupils at technical schools* (PTS) consisting of students aged between 18 and 22 years and training to become secretaries, ceramicists, furriers, or to work in optics, etc.

In order to make what appeared to me to be an essential comparison, I also interviewed two small groups of subjects living in the provinces (Grenoble and Lyon).

The sampling was done on a quota basis. The individuals selected for interview were chosen on a proportional basis, taking into account pre-established conditions such as age, gender and profession. For technical reasons pertaining to both the way the survey was carried out and the precise definition of the populations, it was not always possible to guarantee that the samples were representative. A total of 2,265 subjects were interviewed

2 The notebook-questionnaire

The object of the research was not simply to describe distributions of opinions about psychoanalysis, but also to analyse their insertion into the psychosocial fields of the individuals and groups concerned. The tools developed for observation and quantification had to take that requirement into account. The notebook-questionnaire, which combined interviews with a questionnaire, facilitated a different approach to the same question, on the one hand – using both standardized and free forms – and, on the other, made it possible to use interviews to identify certain aspects that cannot easily be formulated as specific questions. Subjects from the 'student' and 'professional' populations were interviewed a few days after they had responded to the questionnaire.

Taking the view that every group inhabits its own world of opinion as a starting point, I drew up different questionnaires, with fourteen questions common to all of them. This approach made it possible to make useful comparisons and facilitated a specific exploration of the opinions about psychoanalysis expressed by each social stratum. The simultaneous use of different techniques has to be justified. The 'free' interviews, to which I attach as much, if not more, importance as to the questionnaires, were coded in accordance with certain themes and certain categories that allowed me to grasp how they related to one another and to present them in statistical terms. A distinction must be made between two aspects of the coding. One is *group-centred*, and the other *content-centred*. Group-centred coding tends to define the group's modalities of expression with regard to a given object. Does, for example, the group think about the object in abstract or concrete terms, and does it have a 'real' or 'ideal' image of it? Content-centred coding is designed to separate out the themes that appear most frequently in connection with our problem. It thus allows us to define the vocabulary that expresses their content. The categories and themes help us to abstract and generalize by combining highly individualized discourses, and to work statistically, rather as though we were looking at questions and answers.

I also attempted to establish the dimensions of the world of opinion by making a scalar analysis of the material.

The interpretation of the results and the definition of samples implies the choice of variables that can be assumed to explain the trends that have been identified. Age, gender, socio-professional categories and social status are the most easily defined variables. Assessing the effects of membership of political parties raised some delicate problems. It was possible to resolve them in satisfactory terms, but only in the case of the liberal professions. The 'religious' factor is easier to detect. Those interviewed made no secret of their beliefs or lack of beliefs. The distinction between 'believer' and 'practising church-goer' was made by the respondents themselves, who put themselves into one or the other category. Where possible, scales were used to determine two other variables, namely level of information or knowledge about psychoanalysis, and attitude. In all other cases, we relied upon the consensus of opinion.

Different techniques and indices, depending upon the requirements of the survey and our ability to survey each population, were used to establish a list of factors – age, gender, socio-professional category, social status, level of education, membership of political or religious organizations – that explain the findings. I am aware that this survey has its imperfections. The entire survey was carried out with the help of student volunteers who expressed an interest in it.

3 *Content analysis of the press*

The survey of the populations cited was complemented by a content analysis of articles about psychoanalysis, which provided me with a second field of investigation. I analysed much of the press over the period between January 1952 and March 1953. From that date onwards, a specialist cuttings service sent me all press articles dealing, either directly or indirectly, with psychoanalysis. In all, I collected 1,640 articles published in 230 newspapers and magazines, 110 published in Paris and 120 in the provinces.

The method used to study the press coverage was inspired by that developed by Laswell's school and described by Berelson (1952) as a systematic and quantitative technique for content analysis. The research was carried out as follows.

First, an attempt was made to test a certain number of hypotheses. It was, for example, assumed that the so-called left-wing press was more interested in psychoanalysis than the right-wing press. To test that hypothesis, I drew up a questionnaire-grid which allowed me to determine the length of each article, the rubric in which it appeared, the terms in which psychoanalysis was described, the attitude towards psychoanalysis expressed, those features of psychoanalysis to which attention was drawn and the goals that were ascribed to it. Thanks to the questionnaire-grid, it was possible to quantify and classify (a) the *number* of articles and the amount of space devoted to each one, and the context in which the articles appeared; (b) the *terms* in which psychoanalysis was described; (c) the *themes* associated with the subject; (d) *relations* between those themes, such as relations of opposition or conjunction (psychoanalysis is materialist/ psychoanalysis is spiritualist; psychoanalysis/existentialism); and (e) the *evaluation* of themes and of psychoanalysis. The agreement reached by the coders was satisfactory in statistical terms.

Second, message-schemata were abstracted from each group of papers. These are more or less coherent constructs that represent logical or symbolic connections pertaining to psychoanalysis, and the way they are *organized*. The construction of these schemata began with a search for significant *assertions* that appear to sum up a position that is of significance to the vision of the individual who makes the assertion *or* in his or her discourse. The elements of these messages, or assertions in this case, were examined in relation to one another, allowing a structured model of *qualified* relations and assertions to be described. Christian fundamentalists, for instance, see a connection between 'incomplete image of human beings' > 'sexual mechanism' > 'psychoanalysis' > 'materialist psychology', just as they define the relationship between scientific psychology and spiritualist psychology as a 'relationship of *opposition*'. Such assertions and relations may be manifest *or* latent; once they have been identified, one can investigate their organization. Assertions and relations are in fact meaningful only to the extent that they are *independent*, and the way they are organized allows a *set* of relations to be constructed, the 'law' of which, once understood, allows the order to become visible. The various propositions and liaisons are *weighted* to take account of the findings of the first stage of the content analysis. That stage, which is purely taxonomic, provides the general framework for their scientific study; it cannot verify theoretical conjectures about the phenomenon of communication. It is therefore complemented by the more deductive content analysis made during the second stage.

Both the techniques used – the survey and the content analysis – are *observational* techniques. We can get beyond the limitations this places on our theoretical conclusions in two ways: comparison and experiments. In that sense, the findings of this study are at once provisional and open-ended. They are provisional because of the way they were established and they are open-ended in that they can provide the basis for analogous work and experiments capable of grasping the processes that have been explored. The fact that such a field of research had been opened up encouraged me to pursue a *detailed* analysis of the material, both qualitative and quantitative, that had been collected. My main concern was to explore the possibility of carrying out similar studies in general. The only goal of this account of the methodological approaches used is to *illustrate* the way the material was collected, and their purely technical implications are of secondary importance here. My desire to explore future possibilities sometimes led me to stray away from conventionally strict empirical doctrine in the hope that I would one day be better equipped to consolidate observations for which there is as yet insufficient evidence.

The way this book is organized reproduces the way my research was organized. Part I deals with the findings of the survey, and the second with the content analysis of the press. By describing the definition, goal and field of application of psychoanalysis, I sketch its image and the processes that led to its elaboration. An examination of attitudes and sources of information supplies an introduction to a discussion of how it is constituted as a social object. The psychoanalyst, who is the central figure in both the analytic relationship and the collective imagery, is described in a separate chapter. I then go on to discuss in more detail the relationship between psychoanalysis and everyday life, and political or religious values. A look at the way this science is currently 'talked about' or 'thought about' completes the picture I wished to paint of its social representation.

In Part II, I present, to begin with, the general findings of the content analysis of the press. I then study several 'cases' of propaganda, of the diffusion of models of how psychoanalysis is used in literary criticism, advertising, politics and so on.

The unity of this book lies in its goal: describing and understanding how psychoanalysis has entered French society. I did not seek to achieve any stylistic or speculative unity. On the contrary, there are many reasons why it appears to be heterogeneous. The reader should regard it primarily as a social document that reflects some of our society's current preoccupations.[2]

The scope of this work required devoted collaborators without whom it would never have seen the light of day. Mlle Nicole Eizner and Professor Raoul Constenla helped to carry out and analyse the interviews with the 'professional'subjects. Mlle Sonia Askienazy collaborated actively on the content analysis of the press. M. Claude Breteau also worked on it. M. Gérard Salmona coded some of the interviews and helped with the scalar analysis of the findings. But it was Mlle Marianne Gluge and Mme Claudine Hertzlich who were most closely involved in designing the project and analysing its findings. They were such intelligent and productive collaborators that I can say that this is, in part, their book too.

It was the late lamented Professor Lagache who first inspired me to carry out this research. At every stage in my work, he demonstrated the constant interest he took in it. I will always be grateful to him.

---

[2] The document certainly has its lacunae. I would have liked to include a survey of a group of psychoanalysts. The poor response I received made further attempts to do so pointless. When they claim to be the only people who can explain the implications of their knowledge or their practice, psychoanalysts fail to recognize their duties and responsibilities towards the future of their science within the collectivity.

Part I

The Social Representation of Psychoanalysis

Findings of Survey and Theoretical Analysis

1

Social Representation: A Lost Concept

1 Miniatures of Behaviour, Copies of Reality and Forms of Knowledge

Social representations are almost tangible entities. They circulate ceaselessly in our day-to-day world, intersect and crystallize through a word, a gesture, an encounter. Most of the social relationships we establish, most of the objects we produce or consume, and most of the communications we exchange are impregnated with them. We know that they correspond, on the one hand, to the symbolic substance that goes into their elaboration and, on the other, to the practice that produces this substance, just as science and myths correspond to scientific or mythical practice.

Yet if the reality of social representations is easily grasped, the concept is not. There are many reasons for this. Most of them are historical, which is why the task of discovering them must be left to historians. All the non-historical reasons come down to the same thing: its 'mixed' position at the crossroads between a series of sociological concepts and a series of psychological concepts. It is at this crossroads that we have to situate ourselves. There is certainly something pedantic about this approach, but I cannot see any other way of extracting a concept such as this from its glorious past, revitalizing it and understanding its specificity.

Let us go back in time, and to Durkheim, to be more specific. In his view, social representations constitute a very general class of mental and social phenomena comprising what we call science, ideology, myth and so on. They mark the difference between the individual and social aspects of collective functioning and, at the same time, between the perceptual and intellectual aspects:

A man who did not think with concepts would not be a man, for he would not be a social being. Limited to individual perceptions alone, he would not be distinct from an animal. . . . conceptualizing is not the same as generalizing. To think conceptually is not merely to isolate and group the features common to a certain number of objects. It is also to subsume the variable under the permanent and the individual under the social. (Durkheim [1912] 1995: 440)

If Durkheim is simply saying here that social life is the condition for any organized thought – and vice versa, to some extent – his attitude would not raise any objections. Yet, to the extent that he neither addresses the question directly nor explains the plurality of the ways in which thought is organized, even if they are all social, the notion of representation loses its clarity. One might perhaps look here for another reason why it was abandoned. Anthropologists turn to the study of myths, sociologists to the study of the sciences, and linguists to the study of *langue* and its semantic dimension, etc. If we are to give 'social representation' a specific meaning, it is essential to strip it of its role as a general category concerning both intellectual and social productions. In that way, we can, I believe, particularize it and remove it from the middle of a chain of similar terms.

Is it a question of a form of myth, and could we today confuse 'myths' and 'social representations'? The example of myths, the way they regulate behaviour and communications in so-called primitive societies, and the way they conceptualize concrete experience are certainly in many ways analogous with phenomena specific to our society. There is an element of prejudice involved. Who does not speak of the 'myth of woman', the 'myth of progress', the 'myth of equality' and other myths of the same order? This is often no more than a way of reducing the opinions and attitudes we ascribe to a particular group to the opinions and attitudes of the masses – basically, the lower classes – who have not reached the degree of rationality and consciousness of the enlightened elites who baptize, create or write about these mythologies.

Such a transposition is hardly needed for the difference to appear more fruitful.[1] In our diversified society, in which individuals and classes

---

[1] There are thousands of reasons for stressing the difference between myths and social representations. This, however, is the most important. Myth is regarded in and by our society as an 'archaic' and 'primitive' way of thinking and of situating ourselves in the world. It is therefore in some way an abnormal or inferior form. Of course we do not want to admit this, but that would mean ignoring my argument. By extension, we come to regard social representations in the same way. Now, my point of view is very clear: these representations are not an 'archaic' or 'primitive' way of thinking or of situating ourselves and, more important, they are normal in our society. Whatever the future of the sciences may be, they will always have to undergo transformations if they are to become part of the daily life of human society. But there is a more direct sociological reason why our societies take a particular interest in them and give them a special role. They do so because the sciences correspond to needs and practices that might be described as professional, just as science, technology, art and religion have their counterparts in the needs and practices of scientists, engineers, artists and priests. I am speaking of professions whose members are 'representative', and whose

sometimes enjoy great mobility, we are witnessing the emergence of very heterogeneous political, philosophical, religious, philosophical and artistic practices, and of more reliable ways of controlling the environment, such as scientific investigation. Whereas myth was, for so-called primitive man, a total science, or a unique 'philosophy' that reflected his practice and his perception of the nature of social relations, social representations are, for modern man, no more than one of many ways of understanding the concrete world. Both their foundations and their implications are circumscribed. When groups or individuals resort to them, assuming that it is not an arbitrary choice, they do so in order to profit from one of the many possibilities that are available to all. The Hispanic populations of the south-western United States have, for example, no fewer than four registers for the classification and interpretation of illness: (a) medieval folk knowledge about medical suffering; (b) the culture of Amerindian tribes; (c) anglophone folk medicine in both rural and urban zones; and (d) medical science. Depending on how serious the illness is, and depending on their economic situation, they use one or another of these registers in their attempt to find a cure. We can thus detect socially defined circumstances in which they are willing to be guided by either collective representations or scientific data. In this case, as in so many others, the groups are aware of their reasons for choosing one or the other.

We can now understand that the features, social as much as intellectual, of representations formed in societies in which science, technology and philosophy are present, are influenced by them, come into existence as extensions of them and come into conflict with them. We will see later what those features are. For the moment, to take the view that myths and social representations are identical and transferring the mental and sociological properties of the former to the latter without further ado is tantamount to being satisfied with metaphors and facile comparisons, when we should, on the contrary, be concentrating on an essential aspect of reality. The goal of these facile comparisons is often to denigrate our 'common

---

job it is to play a role in the creation of representations. What is a 'popular scientist', a 'cultural worker' or an 'adult education worker', if not someone who introduces or represents science, culture, technology to the public and, insofar as it is possible to do so, represents or introduces the public to the groups that create science, culture and technology? What are they doing, if not playing a part in the constitution of social representations, often, unfortunately, without wishing to or knowing what they are doing? In the general evolution of society these professions can only multiply. They have to recognize the specificity of their practice. We will then see the emergence of a pedagogy that can deal with social representations. Without that pedagogy, the effects of the division between manual and intellectual labour, and between the 'production' and 'consumption' of culture will be increasingly harmful. These comments were prompted by the experience of several students in my seminar at the Ecole des Hautes Etudes and by Philippe Roqueplo's very fine book (1974), which has just come to my notice.

sense' by demonstrating that it is inferior, irrational and, ultimately, erroneous; this obviously does not restore myths to their true dignity. It is not worth dwelling on the issue. We therefore have to take the view that social representations both have an autonomous psychological texture, *and are specific to our society and our culture.*

Are we dealing with a dimension or co-product of science? Durkheim seems to have thought so, since he regards the sciences, and religions for that matter, as no more than particular cases: 'The value that we attribute to science depends, in the last analysis, upon the idea we collectively have of its nature and role in life, which is to say that it expresses a state of opinion' (Durkheim [1912] 1995: 439). Quite so. But the role played by this state of opinion in the structuring and development of scientific theories is of less and less importance. It sometimes ascribes more importance, on the scale of values, to one science rather than another, to biology rather than to physics, to psychoanalysis rather than to ethology, and even decides the level of financial and political investment. That is what its role comes down to, or almost. Everything else is decided on the basis of experiments, calculations and theoretical discoveries. For their part, social representations proceed on the basis of observations and by borrowing notions and languages from here, there and everywhere, from both sciences and philosophy, and draw the obvious conclusions. Many of the formulae that find their application in biology – the struggle for existence, for example – or the social sciences – where there are innumerable examples – extend those conclusions and express them in memorable terms. They remain, however, marginal to the hard core of each science. Similar remarks apply to other concepts of the series: ideology, worldview, etc, which tend to describe in overall terms sets of intellectual and practical activities. From the point of view that concerns us here, such an exercise, which would by definition be fastidious, is pointless. The outcome would be the same as that obtained by comparing social representations of myth and science: we have to conclude that they constitute *a psychological organization, or a form of knowledge that is specific to our society and irreducible to any other.*

At this point, we might ask ourselves why we picked up what is already an old notion. If we refuse to grant it a dominant position as the distinguishing feature of the social, or see it as a category that encompasses every form of thought, and reduced to the more modest role of one specific form amongst many, it overlaps with many other equivalent psychosociological notions. The notions of opinion (attitude, prejudice) and image seem, for instance, to be very similar. This may be true in the narrow sense, but it is false in a more basic sense. Let us look in detail, then, at the reasons why.

Public opinion is, as we know, on the one hand, a socially valued formula to which a subject lends his support and, on the other, a position with regard to a controversial social question. When we ask subjects to answer the question 'Can psychoanalysis have a positive influence on criminal behaviour?', the fact that 69 per cent say 'yes', that 23 per cent say 'no' and that 8 per cent 'do not know' tells us what a collectivity thinks of the application in question. It tells us nothing about the context, the judgemental criteria that are being used, or the concepts that sustain them. Most studies describe public opinion as being unstable and as relating to particular points and, therefore, as something specific; it proves, ultimately, to be one moment in the formation of attitudes and stereotypes. Its partial and divided character is universally admitted. More generally, the notion of public opinion implies:

- a reaction on the part of individuals to an object that is given externally, that is complete, and that exists independently of the social actors, their intentions or their prejudices;
- a direct link with behaviour; the object or stimulus is judged, and that judgement is, so to speak, either an indication as to what action will ensue, or the internalized double of that action.

In that sense, an opinion is, like an attitude, seen purely in terms of the response and as a 'preparation for action' or a miniaturized behaviour. It is therefore given a predictive value, as what the subject is going to do is deduced from what the subject says.

The concept of an image is quite close to that of opinion, at least insofar as its basic presuppositions are concerned. It has been used to describe a more complex or coherent organization of judgements or evaluations. In a fascinating little book, Boulding (1956) calls for the creation of an 'iconics', or a specific science of images. This suggestion points to an obvious gap in social psychology, which should be able to study these images. Boulding's suggestion should be seen as a sign of a renewed interest in symbolic phenomena and of dissatisfaction with the way they have so far been approached. Anyone who looks closely at this question cannot avoid the conclusion that the way they are currently approached is very unsatisfactory. Images are seen as internal reflections of external realities, as the certified copy in the mind of something that exists outside the mind. They are, that is, passive reproductions of immediate givens.

> The individual carries in his mind a collection of images of various aspects of the world. These images are combinatory constructs, and they are analogous with visual experiences. They are, in varying degrees, independent, both in the sense that the structure of the source-images can be inferred or predicted on the basis of the structure of the other, and in the sense that the modification of certain images creates a disequilibrium resulting in a tendency to modify other images. An image is, it is argued, goal-determined and its main function is to select what comes from inside and, above all, what comes from outside. It is further claimed that images act as a selective screen

for the reception of new messages, and that they govern the perception and interpretation of those images that are not completely ignored, rejected or repressed. (Boulding 1956)

We can assume that these images are 'mental sensations' or impressions that objects or people leave in our brains. At the same time, they keep alive traces of the past, take up space in our memories in order to protect them from the hurly-burly of change, and reinforce the feeling that there is a continuity to the environment and to individual and collective experiences. We can, to that end, recall them and bring them back to life in our minds, just as we can commemorate an event, evoke a landscape or recount an encounter that took place in the past. They always act as filters, and are themselves the product of the filtering of the information the subject has or receives about the pleasure he is seeking or the coherence he needs. It is said that images are largely determined by ends and that their main function is to select what comes from outside, and especially from inside: 'Images act as a selective screen whose role is to receive new messages, and they often determine the perception and interpretation of those messages that are not completely ignored, rejected or repressed' (Boulding 1956).

When we speak of social representations, we generally begin from other premises. First, we take the view that there is no definite break between the outside world and the world of the individual (or group), and that the subject and the object are not basically heterogeneous in their common field. The object is inscribed within a context that is both active and unstable because individuals or collectivities to some extent see it as an extension of their behaviour and because, for them, it exists only because of the means and methods that allow them to understand the object. Definitions of psychoanalysis or of the role of the psychoanalyst depend, for example, on their authors' attitude towards psychoanalysis or psychoanalysts, and on their own experience. If we fail to recognize the creative power of objects, events and our own representational activity, we come to believe that there is no connection between our 'reservoir' of images and our ability to combine them, and to combine them in new and surprising ways. Now those authors who see in that reservoir only faithful copies of the real appear to deny the human race that ability, even though it is obvious and even though art, folklore and common sense bear witness to it every day. But the subject is constituted at the same time, since the subject is situated in the social and the material world according to the organization which it gives itself or accepts from the real. There is a community of genesis and complicity between the subject's definition of what it is and what it is not, hence of what is not-subject or another subject.

When, for example, the subject expresses an opinion about an object, we can only assume that he already has a representation of some aspect of that object, and that the stimulus and the response take shape together. The response is not, in a word, a reaction to the stimulus; it is, to a certain extent, its origin. The stimulus is determined by the response. What does this mean in practical terms? It usually means that, when an individual expresses a negative attitude towards psychoanalysis – and says it is an ideology – we can interpret his attitude as meaning that he adopts a stance with regard to a science, an institution and so on. If, however, we look at it more closely, we find that psychoanalysis is confined to the domain of ideology precisely in order to facilitate that negative judgement. If, therefore, a social representation is a 'preparation for action', it is so not only to the extent that it governs behaviour but above all to the extent that it remodels and reconstitutes the elements of the environment in which the behaviour takes place. It succeeds in giving meaning to behaviour, and in integrating it into a network of relations in which it is bound up with its object. At the same time, it supplies the notions, theories and stocks of observations which render those relations stable and efficacious.

The viewpoints of individuals and groups are envisaged as much by their communicative as by their expressive character. Images and opinions are in fact usually specified, studied and thought through only to the extent that they express the position or scale of values of an individual or collectivity. They are in reality no more than samples of a symbolic substance elaborated by individuals or collectivities which, by exchanging their ways of seeing, are trying to influence one another or model themselves on each other. Racial and social prejudices, for instance, are obviously not isolated phenomena; they stand out against a backdrop of systems and reasoned arguments about the biological and social nature of human beings. These systems are constantly mixed, communicated between generations and classes, and those who are the objects of such prejudices are more or less forced into the mould that has been prepared and made to conform to it. The reason why all that is rational is real, as Hegel puts it, is that the 'real' – women, blacks, the poor – has been so worked on as to make it conform to the 'rational'.

The survey itself, which is an observational tool, works in the same way. Someone who fills in a questionnaire is not just choosing a category of answers, but transmitting a particular message to us. They are telling us that they wish things to change in one way or another. They are looking for approval, or hope that the answer will give them some intellectual or personal satisfaction. Such individuals are well aware that, given a different interviewer or different circumstances, their message would be different. Such variations are not indicative of a lack of authenticity on the part of the individual, or of a Machiavellian attitude intended to mask a 'real' opinion. The normal process of interaction is all that is involved, emphasizing one or other aspect of the problem under discussion, or deciding which code is appropriate to the fleeting relationship established for the time it takes to complete the questionnaire. It is this process which mobilizes and gives meaning to the representations in the flux of relations between groups and individuals. As Heider puts it, 'the problem of consciousness or openness to the world takes on a particular meaning when we look at inter-personal relations and interaction'. The concepts of image, opinion and attitude do not take account of these links, or the openness that characterizes them. Groups are viewed as something static and not as something that creates and communicates, but, given that that is what they are, they use and select information that is circulating in society. Social representations, in contrast, are dynamic ensembles, and their status is that of a *producer* of behaviours and relations with the environment, of actions that modify both, and not that of the *reproducer* of that behaviour and those relations, of a reaction to a given external stimulus.

To sum up. We are looking at systems that have a logic and a language of their own, and a structure of implications which bears as much on values as on concepts. They have their own style of discourse. We do not consider them to be 'opinions about' or 'images of'; we consider them to be *sui generis* 'theories' or 'collective sciences' to be used for the interpretation and shaping of the real. They constantly go beyond what is immediately given in a science or philosophy, or in any given classification of facts and events. We can see in them a corpus of themes and principles which has a unity and which can be applied to particular zones of existence and activity: medicine, psychology, politics and so on. Anything that is received or included in those zones is subject to the work of transformation and evolution that allows it to become a piece of knowledge that most of us will use in our daily lives. In the course of this work, the world becomes populated with beings, behaviour takes on a meaning, and concepts take on a certain colouration or become concrete; they become objectified, as they say, enriching the texture of what is, for everyone, reality. At the same time, there are forms in which the ordinary transactions of society find their expression, and we should recognize that these transactions are governed by these forms – which are of course symbolic – and that the forces crystallized in them become available for use. We can understand why. They determine the field of possible communications, of the values and ideas present in the visions shared by groups, and therefore regulate desirable or accepted forms of behaviour. It is these features – their specificity and their creativity within collective life – that make social representations different from the sociological and psychological notions with which we have compared them, and from the phenomena which correspond to them.

2 Philosophies of Indirect Experience

2.1 *The society of amateur thinkers*

It is a truism to note that any order of knowledge presupposes a practice and an atmosphere which are specific to it and which give it substance. And of course a particular role for the knowing subject. We all play that role differently when we are professionally involved in art, technology or science, and when we are forming social representations. In the latter case, each person begins from the observation and above all the testimony which they accumulate of current events: the launching of a satellite, the announcement of a medical discovery, a speech by an important figure, a lived experience described by a friend, a book we have read and so on.

Most of these observations and eye-witness accounts are, however, supplied by those who have catalogued, organized and learned about them in their official capacity. Journalists, scientists, technicians and politicians continually supply us with accounts of political decisions, military operations, scientific experiments or technical inventions. These accounts – articles, books, lectures, etc. – are far removed from us because it is, strictly speaking, impossible for us to grasp their language, to reproduce their contents or to compare them with more direct information and experiences that are more in keeping with our immediate environment. When taken together, they seem to be part of a 'world of discourse' built from raw materials that have been carefully checked in accordance with explicit rules. We are the object of those rules, together with our problems, our future and, ultimately, everything that exists in the same way that we exist. These accounts are, however, also very close to us because they concern us, because their observations interfere in our observations, whilst their languages or the notions they elaborate on the basis of facts that are and sometimes remain alien to us determine the questions we ask. What we see and feel is in a sense overloaded by the invisible and by what is, for the moment, inaccessible to our senses. It is as though they were genes and atoms that circulate in our images, words and arguments.

We are convinced that certain things exist and that certain events have taken place, but we usually do not have the criteria we need to vouch for their material existence. The individual who looks for a satellite in the heavens knows that there *must* be one and *does* find one. For want of more specific indices, he may, however, unwittingly mistake a twinkling star, an aircraft flying at very high altitude or some other meteorological or optical 'object' for a satellite. If he dreams of other human races living on other planets, he may eventually see a spaceship landing on Earth in the same way that our spaceships land on the moon. Taking his desires for reality is just one way of taking his visions for realities. Similarly, anyone who, following psychoanalysis, knows the importance of 'complexes' assiduously sees and encounters them. In both cases, we bank on what we assume to be a reality and, on that basis, think it essential to reconstruct it and make it familiar. Moving from eye-witness accounts to observation, from reported facts to a concrete hypothesis about the object concerned, or in other words transforming indirect knowledge into direct knowledge is the only way we can appropriate the outside world. It is 'outside' in two senses. It does not belong to us – and is assumed to belong to specialists – and it exists outside us, outside the limits of the field of action.

But when it is internalized, and in order to become internalized, it enters the 'world of conversation', the verbal exchanges that have been going on for some time. A sentence, an enigma or a theory that we overhear arouses our curiosity or captures our attention. Fragments of dialogue, half-read books or expressions they have heard somewhere, come back to the minds of interlocutors, merging with the impressions they have; memories gush forth, and shared experiences capture them. This chatter does more than just transmit information and confirm a group's conventions and habits; it allows everyone to acquire an encyclopedic knowledge of the object under discussion. As the collective conversation continues, it flows more smoothly and the expressions used become more specific. Attitudes become organized, values become established, and society begins to be inhabited by new phrases and visions. Everyone becomes eager to transmit his knowledge and to keep his place in the attentive circle that surrounds 'those in the know', and everyone gathers information as best they can so as 'to keep up'. This is how Alexandre Moszkowski, a Berlin critic and man of letters, describes how relativity entered this 'world of conversation', or in other words became public knowledge to those outside scientific circles:

The conversation of educated people circled around this pole, could not escape from it, constantly reverted to the same theme when pressed aside by necessity or accident. Newspapers entered on a chase for contributors who could furnish them with short or long, technical or non-technical notices about Einstein's theory. In all nooks and corners instructional meetings were organised in the evenings; wandering universities appeared with errant professors helping people out of the three-dimensional misfortunes of everyday life in order to bring them to the four dimensional Elysian fields. Women lost sight of domestic worries and discussed co-ordinate systems, the principle of simultaneity and negatively-charged electrons. All contemporary questions had gained a fixed centre from which threads could be spun to each of them. Relativity had become the sovereign password. (1972 : 13–14)

To exaggerate only slightly, each of us can claim to have directly witnessed, in the space of a generation, equally widespread and intense displays of public speech and interest on a number of occasions. We will come back to the meaning of this conversation for the workings of society. It was, however, necessary to indicate how individuals or groups approach and internalize the themes and objects of their world, and to demonstrate that they behave like a clinician who accumulates numerous signs, communicates them to and verifies them with his patient so as to give an opinion on his illness. It is only at a secondary stage that he moves to an analysis. He relies upon what the patient tells him, the cases he has seen and studied, on the cases other clinicians have told him about, and draws what appear to him to be valid conclusions. Thanks to a sort of habit that has become second nature, he can see beyond the symptoms and descriptions, and detect an order that he cannot reproduce experimentally and that he does not wish to demonstrate by means of formulae or statistics.

The practice of knowledge of organizing the relations between the disparate regions of thought about the real has much more in common with how the librarian works than with the work of the clinician. A librarian works on texts that have already been completed, puts them together and combines them by using a code to analyse and classify them; it takes the material form of a set of catalogues. It is not his job to pronounce upon the truth or quality of the texts to which he applies his code and which he includes in his catalogue. He therefore does not work under the same constraints as the specialist who records or dissects in minute detail what he is reading in order to discover whether its content has any value, whether it corresponds to the norms of science, technology or art, and whether he can use it in his turn. Free to construct whatever he wants to construct, the librarian also feels free to associate notions, data and articles belonging to the most disparate domains and schools. The only barriers he encounters are those of the cost and power of his techniques for handling information. The temptation to encyclopedism and to a unique system is very strong. To the extent that we are – outside our professional lives – 'ordinary people', we all behave in the same way faced with these 'documents' which might be articles in a newspaper, an accident in the street, a discussion in a café or a club, a book we have read, a report on television and so forth. We sum them up, cut them out, sort them and, like the librarian, are tempted to make them all part of the same world. We do not have to be as careful as the specialist, and there is nothing to prevent us from putting together the most disparate elements that have been transmitted to us, from including them in or excluding them from a 'logical' class in accordance with the social, scientific and practical rules we have at our disposal. The goal is not to 'advance knowledge' but to 'be in the know', and 'not to be ignorant' of the collective circuit. It is from this work, begun and repeated a thousand times and which displaces the events and surprises that capture our attention to the four corners of the globe, that social representations are born. The spirit at work here transforms members of society into what we might call 'amateur scientists'. Like the 'curious' and the 'virtuosos' who, in past centuries, haunted the academies, philosophical circles, adult education classes, we all try to keep up with the latest ideas and to answer the questions that bombard us. No notion comes supplied with instructions for use, and no experiment comes supplied with a methodology. The individuals who are given them are free to use them as they see fit. All that matters is their ability to fit them into a coherent picture of the real or to slip them into a language that allows them to talk about what everyone else is talking about. This double movement of familiarization with the real by extracting a meaning or order from what we have been told and by handling atoms of knowledge dissociated from their normal logical context is of crucial importance. It corresponds to a constant preoccupation: filling in gaps, abolishing the distance between what we know on the one hand, and what we observe on the other, filling in the 'empty boxes' in one body of knowledge by dipping into the 'full boxes' of a different body of knowledge. We fill the gaps in our science by borrowing from religion, and the gaps in a discipline by borrowing from the prejudices of those who practise it. At the same time, concepts and models that have been set free from their bonds spread and proliferate in astonishing abundance and with great freedom. The only limit is the fascination they exercise and the anxiety they arouse when they seriously call into question things we want to remain unquestioned. As in a game in which we try out and test collective material phenomena before verifying their real existence and putting them into practice 'for real', we venture to make rough drafts and sketches, we indulge in intellectual manoeuvres and rehearsals that make the spectacle of the world look like a world of spectacle. Certainly these 'amateur scientists' – and we are all amateur scientists in some domain or other – live in a world of conversation, with their librarians' habits – part-autodidact and part-encyclopedist – and they remain often prisoners of prejudices, ready-made visions and dialects borrowed from the world of discourse – the famous jargon so hated and so necessary – and all we can do is bow before their superiority. They do, however, show us that, in their everyday lives, individuals are not only passive machines obeying apparatuses, recording messages and reacting to external stimuli which a perfunctory social psychology reduced to collecting opinions and images would turn them into. On the contrary, they have the freshness of the imagination and the desire to make sense of their society and their world.

2.2 Knowledge of what is absent and strange

That is how what we might call the 'sciences' or 'philosophies' of indirect knowledge or observation are constituted. What is the specificity of the mode of thought that is at work here? Classical psychology, which paid a lot of attention to representational phenomena, provides us with some useful starting points. It saw them as processes that mediated between concepts and perception. Alongside these two mental processes, one purely intellectual and the other predominantly sensorial, representations constituted a third process with mixed properties: properties that facilitated a transition from the sensori-motor sphere to the cognitive sphere, from the object perceived at a distance to an awareness of its dimensions, forms, etc. To represent something and to be aware of it are one and the same thing, or almost one and the same thing.

According to Heider,

the perceptive process mobilises stimuli that are situated some distance away, and a mediation that leads to stimuli that are near to hand. Within any organism, there is therefore a process that constructs perception; it leads up to an event corresponding to an awareness that the object or reality is something that is perceived. He uses the expression 'representation of the object and image' to describe that awareness.

In this particular form of cognitive work, transferring something from outside to inside or transporting it from a distant space to a space that is close to hand are essential operations. But we are under no obligation to look at things in this way. Representation is not, in my opinion, an intermediary instance, but a process that makes concepts and perceptions in some sense interchangeable because they generate one another. The object of the concept can, that is, be taken as the object of perception; the content of the concept can be 'perceived'. We 'see', for example, the unconscious, which is located deep in the mental apparatus, and we see that someone 'suffers from a complex'. Some forms of behaviour are not described as timid on the basis of what we can see; they are regarded as obvious *manifestations of* a 'timidity complex' that we can conceive without seeing it, and which is located within the individual.

We can see that a representation is initially an expression of a relationship with the object, and that it plays a role in the genesis of that relationship. One of its aspects – the perceptive aspect – implies the presence of the object; the other – the conceptual mind – implies its absence. From the conceptual point of view, the presence of the object, if not its existence, is useless; from the perceptive point of view, its absence or non-existence is impossibility. Representation maintains this opposition and develops from it: it re-*presents* a being or quality to consciousness, or in other words presents them again and makes them real, even though they are not there and may not exist. At the same time, it removes them far enough from their material context for the concept to be able to intervene and mould them to suit its own purposes. On the one hand, a representation follows the traces of a conceptual thought because the disappearance of the object or concrete entity is a precondition for its appearance; but on the other hand, it cannot disappear completely and the representation must, like perceptive activity, recuperate that object or entity and make them 'tangible'. It retains the concept's ability to organize, relate and filter what is going to be recaptured or reintroduced into the sensorial domain. It retains perception's ability to glance through and record things that are unorganized, shapeless and discontinuous. The variety of approaches and the discrepancy it presupposes between what is 'taken from' and what is 'returned to' the real indicate that a representation of an object is a *re*-presentation that is different to the object. The perception generated by the concept is of necessity different to the perception that initially underpinned the concept. The 'timidity complex' the individual is said to be suffering from comprises the usual psychological indices – blushing, low voice, shaking, etc. – but there are also indices of an affective order – fear, hesitation, avoidant behaviour – that are assumed to be expressions of childhood experiences and to result from the repression of desires of a sexual nature.

Representing a thing or a state does not just mean reduplicating it, repeating it or reproducing it; it means reconstructing it, retouching it and altering its text. The communication that is established between concept and perception, as one penetrates the other and transforms their common material substance, creates the impression of 'realism', of the materiality of abstractions, because we can act with them, and of the abstraction of materialities, because they are expressive of a specific order. Once they have become fixed, these intellectual constellations make us forget that they are our creations, that they have a beginning and will have an end, that their internal existence bears the scars of their transition through the individual and social psyche. 'What', asks Köhler, 'are the objective facts of nature?'.

> What is the best access to objective knowledge about it in this sense? What influences on the other hand are apt to hamper our progress in this field? Since the seventeenth century such questions have introduced a definite set of values which is now so dominant far beyond that circle of scientists proper that the proper attitude of civilized people is thoroughly governed by those particular ideals. A sober attitude towards a real world is instilled in children of our civilization by the words and actions of their parents. Long ago the most basic convictions of scientific culture lost the character of theoretically formed sentences. Gradually they have become aspects of the world as we *perceive* it; the world *looks* today what our forefathers learned to say about it. (1937: 273–4)

Individual or social representations make the world what we think it is or what we think it must be. They show us that at each moment something absent is being added, and that something present is being modified. But the play of this dialectic has a broader meaning. Something that is absent strikes us, and our minds and our group set to work, but that is not because it is at first strange or something from outside our usual world. It is the fact that it is distant that surprises us and creates the characteristic tension. When psychoanalysis speaks of childhood, dreams or the unconscious, it not only suddenly introduces a domain that is far removed from adult human life; it also sheds a light that surprises and shocks. Scientific or technological discoveries are striking in the strict sense of the word. The tension I allude to constantly betrays its origin, namely the incompatibility between the linguistic and intellectual possibility of understanding parts of the real to which the content refers. That content is strange because it is remote, and it is remote because it is strange. We do not normally, by definition, have the data, words and notions to understand or describe the phenomena that appear in certain sectors of our environment. We have other data, words and notions that we are forbidden to use or to take into account in order to define or indicate the presence of phenomena or forms of behaviour that have been concealed or hidden in our environment. There are, on the other hand, sectors in which we have too much information and too many words, and in which the use and abuse of anything and everything is legitimate. Groups as much as individuals experience both a plethora and a dearth of forms of knowledge and languages that they do not have the means to associate with realities, and realities that they cannot or must not associate with those forms of knowledge and those languages. Ellipsis on the one hand and volubility on the other are both expressions of this state of disequilibrium. When an object from the outside world – be it a rocket or relativity – penetrates our field of attention, that disequilibrium increases as the contrast between the fullness of the ellipsis and the emptiness of the volubility becomes greater. If we are to decrease both the tension and the disequilibrium, the strange content must be decanted into a familiar content, and what was outside our world must come inside it. To be more specific, we have to make the unaccustomed familiar and the familiar unaccustomed, and change the world whilst ensuring that it remains our world. This is only possible if we make languages and knowledge from regions where they are abundant pass through communicating vessels towards regions where they are in short supply, and vice versa. We have to make the ellipsis chatter, and make the chatter elliptical. This is not surprising because, as in surrealist paintings of limbs in search of a body, or of a body in search of limbs, concepts without perceptions, perceptions without concepts, words without content and contents without words are in search of one another as they move around and are exchanged in societies that are both differentiated and changing. That is what representations are used for, and that is how they arise.

Let us take an example. When they enter the sphere of an individual or group, notions such as 'unconscious', 'complex' or 'libido' are surprising or shocking. They are surprising to the extent that they designate distinct entities that have nothing to do with immediate experience, and they are shocking because they concern a region we are forbidden to think about or talk about: sexual life. We can, at a pinch, create a corresponding intellectual host-structure within our individual worlds – the soul/body, rational/irrationality dualisms allow us to do this – but not a material support in the sense that a notion from physics, psychology or chemistry has one. We understand what the unconscious, a complex or the libido is, without being able to grasp what any of them *is*. In contrast, neither the relationship between the analyst and the patient – the couch and free association have a lot to answer for here – nor the modus operandi specific to that relationship (the transference and its effects) has an intellectual host-structure in public opinion, because a 'doctor with no medicine' is something of a paradox. Overcoming their strangeness and bringing them into a shared space by staging an encounter between separate and disparate visions that are, in a sense, in search of one another, is the task of representations.

This is a twofold task. On the one hand, the representation divorces concepts and perceptions that are usually associated with one another, and makes the unusual familiar. Thanks to the idea of libido, sexuality, for example, becomes both a localized physiological activity and a generalized desire. Almost the whole of the personality is concentrated and expressed in the act of 'making love', or at least some people convince themselves that such is the case. To take another example, confession is evoked in order to give a meaning to what goes on between a psychoanalyst and a patient. The relationship between confessor and 'confessee' is detached from the religious context on which it is based and from a ritual with which the believer is familiar. We then add our idea of what transference is and liken the rules of confession to the rule of 'free association'. As a result, something that could not be grasped becomes something that can be grasped. It becomes something intelligible and concrete. Psychoanalysis is said to be a confession. Conversely, confession becomes a particular form of psychoanalytic treatment. Like the psychoanalyst, the priest gives someone the opportunity to express themselves, to talk about what is bothering them and even to rid themselves of their worries by doing so. The only thing that is missing is the sacred dimension, which gives way to the profane dimension somewhere along the way. By dissociating psychoanalytic technique from its theoretical framework, confession from its religious framework, and sexuality from the framework of physical need, people are convinced that this separation is valid. They do not, however, forget its approximate nature. At least the therapy proves to be comprehensible, libido is articulated with a concrete substratum, and a concrete look is taken at what was routine, namely confession and especially sexuality. This is where the creative power of the act of representation lies: by taking as its starting point a stock of forms of knowledge and experiences, it can displace and combine them in such a way as to integrate them into one context and shatter them in another.

On the other hand, a representation brings together experiences, vocabularies, concepts and modes of behaviour from very different origins, and causes them to circulate. In doing so, it reduces the variability of our intellectual and practical systems, and of disjointed aspects of the real. The unaccustomed slips into the customary, and the extraordinary is made familiar. As a result, elements that belong to distinct regions of activity and social discourse are transposed, and serve as signs and/or means of interpreting one another. Political schemata and political vocabulary take it upon themselves to classify or analyse psychical phenomena; psychological languages or conceptions describe or explain political processes and so on. Theories and their respective specific meanings both merge and move from one domain to another. At first, these associations appear to be arbitrary or conventional. But they soon become organic and motivated. Who, at least in our society, is not familiar with doublets such as 'psychoanalysis-United States', 'psychoanalysis-conservatism' or 'psychoanalysis-subversion'? The redundancy that results from these associations is an expression of the endless reduplication of the same objects and the same signs wherever it is possible to realize and understand a felicitous combination. Creativity and the redundancy of representations light the way for a great plasticity and an equally great inertia. Of course their properties are contradictory, but the contradiction is inevitable. It is only on this condition that the mental and real world always becomes different, and always remains a little the same, that the strange penetrates the fissure of the familiar, and the familiar fissures the strange.

The notion of representation still eludes us. We are, however, getting closer to it in two ways. By specifying its nature as a mental process that can make something that exists some distance away from us, or that is in some sense absent from us, familiar, situate it and make it present in our inner world. The result is a 'print' of the object, and it remains there as long as we feel a need for it. When it is no longer necessary or loses its vigour, it either disappears into the labyrinth of our memory or is refined into a concept. This print – or figure – is involved in every mental operation. It is the starting point and the point to which we return. It gives the form of knowledge at work in it its specificity and makes it distinct from every other form of intellectual or sensorial knowledge. That is why it has often been said that *any representation is a representation of something*.

We have also been able to clarify the notion of representation by noting that, in order to enter the world of an individual or group, an object enters into a series of relations and articulations with other objects that are already there, borrows their properties and adds its own properties. As it becomes ours and familiar, it is transformed and transforms other objects, as the example of analytic therapy and confession shows. Truth to tell, it ceases to exist as such and changes into an equivalent to the objects (or notions) to which it is subordinated by pre-established relationships and links. Or, which comes down to the same thing, it is represented to the precise extent that it has in its turn become a representation, and appears only in that guise. The smoke that indicates the existence of a fire or the staccato noise that signals that a pneumatic drill is at work are representatives of this kind because they are 'perceived' not as smoke or noise, but as equivalents or substitutes in the 'fire' or 'drill' series into which they have been inserted. In the same way, analytic therapy seems to some people to be almost interchangeable, in terms of its practice and effects, with the confession specific to the Catholic religion. But the establishment of the series and the links that are woven around the object are of necessity an expression of choices, experiences and values. The reason why many people see psychoanalysis as an 'index' of the United States – hence the expression 'American psychoanalysis' – of a political conservatism – hence moreover the expression 'reactionary science' – is that a national political value links it to a notion or a social group. We observe, in short, that representing an object means both according it the status of a *sign*, and getting to know it by making it significant. Because of the particular way in which we master and internalize it, we make it ours. And we really do so in a particular way because the outcome is that *everything is a representation of something*.[2]

It now remains for us to add one last link to the chain. That link is the subject, and the subject's self-representation because, when all is said and done, it is often the individual or group that is absent from the object (and makes the object absent) and that determines its strangeness (and makes it strange). The reason why science, nature or politics are absent from our world, or seem so esoteric to us, is, as we know, that they make a great effort to exclude us, to erase every last trace that might allow us to recognize ourselves in them. A people, an institution, a discovery seems strange to us because we are not there, because they come into being and evolve 'as though we weren't there'. When we represent them, we re-think them, re-experience them and re-make them as we see fit, and in our context ('as though we were there'). We basically introduce ourselves into a region of thought or the real from which we have been evicted and we therefore invest in it and appropriate it. We have a marked propensity for trying to give an existence with us to what existed without us, to make ourselves present where we were absent, and to familiarize ourselves with what is strange. Narcissus certainly wanted to see his reflection in a pool of water because he was in love with himself and his image. But perhaps he was always secretly trying to use the image to take possession of the water, to enter into a flow of things that were already there in their own right, outside him, and without him. He not only wanted to find a mirror in that watery world; he also wanted to be the centre of that mirror in the world. It is pointless to dwell on the issue. Philosophers realized long ago that *every representation is a representation of someone*. This by itself suggests that it is intentional. As is the case with any intention, it is often ambiguous and oblique in its consequences. Here is the source of tension which lies at the heart of any representation, between the facet oriented towards the object – the figure[3] – and the meaning chosen and given to it by the subject.

---

2 We often encounter situations in which 'everyone is a representation of someone' in our social lives. The children of someone from a rich or famous family are, for example, always seen by others not as individuals in their own right, but as the sons or daughters of the person whose name they bear, and we react first to their position or the name they bear. The same is true of foreigners or groups of foreigners: we do not judge them in their own right, but insofar as they belong to a class or nation. Racism is an extreme case in which everyone is judged, perceived and experienced insofar as they are representatives of a series of other individuals or a collectivity.

3 The word 'figure' does more than the word 'image' to express the fact that it is not just a reflection or a reproduction, but also something that is expressed and produced by the subject.

What these remarks amount to is the following: usually, especially in the past, representations were placed as intermediaries in a sort of genetic evolution from percepts to concepts, from the concrete to the abstract, or vice versa. In reality every representation appears to us double. Its two sides can no more be dissociated than the recto and verso of a sheet of paper: a figurative side and a symbolic side. We write

$$\text{Representation} = \frac{\text{figure}}{\text{signification}}$$

as a way of indicating that any figure has an aura of meaning, and that any meaning appears in a figurative or iconic pattern. Most of us regard the unconscious as a sign of psychoanalysis that is laden with hidden and involuntary values, and in our minds we visualize it as a deeper and more heavily veiled level; the *libido* is very concretely associated with the sexual act and with genitality, but at the same time wrapped up in a series of religious and political connotations that place it further up the hierarchy of factors that explain aspects of the way a man or woman acts. As we shall see, the function of the processes at work here is both to outline a figure and to give it a meaning, to inscribe the object in our world, or in other words naturalize it, and to provide it with an intelligible context, or in other words interpret it. Their main function, however, is to outline a figure that reduplicates a meaning, or to objectify, on the one hand – a psychoanalytic complex becomes a psychophysical organ of a human individual – and to create a meaning that reduplicates a figure and, on the other, to anchor the raw materials that go into its composition – the psychoanalyst defined as a magician or priest – in a specific representation. Here lies the source of a basic uncertainty. When we re-present something, we never know whether we are mobilizing an index of the real, or an index that is significant in conventional, social or affective terms. The only thing that can remove the uncertainty is a subsequent development, namely a conscious effort to go beyond conventions and get closer to the intellect, or to go beyond figures and get closer to the real. The forms of knowledge known as representations, whose function and structure we have just examined, are, at least where humans are concerned, primary. Concepts and perceptions are secondary elaborations and stylizations derived from the subject and the object respectively. Anyone who is familiar with the history of the sciences knows that most highly abstract theories and notions first occurred to scientists or science in a figurative mode, and that they were laden with symbolic, religious, political or sexual values. This is true of the phenomena of the evolution of biology, chemistry and electricity. It was only thanks to a series of successive distillations that they could be translated into abstract and formal terms. That distillation is never complete or finished. Many a researcher and many a theory depict atoms as coloured balls of various dimensions and no physicist – despite centuries of trying – can talk about 'force' without referring to the primal image of someone applying pressure to something that resists. When an individual or group form a representation of a scientific theory or phenomenon, they actually revert to a mode of thinking and seeing that exists and subsists, that takes up once more and recreates things that have been concealed or eliminated. In a word, they reshape them by walking backwards down the path they followed. The resemblance to Wittgenstein's famous 'What we do is to bring words back from their metaphysical to their everyday use' (1953: 48) is obvious. This, as is well known, is not yet understood in either psychological or sociological terms. Far from being a drawback, it makes us aware of the fact that many difficulties of our modern age could be faced if more attention was paid to the representational mechanisms which make the absent present and the unfamiliar familiar, recreating unity in a world amidst the worlds that have been isolated and divorced. And it is precisely because they are 'archaic' or 'primitive' that they make it possible to 'transcend' or 'readopt' ways of knowledge which, because they are 'recent' or 'very abstract' lose contact with the practice or experience of the 'many', increase the discrepancy between what we know and what exists.

3 In What Sense is a Representation Social?

3.1 Representation as a dimension of social groups

Our line of investigation here was to make explicit the social psychological meaning of the idea of representation and what differentiates it from the usual cognitive system. At a manifest level, it appears as a body of propositions, metaphors, value judgements or figurative beliefs. The philosopher Stanley Cavell suggests these figurative beliefs:

> The official rhetoric is rational, but it bears to ordinary consciousness the same relation as advanced theology to the words and the audience of the revivalist. . . . What does an ordinary citizen think when he says, or hears, that our defense systems provide such and such a margin of warning, or sees a sign saying 'Fallout Shelter'? We speak about the dangers of 'accidental war,' but what does this mean? Not that the *whole* war will be an accident, but that it will *start* accidentally. From then on it will be planned. We are imagining that, if ordered to, men will 'push buttons' which they *know* will mean the destruction of their world. (1976: 135)

The propositions, metaphors, value-judgements and figurative beliefs are, however, organized in very different ways by different classes, cultures or groups, and make up as many *worlds of opinion* as there are classes, cultures or groups. My hypothesis is that each world has three dimensions: attitude, information and a field of representation or image.

Information – defined as a dimension or a concept – relates to the way a group's knowledge of a social object – in this case, psychoanalysis – is organized. In some groups, such as groups of workers, there is no coherent information about psychoanalysis, and we can therefore scarcely speak of the existence of that dimension. If, in contrast, we look at students or the middle classes, we encounter a more consistent knowledge which allows us to differentiate with precision between different levels of knowledge. Each level corresponds to a certain quantity of information, which can be established by using scales – I have used Guttmann scales – but that rather technical aspect need not concern us here.

In order to illustrate the above, here are – in order – the questions that define the 'information' dimension in one of the middle-class sub-groups (A):

- *How long does psychoanalytic treatment go on for, in your view?*
    (a) 1 to 2 years, more than 2 years
    (b) up to a few months, or no opinion
- *Do you regard psychoanalysis as:*
    (a) a well-established scientific theory; a therapeutic technique
    (b) a science that is still being developed; don't know
- *Could you say when psychoanalysis emerged?*
    (a) correct date
    (b) wrong date; don't know
- *In what situation do you think psychoanalysis is used?*
    (a) failure to adapt (neurosis)
    (b) other specific cases: disappointment in love, childhood disorders, marital conflict
- *Can you remember who founded psychoanalysis?*
    (a) Sigmund Freud
    (b) wrong answer; or no answer
- *Are you interested in psychoanalysis?*
    (a) very; quite; moderately
    (b) not very; not at all; no answer

Informants who give (a) answers know more about psychoanalysis than informants who give (b) answers. The former think that psychoanalysis lasts for over a year, regard it as a scientific theory and as a technique, know when it emerged, take the view that it applies, in general, to a failure to adapt (neurosis), take some interest in it and know that Freud was its creator. People who are less well informed think that analytic treatment lasts for a relatively short time, have the vague impression that psychoanalysis is something that is 'being developed', do not know when it emerged, think that its domain is limited to either disappointments in love or childhood disorders, have little interest in psychoanalysis, and have not heard of Freud. If we take into consideration the *order* of the questions, we find that the question about the length of treatment is the most important since very few people are able to respond correctly to it, whereas the name of the founder of psychoanalysis, being relatively well known, is unknown only to only those who really do know very little about psychoanalysis.

The dimension we have designated the 'field of representation' suggests the idea of an image or social model with a concrete and limited content of propositions relating to specific aspects of the representation's object. The opinions expressed may be coterminous with the set that is represented, but that does not mean that the set is organized and structured. The notion of 'dimension' forces us to conclude that there is a field or representation or an image wherever there is a hierarchical set of elements. The extent of the field and the points that provide its axes vary; they include value-judgements about psychoanalysis, and assertions about psychoanalysis or the types of people who supposedly resort to this particular theory.

The same middle-class sub-group's representation centres on the following questions:

- *What type of personality must you have in order to go into analysis?*
    - (a) strong
    - (b) does not matter
    - (c) weak
- *The image of the psychoanalyst is*
    - (a) complete and positive
    - (b) banal and negative
    - (c) no image
- *Do you think that psychoanalysis has a contribution to make to the education of children?*
    - (a) yes
    - (b) no; don't know
- *Which of the following practices is most like psychoanalysis?*
    - (a) conversation, confession
    - (b) hypnotism, suggestion, occultism, narco-analysis
- *The psychoanalyst's attitude towards the person in analysis is comparable with that of*
    - (a) a doctor, a friend
    - (b) an observer, a relative
- *Do you think that psychoanalysis damages or helps the personality of the individual who undergoes it?*
    - (a) helps
    - (b) damages; it depends; don't know

We observe that the domain of representation that we have identified in this population tends to include the image of the analyst, that of the patient, the action of psychoanalysis and the practice it resembles most closely. The standardized questions do not express the full content of the representation, which emerges from the interviews and more open-ended questions. They simply allow us to establish the existence of an organization underlying the content.

The attitude allows the global orientation in relation to the object of the social representation to be drawn out.

People in this group who view psychoanalysis sympathetically have clear-cut views and:

- think that psychoanalysis has a wide field of application;
- say that most people who go into analysis are artists and intellectuals (and have a positive view of these groups);
- would go into analysis themselves, if need be;
- think that it should be used in careers guidance;
- would agree to having their children analysed if they felt there was a need for it;
- think that anyone who goes into analysis must have a strong personality, or that personality is not important;
- believe that psychoanalysis improves the state of those who undergo it.

People who are hostile to psychoanalysis say that

- psychoanalysis is applicable only in well-defined cases;
- people who go into psychoanalysis are rich;
- they themselves would not go into psychoanalysis;
- the use of psychoanalysis in careers guidance must be viewed with caution;
- they would not have their children psychoanalysed;
- people who go into psychoanalysis are weak;
- psychoanalysis does not help anyone.

Between these extremes, there are of course intermediate attitudes.

The three dimensions of the social representation of psychoanalysis – information, field of representation or image, and attitude – give us an insight into its content and meaning. It is legitimate to ask how useful this 'dimensional' analysis is. The argument about accuracy, which we owe to the quantitative approach, is not decisive. It seems to us that a *comparative* study of social representations, which is absolutely essential to a discipline such as ours, depends upon the possibility of identifying contents that can be related to one another in a systematic way. A few examples will demonstrate that we have achieved this goal.

Let us put side by side the *content* of the scales belonging to two factions of the 'professionals' sample: 'communist-left' and 'centre-right'.

The following questions appear in the scales of both groups

- *If psychoanalysis seems to you to be of increasing importance, to what factors do you attribute that fact?*

The positive values (social needs, scientific value, effects of the war) and the negative values (American influence, advertising) are the same for both factions.

- *Which of the following practices seems to you to have most in common with psychoanalysis?*

Both relatively positive associations (conversation, confession) and relatively negative associations (narco-analysis, suggestion) are the same for both groups.

- *Would you liken the psychoanalyst to a doctor, a chaplain, a psychologist or a scientist?*

People on the left liken psychoanalysts to doctors and psychologists.

As well as answering the same three questions, each sub-group extends the content that expresses its view by answering *specific* questions.

The 'left-wing' faction attaches great importance to problems relating to the application of psychoanalysis, and especially its political application:

- *Do you think that psychoanalysis can have a good influence on criminal or delinquent behaviour?*
- *Is psychoanalysis compatible or incompatible with having an active political life?*

The distinguishing feature of the 'centre-right' faction is that it answers questions about more 'technical' problems:

- *Can psychoanalysis change someone's personality for the better?*
- *Is the psychoanalyst's position with respect to the patient that of a doctor, a friend, an observer or a relative?*
- *Can psychoanalysis be used for political ends?*

The first two questions show that this faction of our sample is more aware of the effect of psychoanalysis and of the transferential repercussions of the analytic relationship. The significance of the last two questions calls for more detailed consideration. The one-dimensional character of the scales presupposes the existence of shared criteria or frameworks of reference for all interrelated questions. Centre-right intellectuals take the view that social problems can, like political action, occur at a psychological level.

Opinions may differ, but the fact that these questions are all part of the same world is part of their conception of society. For 'left-wing' intellectuals, social problems are of a different order – they are economic or political – *and if that is the case, this question cannot be related to the others*, which explains its absence. As to the question 'Can psychoanalysis be used for political ends?' it does not divide this group in the way that it divides the centre-right group. The 'yes' is such a *stereotypical* answer that it does not discriminate and is not very specific.

One might wonder about the meaning of the 'political' question included in the 'communist-left' sub-group's scale. The question does not deal with the application of psychoanalysis for political purposes, but with the possible relationship between an individual's involvement in political life and the fact of being in analysis or adopting the psychoanalytic viewpoint. It is simply a commonplace assertion in a new form: psychoanalysis makes individuals introverted, cuts them off from their group and, because it cuts them off, makes them incapable of being politically active. Opinions differ over this point: some intellectuals will make no concessions to the hypothesis that psychoanalysis causes people to break with politics, whilst others take it as axiomatic. It is, however, an important question for any left-wing ideology, and it has therefore given rise to a lot of debates.

The comparison we have just made can be repeated for every dimension of the groups under investigation, and for the groups as a whole. If we accept that a social representation has three dimensions, we can from the outset determine the degree to which it is structured within each group. This three-dimensionality is present in only four populations: students, professionals, middle classes (A) and pupils in technical schools. Both workers and the middle classes (B), in contrast, have a structured attitude, but their information and field of representation are more diffuse. Whilst there is nothing surprising about this empirical confirmation, it does make me more certain and does justify the approach adopted.

On the basis of the situation we have just described, we can *stress the fact that psychoanalysis always leads to the adoption of determinate positions (attitudes) but does not always generate coherent social representations*. There is nothing surprising about this either. It does, on the other hand, transpire that 'attitude' is the most common of the three dimensions and that it is, perhaps, the first to appear in genetic terms. It is therefore reasonable to conclude that it is only after a position has been taken, and only on the basis of that position, that people seek to inform themselves about and shape a representation of something. Recent research into perception and judgement (Moscovici 1962) fully endorses that conclusion.

A comparison of the content and degree of coherence of a group's information, field of representation and attitude brings us to the last point we propose to study: the way their social representations split groups.

A group is defined on the basis of a bundle of presuppositions which give a preferential weight to a certain number of criteria. In this survey about psychoanalysis, we have followed the general practice of using both socio-economic criteria (middle classes, working class) and professional criteria (students, liberal professions). Isolating these criteria is very difficult and the way they overlap with the cultural content specific to certain groups and common to others makes it difficult to organize them into a hierarchy. Some indices do, however, allow us to identify them with respect to psychoanalysis. The 'working-class' sample is divided into two sub-groups whose features have already been enumerated: subjects who have never heard of psychoanalysis, and subjects who have heard of it. The latter sub-group *cannot, however, be considered to be a group that is homogenous in terms of its representation of psychoanalysis* in general. Workers are not a group that is *univocally* defined with respect to psychoanalysis. Despite the diversity of their interests, political options and social origins, students, in contrast, constitute a relatively well-defined group. The middle classes have only *one* dimension in common: middle classes (A) *have* a structured social representation of psychoanalysis, and middle classes (B) do not. The differentiating factor here is *socio-cultural*: a higher socio-economic level and degree of education in the first sub-group, and a lower level and degree in the second. In this group, it is neither age, profession, degree of religious belief nor indifference to religions that differentiates the two sub-groups and positions them with regard to psychoanalysis. We can therefore speak of a middle-class *attitude* towards psychoanalysis, but not of a shared *representation*. Amongst intellectuals, the divide is *ideological* or, to be more precise, political. Attempts to identify other factors such as gender, religion or profession have not allowed us to distinguish between the sub-groups. When, on the other hand, we divided intellectuals into 'left' and 'centre-right' sub-groups, we did find *two coherent social representations*. In the middle classes, the dividing line is, as we have seen, socio-cultural; in the professionals, which were initially viewed as a single group, the dividing line is ideological, as both sub-groups have a distinct representation of psychoanalysis.

Diversity of structuration, diversity of content, or the inverse: we see that it is possible bit by bit to define the contours of a group on the basis of its worldview or its vision of a particular science. We commonly speak of class consciousness, national consciousness and so forth. We further observe that the representation also translates the relationship of a group to a socially valorized object, notably by the number of its dimensions, but above all by the extent to which it differentiates one group from another, either by its orientation or by the fact of its presence or absence. Because of the reciprocity that exists between a collectivity and its 'theory' (consciousness, representation, etc), its theory is, as our empirical observations confirm, *one of its basic attributes*. Which is another way of saying that it delineates and defines it, and that all other definitions remain abstract and artificial. In this way one of the modalities through which representations are conferred with their collective character is made concrete.

3.2 *The substantive 'representation' plus the adjective 'social'*

What meanings does the adjective 'social' add to the substantive 'representations'? We have already described one of them: the dimension of social groups. But we stated from the outset that this is a superficial meaning. In one way or another, it corresponds to an *expressive* criterion. As we can see, this immediately raises a whole host of questions. What are the precise limits of the social? Can a representation be other than social, and which indices allow us to recognize the degree to which a representation is adequate to a social group, and so on? The battlefield where classical sociology and social psychology meet is strewn with books and systems that have tried to address these questions and to decide between the possible answers. I will not follow their example not because I am any wiser, but because I believe that these questions are sterile and that the scientific tree on which the answers grow bears rotten fruit.

Let us look elsewhere for a better defined point of attack, and look at the *process of the production* of representations. From this perspective, describing a representation as 'social' means opting for the hypothesis that it is collectively produced and generated. As we know, this hypothesis has been challenged by psychologists and sociologists who stress the important and exclusive role the individual plays in the genesis of conceptions that are adopted by society. The Durkheim–Tarde controversy is still present in everyone's memory. Today similar controversies have lost their acuity and are dressed in more subtle forms. Asking 'who produces a representation, a science, an ideology and so on' is now common practice, and the answer is *ipso facto* a group, a social class, a culture and so on. And yet, because they have been repeated so often, and because they form the basis of a consensus, references that were once sources of light and discovery have become sources of obscurity and of boring banalities. In terms of their production or origins – collective or individual – science like representation, technology like ideology are hardly differentiated. It might be more accurate to say that they have not been differentiated. People are content to list the part played by the historical or economic situation, or by social or individual motivations, in the construction of a particular content and the specific form it receives.

And it is in this connection that a change of perspective seems to me to be needed. It is no longer sufficient to qualify a representation as social simply to define the *agent* who produced it. It is now clear that one no longer shows how it differs from other systems that are just as collective. Knowing 'who' produces these systems is less instructive than knowing 'why' they produce them. If, in other words, we are to grasp the meaning of the adjective 'social', we would do better to emphasize the *function* to which it corresponds rather than the circumstances and entities that it reflects. This function is specific to it to the extent that the representation contributes exclusively to *the processes that shape social behaviour and orient social communication.*

It is the specificity of its function that allows us to say that a representation is 'social'. It differs from, for example, the function of science or ideology. The former strives to control nature, or to tell the truth about it; the latter strives, rather, to provide a human group with a general system of goals, or to justify its actions. They will subsequently demand appropriate behaviour and communication. But in order to be able to do that, they must undergo transformations that make them conform to their representational mechanisms. Of course science and ideology also have a contribution to make, as do philosophy and art. But that is not their essential objective. The transition from a scientific theory to its social representation, in contrast, does answer the need to instigate behaviours and visions that are socially adapted to the state of our knowledge of the real. The dimensions of space, as conceived by a physicist, do not spontaneously conform to the sensations of seeing and touching, or to the dimensions we recognize in everyday life. The fact that the earth revolves around the sun is far removed from our sense-data and from our experience of the setting and rising of the sun, which leads us to think the opposite. The reasoning of physics or astronomy – and scientific reasoning in general – apply to pure cases, and to isolated phenomena that exist in a very rarified and stylized environment. If that reasoning were applied to the solution of the complicated but ill-defined problems that assail individuals or groups in a context as un-rarified and non-stylized as the concrete physical or sociological environment, the outcome would be at best comical and at worst the very opposite of the outcome we wanted. As Garfinkel (1967) very rightly remarks, the rational elements in science are neither stable features nor ideals that sanction our day-to-day ways of going about things. He further argues that any attempt to make those elements stable will simply emphasize the absurd character of the environment in which individuals behave and add still more disarticulated features to the interaction system. If we wish to avoid these unfortunate side-effects, a change of level and of the way in which we organize our knowledge is required. If we change them in the way suggested, it should be possible to bring about the necessary adaptation of science to society, and of society to science and the realities it discovers.

Representations do more than avoid such side-effects by bringing about transformations in the cognitive order; they also inscribe them in concrete collective relations. Psychoanalysis, for instance, provokes hostility when it is associated with the American way of life and becomes a negative sign of that way of life because it comes to resemble bourgeois knowledge, as opposed to knowledge that conforms to the values of the working class. Because it makes it possible to translate so many material and social normative conflicts, its representation grounds the scientific raw materials in the wider environment we all share. At the same time, it motivates and facilitates the transposition of supposedly esoteric theories to the level of an immediate and exchangeable knowledge, thereby becoming instruments of communication. On the one hand, the representation substitutes the science; on the other, it constructs (or reconstructs) it on the basis of implied social relations. On the one hand, then, in this way a science acquires a double – the shadow it casts on the body of society; on the other it is itself reduplicated to the extent that it exists both inside and outside the cycle of society's current interests and transactions. An example will clarify the argument. The concepts of the psychical apparatus, repression and the unconscious were used by Freud to describe certain phenomena. The goal of their scientific formulation was to unveil the truth, to explain observable facts and to support a therapy. When the same notions are used by someone who is interviewed for our survey, their objective is to determine behaviour and, usually, to communicate with someone else about a socially important theory, to describe the individuals to whom he relates by describing them as 'repressed' or having 'complexes', or, finally, to give those relations a political or ethical meaning. At a still deeper level, we can say that communication in some sense moulds the very structure of representations. Bartlett (1932) said that 'everyday thoughts are thoughts that are used for immediate communication'. Effectively a social representation condenses a quite direct, diversified and diffuse collective reflection, each of its participants being up to a point an autodidact, and like every autodidact takes both the dictionary and the encyclopedia as an ideal. Hence the narrative, descriptive, arborescent style, with its repetitions and its goings and comings between 'texts' produced by 'thoughts used for immediate communication'. Hence too the impression that they have internalized a vast number of possible dialogues. When they speak, individuals refer 'to them' – psychoanalysts, Americans, rich people and so on – or to what George Mead (1934) calls a 'generalised other', who is the quintessence of all interlocutors, near and far. To correct the imbalance, the individual defines himself as a 'generalised self', and therefore as a spokesman for his group or class, for Christians or 'common sense', and not as a particular person. Indeed when, in the course of an interview or when speaking to someone else, the individual does speak as an individual, he does so in order to distance himself from what he says as a 'generalised self', and in order to become a commentator on his own discourse, which he describes as 'their discourse' or 'everyone's discourse'. As he does so, psychoanalysis – or any other science – becomes a behavioural and communicational substratum, and acquires the 'double' we described earlier. But once he distances himself from it and reinserts psychoanalysis into value-laden relations, he brings pressure to bear on it; a further aspect emerges and it is reduplicated in the shape of a psychoanalysis – or science – of society. Scientists usually take no interest in this aspect, despise it and regard it as null and void. In recent years, they have been able to observe, thanks to the tendency to challenge the sciences, that this attitude is to a large extent false and incoherent.

Resolving problems, giving social interactions a form and supplying a mould for behaviours are powerful reasons for constructing a representation and decanting the content of a science or an ideology into it. As we shall see in a moment, this happens to a varying degree and in roundabout ways. Within a group, this is largely a matter of behaviour and of predicting behaviour, and of sets of categories of thought and exchange corresponding to the social situation of those groups and the religious or political norms they share, or which divide them. Despite those variations, the representation, and the attention it draws to psychical, physical or collective phenomena by functioning as a framework for the interpretation of those phenomena, becomes one of the constituent factors of reality and social relations. It has to be said that those relations and that reality are not 'concrete' on the one hand and 'represented' on the other. Their interweaving is total, and the analytic distinction between the two is fragmentary and artificial.

At the threshold of a study of the social representation of psychoanalysis, it was necessary to discuss a concept that has disappeared from the horizon of the social sciences for about one hundred years. It was necessary to show that it is an autonomous form of knowledge that obeys a good number of demands characteristic of the human mind when it is confronted with events that take place in a familiar world. Its style and logic bear, as will become more obvious later in this study, the mark of its *raison d'être*: consolidating the internal structure of a group or individual, making it real, communicating it and establishing links with others. It provides the resultant socialization with a set of specific figurative elements and a system of meanings that is in working order: 'What is a representation?' 'Why do we produce representations?' are the two questions we have tried to answer. We have paid less attention to the question 'Who is being represented' or 'Who produces a representation?' because, if considered on its own, it seems to me to be both superficial and largely resolved.

I had another reason for stressing this, rather than being content with taking things for granted. I wanted to remind social psychology that, if it really wished to understand the processes it is supposed to be interested in, it would do well to include in its field of study beside behaviour, the knowledge that individuals and groups possess and use about society, the other and the world, as well as the specific organization of this knowledge. But not only this. Behaviour and knowledge are understood, when they are understood at all, in a strictly instrumental way. Recent research into the attribution and perception of interpersonal relations is no exception. Now, social representations urge us to take more interest in the imaginary and symbolic behaviours we observe in the ordinary existence of collectivities. Reviving, on this point, the lost thread of a tradition may have some very happy consequences for our science.

2

Psychoanalysis as She is Spoken

1 The Presence of Psychoanalysis

The spirit of the age is the outburst of ideas acting on our vision of human nature. This age is one of ideological warfare, or what the Germans call *Kulturkampf*, an everyday occurrence that is changing the map of our world, and psychoanalysis is an important part or ingredient of it.

In this chapter, I would like to start clarifying the reasons that lead social groups to elaborate social representations and especially the reasons why French society has adopted a certain representation of psychoanalysis.

1.1 Good and bad reasons for psychoanalysis

That psychoanalysis has spread is a given. For the public, certain phenomena or certain reasons explain why this should be the case. Table 2.1 summarizes them.

First comment: *the scientific value of psychoanalysis is not regarded as the most important reason for its extension, which is attributed to many extrinsic factors (fashion, social needs).*

Although we do not have the tools to make a comparative analysis,[1] it can be argued that when science is associated with certain events or certain social groups, society recognizes the marks of its elaboration and proclaims itself to be the subject of its representation before weighing up the object that underlies it. This is probably especially true in the case of the human sciences, whose intervention is felt at the level of our individual lives. Many socializing operations must, of course, be performed if a science is to become a common and transformed image; atomic physics, for instance, did not originally look like the image that Hiroshima has given it.

---

[1] In the absence of complete studies, some interesting suggestions will be found in Ramsey and Seill (1948), Redlich (1950) and Woodward (1951).

Table 2.1 What are the reasons for the spread of psychoanalysis?

Sample	Individual needs (%)	Social needs (%)	Effects of war (%)	US influence (%)	Fashion publicity (%)	Scientific value (%)	N/R (%)	Total no. of subjects
Representative	5	12	19	11	19	14	20	402
Middle classes	0	22	34	23	30	25	0	331
Liberal professions	12	11	18	12	19	22	4	175
Students	14	20	15	13	26	11	1	140
Pupils in technical schools	0	25	12	0	27	32	4	101
Workers	28	0	19		31	21	0	210

The spread of psychoanalysis is seen as resulting from several causes. This is because, as the configuration of the world changed, it acquired a greater ability to provide answers, and its instrumentalization increased. Since every generation experiences contemporary events in different ways, the *age* of the subjects became the first differentiating criteria in our study. It transpired that, for the oldest subjects in the 'middle-class' populations, it was publicity and its scientific value that explained the spread of psychoanalysis, whereas, amongst students, it was the youngest subjects who answered 'fashion, publicity, American influence', whilst the older (over 25) subjects invoked social needs, the effects of the war and moral distress ($p < 0.05$).[2]

If we look more closely, we can identify two tendencies:

- The oldest subjects give more or less contradictory reasons for the spread of psychoanalysis (scientific value, fashion).
- The youngest subjects in the 'middle-class' sample are the same age as the oldest of the students and, like them, think that it is individual and social needs that have allowed psychoanalysis to spread. We do not, however, find any age-determined difference in the answers given by workers, apart from the fact that more older people give the answer 'effects of the war' ($p < 0.01$). We can therefore say that the answer 'individual and social needs' is characteristic of a certain generation within a certain social class.

Depending on whether they take a favourable or unfavourable view of psychoanalysis, subjects believe that its spread is due to this or that social reason, and they do so with a consistency that merits examination. Before

[2] Probability values refer to χ^2 tests for differences between sub-groups.

clarifying its meaning, I would like to list our findings. For the representative sample and the 'middle-class' sample it is due to social needs ($p < 0.01$) and scientific value ($p < 0.01$); those who are hostile to psychoanalysis explain its spread in terms of 'American influence' or 'fashion' ($p < 0.05$).

We obtain the same answers from students ($p < 0.05$), and similar tendencies can be observed amongst pupils in technical schools ($p < 0.05$), and workers ($p < 0.01$). When we turn to the intellectuals, ideology replaces attitude: Communists and left-wing intellectuals are virtually the only subjects to think that American influence is responsible for the spread of psychoanalysis; subjects on the right or in the centre are more likely to recognize the role of its scientific value ($p < 0.10$). It is assumed, then, that there are both 'good' and 'bad' reasons for the spread of psychoanalysis. People chose one or the other according to whether they are sympathetic or hostile to it. This is recognizably a normal way of understanding and explaining the order of events in our society.

Centuries of teaching logic have done nothing to change this. 'Tell me what you are afraid of, and I will tell you who you are.' Where social representations are concerned, the causal logic is always the same. No distinction is made between the object and its cause, which becomes one of its component elements and qualities: the good cause is linked to good psychoanalysis, and the bad cause to bad psychoanalysis. The object itself is judged, not in accordance with a general criterion, but on the basis of the subject's relationship with it.

The importance of this social mode of establishing links between phenomena has not gone unnoticed by psychologists (Heider 1944) and sociologists (Fauconnet 1928).

Other aspects of the social representation of psychoanalysis are, like the parts of a whole, bound up with the particular aspects such as the 'good' and 'bad' reasons for its spread, as we shall see if we examine these reasons in order:

Individual needs
- Subjects in the representative sample who give this answer are also more likely to think that (a) people go into analysis because they are social failures or have been disappointed in love ($p < 0.01$); and (b) psychoanalysis improves social relations ($p < 0.01$).
- Workers who give the answer 'social needs' think that it is artists and intellectuals, groups which they perceive favourably, who resort to psychoanalysis ($p < 0.10$).

Social needs
- In the 'pupils in technical schools' population, this category of answer is associated with the conviction that psychoanalysis has a contribution to make to the education of children ($p < 0.05$) and to improving social relations ($p < 0.01$), and this latter is also true of the middle classes ($p < 0.01$).

- In the middle-class sample, subjects who explain the growing importance of the discipline in terms of social needs also argue that it is not talked about often enough (p < 0.01).
- In the representative sample, the *scientific value* category goes together with a series of favourable opinions, including:
  psychoanalysis can contribute to the improvement of social relations (p < 0.05);
  its popularization is possible and useful (p < 0.05).

Fashion and advertising
Those who think that the spread of psychoanalysis is due to fashion and advertising also think that it modifies personalities for the worse (p < 0.10), that its effects are mostly political (p < 0.05), and that its goals are doctrinal (p < 0.05) (student sample). They also think that there is too much talk of psychoanalysis (p < 0.05). Amongst workers, that criticism is associated with an unfavourable view of psychoanalysts (p < 0.01).

We can see from these examples that the reasons for the spread of psychoanalysis are integrated into different aspects of its representation. More than the link between a cause and an attitude, it is the plurality of causes which is significant for each group. Their hierarchy is essential, it reveals the constellation in which psychoanalysis is grasped, and in which psychoanalysis is being considered.

1.2 Attitudes and level of knowledge

How much do people know about psychoanalysis? What, in general, is their attitude towards it?

Two methods allowed us to tell how much the public knows about psychoanalysis, and to satisfy our curiosity. In surveys of students, members of the liberal professions, the middle classes and pupils in technical schools, we asked a number of questions ('When did it emerge?' 'How long does the treatment last?') that allowed us to construct an information scale for each sample. Any subject can be ranked on the basis of his or her knowledge of psychoanalysis according to their position on this scale: Good, Average, Poor. Not having the means to make similar statistical estimates for the other populations, we asked the judges to estimate their level of knowledge on the basis of interviews and pre-determined criteria. The highest levels were designated 'A', and the poorest 'C'. The 'worker' sample posed a more delicate problem; the subjects had very limited knowledge, which made it impossible to establish a series of equivalences with the other informants. We therefore put the workers interviewed into sub-groups C1 and C2. As the actual content of their knowledge or ignorance about psychoanalysis is discussed throughout the book, our sole concern here is with the extent of the variation in the amount of their information.

Table 2.2 Level of knowledge of psychoanalysis (%)

	Higher			Lower	
	A	B	C	C1	C2
Representative	14	25	35	13	13
Middle class A		64		36	
Middle class B		27		73	
Liberal professions	24	16	30		
Students	28	34	38		
Pupils in technical schools	22	25	53	35	65
Workers					

For the populations covered by the survey, the distribution of levels of knowledge is shown in table 2.2.

We note first of all that 15 per cent of the 'middle-class' population and 51 per cent of workers have never heard of psychoanalysis. Those workers who do have some knowledge of psychoanalysis are the youngest (under 28), and are better trained. The vast majority of them are men. This is the only population in which there is a major difference between the knowledge of men and that of women.

It also transpires that psychoanalysis is better known in Paris than in the provinces.

Having noted that, we can say that those subjects who are best informed about psychoanalysis are (to restrict discussion to the sample, and without going into detail) aged between 20 and 28 ($p < 0.05$), in managerial positions or civil servants ($p < 0.05$), those who have an average or higher than average level of education ($p < 0.05$), and those who belong to a fairly wealthy socio-economic group ($p < 0.01$). But every population retouches this general picture in its own way. The level of knowledge of a member of the liberal professions often depends upon his or her political options. People on the left ($p < 0.01$) know more about psychoanalysis than those on the right or in the centre. A broad category of intellectuals appear to have hailed psychoanalysis as a revolutionary theme until the Communists expressed hostility to its spread. More Communists than members of all political and religious groups are at level C ($p < 0.01$), or at the bottom of the scale, even though the 'left-wing' informants group, to which they belong, is less well represented there. The contradiction between their interests as leftists and their estrangement from the Communists explains why they are concentrated at both extremities of the scale. The political dimension does not affect the other populations interviewed.

When we state that intellectuals, students, pupils at technical schools and, to a lesser extent, the middle classes have a fairly good knowledge of psychoanalysis, we are making a *social* and *comparative* estimate and this

Table 2.3 Variations in attitude and populations

	Attitude towards psychoanalysis		
Population	Favourable (%)	Neutral (%)	Unfavourable (%)
Middle class A	22	38	40
Middle class B	30	34	36
Liberal professions	36	40	24
Students	66	0	34
Technical schools	53	30	17
Workers	43	32	25

finding only has value in relation to the totality of subjects interviewed. A scientist or psychoanalyst would be entitled to reject this statement. The dimensions of our survey suggest that psychoanalytic knowledge is widely distributed across various social groups.

Freud is a well-known figure: 64 per cent of subjects in the 'middle-class' sample could name the founder of psychoanalysis.

The public tends to confuse the *historical* moment of the appearance of psychoanalysis with that of its *social emergence* and, whilst 54 per cent of the middle classes, student and pupil populations did accurately date the beginnings of psychoanalysis (late nineteenth and early twentieth centuries), a significant proportion (37 per cent) dates its emergence to the late 1930s. Psychoanalysis is therefore perceived to be a very recent discovery and, according to many, this explains why it is still not widely known. The fact that the young generations pay it more attention seems to confirm this hypothesis.

Is there a corollary between a subject's level of knowledge about psychoanalysis and his or her attitude towards it?

We first note:

- a rather neutral and unfavourable attitude in the middle classes and amongst members of the liberal professions;
- a favourable attitude amongst students, workers and pupils in technical schools.

Notwithstanding the widespread opinion to the contrary, women do not have a more sympathetic view of psychoanalysis, and men are not more hostile to it. Neither their family situation, their level of education nor their socio-economic positions influences subjects' attitude towards psychoanalysis, and nor does the fact that they live in Paris or would rather read a newspaper than listen to the radio. In all groups, with the exception of

Table 2.4 Attitude and level of knowledge

		Attitude towards psychoanalysis		
Population	Level of knowledge	Sympathetic (%)	Neutral (%)	Unsympathetic (%)
Liberal professions	High	36	43	21
	Average	32	40	28
	Low	42	37	21
Students	High	63	0	37
	Average	65	0	35
	Low	70	0	30

intellectuals and students, it is the youngest subjects that are most sympathetic towards it ($p < 0.05$). We have already noted that psychoanalysis is popular with students, workers and pupils in technical schools, or in other words with populations that are young in either cultural or chronological terms. An *internal* analysis of each population merely confirms this finding. There is therefore no clear correlation between what subjects know about psychoanalysis and their attitude towards it.

We merely note some correlations:

- In populations with a fairly good knowledge of psychoanalysis (students, liberal professions, middle classes), there is no clear link between knowledge and attitude. There may even be a tendency for those who know most about it to be unsympathetic.
- Among the 'workers' and 'pupils from the technical schools', the subjects who are sympathetic to psychoanalysis are those who know most about it ($p < 0.05$).

The explanation of these findings must take several factors into account. Observation allows us to make a first partial comment: left-wing intellectuals know most about psychoanalysis and they currently distance themselves from it to some extent.

Is this a more general phenomenon? The best-educated groups become acquainted with theories because they are accustomed to doing so or because they must do so for professional reasons. They also become 'saturated' with them more quickly (this indicates that the objects have become very familiar). When members of less-educated groups look in depth at certain general cultural questions, they make a special effort and are motivated by a genuine interest in them. That a worker – or a pupil in technical school – has some knowledge of psychoanalysis does not mean that he is receptive to contemporary culture or prepared to become involved in it.

To sum up: the average attitude towards psychoanalysis tends to be neutral or positive, with some major variations depending on

- age of subjects: younger subjects are more sympathetic;
- socio-professional group: intellectuals are relatively neutral; the lower and upper middle classes are neutral or view psychoanalysis with disfavour; students, pupils in technical school and workers are more sympathetic;
- ideological options: the great majority of believers (intellectuals, middle classes) view psychoanalysis sympathetically (p < 0.10) whereas most communist intellectuals do not (p < 0.01). Those who cannot be categorized as either 'right' or 'left' tend to be neutral.

There is no univocal relationship between knowing about psychoanalysis and being either in favour of it or hostile towards it. This brings us back to a fact that is so well known as to need no comment: the positions adopted by individuals do not depend upon how much they know.

2 The Taboo on Communication and the Attractions of Ignorance

2.1 The contagion of knowledge

So far I have shown that the public is receptive to psychoanalysis, and yet its spread is seen as having harmful effects. That is hardly logical. This paradox inevitably requires us to investigate the sources from which our informants derive their knowledge of psychoanalysis and on which they rely.

As the number of different answers they give shows, they have multiple sources (table 2. 5), which can be classified on the basis of their social function.

- institutional (school and university) and non-institutional communications;

and on the basis of the reciprocity or non-reciprocity of the exchanges in which they are involved:

- directional communications with a direct impact (press or radio) or transitive communication (conversation).

As well as being a place for the mediation between various kinds of communication, the source of information also has the sense of being a channel of communication, since at the same time it is the point of departure for the information and supports its communication.

Table 2.5 Sources of information

Population	School/ university (%)[a]	Books (%)	Entertainment radio press (%)	Conversation (%)	N/A (%)	Total no. of subjects
Representative	2	27	31	24	16	402
Middle classes	0	33	67	34	0	331
Liberal professions	40	27	13	20	0	175
Students (survey)	45	16	18	21	0	892
Pupils at technical schools	29	19	19	34	0	101
Workers	0	19	70	40	0	210

[a] Totals above 100% are due to multiple answers.

Every population has its dominant modes of communication, depending upon its social situation and degree of education. Radio[3] is rarely mentioned, and always by individuals belonging to the middle classes. The press and entertainment provide workers and the middle classes with their introduction to psychoanalysis, but are quite secondary for students in technical schools, intellectuals and students. The students are more likely to mention institutional sources of information (school and university), whilst intellectuals and the middle classes derive their knowledge mainly from books (a directional and non-institutional form of communication, which appears to play a less important role for other populations).

There is a relationship between the hierarchy of professional groups and that of sources of information. At the top of the hierarchy, students and members of the liberal professions came into contact with psychoanalysis at school or university, by reading about it, or in the course of private conversations. Students at technical schools have more in common with 'intellectual' groups, as their notions about psychoanalysis were acquired at school, but they also mention conversation as a source of information. The middle classes mention books almost as often as the liberal professions, but conversation, radio and the press play the same role as they do amongst workers.

(It should be noted in passing that the press, cinema and radio have allowed psychoanalysis to penetrate France on a huge scale; this reveals not only an interest in the subject but also a propensity for spreading it.)

---

[3] Given the low percentage of subjects who said 'radio', that medium has been included in the 'entertainment and press' category.

Although it is not perfect, we find, then, that the order in which sources of information appear relates to the stratified order of society. It is, however, noteworthy that conversation plays an important role for *all* social groups, and I would like to dwell on this point at greater length. The proportion of subjects for whom conversation is their primary source of information underlines the extent to which *psychoanalysis has penetrated interpersonal relations*. Most of the people interviewed are aware of it; it is of interest to them; they talk about it; it is, in a word, a topic of conversation. Only 18 per cent of middle-class informants reply 'not at all' when asked 'Do people around you talk about psychoanalysis?'; 40 per cent think that there is 'little' talk of it, and 42 per cent say 'a lot', 'quite a lot' or 'average'. Young people (aged between 20 and 35) are much more likely ($p < 0.01$) to say that psychoanalysis is talked about 'a lot' or 'quite a lot' in their circles. Mature (35 to 50 years old) subjects, in contrast, insist that they talk about it 'a little' or even 'not at all' ($p < 0.01$). Although conversation is not, as it is sometimes said, a specifically female speciality (women workers and students at technical schools are more likely to say that they learned about psychoanalysis from conversations, but that is not sufficient proof), women do display a slight tendency to say that those around them are drawn to psychoanalysis. Whereas men say that the frequency with which it is discussed is 'low' or 'poor'($p < 0.01$), women say that it is 'average' ($p < 0.01$).

Freud's theories are more likely to be discussed in better educated circles ($p < 0.01$).

Subjects' views about how widely psychoanalysis is discussed in their immediate circle are not determined by their attitudes towards it. If, however, a subject's own attitude is irrelevant, the attitude *attributed* to those around them is not:

- When subjects perceive the circles in which they move as 'sympathetic' or 'quite sympathetic' towards psychoanalysis, it seems to them that there is 'a lot' or 'quite a lot' of talk of it ($p < 0.01$).
- When the circles in which they move are judged to 'have reservations', they say there is 'little' talk of it ($p < 0.01$).
- When the circles in which they move are thought to have no interest in psychoanalysis, it is 'not talked about at all' ($p < 0.01$).

If psychoanalysis is to be an elective communicational object, the field of interest that is established around it must be seen as positive.
What is more:

- Those who think that there is 'a lot' or 'quite a lot' of talk about psychoanalysis in the circles in which they move also think that a 'a lot' or 'quite a lot' of people are in analysis ($p < 0.05$).

Table 2.6 Is there more talk about psychoanalysis than there was ten years ago? (%)

Sample	Yes (%)	No (%)	N/A (%)	Total no. of subjects
Middle classes	79	10	11	331
Liberal professions	57	18	25	175
Workers	74	6	20	210

An acquaintance with people who have been analysed reinforces the connections we have established: subjects who move in circles where people talk about psychoanalysis know more people who have turned to psychoanalysis than subjects who move in circles where people do not talk about it (p < 0.01).

If there is 'little' talk of psychoanalysis in the circles in which they move, subjects believe that 'relatively few' people go into analysis (p < 0.01).

These opinions support the field of interest that has developed around psychoanalysis and give it a sort of 'density'.

One conclusion clearly emerges: a subject's perception of a science is determined by the group to which they belong, the information they have about it and their attitude towards that science. A subject's perception of its presence is determined by its presence in their immediate circle's field of interest, and by the field's density (information, the circle's attitude, possible willingness to go into analysis, acquaintance with people who have been analysed). This presence is active. It is also 'spoken'. More and more so, if public opinion is to be believed. Subjects from three 'adult' populations – liberal professions, middle class and working class – were asked to say if, and *why*, there was now more talk of psychoanalysis than there was ten years ago. The answers were on the whole positive (table 2.6).

Why is psychoanalysis being discussed more widely? An analysis of the interviews provides an answer for each sample. Most intellectuals mention fashion and snobbery (18 per cent), American influence (15 per cent), the war and its effects (16 per cent), cultural progress (13 per cent) and the needs of the ruling classes (8 per cent). Other subjects say that there is as much talk of psychoanalysis as there was before the war, or that they are not in a position to express any views.

These fragmented answers do not do justice to the real argument:

'There is a lot of talk of psychoanalysis. A relatively new science, American propaganda, the American way of life is spreading to Europe.' 'There is not that much talk about it, it's only in certain circles – snobbish ones. Or because they laugh at it, rightly so, because it's a joke. No one laughs when they talk about Marxism, for example.'

The channels of communication help psychoanalysis to spread:

> 'There is more talk about it than there was before the war. The influence of American films has brought it to peoples' notice. People are interested in it.' 'There is too much talk of it; on the radio, and in publications like *France-soir*, *Samedi-soir* and *Reader's Digest*; it also corresponds to a real turmoil. It helps people to see things more clearly. Their immediate impulse is ask themselves what risk they run when they don't ask questions about society.'

It is the controversial and mysterious aspect of psychoanalysis that captures the public's interest. And the public accepts that this is the case:

> 'There is more talk of psychoanalysis; the economic situation, the crisis, unbalanced individuals; psychoanalysis can look like the solution.' 'There is a lot of talk about it; it's because of the magical, sacred character that surrounds psychoanalysis (the unfathomable, the unknowable). That has a great influence on the popular imagination. And it's entertaining.'

That so many reasons are given seems to suggest that there are many different forms of psychoanalysis: a scientific psychoanalysis, a fashionable psychoanalysis, a Hollywood psychoanalysis and a European psychoanalysis, a psychoanalysis for the press and another for class ideologies, and a psychoanalysis that provides a solution to psychological problems. If we were not talking about representations, we might well wonder which is the real psychoanalysis.

And yet, no matter whether it is as a result of American influence, the tragic aftermath of the war, or rising cultural standards, psychoanalysis is associated with a specific moment in the history of France. It is tied up with the great, but still ill-defined, turning point of the post-war years.

Although they take a different form, the comments made by workers are similar to those made by the other groups. The themes are the same, but their proportion changes. The 'growth of knowledge' outstrips all others, and is mentioned by 41 per cent of workers; 30 per cent invoke social upheaval, the war and American influence; 6 per cent mention fashion and advertising, whilst 22 per cent were not in a position to answer the question.

Psychoanalysis is a new science, or a science in the making:

> 'They're still doing the research, so not a lot is known about it yet. It's very new.' 'Didn't exist.'

As for the war:

> 'The war influenced people. They've lost their way. Social relations are much more strained.' 'After the war, people felt ill at ease, and they automatically asked themselves why they've reached this point.'

But psychoanalysis is also penetrating society because society is taking an interest in new problems:

> 'This sort of health care was not available before the war. But it seems that lots of people who are not quite mad are a bit abnormal, and it's because of their childhood.' 'Before the war, less care was taken of the mad, and they were locked up.'

This change of perspective is seen as a process of enlightenment:

> 'Basically, people were less intelligent, so they had less to say about it.'

In the past, advertising, the press, fashion and the 'American way of life' did not have the same influence:

> 'It was not in fashion, as it is nowadays. The papers talk about it more, and American influence also has something to do with it.' 'Before, the Americans used to leave us in peace, and hadn't started exporting Coca-Cola, chewing gum and psychoanalysis.'

Despite the diversity of their experiences, we find that intellectuals and workers all make the same observations, as do subjects in the middle-class sample. The themes expressed in that sample appear in the following order: novelty of psychoanalysis (16 per cent), popularization (16 per cent), development of psychoanalysis (16 per cent), war and insecurity (15 per cent), American influence (11 per cent), general growth of knowledge (11 per cent), fashion (10 per cent), press, radio (8 per cent).

On the whole, people think that they are living in troubled or *abnormal* times and think it *normal* that psychoanalysis should have a role to play. In this social space, which is filled with worries and conflicts, psychoanalysis looks like an oblique line, but an individual leaning in the same direction perceives it as a vertical. It is accepted because its intervention seems appropriate. In the fragments from the interviews I have cited, it is seen now as a remedy for a situation (upheaval, war), now as a response to a need (for knowledge) and sometimes as an index of some form of social action (political or cultural action). For most people, its presence has a meaning. This correspondence between psychoanalysis and specific needs or events reveals the *concrete basis* of its representation. When it is 'spoken' through events (war), relations between groups (French, American) and conceptions, psychoanalysis becomes structured and imbued with elements that are, a priori, extrinsic to it.

Here we hit upon what is, to my mind, the most sensitive index of the presence of psychoanalysis in French society: it is primarily a topic of conversation. It is neither a matter of factual information, nor a matter of systematic knowledge, but a matter of saying something about it or uttering a judgement. As people talk more and more about it in daily life, it gradually enters the common language and fills the time that people devote to talking about everything and nothing. Sociability itself is the main topic of these conversations alongside the weather, sport, etc. Such *phatic* communication is both exciting and subliminal, and often decisive in shaping our knowledge and behaviour. It is true that in everyday life 'the most important vehicle of reality-maintenance is conversation' (Berger and Luckman, 1967: 172).

It is not, as one might think, an informal communication. It is surrounded with a very specific ceremonial: the order of precedence, the available time, the bodily posture of the individuals. We do not 'chat' with everyone, at any time, or about everything. The gestures or the quality of the vocabulary or grammar count. Can it be called an effective or non-instrumental genre of communication? Certainly not. The partners involved try to state their differences or to reach an agreement, and also to impress themselves and each other with their intellectual qualities, competence and so on.

Within these limits, the goal remains the same: to maintain or modify the ongoing interaction. The question 'right or wrong' is deeply embedded in another one: to take part or not to take part in the making of social reality. And the answer depends on whether or not we share or do not share a certain knowledge, something foreign or familiar to us. Someone who knows nothing about psychoanalysis begins to learn about it by listening to those who do in their 'social circle'. 'Stories' are embellished with jokes or funny anecdotes, we observed, creating a density around the object, that is, psychoanalysis, and giving it a 'spoken' reality. It is as though the object were exerting its own subtle pressure at a time when individuals have not yet acquired the ability to recognize it, and yet it becomes one of the entities existing for them. People can even talk about it when they do not know what they are talking about. We could say that conversation in groups is an experimental activity. It involves a high level of repetition, a high failure rate and many approximations in asking questions and giving answers. It is as if we are not greatly concerned with efficacy when we are chatting, nor trying to inform or convince our partners so as to change their opinions. Though this is what we seem in a sense to achieve. So we could say that conversation is a reality and an end in itself. Verbosity is the price to be paid for having conversations as well as an obstacle to conversation. It is an indicator that nothing is completely forbidden and nothing is really deviant, because nothing seems more important than to keep on talking. Perhaps this is what is misnamed as rumour or social noise. As important as other communications genres, conversation is the main one that gives large sections of the public a privileged access to psychoanalysis.

2.2 *The rejection of popularization*

Knowledge does not, however, exist simply in order to be transmitted; everyone is convinced that it is transmitted with an end in view. Whilst the distinction between information and influence is meaningless at the sub-communicational level (communicating means breaking the silence, satisfying one's curiosity, experiencing one's complicity with the world, and nothing else matters), perceptions change when the exchange is no longer reciprocal and when it is books, papers or teachers who transmit the information. We all feel that we are in the presence of an organized enterprise that *wants to* let us know, demands a response and requires our involvement. The diffusion of a science is valuable because it is informative, but anyone who is in possession of knowledge is also in possession of power. He is competent and dominant; he is an expert and not just a sender, and the other is no longer just a receiver, but a layman. Acceptance of knowledge therefore implies dependence on the group that identifies with it and hides behind it.

If we wish to escape this dissymmetrical relationship, we can react in only one way: we must reject the information. When it is popularized, psychoanalysis becomes disturbing: 45 per cent of subjects are opposed to its diffusion, 36 per cent are in favour, and 19 per cent express no opinion. Those who belong to the 'middle' category are much more in favour of the popularization of psychoanalysis than subjects who are well off in economic terms $p < 0.10$. Those subjects with the highest level of education are most in favour of the diffusion of psychoanalytic ideas ($p < 0.01$); those with least education are neutral, and those with an average level of education are reluctant to voice any opinion ($p < 0.05$). Women appear to be generally in favour ($p < 0.01$), whilst men take refuge in abstentionism.

What is the meaning of these views about the popularization of psychoanalysis? An analysis of the interviews allows us to refine the summary categorization of 'for' or 'against'.

Popularization seems to offer those who accept it (20 interviews) more information, and a possible habituation to new practice. This may lead individuals to become part of a new culture, and to learn to regard psychoanalysis as a normal option, should they need it (16 interviews).

> There is nothing wrong with popularization. It shouldn't go too far, but it's no bad thing for everyone to learn what it is' (PTS). 'It's a good thing, why not? People are informed and know that they can consult an analyst' (LP).[4]

---

[4] The adoption of a few conventions will make the text easier to read. One such convention allows us to indicate which population the subject expressing an opinion belongs to: W = worker; S = student; LP = intellectual (liberal profession); PTS = pupils in technical schools; MC = middle-class informant (office worker, artisan, civil servant, etc.).

Many respondents express reservations about the activity of popularization. They are mainly concerned about the *quality* of the popularization
(25 interviews). The very word 'popularization' has a pejorative meaning
and arouses opposition.

> 'Popularization: it inevitably distorts things, but, truth to tell, it's why I know
> about psychoanalysis' (LP). 'I'm opposed to popularization in general; it dis-
> torts things, but it may be necessary to stop people being frightened, to get
> them used to this new form of treatment' (LP). 'Same problem with all pop-
> ularization' (PTS).

Popularization in general is judged to be simplistic and superficial (64
interviews):

> 'I don't know. it all depends on what psychoanalysis really is. I don't know
> enough about it, but as a general rule we should distrust popularization
> because it's always superficial' (LP). 'At the moment, popularization is very
> bad; we have to change the way it's done. It would be useful if it was done
> properly' (PTS).

Quality seems to be essential to most subjects. They therefore ask *who* is
doing the popularization. It sometimes seems to them that it has to be
guaranteed by a specialist:

> 'Useful, provided it is done by scientists and not the common herd. Scientists
> know how much to say and how to measure their words' (LP).

Until now, the popularization of psychoanalysis seems to have raised only
minor problems for our subjects (approval of or reservations about the
quality of the information or the character of the informant); if we attempt
to go further and look at the symbolic level, we encounter a series of value
judgements about knowledge (knowledge about human beings in particular, and knowledge in general).

Popularization now becomes a sign that knowledge has been *debased*
and that it is *aggressive*. Every individual lives inside a circle of relatively
stable objects; they are his immediate and self-evident truths, and they
provide him with daily confirmation of his existence.

It is this environment that assures the subject or group of its social and personal identity. Other people are there to make ritual responses to his prompt-
ings in the form of more or less ceremonial actions to tell him once more that
he is indeed what he is: French, Catholic, of sound mind and so on. The world
of knowledge can undermine this evidence and destroy the integrity of this
identity. Groups and individuals make a careful distinction between:

(a) what we are supposed to know, and what we are not supposed to know;
(b) what we talk about and what we do not talk about.

Which implies, of course, that what should not be talked about is talked about, and that we know what we should not know. Those who regard the spread of information as the solution to human problems and who believe that difficulties of a technical nature are the sole obstacles to its diffusion fail to recognize one major psychological phenomenon: for human beings, having access to knowledge is transgressive – in the strict sense of the term. But whilst it is true that, in order to have access to certain *spheres* of knowledge, certain intellectual or moral aptitudes are necessary, that objective basis is, so to speak, diluted by a value system with a strong affective charge which insists that all knowledge is the knowledge of an elite and that sees all popularization as a sign that knowledge is being debased (18 interviews).

> 'Popularization is not a good thing for anyone who has to act in his life, as it takes away the rather magical prestige that surrounds science; it plunges them into a meditation, and they can't find their way out again. It is bad for people to know a little without having full knowledge' (LP). 'There are two reasons why psychoanalysis should not be popularized: it is a scientific method and it is an exceptional method. People who believe in psychoanalysis are obsessed with it and drive those around them mad. It's a deplorable weapon when it is *democratized*' (LP).

Understanding psychoanalysis means knowing oneself thanks to psychoanalysis, seeing oneself in a new way, and changing the way one relates to reality or one's image. Popularizing psychoanalysis is seen as something dangerous because it is not just a way of giving people a mode of information; it also gives them a tool that can influence people. The fear of internalizing psychoanalytic concepts is all the greater in that it is the representation of society that is at stake (33 interviews).

> 'Popularization? No. Encouraging people to look at themselves too closely is a very bad idea. It's the best way to create misfits, and there are enough of them as it is' (LP). 'No, it would be like medicine, which convinces everyone that they're ill. Creates neurotic patterns of behaviour' (LP). 'There's a danger of creating new needs; we've managed perfectly well without it so far' (PTS). 'As far as the general public is concerned, these ideas just disturb people and fill their heads with wild imaginings' (LP). 'It's a threat to normal people; we're better off not knowing some things' (PTS).

Some intellectuals also stress the ideological implications of popularizing psychoanalysis:

> 'I'm opposed to the popularization of psychoanalysis; it's further proof that its real purpose is social mystification.' 'It doesn't just prove to the petty bourgeois that they're something exceptional, it also corrupts the marginal fringes of the proletariat.'

Those who are in favour of the popularization of psychoanalysis regard it as a science with an obviously deontological status. They regard it as an instrument that can raise the cultural level in general.

They see psychoanalysis as a possible therapeutic choice for people who are trying to come to terms with the ordinary difficulties of life. Its popularization appears to them to be quite in keeping with the ideal of the freedom of information that our society demands.

It should be noted that everyone regards popularization as something that is both serious and pragmatic. Those who think that psychoanalysis can help individuals and those who tell us that it will distract them from social issues, those who worry that it will spread morbid ideas, and those who tell us that it provides an answer to the worries resulting from the war, and those who are in favour and those who are against, all view it as a conception that is powerful enough to alter the structure of the living world.

A prejudice against psychoanalysis usually goes hand in hand with a poor opinion of the quality of the available information. It is impossible to judge the competence of those who supply it, and they constitute a disturbingly powerful but generalized 'they'. Such fears are justified to the extent that psychoanalytic models are rarely diffused for purely pedagogical purposes.

That explanation does not, however, apply to all the opinions expressed and does not exhaust all the hypotheses we require if we are to understand them. If we are to do that, we have to recall that knowledge has always, since ancient times, been perceived as the prerogative of a restricted group. Sacred and profane esoterism has always had a particular resonance, and it still does. Subjects who regard the popularization of psychoanalysis as a debasement of knowledge or as the destruction of a 'magical' atmosphere, to use the expression cited earlier, argue that it is the preserve of knowledge. For similar reasons, there is a reluctance to see it becoming common property, and a rejection of every propagation that does not reserve it for the elite.

Other positions are based upon the postulates that:

'We're better off not knowing about some things.' 'Erecting barriers around certain questions is the only way we can lead a balanced life.' 'A failure to recognise, or a failed self-recognition, is in man's best interest.'

Psychoanalysis's baleful influence spreads to the extent that individuals begin to want to analyse themselves, or in other words to internalize the knowledge they have acquired. When this happens, psychoanalysis is no longer a matter of diffusing information, but a factor for change. The affective incidences of a dichotomy of 'good' and 'bad' knowledge usually find expression in the frequent repetition of the word 'threat'. Whilst I do not wish to make an in-depth anthropological analysis of the roots of this bundle of attitudes and whilst I am not competent to do so, we can still demonstrate the existence of a real *taboo on communication*. *The taboo is not on knowledge itself, but on its diffusion.*

The universality of this taboo appears to me to be just as strong as the taboo on incest. It can take many different *forms* in different societies, and can apply to very different contents (science, politics, philosophy, techno-logy). Eve's apple and the Prometheus myth are precedents and provide ample material for a more in-depth study. Most societies give this taboo an institutional form. No matter whether they are sacred or profane, those institutions can themselves take novel forms and can affect very distant epistemological regions. If we are to understand this taboo's function, we must look at its positive aspect: it is a rule that governs the exchange of messages.

2.3 The threat of a double-edged language

The transition from one culture to another obeys the rule that divides the world into zones in which the circulation of information is declared 'good' or 'bad', and communication 'free' or 'restricted'. Social organization depends upon the nature of knowledge, irrespective of man's ability to access it. Societies often forbid their members to have a certain vision of things or to become part of an emerging culture (the Church, for instance, did so when it prevented Catholics from reading the works of Galileo and Copernicus). When a new science develops on the fringes of an individ-ual's intellectual field, it is a harbinger of conflict. It raises questions to which we do not have answers, and gives answers to questions we had not foreseen. Psychoanalysis demonstrates the polymorphous perversity of innocent children; it introduces drives into what we thought was con-scious, rational behaviour and gives it a double; it extracts traces of the past from our present intentions. Both the physical sciences and the social sciences are undermining our terra firma. Once, we were simply asked to react; we are now being asked to make choices. What is much worse, we do not know if this inescapable diversification is a symbol of multiple real-ities or a symbol of the multiple dimensions of a hidden reality. Does new knowledge introduce groups and individuals to a different world, or to differences within the same world? Do the teachings of established reli-gions, sciences and philosophies deal with particular spheres of man, nature and society, or with man, nature and society in general? The revival of these divisions takes us back to plurality, unity lost to discontinuity in the circles of the real in which individual and collective beings move. What appeared to have a single, motivated and physical meaning proves to be a social construct that is variable and arbitrary. Norms that were supposedly universal because they were common to all and because there was no alter-native become specific and dependent on the relationship between science and society. We thought we knew the difference between the normal and the pathological; psychoanalysis convinces us that the boundary between the two does not lie outside us, but within us. 'Finally, it is our heritage from Freud that the all-or-none distinction between mental illness and mental health has been replaced by a more humane conception of the continuity of states' (Bruner 1957: 283).

Knowledge can challenge the legitimacy of our aptitudes, our actions or the code we use to interpret our relationship with others or with our history. It may become a source of tension and anxiety, distort links between groups and point them in new directions. Our communist informants say that they are worried: won't psychoanalysis interfere with the interests of the working class and make it lose sight of its political interests? All these reasons explain why we tend to reject science or the intellectual models that appear from time to time. We reject them in vain, as they find their way into our conversation and are spread by rumours. They exist, and they are both familiar and insistent; in a sense, we have all appropriated them already. How can we reject the satisfaction they seem to afford certain social groups? Because we want to escape the power of those who have mastered knowledge, we all feel obliged to seek knowledge and to overcome our tendency to avoid it. For it is not truth that frightens us; what does frighten us is the thought that we might fall into the cycle of submitting to those who speak in its name.

If, moreover, knowledge remains the object of a particular group, there is a threat to the social structure. If a group retains the visions and the practice of the real that it had before the new concepts appeared it loses control of the social structure as a whole, and of its relationship with part of society; if it does not wish to cut itself off from various sectors of reality, it must renounce the very thing that gave it its identity, either in whole or in part.

The conflict between the fear of knowing and the need to know (Maslow 1963: 125) affects, as we have seen, individuals' psychological and social integrity. By tracing its limits and delineating what is external to the group and what is internal to it, the taboo on communication channels that conflict. As the taboo is reinforced through repetition, it takes on connotations specific to the world of rules, with its unavoidable rewards and punishments. When this taboo comes into play with respect to a science, it does so because that science threatens the identity of those to whom it applies. Their representation of that science is a form of defence, a way of overcoming and warding off the threat. Thanks to the representation, 'the voice of the intellect', which is 'soft', 'does not rest until it gets a hearing. Finally, after a countless succession of rebuffs, it succeeds' (Freud 1927: 53).

3

Ideas That Become
Common-sense Objects

1 Objectification

How does a representation of a social object take shape in such a way as to ward off the threat it represents and to restore the identity it calls into question? I cannot answer this question completely. What is more, the verb 'take shape' does not have a genetic meaning here. It designates, rather, a probable sequence of events, and it is to be hoped that experimental observations will one day confirm its stages. Yet, these are not mere hypotheses. The sequence was established by correlating a series of analyses, and the material from the surveys is there to support my assertions and, if need be, to correct anything artificial that they may contain.

Social representations take shape according to two basic processes: *objectification* and *anchoring*. The social body's slow investment of psychoanalysis and the way referential values influence its evolution relate to its anchoring. Objectification helps, as we know, to make a conceptual schema real and to reduplicate it in a material counterpart. The initial outcome is a cognitive mechanism: the stock of indices and signifiers that an individual receives, sends and shuffles in the infra-communicational cycle may become superabundant. In order to reduce the discrepancy between the mass of words in circulation and the corresponding objects, and because we cannot talk about 'nothing', 'linguistic signs' become attached to 'material structures' (we attempt to link words to things). This approach is all the more indispensable in that language – and especially scientific language – presupposes a series of conventions that establish its adequacy to the real. According to Freud, for example, the 'Oedipus complex' designates a specific way of organizing relations between parents and children. Psychoanalysts use the formula to group a set of relations between individuals, and to interpret certain symptoms. But its usage certainly does not imply the presence of the complex. Individuals and groups who know nothing about the rules specific to psychoanalysis and who do not observe that convention take the word to be indicative of a material phenomenon whose existence can be verified. When the technical norms of language and the current lexicon become divorced, what was a symbol comes to look like a sign. It is then quite natural to try to find out what it is a sign *of* and to make it correspond to some 'reality'.

As a result of this decentralization, elements of a scientific language pass into everyday language, where they obey new conventions. Invested with a new power, the words 'complex' and 'repression' now designate obvious manifestations of the real.[1] Even if psychoanalysis had, like Aristotelian physics, been forgotten about long ago, it would still impregnate our worldview and its vocabulary would still be used to designate psychological behaviours. Objectification means reabsorbing surplus significations by making them material (and distancing ourselves from them). It also means transferring something that was no more than an inference or symbol to the level of observation. As Gibson remarks: 'Visual perceiving often enough does not feel like knowing; instead it feels like an immediate acquaintance or a direct contact' (1960: 220). Ideas are no longer perceived to be products of the intellectual activity of certain minds, and are seen as something that exists outside. Something that was known has been replaced by something that is perceived. The gap between science and the real narrows, and what was specific to a concept comes to look like a property of its counterpart in the real world. This is why everyone in our society can recognize an individual's 'complexes' as personal *attributes* of that individual. That recognition is not moreover necessarily associated with psychoanalysis.

I will now attempt to analyse the implications of objectification, and the forms it can take.

We saw in the previous chapter how the diffusion of a science calls into question the integrity of the collectivity because it escapes its control, and how it creates a link of dependency on the group that represents it. If a scientific conception is to be harmonized with behaviours with which we can identify, it must become detached from this group of 'experts'.

Because it objectifies the scientific content of psychoanalysis, society no longer positions itself with respect to psychoanalysis or psychoanalysts, but with respect to a series of phenomena, and it feels free to do what it likes with them. The testimony of human beings mutates into the testimony of the senses, and an unknown world becomes familiar to all. Once individuals can relate to this environment without the mediation of a specialist or his science, they move from a relationship with others to a

[1] 'The normal observer naively assumes that the world is exactly as he sees it. He accepts the evidence of perception uncritically. He does not recognize that his visual perception is *mediated by indirect* inference systems' (Segall, Campbell and Herskovitz 1966: 5).

relationship with an object, and this indirect appropriation of power is an act that generates culture:

> Reification – the making of ideas into things located outside of individual mentality – is *proscribed* (sometimes but not invariably) in the logic of science and even in some part of common sense. But it is prescribed as a canon of the common sense of cultural involvement . . . Collective reification, then, is the most revealing concise account of how a cultural idea is treated in terms of its behavioural sources. How persons succeed in projecting notions on to a public is the core problem for the empirical research relating culture to behaviour. (Rose 1962: 172)

We can understand the importance of this: most of the stimuli that are said to provoke our reactions are in fact the result of a twofold effort on our part. We have already spoken of the first, namely the leap into the imaginary that transposes objective elements to the cognitive milieu and prepares them for a fundamental change of status and function. When they have been *naturalized*, the concepts 'complex' or 'repression' are assumed to take on the features of an almost physical reality. The intellectual character of the system to which they belong ceases to be of any importance; the same applies to the social aspect of their extension. The second effort is an effort of classification which locates and classifies parts of the environment and through the divisions it makes introduces an order that adapts to the pre-existing order, thus attenuating the shock occasioned by all new conceptions. The adaptation of the environment to beings, gestures or phenomena corresponds to a psychological need. We must interrupt the incessant flow of stimuli in order to orient ourselves and decide which elements are accessible to us in sensory or intellectual terms. A grid is imposed, and it allows us to name, and therefore to define, various aspects of the real. If a new grid appears, its new terminology will be associated with the existing entities it helps to redefine.

Thanks to the appearance of psychoanalysis, we no longer simply say of someone that he is stubborn or quarrelsome; we also say that he is aggressive or repressed. The categories of normal and pathological have changed. Naturalization and classification are the two fundamental mechanisms of objectification. One makes symbols real, and the other gives reality a symbolic appearance. One broadens the range of beings that can be attributed to an individual (and in that sense we can say that images play a part in our development), whilst the other detaches certain of those beings from their attributes so as to keep them within a general picture that is in keeping with the system of reference established by society.

In this and the following two chapters, I will attempt to show that culture is elaborated in this way by bringing every part back to a common denominator.

2 From Theory to Social Representation

2.1 What is psychoanalysis?

How is a scientific theory transformed into a social representation? I admitted at the outset that this is the main problem I have to address in my work. Elaborating what an explanatory science is might, perhaps, be one way of answering the question. But I am aware of the traps that lie in store for anyone who attempts to do so, and I would rather avoid the philosophical and epistemological obstacles by starting with a hypothesis: *psychoanalysis is an explanatory science.*

Demonstrating that all the laws of a theory are underpinned by one basic principle is all it takes for us to be able to describe it as 'explanatory'. If, for example, we refer to the Newtonian system, we find that it evokes the principle of universal gravitation to explain most movements on our planet and the actions of the planets. In the absence of such a principle, the various relations remain local relations; they can, in other words, all be examined separately, or in any combination we wish to choose. The fall of bodies, the trajectory of the planets and gravitation were so many phenomena known in isolation before the Newtonian synthesis gave them a unitary character (Koyré 1950).

That the actual nature of universal gravitation was not correctly recognized does not change its epistemological function.

'Libido' is to psychoanalysis what universal gravitation is to the Newtonian system, or at least Freud's first formulations (whose presence we note in our society) were based upon that fundamental phenomenon. The classification of the neuroses, the symptomatology, relations between parents and children, and the interpretation of dreams and symbols all derive from it or culminate in it. The first 'version' of psychoanalysis was structured around this principle, even though the notion of *libido* was itself never absolutely clear.

Let us look now at how psychoanalysis is defined by the public and at what schema of mental functioning is attributed to it. Nine hundred and fifty people from all social categories answered the open question: 'What, in your opinion, is psychoanalysis?'

The contrast between the evasive nuances of some statements and the stereotypical generality of others make it difficult to fit them into our categories. We will begin with an account of the content of the freely formulated statements. Psychoanalysis is, first and foremost, a *science* or a *theory*:

'The scientific study of the individual' (W). 'Psychoanalysis is a scientific theory' (S). 'A science that allows us to understand man' (LP). 'A relatively modern science that deals with problems that used to be the preserve of occultists' (MC).[2]

The definitions cited demonstrate that their authors are not in a position to give detailed accounts of the content of psychoanalysis. Their sole concern is to locate it within a familiar domain. In some cases, *therapy* is the dominant notion. This notion rarely appears in isolation, but the frequency with which it appears shows that psychoanalysis is very often regarded as a practice. Regardless of whether the therapy's effects are described as beneficial or harmful, the respondents were much more struck by the science's action than by its content:

> 'Psychoanalysis is a form of therapy for the neuroses' (W). 'Psychoanalysis is a form of therapy which, because it is based upon a psychological understanding of the individual, can succeed in ridding the individual of certain anxieties: the treatment consists in conversations designed to awaken the individual's complexes and to explain them to him so that he can get rid of them by becoming aware of them' (MC). 'Psychoanalysis is a therapeutic technique for use with people who are unbalanced but not mad' (MC).

The distinction between science and therapy sometimes becomes blurred and is replaced by a sort of *undefined practice dealing with the human personality in general*:[3]

> 'Psychoanalysis is a method for investigating and understanding the personality' (S). 'Psychoanalysis studies human life' (MC). 'An analysis that can be applied to anything; an in-depth analysis' (W).

No matter whether it is described as a science, a form of therapy or an undefined practice, psychoanalysis is always perceived through the intermediary of certain attributes that do more to make it stand out than to circumscribe its domain. The 'novelty' that makes it stand out from the indeterminacy of other psychological conceptions is one of the signs which, together with certain of its novel features, capture the attention. They are enough to individualize it.

> 'It is a new American system which consists in getting people to lie down in a darkened room and getting them to recount their dreams' (W). 'A new fashion

---

[2] The frequency with which these definitions appear is as follows: students: 17 per cent; intellectuals: 10 per cent; middle-class informants: 24 per cent; pupils at technical schools: 24 per cent; workers: 8 per cent.

[3] In the 'intellectual' samples (liberal professions, students, pupils in technical schools) this answer has a frequency of 25 per cent; in the other sample, it has a frequency of 17 per cent.

that tries to find out what is going on in people's minds and in the minds of people with depression' (MC). 'A modern invention that tries to make people believe that the reason they are ill is that they were unhappy in the past' (W).

The fact that psychoanalysis is a technique using language adds to its novelty:[4]

> 'Psychoanalysis is medicine without medication' (W). 'The study of the character or behaviour of individuals; ultimately, psychoanalysis means telling your life story' (MC).

Psychoanalysis is understood in terms of its extrinsic ritual manifestations, and the detailed descriptions give no hint of any specific understanding of the theory. The descriptions become more precise when it is recognized that psychoanalysis has *a particular conception of the nature* of the 'soul', 'character' or 'individual'. In everyday language, these terms designate a vague organization that is assumed to represent not an individual with all his or her attributes, but that individual's *essence*. Because it is apprehended thanks to the chiaroscuro of a fleeting perception or a linguistic habit, the only difference between this essence and a strictly defined personality structure is a socially conventional distinction that is, to a greater or lesser extent, organized. Saying that 'Psychoanalysis is a science of the soul', 'psychoanalysis is the study of character' or 'psychoanalysis is the study of the personality' does not cause subjects who express these views any problems:

> 'Psychoanalysis? A series of concepts that overlap with the realities of the eternal human soul' (LP). 'A new way of deciphering the human soul discovered by doctors' (MC). 'Studies the soul and the effects of human behaviour by looking at the soul, the environment and past experience' (MC).

Basically, it is always the same theme: psychoanalysis is a theory of the personality; it is a particular theory because the notions of the soul, personality or character are replaced by other specific notions:

> 'Psychoanalysis is the study of the subconscious and conscious mind' (W). 'Psychoanalysis is a scientific theory that tries to lay bare the unconscious and conscious phenomena that determine how we behave' (S). 'The study of the individual's conscious and subconscious complexes' (S). 'It is the study of the unconscious, of things we cannot discover simply through introspection' (PTS). 'A science that tries to reveal our deepest secrets and to explain our every action in terms of subconscious relations' (LP).

---

[4] This theme is relatively rare. It appears mainly in the definitions given by subjects from the 'middle-class' and 'worker' samples.

Because it is a science of the personality with novel structural characteristics, psychoanalysis is associated in the public mind with the various ways
in which human beings relate to themselves thanks to an imaginary
dimension of *depth* (relations are, so to speak, so many focuses of their
attention): hidden–visible, voluntary–involuntary, authentic–false, superficial–fundamental, etc. Public opinion is shaped by these relations. It
organizes similarities, and elements of the representation emerge from
them in the shape of simple outlines. Pairs of opposites that correspond
word for word (visible–false, hidden–authentic) are subsequently *embodied* in an agency of the personality; relations between them allow us to
understand its workings.

What is psychoanalysis?

'Discovering all the circumstances in his earlier life that make an individual
react in ways that do not reflect his *true* personality, and inducing, through
the intermediary of educators, an inner tension in a being who is handi-
capped' (MC). 'The internal study of the subject and the study of the involuntary being that dwells inside the subject, as opposed to the voluntary
being' (W). 'A science that allows us to understand our innermost and most
secret reactions, even if they are subconscious. We all wear masks, without
even realizng it. Thanks to psychoanalysis, we can take off our masks' (S).

According to these statements, psychoanalysis is a reworking, both codified and rational, of the ancient myth that 'powers' and 'forces' are inherent in us all. By the same token it embodies the hope that we will be able
to escape the oppression that day-to-day life brings to bear upon the finite,
microscopic life of the individual. 'Inner', 'implicit', 'possible' 'external',
'explicit' and 'attainable' all overlap in the desire to live, to be free and to
re-establish a truth that lies 'beyond' appearances. *The distinguishing
feature of psychoanalysis is that it is a sign of the re-establishment of subjectivity
and the laying bare of an authentic personality.*

'Psychoanalysis helps us to see what we cannot express and what we dare
not say' (W). 'Trying to find in people's actions and reactions something
secret that they cannot discover by themselves' (MC).

The way psychoanalysis is explained in terms of this image of personal life
allows us to arrive at a better understanding of the role that the conscious
mind and the unconscious play as the dramatis personae of the psychic
organization.

We have already outlined the features of the psychic organization that
are associated with psychoanalysis.

'Psychoanalysis studies the subconscious and tendencies that are usually
repressed' (LP). 'The study of the unconscious and of the way it relates to the

conscious mind and to the individual's antecedents' (MC). 'There are two things: the conscious mind and the unconscious' (W).

The unconscious and the conscious mind are often seen as a transposition of the pairs of categories we have outlined: hidden/apparent, involuntary/voluntary, inner/outer. As a result of this mutation, they acquire a conceptual dignity. The concepts of the conscious mind, the unconscious and repression are themselves steeped in concrete imagery and have the same dynamism as any contradictory concept. The fact that psychoanalysis is described as a science of the unconscious and of its relations with the conscious mind is a reflection of both the theory itself and of a stylized and pre-established conception of existential processes.

All these descriptions give rise to the personality structure that is associated with psychoanalysis.

The psychic organization is made up of two parts: the unconscious and the conscious mind (inner/outer, hidden/apparent), and one exerts pressure on the other; alternatively, the notions of repression and suppression are seen as expressions of a relationship of alterity.

If we ask about the result of its workings, we immediately get the answer: a complex.

The overall schema is shown below.

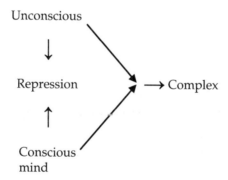

The interviewees were asked which 'psychoanalytic words' they knew. The most frequent words appeared in the order as shown in table 3.1.

The terms are the same as those in the schema. This calls for certain remarks. The psychical apparatus identified in this schema is the first apparatus described by psychoanalysis before 1920. Major modifications have been introduced since that period (Lagache 1956). This survey was carried out between 1951 and 1955. We therefore note that there is a historical discrepancy between the *theory and its representation*, and it cannot be explained by reference to the ignorance of the public. Students who have just come into contact with psychoanalytic theory and intellectuals

Table 3.1 Knowledge of psychoanalytic terms

Population	Frequency of appearance			
	1	2	3	4
Students	Complex	Repression	Unconscious/ Subconscious	Libido
Middle classes	Complex	Repression	Subconscious/ Unconscious	Libido Libido
Liberal professions	Complex	Repression	Unconscious/ Subconscious	Libido
Technical schools	Complex	Unconscious	Libido	Repression

who have an in-depth knowledge of it both use the model of a defensive conflict, and equate it with a conflict between the unconscious, the conscious mind and repression. We can conclude that the image of psychoanalysis initially crystallized around certain notions which could not then be rejected.

It can therefore be assumed that this schema is *meaningful*, or in other words that it corresponds in a striking way to the dynamics of the person just as they emerge from everyday experience. Its congruence with a dichotomous vision of that which is intimate is evident (a vision of two conflicting forces). Despite its revolutionary implications, the idea of an active unconscious is not alien to what individuals consider to be an intuitive experience. And whilst it is because it is highly structured that this model has become so widespread, it is also because it is similar to more familiar models. The concrete character of the elements of this 'psychic apparatus' stems from their power to express familiar situations. Their scientific origins and the links between them help to clarify a host of 'theories' that operate at a common-sense level. This metaphorical counterfeit money conflates 'complex' and 'unconscious' and then introduces divisions useful for the formation of an image that benefits from the familiarity of the sign and the prestige of science.

2.2 The mingling of concepts

The reason why there is a discrepancy between the theory and its representation is, then, that the first conceptualization of psychoanalysis is significant and that it is difficult to change images and symbols quickly. Freud's first formulation gave an important role to the 'libido'.

Now sexuality has no role to play in the schema we have described. Only 1 per cent of subjects mention libido in their definitions of psychoanalysis.

This is because the dominant values of our society refuse to recognize that the sexual drives are major psychological forces. If the individual experiences the world as a conflict between two terms, one authentic and inner and the other outer, a personality structure that reproduces that contradiction is in itself productive of a dynamic, and the energetic sexual element is an afterthought that adds nothing to the coherence of its structure.

If we eliminate the libido and its function – epistemological or real – and deny its existence without replacing it with other principles, we transform psychoanalytic theory into a *set of relations* (interpretations, phenomena, properties) that can retain a certain autonomy and that can, if need be, be integrated into a different conception. This bracketing out of its essential principle takes away a theory's unitary structure. Such is the object, and the outcome, of the clash between psychoanalysis and the norms of our society. Thanks to the social diffusion of psychoanalysis, some psychoanalytic concepts and notions have been, and are, accepted (Bastide 1950), but its very principle is denied or concealed:

> 'I think that Freud exaggerated greatly when he turned sexuality into the main driving force within our psyche. Other drives, such as hunger, are just as powerful. Some neurotics (and I see a lot in my line of work) are sexually unbalanced, but that might well be because they're neurotics' (LP). 'The sexual problem is not as important as Freud claims. I do not think that the sexual act can free an individual from his complexes. I know people who do not have sexual relations and who are well-balanced' (LP).

Without its theory of sexuality, psychoanalysis becomes socially acceptable and, once that basic principle has been removed, the group can go ahead and rearrange the topography of its concepts as it sees fit; each of the familiar relations can now be 'manipulated', and accepted or rejected, irrespective of their original unity or order. There is nothing new about this work of conversion. And Freud was too alert to the traps that reason sets for science not to know it:

> A sort of buffer-layer has formed in scientific society between analysis and its opponents. This consists of people who allow the validity of some portions of analysis . . . but who on the other hand reject other portions of it . . . One person will take objection to sexuality, another to the unconscious; what seems particularly unpopular is the fact of symbolism. Though the structure of psychoanalysis is unfinished, it nevertheless presents, even today, a unity from which elements cannot be broken off at the caprice of whoever comes along: but these eclectics seem to disregard this. (1933: 138)

Where the social elaboration of a representation is concerned, we are not so much dealing with eclecticism, as with an attempt to instrumentalize the scientific model and to rebuild it around whatever values and categorical systems are available. As the theory becomes a set of relations, it loses its coherence; when they are taken separately, its internal principle, its dimensions and the impact of these relations come to depend on the group's social rules. Communist subjects place significant limits on the frontiers of the set by claiming a monopoly on the political domain. Believers are more open to certain of its aspects, and especially those pertaining to the unconscious, and more reticent about others. These are of course extreme cases. Do we have to dwell any longer on the effects of the elimination of this explanatory element? Once we cease to take sexuality into consideration, partial interpretations become permissible, and it is possible to establish a schema of the human psyche that has its roots in psychoanalytic theory but which gives no role to the libido. *In this specific case, the transformation of a structured theory into a set of relations with a variable degree of autonomy and a variable extension is the first precondition for the constitution of a social representation.*

By placing such emphasis on a whole series of phenomena bound up with sexuality, psychoanalysis has, on the other hand, stimulated an awareness of their 'taboo' nature and of their repercussions on the personality; the whole of psychoanalysis is therefore associated with the sexual behaviour of the individual.

> 'Adolescents should be taught about psychoanalysis as soon as they reach 15. Greater openness in relations with the family, and with women. I notice that my students (who are 20) are still embarrassed about some things, and about calling a spade a spade' (LP).

When asked about the relationship between psychoanalysis and religion, one subject replied:

> 'A theologian told me that our private parts are best left in the dark, and that we shouldn't talk about them too much' (MC).

Descriptions of analytic therapy are organized around the same symbolism. The analytic couple are viewed as heterosexual, and the analytic couch in a private room completes the picture:

> 'Psychoanalysis? It's a fashionable treatment for fashionable women. They lie on a bed, tell lots of stories about their lives and sometimes sleep with the psychoanalyst' (W). 'Psychoanalysis? A sort of magnetism for pseudo-hysterical women. Not scientific . . . The essential thing about women is their libido. The more primitive the woman, the more libidinous she is and the more she likes the sound of her own voice . . . The patients are women with nervous problems who don't know what to do with themselves' (LP).

Sexuality is not always viewed so unfavourably:

> 'Psychoanalysis certainly has a lot to offer where sexual problems are con-
> cerned. I'd happily go in for it myself, I think it can resolve a lot of things'
> (MC). 'There is a lot of talk of psychoanalysis amongst the general public.
> Freedom from social prejudices where sexual taboos are concerned' (LP).

The representation denies the existence of libido on the one hand, and
makes psychoanalysis the *emblem* of all things sexual on the other.
Psychoanalytic theory has influenced individual modes of behaviour. Its
emergence has led to a relaxation of the taboos surrounding our sexuality.
Those who have followed this development seem to think that it is now
over. It is as though the notion of 'libido' were no longer of any use once
sexual taboos had been relaxed.

The respondent's comments on sexuality are significant:

> 'Psychoanalysis is a theory that is still being worked out. Freud lived in a
> certain society and things have changed a lot since then, especially relations
> within the family – and psychoanalysis is based on that – and social relations
> in general, probably partly as a result of the influence of psychoanalysis.
> Freud's concepts are not immutable invariants, and some of them are no
> longer valid or will cease to be valid. Sexuality is no longer as taboo as it used
> to be; symptomatic forms of sexualized behaviour no longer have the same
> meaning, and never will have again' (LP).

To the extent that it has become the index of a certain sexual freedom,
psychoanalysis is taken as a whole. Whilst it has become diversified and
looser at the level of its content, psychoanalysis has, socially speaking,
acquired the symbolic unity we have described. We can therefore infer that
it is the contexts that allow a theory to penetrate a society that define the
dominant meaning associated with its representation.

We can therefore assume that the transition from a scientific doctrine to
its representation implies:

- that it changes into a set of relatively autonomous relations that can
  establish a behavioural framework related to the phenomena it has
  revealed, and that those relations are compatible with the dominant
  system of values;
- that it acquires a unitary meaning related to the circumstance of its
  social penetration, and to the essential aspects of the reality to which it
  applies and on which it is assumed to work. The clash with established
  values means that the science's basic principle must be eliminated,
  whilst its unitary representation makes reference to the eliminated
  principle. The kernel becomes a ghost, but it remains a very active
  ghost.

It is as though we were in the presence of both a *set-of-relations-psychoanalysis* that allows us to understand personalities and behaviour, and an *emblem-psychoanalysis* whose import is determined by collective norms.

Does the formation of the social representation of a scientific doctrine obey the same rules as the formation of any social representation? There is nothing to prove that it takes shape in a different way. The discrepancy between the conceptualization of psychoanalysis and its representation is indeed, as I have stressed, a sign that the representation develops autonomously. And yet it is marked (and facilitated) by the inherent autonomy of science.

Social controls and scientific controls obey the same objectives and specific rules. The fact that a science is present within a society modifies both its vision and its approach to the real. Social representations have a variable degree of objectivity in relation to that of the science which is their source. Both practices and current values can reorient it in one direction or the other. The need for the reorientation, the resultant conflict and the transformation of practices and values are part of the history and structure of the social representation of a science. If the representation can, in its turn, orient, restrict or encourage the development of the science, it does so because society requires it to do so, and I see that as a proof of that society's vitality.

3 The Materialization of Concepts

3.1 *The figurative model*

I will refer to the schema of the organization of the personality that has just been described as the *figurative model*. This is the model that is always referred to when an attempt is made to use psychoanalytically derived concepts to explain the behaviour of children, the resolution of conflicts or the effects of therapy. The model cannot be said to be wrong. But it reproduces psychoanalytic theory in a selective way. This reconstruction makes it possible to grasp the abstract and general forms typical of mature scientific thought. If I say that the model we have described is figurative that is because it is not just a way of coordinating data, but the product of a coordination that defines every part of representation in concrete terms.

In this model the unconscious, for example, is

(a) first, *part* of a whole:
'The goal of psychoanalysis is to resolve psychical problems that result from a conflict between the two *parts* – conscious and

unconscious – of an individual or, to some extent, between those two parts of the individual and his environment' (S). 'Psychoanalysis is designed to cure illnesses which are a combination of the subconscious and the conscious mind' (W).

(b) then described as an autonomous agency:

'Psychoanalysis studies the role the unconscious plays in generating behaviour' (S). 'A science that allows us to discern things that people are incapable of formulating and that are probably being *thought by the unconscious*' (MC). 'Psychoanalysis? Making the unconscious conscious via the subconscious' (PTS).

(c) finally, a 'force' that is in conflict with another 'force' known as the conscious mind. This personalized conflict takes place through repression. Discussions of 'complexes' display the same tendency, which is analogous with the 'thickening' of phenomenological descriptions.

'Gives people with a *complex* a new taste for life' (W). 'Psychoanalysis? A form of treatment that *takes away* peoples' inferiority complexes so that they can live their lives like anyone else' (MC).

It would be pointless to give more examples. The mutation of the abstract and its impregnation with metaphorical and visual elements individualize an important moment in the process of objectification: the theoretical edifice is *schematized*. The resultant schema or figurative model plays several functions:

- It is common to both the scientific theory and its social representation; its accuracy is of course relative, but it is still a *concentration* of most of the important concepts pf psychoanalysis.
- It changes the 'indirect' into the 'direct'; in other words, what is, in the theory, a general or abstract expression of a series of phenomena becomes an *immediate* translation of the real in the representation.
- The model brings together the elements we have described to form an autonomous sequence with its own dynamic: conflict between the implicit and the explicit, between inner and outer. This unitary model is inspired by psychoanalysis, but it excludes something that contradicts its dichotomous system of classification and social norms, namely the libido.

Because it penetrates the social environment as an expression of 'the real', the figurative model is, by that very fact, made 'natural', and is used as though it were a copy of that reality. The combination of the collective generalization of its use and the immediate expression of concrete phenomena allows the representation to become a stable cognitive framework and to orient perceptions of or judgements on inter-individual relations or behaviours.

3.2 *Science and inverted animism*

The naturalization of ideas takes on its full significance here, as it confers a full reality on what was an abstraction. As a result, 'complex' and 'unconscious' are no longer merely notions, but terms that have been materialized, or almost physical organizations. The following extracts from interviews illustrate the point:

> 'Psychoanalysis is applicable in certain rare cases, such as real mental illnesses. Cures are more frequent in cases of neuropathy: *moral shocks that have partly fallen into the unconscious* – that is when the repression is more pronounced' (LP). 'The *acquisition* of complexes has to be avoided in education' (LP). 'The unconscious is disquieting' (W).

There is also talk of the 'division' or 'mixing' of the unconscious and the conscious; a complex is not an expression of a relationship, but something quite specific, namely a sort of state or organ:

> Children's reactions have to be studied *in the light of their complexes*. But there is also such a thing as an underlying personality and, whilst it might well be disturbed *by complexes*, it is still something *else*' (LP). 'Psychoanalysis is a treatment for *taking out* people's inferiority complexes (W).

('Take out' has the same meaning here as in the expression 'take out an organ'; analytic treatment is being likened to a sort of neurosurgical procedure.)

This slippage from the concept to the collectively created entity is facilitated by linguistic habit. As Asch (1958) has demonstrated, the transposition of metaphors from the psychical domain to the sensory and physiological domain is very common. Representations of the object of any science also have an influence. Being midway between psychiatry and biology, psychoanalysis is inevitably seen as a science that acts upon organs, even if they are invisible. Because it makes them similar to other scientific denominations, the naturalization of psychoanalytic notions gives them an almost palpable presence. In our culture, the paradigm for all science is supplied by mathematico-physical science, or in other words a science of quantifiable and measurable objects. The effectiveness of a science is *socially* evaluated on the basis of its proximity or non-proximity to those norms. Science, *sit venia verbo*, is concerned with something that is not a subject. The operational value of the scientific imperative goes beyond the methodological framework, and its initial effect is to impose *social controls* on any activity that claims to be a science.

To the extent that the content of a science presupposes the existence of a certain type of reality, it encourages the creation of beings (through the identification of the concept with the real). Given that a science speaks of organs and that psychoanalysis is a science, the unconscious and the complex must be the organs of the psychical apparatus. Complexes can be taken out, removed and acquired; the living is assimilated to the inert, the subjective to the objective, and the psychological to the physiological. This *inverted animism* is a product of the predominance of the ideal-type we have just described. For certain of our informants, psychoanalysis is already a quasi-medical science with physiological effects; for others, it will become a science when it can operate at a physiological level:

> '[Psychoanalysis] is essentially a medicine; it makes allowance for the phys-
> iological aspect of mental problems' (LP). 'A science that is still in its very
> early stages, it will develop as the physiology of the brain becomes more
> sophisticated' (LP).

Of the 'middle-class' sample, 36 per cent criticize psychoanalysis for not having laws, and for not being quantitative or physiological. The same criticisms were put forward in scientific circles, but had no specific effects. The concepts of psychoanalysis contradict the scientific model. It is expected that psychoanalysis will *become* a science in order to overcome that contradiction; if it does not, it will be no more than a form of therapy. It must, in any case, act upon something, such as an entity or an organ and, if it is to obey the rules of knowledge, its concepts must be translations of beings. The psychic apparatus becomes just an apparatus.

As we will discover, the creative power of the resultant model of science operates at the level of an inverted animism that allows the public to represent the content of a theory to which it still ascribes a scientific meaning. The process that is at work here appears to involve two convergent movements; one moves from the theory to its image, whilst the other moves from the image to the social construction of reality. Initially, a scientific conception is compared with systems of value, and a choice is made between its elements. The second movement has more complex implications. For the reasons expounded at the beginning of this chapter, the group identifies the relations and terms that come together to form a model with an objective reality. This 'naturalization' gives the social representation the status of something self-evident. It is no longer just science's double; it also becomes an autonomous 'profane theory'. When someone tells us that psychoanalysis is 'about complexes', he or she is reclassifying opinions about 'the complex', which was hitherto only loosely associated with any specific science. It is unclear whether this 'copy' of a scientific theory is part of science, or part of the real. Somewhere along the way, it becomes an instrument that can be used to categorize people and behaviours.

4

'Homo Psychanalyticus'

---

1 Classifying and Naming

Once the kernel of the social representation has been naturalized, individual behaviours must be located and fixed, and they must be organized in such a way as to be in keeping with that kernel. This is a task for classificatory thought. It completes the picture of the major agencies of the psyche, indicates which of them are present and decides whether they should or should not figure where they currently figure. Psychoanalytic concepts no longer look like stable images, and turn into linguistic categories (*social categories*) that can differentiate between individuals, appearances and events, and that can be confirmed by them. As it is used, each term is consolidated and becomes a 'natural' cognitive tool, and the group accepts it on that basis. Classification allows us to attain several of the objectives we need if we are to orient ourselves in our relations with others and with the environment.

(a) We choose between various systems of categories (and thus indicate our preferences): describing an individual as mad or neurotic means choosing between a classical and a psychoanalytic system for describing mental health.
(b) Defining common characteristics allows us to establish an equivalence (or difference) between individuals. We can, for example, describe all so-called 'shy' people as 'repressed', and make a distinction between them and those who do not present such symptoms.
(c) We recognize that some behaviours are significant, and give them a *name*. The expression 'Freudian slip', for example, now allows us to catalogue slips of the tongue, mistakes over pronunciation and grammatical inversions. For the general public, they necessarily point to a hidden intentionality or a conflict. They are seen, *stricto sensu*, as the opposite of accidents. They are deemed to be signs and not just facts.

If we go into detail, we can observe the impact of two forms of classification. One attempts to place the object within a defined context. With the help of notions borrowed from the figurative model in particular, an individual can be judged to be 'repressed' or 'unconscious'. Everyone can be compared with everyone else in this first dimension, and then in a second dimension of more or less 'repressed' and so on. This is equivalent to adding another label to those we already use, and to diversifying the tree diagram of 'classes that exist'. Other forms of classification emphasize 'having'. It is often said that a given individual *'has'* or *'does not have'* an Oedipus complex, an Electra complex, an inferiority complex and so on. Ultimately, the entire population of a society could initially be differentiated on the basis of the presence or absence of complexes, and then the presence or absence of certain kinds of complex. It might be objected that this is, after all, merely a question of vocabulary; we say that someone has an inferiority complex rather than saying that they are not intelligent, or that they have a superiority complex because they are proud. It would be a mistake to remain at this superficial level. The classificatory approach succeeds in inserting the new system of categories into existing categories, and in ruining the earlier classification. The process is subtle but has far-reaching implications. The public sees the change of categories as a mere change of designation, and is reassured. It fails to see that the shift between the two vocabularies transforms relations. It results in a situation in which non-psychoanalytic categories are translations of psychoanalytic categories. If, for example, we say of someone that he is shy, the description refers to a gauche attitude, and a reluctance to say or do anything; if we say that the individual suffers from a 'timidity' complex, the same gestures and the same reluctance become signs of different 'materialized' referents (a complex, the conscious mind, the unconscious). To take another example: the term 'conversation' provides a good definition of how two people exchange opinions, but it would be a very poor definition of what goes on between a psychoanalyst and his patient. In both these cases, established systems of categories no longer refer directly to a reality; they have acquired a symbolic character thanks to a constellation of concepts. This resolves the tension that might result from the simultaneous presence of several pictures of 'the real'. The new *corpus* of notions is established as a general code that is 'naturalized' in the perceptual world of the individual. The old code is 'denaturalized' and serves as an intermediary that helps us to understand a reality other than the reality specific to it. This is of course the goal of classification: to bring about the transposition of ideas, to make them a real part of everyone's environment, and to standardize the parts of that environment. The chain of events then becomes comprehensible, and we are able to predict how people will behave. When an individual is classed as 'neurotic' or 'repressed', we can, in theory, explain why he is in that state by referring to his relationship with his family or the evolution of his childhood conflicts. We believe that we can predict the attitudes he will adopt in particular situations. If we tell someone that X is 'neurotic', that person will be able to tell how X will react by cataloguing X inside the social space modelled by psychoanalysis. The classes we use are therefore conventions that allow us to move from the world of the unobserved to the world of the observable without any great risk of being contradicted because we all share the same conventions. The discriminatory aspect usually goes hand in hand with the normative aspect of categorization. In our society, categorization is not a neutral operation. A judgement *about* someone is contaminated by a judgement *on* someone. When we use stereotypes in the normal way and say of an individual that he is 'neurotic', we are also trying to deny that individual access to a determinate zone of social life. Thus, the symbolic armature of the representation acquires an armature of values. I will attempt to demonstrate this with respect to systems of classifications that derive from psychoanalysis.

2 The Internal Boundary Between the Normal and the Pathological

Determining the boundaries between the normal and the pathological is one of society's most important tasks. It is a draconian way of excluding certain of its members (Canguilhem 1966). On one side of the line, life; on the other, death. On one side, law and responsibility; on the other, moral or legal incapacity. Psychoanalysis upsets relations between the normal and the pathological by displacing what appeared to be firmly established barriers. In the nineteenth century, a radical distinction was made between madness and mental health. Society sharply contrasted individuals who were 'of sound mind' with those who were affected by madness. Justified by science, institutionalized by medicine and validated by prejudice, this break excluded psychologically disturbed human beings from the circle of humanity. They represented a non-social world and were at a developmental stage that had been transcended by civilized white adults. They were placed on the same level as children or primitive peoples, when, that is, they were not likened to animals. 'For classicism, madness in its ultimate form is man in immediate relation to his animality, without other reference, without any recourse' (Foucault 1967: 74).

The madman signalled the presence of another world, a different collectivity or a different dimension of the collectivity; he revealed the fragility of what had been regarded as immutable values. Because the mad were outside the organized community of normal human beings, they were the embodiment of a disorganized aggregate of beings who had not achieved human dignity. The hospitals and asylums reassured society by proving to it that it was well defended.

Mental illness was a challenge to an individuality which, in normal human beings, found expression in self-control, independent decision-making and an awareness of the underlying reasons why decisions were made, and which was not without a hint of a self-satisfied submission to the imperatives of the real. The madman refused to control how he behaved and to take independent decisions, and mocked individuality. Madness was un-reason, the night of reason, but also the reason of night. It obeyed the vital laws of a logic that was different from the logic of normal laws. People of sound mind and madmen belonged to two different intellectual worlds, and communication between the two was neither possible nor desirable. One was what the other was not. Classical psychiatry was a form of medicine for 'cretins' and psychiatrists were completely detached from their patients; those diagnostic objects could not be the subjects of an exchange.

I am, of course, over-simplifying. Psychoanalysis has changed the way we see things. By including the drives, childhood and so-called primitive instincts in the psychical apparatus and by giving them both a positive role and a scientific theoretical status, the 'non-human' has been reintroduced into the social cycle. Mental imbalance presupposes that the evolution of the determinate proportionality of relations specific to childhood and those specific to adulthood has departed from the 'normal' schema. A return to that schema signals a return to health and goes hand in hand with the reconciliation of these two moments in the life of an individual. That the conscious mind is in control does not mean that the past has been forgotten, but that it can be remembered. Progress towards rationality does not mean the rejection of desire, but the fulfilment of the truth it expresses. What might be called the spatial discontinuity between the child/adult, drive/reason elements is replaced by a genetic continuity. The normal and the pathological look more like two different combinations of the same terms. Each combination produces an equilibrium corresponding to certain imperatives in the individual's life. Although ill-adapted to society, neurotics are well adjusted to the forces that act inside them or that have always acted on them. They cannot be excluded from the social group because they indicate one of the escape routes that the social group provides so as to enable its members to tolerate its demands and tensions.

New qualifications are used for social purposes. The categories of neurotic/non-neurotic, complexed/non-complexed no longer underpin the 'mad/of sound mind' dichotomy's definition of the normal and the pathological.

By demonstrating that family life can be just as great a source of disequilibrium as biological factors, psychoanalytic science expands the circle of illnesses that can be cured, and penetrates the 'normal' world. In return, it finds that its place in the social space of practice and knowledge is not the same as psychiatry's. The goals of psychoanalysis now extend far beyond the therapeutic field, or so it would seem when we ask our informants to define its goals.

As table 4.1 shows, they refuse to recognize the specificity of psychoanalytic activity and extend its intervention beyond conventional pathology.

Table 4.1 Goals of psychoanalysis

Therapeutic (%)	Cognitive (%)	Social and psychological (%)	N/A (%)	Total no. of subjects
31	47	15	7	402

'The goal of psychoanalysis is to explore the depths of the unconscious. So-called unconscious factors really do have a big influence on the way we behave. The group of states they call "complexes" are repressed because they go against our religious or moral beliefs, social conventions and our imme- diate interests. But those repressed considerations do tend to enter the domain of consciousness, to re-emerge and to intervene in the way we behave' (S). 'From a medical point of view, liberating us from harmful uncon- scious ideas' (LP). 'Solving the problems of the unconscious' (PTS).

These statements make therapy sound like something that acts upon the agencies of the personality depending on how we see it. That action is seen in more dynamic terms when the subject takes more account of the *work- ings* of the model we have described. We have already seen that, accord- ing to popular opinion, 'the conscious mind' and 'the unconscious' act upon one another and can interfere with the free lives of individuals because of the way the process of repression generates complexes. The goal of analytic treatment is to set the subject free, and to give the subject a new taste for life:

'The most striking thing about psychoanalysis is the hope of finding resources that can be used for good purposes. Everyone believes that their real potential is limited and hopes that there are, in the subcons- cious, resources that can help them make a success of their lives' (S). 'Psychoanalysis is a way of restoring a balance, of freeing oneself so as to start all over again after having resolved all one's complexes' (MC). 'The goal of psychoanalysis? Giving people more confidence' (S).

Sometimes, of course, informants openly emphasize its impact at the pathological level:

'Curing mental illnesses, and especially those that don't look like mental ill- nesses' (LP). 'Allow people who are anxious and neurotic to get rid of their anxiety' (W). 'Curing mental illnesses, undoing repression, getting rid of complexes' (S).

Whether or not these pathological considerations are immediately obvious or not, it is clear that what psychoanalysis is being asked to do is to help to realize an ideal personality. And we can summarize that ideal by saying that it is the ideal of an *autonomous person*. Individuals feel that they are dependent, limited and determined by a series of rules and events that society, education and 'others' force upon them. These 'others' are not, however, always explicitly mentioned by name, and are often simply symbolized by the unconscious. The idea that our behaviour and the important acts in our lives are oriented not by our autonomous or independent personalities, but by other powers, leaves an impression of incompleteness or incompletion. Individuals therefore feel that they have not realized all their potential, that there is a gap between their aspirations and their achievements, and that they can neither accept the implications of that gap nor take responsibility for it. It is thought that psychoanalysis opens up the possibility of self-knowledge and self-recognition:

> 'The goal of psychoanalysis? Understanding yourself and others' (W). 'A new way of deciphering the human soul that doctors have discovered, a way of understanding yourself and others' (MC). 'Allowing a person to arrive at a better understanding of themselves and to fight and defeat themselves' (S).

Analytic treatment can even look like a step in the direction of greater *self-control*. The subject's relationship with society is contradictory, and the degree of self-awareness facilitated by analysis must make it possible to abolish, if not the contradiction itself, at least the feelings it provokes. It must give a meaning to both action and that which is acted upon. According to some people, psychoanalysis promotes better social adaptation (and gives individuals who go into analysis a certain intellectual lucidity):

> 'Helping individuals who are unbalanced from a psychological point of view to adapt to normal social life and to achieve a better equilibrium in their inner lives' (S). 'A method that allows people to recover their equilibrium and that can help people to adjust to society' (MC). 'Adapting the personality to the social environment, developing the personality' (W).

Psychoanalysis is, however, also seen as an assault upon the personality to the extent that it acts upon it. It can be rejected completely, or there may be an attempt at mediation. When that is the case, the purpose of analysis is said to be to allow individuals to make use of the information it supplies:

> 'Understanding man in general' (LP). 'Revealing what we don't know, what is not conscious, what we cannot see by ourselves' (MC).

Certain people expect more from social change than from changes within the individual, and call psychoanalysis into question. It becomes a screen, a false theoretical orientation, or a worrying practice that is inspired by the ideology of privileged classes that want to cling to the social *status quo*. Its

Table 4.2 Goals of psychoanalysis by level of knowledge

Level of knowledge	Goal		
	Therapeutic (%)	Cognitive (%)	Social or psychological (%)
High	37	49	14
Average	44	44	12
Low	24	54	22

therapeutic ambitions are frustrated by doctrinal connotations that give rise to illusions:

> 'Psychoanalysis claims to be a therapy, or even a worldview (amongst other things, it claims to be able to explain the origin and development of society in terms of conflict with the libido). It is in fact a falsifying tool that uses so-called complexes to cover up social conflicts. The use that is being made of it today, especially in the USA, is the best proof of that' (LP). 'I also think you can say that one of the goals of psychoanalysis (it's an indirect goal, but the ruling classes in Western countries have seized hold of it) is to stupefy the public, and to distract it from the real problems of the (political) struggle' (S).

It is relatively uncommon for the goals of psychoanalysis to be confused with those of tests (8 per cent). If we look at how the replies are distributed we find, paradoxically, that it is those informants who know least about it who are more likely to say that its goal is cognitive (table 4.2). The paradox is, however, superficial. The same informants are also more vague about psychoanalysis because they see it as a general scientific activity, and it is only informants with a better understanding of it that can see how far it has penetrated the therapeutic domain. We also find that when informants emphasize the non-therapeutic functions of psychoanalysis, this may be a sign that they reject the discipline, that they deny the one thing that might give it a particular effectiveness. Subjects who take an unfavourable view of psychoanalysis are less likely (30 per cent) to say that it has therapeutic goals than those who take a favourable (39 per cent) or neutral (44 per cent) view.

One essential conclusion is inescapable: it is recognized that psycho-analysis has a variety of goals that go far beyond a strictly therapeutic framework. The instability that characterizes the boundaries between the normal and the pathological can also be observed in perceptions of those situations that require a psychoanalytic intervention. In order to demon-strate that instability, we asked 'In which situations should one go into analysis?' In order to avoid stereotyping, we were obliged to work with a very wide range of replies. Table 4.3 gives an approximate idea of the extent of psychoanalysis's field of application.

Table 4.3 In what situation should one go into analysis?

Sample	Mental or childhood disorders (%)	Disappoint-ment in love (%)	Social failure (%)	Family problems (%)	Failure to adapt (%)	N/A (%)	Total no. of subjects
Representative	15	20		0	35	30	402
Middle classes	25	20	25	17	53	9	331
Liberal professions	28	17	2	0	64	0	174
Students	0	14	36	24	0	26	101
Pupils in technical schools	24	8	24	27	0	17	101
Workers	44	5	22	44	0	17	210

Women think that social failure and disappointment in love are the factors most likely to lead to a breakdown requiring analytic intervention (p < 0.01). According to better educated respondents, it is probably their failure to adapt that leads people to go into analysis (p < 0.01); those subjects with a lower level of education prioritize mental and childhood disorders. A close link between socio-economic position and level of education implies similar answers. The role played by the source of information is not irrelevant, and helps to further clarify the above remarks. People whose knowledge of psychoanalysis derives from the press, the radio or entertainment think that it is applicable in cases of mental illness, social failure and disappointment in love (p < 0.01). In contrast, people who have acquired their knowledge of psychoanalysis from books, from conversation or at school or university have a greater tendency to speak of a failure to adjust. Families and lifestyles combine to make specific choices predictable. Middle-class people living with their parents are the most likely to say that a therapeutic use should be made of psychoanalysis in cases of social failure or disappointment in love, or of conflict between parents and children (table 4.4).

Pupils in technical schools who have *brothers and sisters* give 'family reasons' for going into psychoanalysis: failure to get on with one's family, and childhood problems (p < 0.01). Those who have no brothers or sisters mention social failure and disappointment in love as sources of disequilibrium (p < 0.10). Whatever hypotheses we advance to explain these variations, we note that the family constellation can determine the choice of the particular situation that will encourage someone to go into psychoanalysis. Psychoanalysis itself attaches great importance to the family origins of personality disorders. The experience of life in a group as restricted as the family influences the subject's choice when that subject is asked why people should turn to a form of therapy that places the emphasis on the

Table 4.4 In what situations do people turn to psychoanalysis?

Situation of subject	Disappointment in love (%)	Social failure (%)	Conflict with parents (%)	Other (%)
Lives alone	15	20	13	52
Lives with parents	25	32	23	20
Lives with spouse	19	25	17	39

family. The better the subject's understanding of psychoanalysis, the more likely is it that the answer will be 'failure to adjust' (p < 0.01). Subjects who know less about it think that its action is to be recommended for failure or mental problems (p < 0.01). It is very tempting to see these findings as revelatory of a culture gap between the sub-populations under investigation: people with less education and a lower economic status still view psychoanalysis through the prism of classical psychiatry.

It might, then, be thought that, in less well-off circles, acute cases or an obvious failure to adjust are seen as the only reasons for calling in a specialist. But if we look at our overall findings, it is clear that, except for working-class subjects, mental problems are not the privileged objects for psychoanalytic interpretation; reference to various failures to adjust are more common. Biology, psychology and psychoanalysis have done a lot to popularize the concept of 'failure to adjust', which is used to refer to inadequate regulation in any given domain. The fact that psychoanalytic intervention is thought of as particularly desirable in such cases is a further sign that the frontiers between the normal and the pathological have become blurred.[1] We must at least assume that this is the case, as the absence of any comparison with similar studies is an insurmountable obstacle.

3 Who needs Psychoanalysis?

3.1 The strength and weakness of the ego

If we say that an individual is 'complexed', ' repressed' or 'neurotic', we are classifying him or her by taking our inspiration from the content of psychoanalysis. The formation of types of attitudes or reactions based upon psychoanalytic concepts reinforces the social presence of the representation.

[1] It should also be noted that a notion as non-specific as 'failure to adjust' is more likely to appeal to our informants in that it can refer to the ill-defined boundary between mental health and mental illness. Ultimately, it can be assumed that a certain verbalism works in its favour.

The individual is observed and understood in terms of characteristics specific to the dominant typology, and collective pressure may sometimes be
exerted so as to make real behaviour coincide with generally accepted
categories.

This form of classification refers to a certain dimension of the personality. It is bound up with the extent to which an individual can or cannot
overcome the defensive conflict (unconscious-consciousness-repression)
or adapt to the demands of society (stay on the normal or pathological side
of the divide). If we now ask the specific question 'Who needs psychoanalysis?' or 'How do you see the person who turns to analysis?', we find
that the idea that underpins all the answers is that of the strength or weakness of the personality. Strength is seen as normal and weakness as a sign
of fragility and imbalance.

> 'They say that psychoanalysis can produce results with weak personalities,
> with young people whose personalities are not yet fully developed. It tends
> to correct morbid tendencies. It is a therapy for the mind, and it only works
> with people who are easily influenced. The best proof of that is that the *strong*
> don't need it' (LP). '[Psychoanalysis] is useful for people who are not capable
> of making their own self-criticism, of getting to the bottom of their problems.
> Weak people can turn to it' (LP).

The notions of weakness and strength are, then, bound up with the idea
of maturity and immaturity, and with the idea of the plasticity of the psychical organization; the probable effect of psychoanalysis is to crystallize
and complete it.

Analytic action, which has the twin goals of structuring the psychical
organization and freeing the individual from conflict, gives the impression
that there is an optimum age for going into analysis. There are two
optimum moments: during adolescence or between the ages of 20 and 30
(table 4.5).

We find that, in the 'adult' sample populations (intellectuals, middle
classes), a lot of people are not willing to take a stance or do not have any
clear idea about this issue. If they do, it is obvious: psychoanalysis should
be applied before the personality has crystallized. The choice of adolescence, which is more common amongst the young populations (students
and pupils at technical schools) corresponds to a symbolic equating of the
age at which the problems of individual autonomy arise with the help that
psychoanalysis can provide. On the whole, adolescence (and childhood) is
a category chosen by subjects with a sympathetic view of psychoanalysis
($p < 0.01$). This choice appears to be determined by the general feeling that
psychoanalysis has a contribution to make to education.

To go back to the dimension of the strength or weakness of the ego. This
was often mentioned in the interviews. In order to get some idea of its
importance, we asked the 'middle class' sample: 'In your opinion, do you

Table 4.5 What is the best age for psyschoanalysis?

Sample	Childhood (%)[a]	Adolescence (%)	Aged 20–30 (%)	Maturity (%)	N/A (%)	Total no. of subjects
Middle class 'A'	9	30	38	17	21	161
Middle class 'B'	10	26	26	6	32	170
Liberal professions	7	25	30	8	30	175
Students	4	50	35	4	7	140
Pupils at technical schools	12	45	34	6	3	101

[a] Totals over 100% are due to multiple answers.

need a strong personality or a weak one to be psychoanalysed? Or does it not matter?' The findings were as follows: 'does not matter': 41 per cent; weak: 34 per cent; strong: 18 per cent ($p < 0.01$).

Younger subjects stressed the need for a strong personality; subjects approaching maturity stressed the need for a weak personality.[2] Those who knew most about psychoanalysis stressed the need for a strong personality, whilst those who knew less about it tended to believe that it did not matter, or that the personality should be weak ($p < 0.05$). These answers are also bound up with attitudes towards psychoanalysis (figure 4.1). There is a striking parallelism between weak personality/ unsympathetic attitude, and strong personality/sympathetic attitude. The fact that someone with a strong personality goes into analysis has a positive meaning to the extent that the same subjects express the conviction that psychoanalysis *strengthens* the personality ($p < 0.01$); they are also more likely to believe that it provides individuals with *guidance* ($p < 0.01$).

Younger subjects stress that anyone going into psychoanalysis requires a strong personality because they see it as an *ordeal*. The favourable or unfavourable aura surrounding psychoanalysis also coincides with the subject's self-image. Those who take a sympathetic view of psychoanalysis and *those who say they might be prepared to undergo analysis* tend to identify themselves as having a strong personality, whereas those who take an unfavourable view of it or who are not prepared to undergo analysis say that anyone resorting to psychoanalysis should have a weak personality (table 4.6).

[2] 7 per cent of subjects did not answer this question.

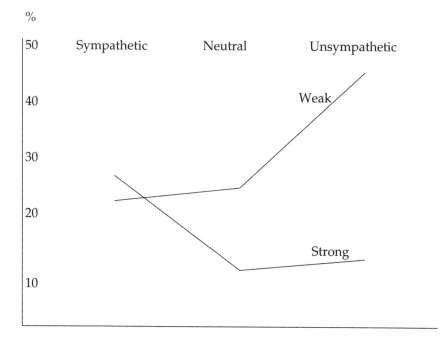

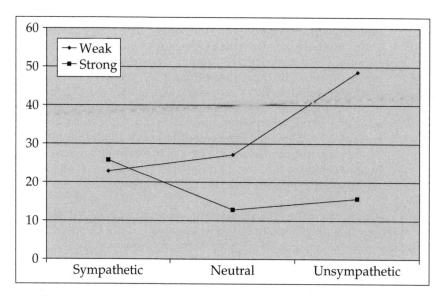

Figure 4.1 Average population: answers 'strong personality' and 'weak personality', as determined by attitude

Table 4.6 Psychoanalysis and personality types

Would you be prepared to go into analysis?	Personality required		
	Strong (%)	Weak (%)	Does not matter (%)
Yes	51	20	48
No	28	65	33
N/A	21	15	19

Thirty people in the 'intellectuals' sample also described their impressions of the outcome of psychoanalysis:

- Seven saw the outcome as positive but did not give many details: 'He's better', 'She's calmed down'.
- Twenty-three gave a negative answer, usually in one of two ways:
  a) Psychoanalysis does not make things better, and can even make them worse:
     'Patients who have been psychoanalysed often come back to me sicker than ever.' 'It has no therapeutic value because it shows the individual what is morbid about him without showing him what promise the future can hold.' 'A woman friend who went into psychoanalysis came off very badly.'
  b) Even if people are cured in an individual sense, they are asocial:
     'After analysis, people usually develop a liking for their problems: and become polarized around themselves – excessive egocentrism. When it comes to specifics, they may well be liberated and cured, but in terms of the personality as a whole, the outcome is unfortunate and they aren't nice to know.' 'I knew someone who was psychoanalysed, with bad results – it was no longer a therapy, but an end in itself, he needed to talk about himself.' 'My brother was psychoanalysed. There was a definite improvement, but he seemed to turn in on himself, developed tunnel vision and now explains everything in terms of complexes.'

Many fewer people in the 'middle-class' sample were able to describe how they saw psychoanalytic treatment (18 interviews). There were few (6 out of 18) accounts of a successful analysis. Here are a few examples:

'The first case of psychoanalysis I ever knew about concerned someone in my family: a completely selfish man who made his wife's life impossible by suffocating her and demanding total subservience; the analysis showed him that his childhood had been suffocated by his mother in the same way . . . two people in my family have been analysed, and there's been a definite improvement.'

Lack of sociability is usually seen as representing a failed analysis:

> 'I know only one person who has been psychoanalysed. He was someone with a failure complex and never succeeded in anything he tried to do. Things are obviously much better now, but he has become unliveable with because he is so arrogant. In fact, I'm not sure that there's been any improvement.' 'I know cases of people in my family who've been analysed; they turned in on themselves and became excessively introspective. Danger: they don't want to take responsibility for anything (that's because, when I was 3. . .).'

Success means adaptation, self-confidence and an ability to get on with others and to forget about oneself. The alternative is the aggravation of the symptomatology, introspection and concentrating on one's own problems. People who have been psychoanalysed are arrogant, uncommunicative, given to introspection and always fail to communicate with the group. In some sense, people who have been psychoanalysed have become different and escape the collective norm of being open with others.

3.2 Therapy for women

When the question of who turns to psychoanalysis is raised, a clear distinction is made between men and women. This question has to do with the most tenacious stereotypes about women and psychoanalysis. These stereotypes are very widespread and form one of the links between psychoanalysis and social reality.

When asked if it is women or men who turn to psychoanalysis, 41 per cent of informants replied 'women' and 7 per cent said 'men', whilst 52 per cent stated that they either had no views on the matter or did not wish to reply.

Whilst there does seem to be a general agreement over this point, there is still a constant tendency for both men and women to think that people of their own gender are more likely to turn to psychoanalysis. Despite the general consensus, slightly more men believe that more men do so, whilst slightly fewer women think that it is mainly women who go into analysis (table 4.7).

It was mainly male subjects who gave the impression of resisting the stereotype and the predictable answer 'women'. This impression, which was given in many of the interviews, was partly corrected by the fact that, in most groups, it was men and not women who refused to choose between men and women (table 4.8).

There is no link between answers to this question and attitudes towards psychoanalysis, but the idea that women go into psychoanalysis still has negative connotations. For example, subjects who reply 'women' also

Table 4.7 Who resorts to psychoanalysis most often?

	Men (%)	Women (%)
Men	14	9
Women	58	68
N/A	28	23

Table 4.8 'No answer' to question: 'Do more women or more men go into analysis?' (% by gender)

Pupils in technical schools		Students		Liberal professions		Middle class 'A'		Middle class 'B'		Representative sample	
M	F	M	F	M	F	M	F	M	F	M	F
29	27	35	28	34	23	47	32	37	33	57	46

think that it is rich people who go into psychoanalysis. The general public believes that it is *partly* because of its aura of sexuality that women are drawn to psychoanalysis. The way the press, the radio and entertainment have popularized psychoanalysis probably reinforces this link: a greater proportion who have acquired their knowledge from these means of communication answer 'women' ($p < 0.01$). A stereotype of 'psychoanalysis-therapy for women' becomes apparent not only through the very high frequency of the response, but above all by its *isolation*, it does not vary with the other elements of the structure of the social representation. Why should women be attracted to psychoanalysis? Table 4.9 shows the results of interviews carried out with middle-class subjects.

Women go into analysis because they are weak, egocentric, exhibitionist and because they have the time to do so. Men, for their part, do so because they are strong and because they want to succeed in the struggle for existence.

3.3 Money is time

In a world in which the demands of production force people to live at an increasingly fast pace psychoanalysis is seen as a 'class medicine', as a luxury therapy. Nothing could be more asocial than this retreat into an analysis in which one man spends years dealing with one individual, reflecting upon one life, and restructuring it. In psychoanalysis, the time–money ratio established by our society is inverted: a person who has money has time. Our informants believe that the only people who have

Table 4.9 Who resorts to psychoanalysis?

Reasons	Men and women	Men	Women
Free time, more time to devote to self	0	0	22
Activity; struggle for existence	0	6	2
Introspection; like self-analysis	0	6	2
Displays private life	0	1	8
Need for direction	0	0	9
Mental strength, ability to take decisions; rationality	0	7	1
Mental weakness: repression, psychological complexity, sensitive illness, sexual problems	13	3	71
Egocentrism, need to be centre of interest	0	0	25
Is an inferior being	0	0	8

Table 4.10 Which of the following categories do you think people who go into psychoanalysis most often belong to?

Sample	Rich (%)[a]	Artists (%)	Intellectuals (%)	Petite bourgeoisie (%)	Workers (%)	N/A (%)	Total no. of subjects
Representative	24	15	29	7	3	22	402
Middle classes	44	21	43	11	5	0	331
Liberal professions	59	16	3	6	0	16	175
Students	52	14	11	15	0	8	140
Pupils in technical schools	25	14	11	12	0	8	101
Workers	24	20	32	–	9	15	210

[a] Percentages over 100% are due to multiple answers.

enough free time to take an interest in themselves[3] are people whose wealth and role allow them to escape the temporal rhythm of our society: intellectuals (cited by 29 per cent of subjects in the representative sample) and the rich (24 per cent) (table 4.10).

It is mainly workers and pupils at technical schools who mention the intellectual aspect of psychoanalysis. The view of subjects from the middle

[3] 'Having time to take an interest in oneself' is often a covert way of expressing the moral principle: 'You must not take an interest in yourself'.

classes are more divided. Of the 123 subjects who thought that intellectuals turn to psychoanalysis:

- 60 used the expressions 'cleverer', or 'know more' in their interviews;
- 43 insisted that intellectuals are more likely to go into analysis, and that they are more complicated;
- 7 stated that intellectuals are more likely to go into analysis because they have more free time (in every case, they are associated with the 'rich').[4]

For their part, students and intellectuals believe that it is mainly 'rich people' who can go into long-term psychotherapy. This answer was also dictated by ideological considerations, as part of this population believes that psychoanalysis has the function of a class ideology.

Informants from the 'middle-class' sample thought that more rich people go into analysis because:

- they have more money (59 subjects);
- they have more time (23);
- they have more leisure time, are idle, have no specific occupation (23);
- they are neurotic or unhinged (14);
- they are curious and they're snobs (11).

We find these arguments in all the other groups, and they are also used with reference to 'artists':

- artists go into analysis because they have time and money, and because they are snobs (20 subjects);
- artists live eventful lives, are unstable, neurotic, unhinged; that is why they go into analysis (18);
- it is their intelligence and their understanding that allow them to go into psychoanalysis (mentioned 11 times).

The only people who turn to psychoanalysis because of their problems or their situation are, finally, 'petits bourgeois'. More of them are *forced* to turn to it because, it is thought, the petite bourgeoisie is a class that is in a contradictory position.

The majority of our informants do not, however, think that this is the group in which most subjects go into analysis. Like workers, the petits bourgeois 'cannot afford it' and 'have better things to do'.

In *all* populations, *those subjects who know most about psychoanalysis think that the majority of people who go in for psychotherapy are 'rich'* ($p < 0.05$).

---

[4] The other answers were unclassifiable.

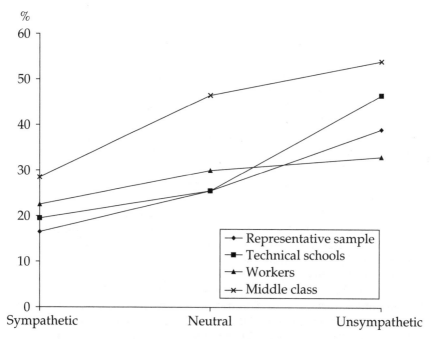

Figure 4.2 Answer 'rich people', as determined by attitude

These subjects probably have a clearer idea of the role money plays in analytic therapy. Neither the level of education nor the economic status of the people interviewed clearly determines the way they answer this question. Leaving aside intellectuals, we can, however, say that in general terms, informants who view psychoanalysis unsympatheti-cally are more likely to say that it is 'the rich' who turn to it more often (figure 4.2).

People who are sympathetic to psychoanalysis, in contrast, believe that many intellectuals turn to it.

Attitudes do not affect the answers given by the 'liberal professions' sample, but ideology is a differential: Communists and subjects with left-leaning political views ($p < 0.05$) are more likely to say 'the rich'.

Taking into account the other questions that were asked, we can outline the following typology:

Those subjects in the various populations who think that rich people turn to psychoanalysis:

- think that the spread of psychoanalysis is a fad ($p < 0.01$);
- compare analytic therapy with suggestion ($p < 0.01$);
- are likely to think that it is an assault on the personality ($p < 0.05$);
- have a negative image of psychoanalysis.

Subjects who think that it is mainly 'intellectuals' who go into analysis:

- think that the spread of psychoanalysis is due to its scientific value (p < 0.01);
- are, in relative terms, more likely to think that psychoanalysis has *positive* effects and that it *helps* the development of the personality; have a positive or idealized image of psychoanalysis.

To sum up. The struggle for existence and the imbalances and failures that result from it allow us to evaluate the 'strength' or 'weakness' of an individual. The fact that an individual turns to psychoanalysis can be a sign of either strength or weakness. Either the individual in question is strong and can therefore accept help when it is needed, or (and this is the more common view) that individual is a weak person who cannot manage on his or her own. Women's resort to psychoanalysis is semantically overdetermined by their membership of the 'weaker sex'. Illness also means emasculation, sensitization and exclusion from the social circuit; it suits women better.

The time–psychoanalysis and time–money relations may first initially appear in isolation. Women and artists can turn to this *lengthy* therapy because their time is not measured. And for precisely that reason, they are marginal to a society designed on a model that is virile, active and practical. Psychoanalysis is a costly form of therapy for rich people. It meets the needs of 'rich women'. This is a fairly widespread view, and it tends to devalue the image of psychoanalysis. We are also told that adolescence is the best time for psychoanalysis; this is an age *when the individual has yet to enter the social circuit*, and psychoanalysis is seen as a means of promoting adaptation. What is more, the introspection, inactivity and sensitivity that are attributed to women and adolescents are not specific symptoms, but signs of a failure to adapt to society. Intellectuals make up a particular group which is not marginal, but *specialized*. For them, the question of time does not arise, because intellectual work is something that exists 'outside time', and they supposedly earn their money without making any effort. They are, however, the embodiment of culture and it goes without saying that it is their intellectual aptitudes that will lead them to psychoanalysis because they and psychoanalysts operate in the same sphere.

How much importance is given to money or intellectual ability varies from one population to another. The emphasis placed on one or other of these factors is a form of compensation and is clearly bound up with the subject's attitude to psychoanalysis. Workers emphasize the intellectual potential that is needed to undertake an analysis, whereas intellectuals place the main emphasis on the financial resources it requires. Inferences of an ideological nature accentuate the link between social category and psychoanalysis.

Everything combines to make the properties of psychoanalysis coincide with those of groups defined by privileged criteria such as age, gender and behaviour. These groups are not divorced from one another. They seem, rather, to be differentiated around signs that have been adopted collectively. Psychoanalysis has the power, which can be used for both good and evil, to displace individuals within these distinct worlds, and it therefore has a regulatory power. This conviction has a very narrow experiential basis. How can an informant objectively justify his or her opinion that psychoanalysis is applicable in one case rather than another? How does an informant *know* that intellectuals or rich people are more likely to go into analysis? These are naïve questions, but they demonstrate how we tend to transpose things we are familiar with at the imaginary level to the level of concrete existence. These precarious combinations of symbolic structures and experience might be seen as expressing an ideological realism similar to that of children, who draw pictures not only of what they can see of an object, but also of what they know about it. Because it defines the indefinable and always reduces particulars to generalities, classificatory understanding encourages this *intellectual realism*. Both representations and society tend to produce an excess of logic in order to obtain an excess of reality.

5

A Marginal Hero

1 The Psychoanalyst: Magician or Psychiatrist?

How are we to locate psychoanalysts in professional terms? What criteria define the recent image that films, the press and caricatures have moulded in such a way as to make the psychoanalyst a central figure in our culture without taking away the mystery that surrounds him? If the sector occupied by the psychoanalyst remains ill-defined it is because it is adjacent to the supposedly inviolable domain which everyday language calls the 'soul', and because it is concerned with individuals who are disturbing. Are not the mentally ill representatives of a deviance that is latent in all of us? And if we are all potentially unhinged, what about the psychoanalysts? Given that they have to be analysed before they can exercise their profession, they must share the illness to some extent. That in itself is enough to make them marginal, as compared with other practitioners, and to signal the difference between them and psychologists or psychiatrists.

The ambition of classical psychology and psychiatric medicine was to be limpid, rational and clinical. Thanks to detailed observation of the symptoms, an accurate recording of the patient's obvious messages, and a study of his reaction to certain stimuli, the clinician controls his patient with a gaze laden with objectivity. After asking a lot of questions, he allows himself to give a diagnosis that puts between him and his patient all the distance that separates the normal from the pathological. Psychoanalysis replaces the surveillance of the gaze with the lazy mobility of an attention which, whilst it is evenly suspended, is still vigilant. It prefers to examine the free associations that lead to the latent message. The autonomy of meaning attributed to the patient's words is not that of a strictly clinical atmosphere, yet the actual formula for psychoanalytic therapy remains clinical.[1] It is this

---

[1] This is because it brings together two individuals and because it is based solely upon their verbal behaviour.

contradiction that makes both the therapy and the therapist so strange. When he meets his analyst, the patient discovers himself to be a subject and ceases to be a 'case' suffering from an illness with specific symptoms.

Despite the ritual nature of the sessions and the strict definition of therapist–patient relations, there must therefore also be a degree of freedom. This makes it difficult to detect the boundary between subjectivity and objectivity that any self-respecting science must, or so it is thought, establish. We have the confused feeling that we are witnessing the birth of a new form of interaction between a psychoanalyst in possession of knowledge that leads to well-being, and a neurotic who is consulting him because he lacks that knowledge. One symbolizes the strong ego, and the other the weak ego. There is something disturbing about this inequality. Speech is obviously not something that is being used to transmit knowledge or to make a diagnosis; it is in itself a form of action, but why is it so effective? Is the important thing about it the joint celebration of an encounter that the patient – and the analyst? – wants, or the exchange that results from that encounter? Is the speech phatic, or is it purely affective? Or is it thematic and intended to convince in a bid to change attitudes? We usually know where we stand with a doctor: doctors give advice and the drugs make us better. The doctor's role is clear; his practice is objective and has nothing to do with his personality. The psychoanalyst, in contrast, seems to be a new incarnation of the old image of the medicine man. His training means that he is still associated with scientists and psychiatrists, but his exceptional position as a doctor with the power to use his personality to heal arouses a public response similar to those that were aroused by magicians in other societies. As Fenichel remarks: 'The influence of magic is greater in medicine than in pure natural science, which stems from the activity of the medicine-men and priests. Within medicine, psychiatry is not only the youngest branch of this magic but it is also the one most tainted with magic' (1946: 3). Because he relates the phenomenon of 'the taint of magic' to evolutionary factors alone, Fenichel seems to take no account of the social and emotional context. One does not see clearly what a scientific, and non-magical, doctor–patient relationship might look like. The conflict between the various demands a patient makes of a doctor is resolved in what seems to be a magical way because there is no index to guarantee that the solution that has been adopted is the one that should have been adopted. This uncertainty is still greater when we are dealing with a new science like psychoanalysis, in which the analyst–patient relationship cannot be defined with any certainty: is it therapeutic or interpersonal?

2 Social Relations and Role Playing

2.1 *The psychoanalyst in professional space*

Freud often reminded his readers that the analyst had to be highly educated if he was to be able to operate in his world of significations, and that the psychopathological knowledge of the doctor and the psychiatrist were not enough to qualify him for his task. But Freudian doctrine is unclear when it comes to defining the psychiatrist's social role, and psychoanalysts themselves are not sure where they stand on this issue. We attempted to discover which professional role was closest to that of the psychoanalyst, and asked if society found it easier to associate psychoanalysts with doctors, priests, psychologists or scientists. Our findings show that the psychoanalyst's position is *sui generis*, and the hypothesis that society required a psychoanalyst to be a doctor was not convincingly proven.

At the time when this survey was carried out, there was a lot of interest in this question; the courts were attempting to decide whether a psychoanalyst had the right to practise in defiance of the rules drawn up by the medical profession, and the press was publishing accounts of the court case. We asked informants from the 'middle class', 'liberal profession', 'student' and 'pupil' samples if they thought analysts had more in common with doctors, psychologists, priests or scientists. A relatively high number said 'psychologists'. As a psychologist does not have the codified status of a doctor or priest, the public used the similarity between them to express its awareness that there is something peculiar about analysts, and they do not have a precise status.

Because there is no association with 'doctors', analysts also stand out from other specialists.

Neither the doctors nor the medical students we interviewed saw analysts purely as doctors. For all the populations we interviewed, the 'doctor' answer implied ($p < 0.10$) that it was the therapist's attitude that was being compared with the attitude of a doctor. It seems that analysts are likened to doctors by those who would like to see them adopting a

Table 5.1 Who can the psychoanalyst be compared to?

Sample	Scientist (%)[a]	Priest (%)	Psychologist (%)	Doctor (%)
Middle classes	8	13	51	45
Liberal professions	5	9	51	35
Students	not asked	5	50	45
Pupils in technical schools	35	8	18	39

[a] The totals exceed 100 because multiple answers were given to this question.

medical attitude. A certain idea of what his practice entails sometimes produces a specific idea of what an analyst is: intellectuals and students at
technical schools compared the role of the analyst to that of a priest
because they likened analytic practice to confession ($p < 0.10$).

There seem to be two possible roles for the analyst: psychologist or
priest. None of the indices used in this survey allows us to state that one
role is more highly rated than the other. But the answers to another of our
questions do provide elements of an explanation by telling us why analysts are compared to doctors, psychologists or priests. Comments from
the 'middle class B' sample demonstrate this quite concretely. The analyst
can be compared to a doctor because:

> 'He treats a part of the body that is also the intellectual organ.' 'Because
> a subject who goes into analysis needs a new form of medicine.' 'It's
> natural, because he is a doctor who treats both the conscious mind and the
> subconscious.'

The same arguments are invoked when the analyst is likened to a psychologist, but the respondents also speak of the personal *qualities* they
think are common to both professions:

> 'Because he has to know everything, guess everything and always know
> when to intervene.' 'Because he has to know people well enough to under-
> stand them.' 'What you really need in psychoanalysis is psychology; it's
> much the same orientation.'

Comparisons with priests are not common, and are mainly restricted to the
patient's position during the analysis:

> 'Because he listens to things you would not dare say to a priest.' 'Listens to
> people's confessions.'

When, that is, we do not have a reminder of some magical practice:

> 'Because they [psychoanalysts] are magicians.'

We recognize here an element whose presence was noted at the beginning
of the chapter.

2.2 The analyst's attitude to his patients

It is because the psychoanalyst has a social *role* that he has become a
figure who stands at the confluence of the science he embodies and
the motivations of the human group he provides with an answer. The

Table 5.2 Preferences for an analyst of the same sex or opposite sex; men and women

	Liberal professions		Students		Pupils at technical schools	
	Men (%)	Women (%)	Men (%)	Women (%)	Men (%)	Women (%)
Same sex	27	14	52	18	42	17
Opposite sex	16	28	14	37	22	43

representation of psychoanalysis, the way different roles are distributed in society and the relations the analyst is assumed to have with them determine the concrete aspects of his persona. But let us not anticipate. A subject's image of the psychoanalyst is not unrelated to that same subject's conception of psychoanalysis. This is obvious from the answers we received to questions about the age and gender of the analyst. Subjects under 30 and over 50 thought that the analyst's age mattered ($p < 0.05$). Men attached more importance than women to the analysts' gender (61 per cent, as against 54 per cent). Subjects who knew more about psychoanalysis thought that the age and gender of the analyst influenced the way the analysis unfolded ($p < 0.05$). These figures apply to the 'middle-class' population. The worker population has no views on the matter. Whilst they attached some importance to the therapist's gender, intellectuals, students and pupils at technical schools thought that his or her age did not matter. In these populations, it was mainly men who said that they would prefer an analyst 'of the same gender', whilst women either thought that an analyst of the 'opposite sex' would be preferable, or said that it did not matter.

We can interpret these findings immediately: there is a marked preference for male analysts. Does some cultural norm rate male doctors more highly? If that were the case, the same norm might influence the choice of an analyst. The analytic relationship finds it difficult to escape the atmosphere of 'sexuality' that surrounds psychoanalysis. Whilst the stereotype of the heterosexual psychoanalytic couple (the analyst and his woman patient) is based upon the supposed willingness of women to go into analysis, it also reflects the general preference for male psychoanalysts. Perhaps a conviction that psychoanalysis treats disorders with a sexual component is another reason for the importance that is attached to the gender of the analyst. The few attempts we were able to make to unravel these two interpretations showed only that the reasons were so tangled that it was futile to try to sort them out. If the specialists are to be believed, the gender of the therapist has no influence on the way analytic therapy progresses (Glover 1940). The public seems to have other criteria. It refers,

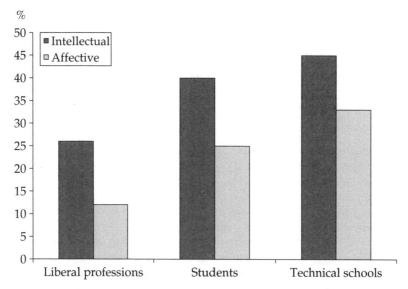

Figure 5.1 Answers 'sex of analyst does not matter' / nature of contact desired

for instance, to the nature of the 'contact' between analyst and patient. Is it affective, intellectual or both? Students, pupils at technical schools and members of the liberal professions who say that it is 'both intellectual and affective' (33 per cent, 48 per cent and 55 per cent of subjects respectively, $p < 0.01$) are expressing an idea about transference which, whilst it is not false, is superficial.

Intellectuals and technical school pupils who describe the contact between analyst and patient as 'affective' also say that they would prefer an analyst 'of the opposite sex'. When the contact is seen as purely intellectual, less importance is attached to the gender of the analyst.

As is often the case when such complex psychosociological phenomena are involved, it is impossible to say if it is because a subject thinks that the relationship with the analyst is affective that the subject expresses a preference for an analyst of the opposite sex, or if, on the contrary, it is because the analyst is seen as belonging to the opposite sex that the relationship is described as affective (or 'intellectual', if the subject imagines an analyst of the same sex). All I can suggest is that *the features attributed to the therapist are not unrelated to the nature of the relationship he or she is assumed to have with his or her patient.*

Let us now put ourselves in the place of the analyst; how is his attitude towards his patient viewed? Public opinion gives the analyst four main dramatic roles: doctor, friend, parent and observer. Leaving aside pupils in technical schools, a large number of people tend to compare the attitude of the psychoanalyst to that of a doctor (table 5.3).

Table 5.3 What is the analyst's attitude towards his patient?

Sample	Doctor (%)	Parent (%)	Observer (%)	Friend (%)
Middle class	40	3	37	39
Liberal professions	45	0	29	26
Students	55	0	34	12
Pupils in technical schools	23	0	43	34

For a high percentage of subjects, the analyst's role is that of a friend or just an observer. It is the diversity of the roles attributed to the analyst that make him seem unlike a doctor, and his roles are not restricted to the pathological domain.

The way in which younger subjects categorize analysts depends in part upon their lifestyle. Students who live alone ($p < 0.10$) and technical school pupils who have no siblings ($p < 0.01$) tend to see the analyst as a friend. The analytic relationship is viewed as something that can remedy the disadvantages of loneliness and affective isolation.

The role subjects expect the psychoanalyst to play also depends upon their attitudes towards psychoanalysis. Informants who are not sympathetic to psychoanalysis want the analyst to be a mere observer who keeps his distance and intervenes as little as possible ($p < 0.10$, middle class A; $p < 0.05$, students; $p < 0.20$, pupils at technical schools). Sympathetic informants, in contrast, expect the analyst's interventions to resemble those of a doctor. Intervention is valued because it is medical. It gives the analyst a status that inspires confidence.[2]

> 'You cannot trust anyone but a doctor.' 'A doctor is competent, knows his subject and has experience.' 'For a patient, a doctor is a God who walks the earth, so he is more effective.'

It is because he is an understanding adviser who keeps secrets that the analyst can be cast in the role of a friend; the analytic relationship is then said to be both 'intellectual and affective':

> 'You're dealing with intimate and emotional things, so the person in analysis must feel they can trust him.' 'Because it's easier to talk to a friend.' 'You pay him enough for him to give the impression of being a friend you can tell your troubles to and how no one around you understands you.'

When the analyst is seen as an observer, he is expected to be impartial, objective and very lucid. An analyst defined in these terms is seen as a very good listener and judge:

[2] I reproduce only comments made by informants in the 'middle-class A' sample.

'You see him as an observer because he then has to pass judgement.' 'So as to be perfectly impartial.'

One informant who sees the analyst's function as that of an observer has nothing to say about the analyst–patient relationship, but is at the same time more interested in what the analyst does:

'[An observer] because he is looking at the subject's every word so as to find the repressions that cause complexes.'

Subjects who see their therapist as a friend and who hope that he will become involved in their personal drama do not display the same understanding of the analyst's work.

The three roles attributed to the analyst – technician, judge and understanding man – provide the signposts that allow us both to locate the analyst and to establish how his figure is defined by a set of characters who capture the public's imagination and attention.

3 How the Audience sees the Actor

In order to get a more accurate picture of how the psychoanalyst is seen, we asked our informants to describe him.

When the content of the survey's findings was analysed, two criteria were used. Images of the analyst were classified as positive or negative, and as abstract or realistic. The choice of criteria is not perfect, but it does give us some useful information. In 47 per cent of cases, the representation of the analyst was fairly neutral; in 19 per cent of cases it was fairly positive; 13 per cent of subjects had no image of the analyst, and 11 per cent had a negative image. Real or banal images[3] were relatively common (19 per cent), but most (44 per cent) images were idealized. Women tended to have a more idealized image of the psychoanalyst ($p < 0.05$), and more men tended to have no image ($p < 0.01$). The social status of informants was a relevant factor: the only groups in which we found subjects with no image of the psychoanalyst were the worker group and the 'middle-class B' group (36 per cent of subjects).

Whilst attitude has an influence on idealized images (sympathetic subjects have a more positive image of the psychoanalyst), the same is not true of real images. We can infer that when there is a concrete image of an individual, the subject's attitude towards that individual is irrelevant; idealized images, in contrast, are closely related to the subject's attitude.

---

[3] 'Banal' images are given by subjects who liken psychoanalysts to 'some kind of practitioner'.

We also find that individuals whose knowledge of psychoanalysis derives from the radio, the press or films come up with a concrete image of the psychoanalyst ($p < 0.05$), whereas those who learned about it at school or university or from books come up with an ideal image ($p < 0.05$).

Whilst some channels of communication define the psychoanalyst's '*action*' and the demands that result from it, others turn him into a concrete character.

A more detailed sketch of the image of the psychoanalyst shows that it is organized around three criteria: (a) normality; (b) professional functions; and (c) a moral and physical assessment of his personality. So as not to overburden this account, we will rely solely upon the material supplied by the 'middle-class' and 'student' samples. Forty-two of the middle class subjects stress the criterion of normality:

> 'A normal man like any other.' 'Driven almost mad by living with the abnormal.' 'An absolutely normal guy.' 'I see him as a man so dangerous that he should be locked up; because he's mad, he judges others by his own standards and the less insane you are, the more you find him deranged.' 'A maniac who takes an interest in the sexuality of others because he is obsessed with his own.'

The figure of the psychoanalyst is sometimes surrounded by a reassuring aura of wisdom and stability, but it is sometimes plunged into a strange and dangerous world. A psychoanalyst claims to be able to communicate with his patients and can therefore either remain balanced or be contaminated by them, unless of course he isn't trying to generalize on the basis of his own failings.

When the emphasis is placed on his professional attributes – 'he's a doctor', 'a philosopher', 'a scientist' – the analyst resembles well-known images and exudes a feeling of familiarity (89 interviews). But he is often given a few *supplementary* characteristics that transform him into *something else*:

> 'I see him as a somewhat special doctor.' 'Like a philosopher who uses a scalpel to understand his own philosophy and that of others.' 'A doctor who is understanding but stern.' 'A specialist doctor, a sort of humanist with a special responsibility for providing support and moral comfort; it's a vocation, not a job.'

The ethical viewpoint introduced in the last interview is important: the psychoanalyst must have a vocation, and must have the gift of a particular abnegation and a purity of intention that must also characterize his relationship with his patients. How are we to explain why this moral requirement is applied to the psychoanalyst with such rigour, when it also goes hand in hand with the far from uncommon accusation of *charlatanism*?

A psychoanalyst has a disturbing power because he can influence the destiny of individuals and because society has no means of controlling his actions. When people say that an analyst is a charlatan, the word contains several kinds of accusation. He is being criticized for being a *simulator* or creator of illusions. He does not believe in what he is doing (whereas the patient really does) and his personal goal is to make money and influence people.

The fact that the two people involved in the analytic relationship have different goals means that their roles are dissymmetrical. The lack of symmetry is concealed by the analyst's sleight of hand (simulation) and by its theoretical justification:

> 'You pay him quite a lot of money for him to give the impression that he is a friend you can tell your troubles to and tell him how no one at home understands you' (MC).

Why would a psychoanalyst be so interested in money if he was not a charlatan? When we think in financial terms, the analyst's charlatanism takes on another meaning. From this point of view, analysis is seen as a passing fad, and the psychoanalyst is believed to be extorting as much money as possible from his rich and snobbish clients in a relatively short space of time. This is just one more image of the analyst. He is also seen as a specialist; any medical activity should, it is believed, be disinterested, and the health of the patient comes before any material consideration. Paying a doctor a fee can be justified on the grounds that we are handing over abstract money in exchange for a prescription for drugs; in analysis, we find nothing of the kind, and that appears to detract from the objective nature of the relationship. Nor do we find the same abstract exchange. In the course of an analysis, the patient – as our informants well understand – hands over much more than money and expects much more in return. The point is that exchanging money for affectivity, or an abstract value for a concrete existence, means swapping things that are heterogeneous. There is no sense of equivalence, and the exchange is therefore unsatisfactory, devalued and illicit. A charlatan is someone who enters into this exchange but, by definition, gives nothing in return. He encourages it and takes advantage of it, but he also flaunts the fact that he exists outside the usual circuits of exchange.

Simulation, worldliness and the heterogeneity of the exchange between patient and therapist – these are the essential significations that support the impression of dishonesty or charlatanism where the psychoanalyst is concerned. When, in contrast, those who expect him to be honest also hope that he will resist all the temptations society offers him. Thirty-six subjects in this population began their descriptions of the psychoanalyst with a reference to the probity they either expected of him or questioned, when asked 'What is your image of the psychoanalyst?':

> 'A man who wants to make money.' 'Someone who is especially human and honest.' 'A charlatan who's rolling in money.' 'A man like any other, but who likes money more than most people.'

Great affective (26 subjects), intellectual (25) and professional (15) qualities are expected of psychoanalysts:

> 'A very gentle, very human man, but one who always gets you to say what he wants.' 'A psychologist crossed with a doctor; must have a lot of tact.' Like an exceptionally intelligent and indiscrete inquisitor.' 'A man with a special frame of mind and a strong personality. Great experience of life in general.' 'Authority, influence over the patient.'

Physical appearance (19 subjects) and power over individuals (25) also figure in the description of the analyst. His physical image includes a number of Freud's own features and features of scientists in general: glasses, a beard, maturity. The image is primarily male. Those subjects who compare psychoanalysis with psychiatry also recall that it developed out of hypnosis and emphasize the penetrating gaze of the analyst who delves into individuals' private lives:

> 'A psychoanalyst is a man with a penetrating gaze.' 'Very understanding, guesses what no one dares to say.' 'A man with magnetic powers and very disturbing eyes.' 'Bearded, wears glasses.'

The beard is symbolic of age and a paternal attitude:

> 'A psychoanalyst? Someone old – like a seer.' 'Like the ideal father I'd like to have had and who carefully looks into my problems so as to solve them.' 'A mature man aged between 50 and 60.'

The psychoanalyst is also a judge, a distant inquisitor and a threatening figure:

> 'A cross between a judge and an examining magistrate.' 'The psychoanalyst is a serious, intelligent gentleman who is *a bit frightening*.' 'A man like any other, except that you can't look him in the eye.' 'Someone who is obviously very psychological, very sensitive, even though he looks *calm, neutral, cold,* even.' 'Human, intelligent and *distant*.'

The authority and rectitude that are expected of the psychoanalyst and that are attributed to him can be a source of reassurance, and they compensate for the worries his activity provokes.

Is this image really specific to the psychoanalyst, or is it just a variant on that of the doctor? We could learn a lot from a comparison of the two.

The image of the psychoanalyst is the same in all the populations surveyed, and the differences we find in the various samples are just differences of emphasis. Some students (43 interviews) put the emphasis on his professional function:

> 'A specialist doctor. A doctor who has studied a bit of biology and mental pathology, and a lot of psychology and literature.'

The problem of normality was raised twenty-five times by subjects from the same population:

> 'A psychiatrist with a lot in common with his patients.' 'Both a psychologist and a doctor . . . Main qualities required: integrity, intelligence, patience, *nervous stability.*' 'Half way between Knock and a witch doctor, or at least more pathological, more obsessed – especially with sex – than his clients. I've never actually met one, as it happens.' [4]

The *good* honest analyst and the *bad* charlatan were explicitly contrasted nineteen times:

> 'There are two possible images, more so here than elsewhere: the sincere doctor and the charlatan.' 'A doctor crossed with a psychologist; his first quality has to be honesty.' 'A charlatan who more or less believes in what he does and who finds madmen where there are none. A psychiatric Knock, but not as clever as the original.'

When the good therapist is not contrasted with the bad therapist, it is thought that an analyst must be intelligent, thoughtful, sympathetic and, in a word, human (115 subjects).[5]

> 'Both scientific and human, rather like a doctor.' 'A calm, educated man, relaxed, a good talker, high level of mental concentration.' 'He has to like human contact. Must have a good knowledge of psychology and medicine. And above all be as suspicious of his own motives as he is of those of others.'

The importance of the analyst's physical appearance was mentioned twenty times:

> 'A strange man, piercing eyes, wears a head-torch, an almost demonic look, more curious than interested in curing people. That's inevitably a superficial

[4] Knock is the eponymous doctor-hero of the play by Jules Romains (1923) [Translator].
[5] The students had multiple images of the analyst, which explains why there are more themes than subjects.

idea.' 'Cold, starchy, used to dissecting peoples' actions, must lack spontaneity.' 'A gentleman in a white coat and with eyes that can see into the
depths of your soul.'

His lucidity and the way that he listens mean that the analyst is a disturbing man who is steeped in things that are inaccessible to ordinary mortals.
This strangeness and superiority are an integral part of his personality and
profession, whereas his coldness and impartiality are an expression of the
strength of his ego:

> 'A cold, impassive man, who plays with the lives of his clients with feigned
> indifference. And who worries about how to reconcile his personal life with all
> the responsibilities he shoulders in the lives of other people.' 'A rather digni-
> fied man, who is persuasive, authoritative, self-possessed and perspicacious.'
> 'Someone who looks for hidden meanings in everything.' 'A reputation for
> indiscretion, but most people have boundless confidence in him. Often has a
> superiority complex, because psychoanalysis was for a long time seen as a
> taboo subject and because he discovers secrets – fear and pretension.'

Whilst the representation of the social persona of the analyst is general, the
raw material it is made from consists of a variety of notions, values and
perceptions. It is recognized that there is something special about the
analyst that sets him apart from doctors, priests and psychologists, and a
careful distinction is made between him and his patients. But classificatory
thought has a role to play here, and attitudes impinge. People look for the
secret motives (curiosity, greed) of imaginary individuals when they try to
justify the way they have grouped together some images and separated
others. The images take shape within certain classes – power, friendly
involvement, trust – that are also zones of relational perception. The
description of the stimulus (the psychoanalyst) and the judgements are
linked together on the basis of behaviour, norms or situations. Every
subject always finds one element more important than the others: the dominant image is also a contrasting image. It therefore cannot be argued, as
has been claimed,[6] that our perception of others is always general, closed
and structured. It always involves a polemical intent to exclude that
delights in emphasizing contradictions. In cases where the emphasis is
placed on the psychological aspect of the analyst's persona, the description

---

[6] There have been many studies of how we perceive the personality of other people
since Asch carried out his first experiment (Asch 1946). There is a growing tendency
to take interpersonal behaviour into account (see, for example, Tagiuri and Petrullo
1958). Asch's point of view was greatly influenced by gestalt psychology, and the distinction between static and dynamic perception and inner and outer perception of
the personality escaped him. He also placed too much emphasis on the global nature
of that perception, and did not make due allowance for contradictions or for the dominance of certain elements.

tends to be dynamic and judgemental, but it remains enumerative and static when the physical aspect of what the analyst is wearing comes to the fore. One form of description can be translated into the other: saying that the analyst is an inquisitor is equivalent to emphasizing his glasses or the way he looks at people. The world of fear and hopes in which the persona of the analyst is embedded means that he casts a disproportionately long shadow. A representation that establishes an absent reality and then takes its place is a form of transgression that establishes a link between the fragmentary perceptions we have of the analyst and the real analyst. The collective perception is that the therapist and his patient must be inter-changeable in some way. Both analysts and psychiatrists feel obliged to conform to their image of 'not being like everyone else', and feel isolated as a result of this social pressure. That is, at least, the conclusion reached by Dr Bonnafé (1948) in his account of an experience shared by psychi-atrists and psychoanalysts in the course of one of his lectures. Does the col-lective representation have a basis that can be objectified? A vocation for psychiatry does sometimes appear to be inspired by some psychological or physiological weakness, and an element of sadism can sometimes be observed in the way psychiatrists behave, as it is not unusual for a techni-cal function to become confused with a human function. Interacting with a patient can be uncomfortable and it may encourage the psychiatrist to eliminate the interpersonal aspect and adopt a semblance of objectivity that is in fact a way of breaking off contact and asserting a feigned superi-ority. We should not, however, make too much of comparisons between psychoanalysts and psychiatrists.

The activity of psychiatrists is associated with asylums and 'madness', whereas psychoanalysts are in private practice and work with individu-als. Yet despite that distinction and in the absence of more detailed accounts, the therapist does appear to have a twofold problem: adapting to his social role and the necessity of acting in ways that bring the repre-sentation of his persona into line with his actual work. 'The psychiatrist is shaped by the gaze of the other who sees him primarily as "the man who deals with madness". He is incorporated into the notion of alienation, but he is not its prisoner. His two basic mistakes are passive acceptance and a failure to recognise it for what it is' (Bonnafé 1948). As for social psycho-logy, it shows that there is a recognized correlation between social moulds and individual attitudes. The dialogue between a self-image and the image of the other can also modify both.

The implications of such modifications and their symbolic connotations cannot be studied within the confines of the present study. We took as our starting point the problem of how the representation of a figure – the psy-choanalyst – related to its real model. We have seen that there may be a link between the analyst's attributes, his behaviour and his vocation. But we are on shaky ground here. We will therefore restrict ourselves to describ-ing the psychoanalyst and to looking at what makes him special.

6

The Psychoanalysis of
Everyday Life

1 Description of the Second Major Process:
Anchoring

We have seen what definitions the public gives of psychoanalysis, what goal it assigns to it, and what images it has of the groups that turn to it and of those who practise it. We have also observed that psychoanalytic theories have given rise to a new collective model of psychical life, a new way of categorizing individuals and a new way of relating the normal to the pathological. We have seen that there is a propensity to substantialize abstract ideas and to change concepts into linguistic categories. We have in fact been describing the main stages in the process of anchoring. *Anchoring* designates society's insertion of a science into a hierarchy of values and into its operations. In other words, society uses the process of anchoring to change a social object into an instrument it can use, and to insert that object into existing social relations on a preferential basis. We might also say that anchoring transforms a science into a framework of reference and a network of meanings, but that would be to anticipate. Let us simply recall that a social representation emerges when there is a threat to the collective identity, and when the communication of knowledge submerges the rules society has set itself. Objectification overcomes this difficulty by integrating the abstract theories of a specialist group into elements of the general environment. The anchoring process that transforms science into a knowledge that is of use to everyone seeks to achieve the same result. To cut a long story short, objectification transposes science into the domain of *being*, and anchoring defines it within the domain of *doing* so as to get around the taboo on communications. Both operations can be justified: a science is imported because it is assumed that its concepts reflect the objective environment, or because it is assumed that they can be put to some use. We anchor genetics, for example, when we claim to be able to explain its diffusion in terms of its relations with biological warfare or medicine, and ignore its theoretical implications and the way they might modify our conceptions of nature, man or religion. This is a very basic approach. Ever since the first stone was changed into an axe, and ever since the first silex was used to make fire, human beings have always transformed things and other human beings into useful tools.

In certain contexts, tools can become political or religious symbols. In order to transform the materials supplied by science, society uses certain 'investment' mechanisms. Investment has to be understood primarily as the process of circling around an object so as to discover what is strange about it, in much the same way that we circle around a town or an animal. This is not a defensive manoeuvre but a form of contact that allows us to avoid having to make hasty decisions before we finally decide whether to reject or familiarize ourselves with the object. As we tame it, the object comes to be associated with known forms and is reconsidered in their light. Psychoanalysis, for example, is likened to more familiar practices (conversation, confession). Investing a science also means making a personal investment in the attempt to adopt or reject it. Everything that was foreign to the individual comes to look like something he has made himself; psychoanalysis becomes part of his history and gradually comes to influence it.

Psychoanalysis looks to those who encountered it as adolescents like something they themselves have done to their own personalities. As a result of that biographical accident, it looks like a solution to certain problems, or an answer they could not have assimilated had it not involved a major mobilization of intellectual and affective energy. The expenditure of energy that goes into investing a social object integrates it into the field of a group or individual's productions. In the course of this work it is transformed into a formula that can resolve or express problems. Psychoanalysis becomes a system of interpretation and mutates into a language that allows those problems to be communicated. At this stage, it ceases to be 'what we talk about' and becomes 'what we use to talk'. To the extent that it has penetrated a given social stratum, it allows that stratum to influence others, and in that sense acquires an instrumental status.

When, for example, the behaviour of an individual has to be judged, it is explained in psychoanalytic terms. In this case, language is an effective way of persuading the other to become involved in a particular action.

All these factors mean that psychoanalysis becomes what I will call a *referential tool*, or a model for action that has a symbolic and an imaginary dimension and that does not exist solely at a conceptual level.

So far, I have described only one aspect of the process. If psychoanalysis is a tool that circulates in society and has an impact on society, it must be *someone's* tool. That 'someone' might be Freud, psychoanalysts in general, a social class or an entire nation. A multitude of links connects psychoanalysis to a network of meanings that convey norms and values, and to groups or domains of application that are never neutral. The 'pychoanalysis-America' association is, for example, an integral part of the social image of psychoanalysis, and even psychoanalysts subscribe to it when they make a distinction between 'good' and 'bad' psychoanalysis; the 'good' psychoanalysis is, of course, that practised in France, whilst the 'bad' is practised in the United States.

We could use other examples to demonstrate the extent to which these meanings have become inseparable from psychoanalysis. We also find that psychoanalysis has been diversified: there is a psychoanalysis that suits Christians and a psychoanalysis for Marxists, one for the French and one for the Americans, one for ethics, one for politics and so on. This list is by no means restrictive.

To a certain extent, we are still talking about the same psychoanalysis. The social object has not been dissolved. Whilst not every group has *its* psychoanalysis, there is a sense in which psychoanalysis does belong to it (this does away with anything that might directly contradict the obvious signs of its identity). The group therefore generates its own set of broad collective meanings, and that inverts the tendency towards objectification. Thanks to the process of objectification, society's task of selection and organization is concealed in the texture of the environment, and the social is recuperated in a substantialized form. The network of meanings that is established around a science transforms scientific objectivity into a social fact. It is as though everything that looks provisional and approximate to science became solid and materialized at the level of society, whereas everything that was solid and materialized at the level of science came to look relative and fluid to society.

These developments naturally correspond to a particular society's situation. Whilst objectification shows how the elements of a science that are represented are integrated into a social reality, anchoring allows us to understand how they help to model social relations and how they express those social relations. Society's object is transformed as a result, and the subject is, perhaps, transformed to the same extent. In this chapter and the three that follow, I will explain how these developments take place and the way in which they are experienced.

2 Current Activities and Analytic Therapy

The presence of psychoanalysis in everyday life takes thousands of forms. It is associated with a perception of the 'analytic situation' which assumes that the patient supplies the therapist with a certain 'raw material'. Referring to the objective reality of analytic treatment (someone lying on a couch and telling an analyst he or she cannot see whatever comes into his or her head), we asked our informants if they thought that the patient had to talk about 'whatever came into his mind' or his 'dreams' and 'memories', or 'answers questions'. While I was preparing for this survey, it

Table 6.1 Raw material supplied to the psychoanalyst

Sample	Dreams (%)	Answers to questions (%)	Whatever comes into your mind (%)	Childhood memories (%)	Everything (%)	N/A (%)	Total no. of subjects
Liberal professions	8	23	20	15	26	8	175
Students	9	38	29	20	0	4	140
Pupils in technical schools	31	18	32	15	0	4	101

occurred to me that this question should be put only to groups that were likely to give satisfactory answers, namely students, pupils at technical schools and intellectuals. Yet the results showed that the answer that corresponded most closely to the basic rule of free association ('whatever comes into your mind') was not actually given by the majority of subjects (table 6.1). The more restrictive 'answers to questions' category was, in contrast, frequently chosen.

The students put 'answers to questions' first. But, no matter what order they appear in, these answers betray the existence of two distinct images of the analytic exchange: one of full self-expression, and one of a sort of contractual communication in which the patient says only what he is expected to say or what he judges to be pertinent to psychoanalysis (dreams or childhood memories) or what might help the ongoing treatment.

The issue of the raw material that has to be provided for the psychoanalyst does not affect the overall representation of the analytic situation and its correlates. Things look very different if the subjects are asked: 'Which of the following practices seems to you to be most like psychoanalysis?'

Two answers predominated: conversation and confession. Other possible answers were included to take into account differences in the degree of knowledge and linguistic level among the populations: 'psychiatric' (hypnotism, suggestion, narco-analysis) 'magical' (occultism, chiromancy). The order in which each population rated the various categories of answers calls for some general remarks (table 6.2).

The level of education of those populations that likened psychoanalysis to conversation did not allow them to have any great familiarity with it or with activities of an intellectual nature. In this case, what is being stressed is that psychoanalysis is a technique that uses speech; the emphasis is placed upon its novelty and distinctiveness. The term 'conversation' says nothing about the transferential aspect of the relationship; once again, lack of information is the explanation for this. Students, members of the liberal

Table 6.2 Which practice seems to you to be most like psychoanalysis?

Sample	Conver-sation (%)[a]	Confession (%)	Suggestion (%)	Narco-analysis/ hypnosis (%)	N/A (%)	Total no. of subjects
Representative	27	20	22	18	13	402
Middle class 'A'	42	45	29	19	7	161
Middle class 'B'	35	28	25	12	9	170
Liberal professions	31	37	13	19	0	175
Students	29	43	0	23	5	140
Pupils in technical schools	55	22	14	4	5	101
Workers	32	18	28	8	14	210

[a] Totals greater than 100% are due to multiple answers.

professions and the 'middle class A' population, or in other words those populations with the highest intellectual level, compare psychoanalysis to confession. Informants in these populations are less struck by the 'spoken' aspect of analysis than by the attempt to achieve greater self-awareness that it demands ('There's a greater awareness', 'You try to tell the whole truth'). They also note a functional equivalence between the analyst and the priest or between analysis and religion, and to some extent think it possible that one practice could be a substitute for the other. An association with drug-based hypnotic treatment (narco-analysis) is fairly common in populations with a good understanding of psychoanalysis and an awareness of the technical and historical links between the two. In another sense, and especially for the 'worker' population, 'suggestion' presupposes on the one hand that analysis can be assimilated to an older psychiatric practice, and on the other that it is an expression of the 'influence' the worker population assumes to be a necessary part of all treatment (or of any one-to-one relationship).

An examination of each category of answers allows us to broaden the discussion.

Conversation
As a rule, the people we asked had difficulty in telling us why they compared analytic practice to a more common practice. It can be assumed that, for most people, the term 'conversation' implies the possibility of dialogue and freedom of expression. This is presumed to be a primordial characteristic

of analytic treatment: communication and the re-establishment of a relationship.[1]

> 'Psychoanalysis means telling your story' (W). 'Being able to talk to someone is a relief in itself' (MC). 'The patient is free to say what he likes, and must tell all' (S).

These statements imply communication and its attributes. The 'positive' properties of the analogical link expressed in conversation explain why, in each population, this answer is most frequently given by informants who are sympathetic to psychoanalysis ($p < 0.05$). Communication is, however, no more than one aspect of the therapy; it is the aspect that is most easily understood, and the first aspect we become aware of when we come to know a little about psychoanalysis. With the exception of the 'worker' population ($p < 0.10$), sub-groups in all the populations who knew less about psychoanalysis were in fact more likely to say 'conversation'.

A consideration of general attitudes or degrees of knowledge is not, however, enough. An association with the 'good' image of the psychoanalyst indicates that 'conversation' is seen by certain populations as a positive context. The technical school pupils and students who chose this answer often saw the psychoanalyst in the role of a friend. Students and workers who regard analytic practice as a dialogue are generally less likely to have a negative image of the analyst ($p < 0.05$).

Sources of information also seem to play a role. In the representative sample, subjects who heard of psychoanalysis 'in conversation' give 'conversation' (and 'suggestion') as their first answer. The similarity that is established between the source of the communication and analytic practice is both the result of the subjects' low level of knowledge and a transposition of the situation in which they heard about psychoanalysis. As we shall see below, certain indices lead us to state that subjects who *talk* psychoanalysis also *do* psychoanalysis in a rudimentary fashion by 'interpreting' the gestures or behaviour of the people they are talking to. 'Speaking', 'doing' or 'giving examples' are ways of describing the analytic situation.

Confession

Confession is a practice that has deep roots in France, and the role it is assigned (direction of conscience, freeing people from conflicts) predestined it to be an image of analysis. The priest has a lot in common with the analyst, namely a spiritual bond with the believer whose inner peace he restores; he is also someone to whom the believer can 'entrust' his problems,

---

[1] 'They overlook the fact that the formulation of the basic rule introduces an invitation to freedom . . . What the patient is being given is a chance, or even the possibility, of a free existence' (Lagache 1954: 24).

and his function is that of a regular listener in a secret place specially designed for that form of communication. The similarity between confession and analytic practice is all the greater in that we are not just talking about communication but about a slightly unequal relationship of dependency in which communication is valid only if it employs a systematized language that restricts freedom of expression.

'A psychoanalyst is a professional confessor' (S).

In this relationship, the presence of the priest or analyst makes the subject fade into the background:

'Confession, because there is an intervention by an other who acts beyond consciousness' (LP).

Psychoanalytic treatment is also likened to confession on the grounds that it is a practice specific to a given ideological and social system that allows the individual to come into contact with the representative of a whole series of social values:

'Confession because, when all is said and done, confession used to play the same role as psychoanalysis: it alleviated repression' (S).

As we can see from table 6.3, individuals who are better informed about psychoanalysis (middle class A, liberal professions, students) are more likely to compare psychoanalysis to confession. Similarly, subjects whose first contact with the theory came at school or university or from books tend to see a greater similarity between analysis and confession.

Whilst those who choose this category of answer have a good understanding of psychoanalysis, their attitude towards it is either *neutral* or *negative*. When certain populations compare analytic practice to confession,

Table 6.3 Representative population: Analytic practice and sources of information

	Confession (%)	Conversation (%)	Suggestion (%)	Narcoanalysis/ hypnotism(%)	N/A (%)
School, university, books	34	33	19	9	5
Entertainment, radio, press	24	26	33	16	1
Conversation	15	37	30	6	12

they are implying that it is mainly 'rich people' who go into analysis (liberal professions, $p < 0.01$; technical schools, $p < 0.10$). Sometimes, it is the answer 'rich people' that is associated with confession and suggestion (representative sample, $p < 0.01$). Priests, for their part, are more likely to compare analytic treatment to confession (31 per cent) than to conversation (23 per cent).

The symmetry between the two images of psychoanalysis is striking. Those who compare it to conversation are less well informed, and therefore associate it with a less structured and more spontaneous practice. In a world in which silence and conformity are so many imperatives that allow society to display its power, being able to talk is a major step forward:

> 'To the extent that talking to other people of your acquaintance about what is bothering, worrying or boring you does you good in itself, even if it does not provide a concrete solution at the time' (W).

Conversation is seen as a free and relaxed activity that allows all individuals to discover that they are less lonely and more independent than they thought. Those who take a positive view of psychoanalysis see this loosely structured image as a field in which they are free to make what they like of the analytic situation.

When, in contrast, psychoanalysis is compared to confession, it is placed within a specific cultural context. The more specific image goes hand in hand with more precise knowledge. Comparing analysis to confession may look sacrilegious to some practising Catholics, but they sometime see it as a positive comparison too. Non-believers associate confession with the survival of relations that deny the possibility of free individual development. When communication does take place, it is a tool, a means to an end or a reproduction of an externally determined relationship. The fact that there are so many reasons and so many types of subject who give the 'confession' answer explains why attitudes are less clearly defined, though they tend to be sympathetic.

Hypnotism, narco-analysis, suggestion, occultism and chiromancy
It is relatively unusual for psychoanalysis to be associated with *occultism*. Hypnotism, narco-analysis and suggestion are normally seen as coming within the domain of classical psychiatry. They are also compared to the effects of 'influence' or 'persuasion', which are quite widespread in social or religious life. The attitude of subjects who choose these answers is usually rather neutral or negative ($p < 0.05$), and their level of knowledge is quite poor ($p < 0.10$). The relationship between psychoanalysis and narco-analysis is more likely to be grasped by doctors and medical students. In these categories, the 'suggestion' answer was given quite often. In a representative sample from the Parisian population, most subjects

who compared analysis to suggestion were older ($p < 0.01$), and had an average or lower than average level of education.

The categories we gave the subjects – conversation, confession and suggestion – are a formalization of a content that appeared spontaneously and which I attempted to organize. Asking the subjects to compare psychoanalysis to other practices was, basically, a rehearsal for the transposition of pre-existing associations.

Subjects use these associations to organize new practices that have recently appeared in their world and to produce a unitary image of their world. In this case, producing a unitary image simply means adding a dimension that transforms analytic treatment into a sort of conversation or confession, but which also turns conversation and confession into variations of analytic treatment; the image functions as a set that allows one thing to be substituted for another. Analytic practice thus becomes something that is, like a familiar product, available to all.

3 Self-analysts

3.1 In search of an identity

Ultimately, there is, therefore, nothing exceptional about analytic practice. In a sense, we all practise psychoanalysis without realizing it, in the same way that Molière's Monsieur Jourdain spoke in prose without knowing it. Psychoanalytic language and psychoanalytic notions can be integrated into 'conversations' or 'confessions' that can sometimes look like analytic sessions. The same language can be used to make a self-diagnosis (Anzieu [1959] 1986). Perhaps the time will come when analysts will have to invent a new language to avoid the opacity of a language that is now widely spoken. I am thinking of the cartoon in which the analyst turns to his patient and says: 'Let's start with your diagnosis, Madame.' As we shall see, the original theoretical and practical elements of psychoanalysis have, somewhere along the way, fused to form an *interpretative system*.

Any theory is, a priori, an interpretative system but, in the case of a social representation, the system plays some rather special roles, first because its strict conditions of applicability are not respected and, second, because its supposed use and effectiveness are based upon a social consensus and are not subject to any verification. The interpretative system is therefore at once too poor because, for intellectual or normative reasons, it jettisons many of the notions the theory requires, and too rich because it extends far beyond the field specific to the original theory and the phenomena for which it seemed adequate. Because it ignores the distinction between theory and practice, the interpretative system is, finally, applied to an imagined reality but the revelation of that reality does not require any specific action. The way it is repeated in the most disparate situations eventually influences the way we behave and the way we see social relations.

When a social representation becomes an interpretative system, it mediates between members of the group. There is nothing vague or precarious about the internalization of such behaviours and perceptions; they are organized. The information at the group's disposal penetrates everyday life and generates appropriate behaviours by putting interpersonal relations and the way in which they are lived into a different context. The same process that makes a theory 'subjective' correlates it with its objective or, basically, external aspects. It is when it puts its hallmark on microcosms that a representation becomes truly social. If we do not understand its role in everyday life, we cannot have any clear conception of it (unless we assume the existence of a group mind specializing in the construction of social models). When I asked informants different questions with a similar content ('Do you believe that psychoanalysis can modify the personality?' [students], 'Do you think that psychoanalysis can have an influence on someone's ethical and physical life?' [workers]), I was trying to discover what they thought about the day-to-day influence of a social representation.

An analysis of the answers (table 6.4) shows that most subjects reacted positively. As we move from the 'non-intellectual' populations to the 'intellectual' populations, the proportion of negative answers rises. When we ask informants about the extent to which psychoanalysis can transform the personality, we find that, in the representative population, the proportion of subjects who think it has a profound influence (33 per cent) is greater than the proportion that finds that it has little influence. Very young informants are the most likely to think that the influence of

Table 6.4 Do you think psychoanalysis can influence the personality?

Sample	Yes (%)	Yes for better (%)	Yes for worse (%)	No (%)	N/A (%)	Total no. of subjects
Representative	58	29	5	3	5	402
Middle classes	0	72	19	4	5	331
Workers	25	43	9	10	13	210
Pupils at technical schools	28	44	9	6	13	101
Students (survey)	19	28	9	34	10	892
Liberal professions	50	0	0	37	13	175

psychoanalysis is profound. Levels of education, socio-economic status and the extent of knowledge of psychoanalysis divide the population into two sub-groups, one of which regards analytic intervention as something that *just helps* to transform the personality, whilst the other sees it as something that modifies it *profoundly*.

The first sub-group is made up of better-educated people ($p < 0.05$) who are well off ($p < 0.01$), and who have a better understanding of psychoanalysis ($p < 0.01$); the second sub-group is made up of people who left school earlier, who are lower down the socio-economic hierarchy and whose understanding of psychoanalysis is more limited.

These findings can be interpreted in one of two ways. The first, and more obvious, which takes into account the correlation between education, socio-economic status and knowledge of psychoanalysis, invites us to infer that people who know a lot about the science's modus operandi tend to have reservations about its effectiveness. The second offers a broader understanding. We cannot rule out the possibility that the higher social categories to some extent distance themselves from psychoanalysis not simply for ideological (political) reasons but also because, to the extent that they are, in psychological terms, more comfortable with their social situation, the need for change looks less plausible to them. Social categories living in dependency and insecurity are, in contrast, more genuinely aware of the need for their situation to change and therefore believe that psychoanalysis can have far-reaching effects.

This becomes particularly clear when we look at the workers' answers. The proportion of 'yes' responses – 25 per cent without further qualification, 43 per cent 'for the better' and 9 per cent 'for the worse' – is one of the highest (77 per cent). The high frequency of affirmative answers from this population reveals a further factor that can influence opinions about a social object. The problem is as follows. How is it that this population can have such a positive opinion of psychoanalysis when it knows so little about it and has been subjected to ideological influences that should lead it to reject it? Have its political representatives underestimated the extent to which psychoanalysis has penetrated this social category? The fact remains that the Communist Party's anti-psychoanalytic propaganda does not seem to have been carried out with any great intensity in working-class circles, and most worker informants see psychoanalysis as a *scientific theory like any other*, and regard it as a tool that can help individuals to resolve their personal and social problems. If it were seen as an ideological system (which is how intellectuals and students see it), it is likely that workers' attitudes towards it would be different and that it would not be valorized in the same way.

This leads us to note that attitudes towards a social object *also depend upon the context in which that object is seen*. The importance of the context has been recognized in psychology, as well as in history and anthropology, but studies of opinion rarely take into account the framework in which social objects are placed. The following findings appear to confirm our hypothesis that the worker population's views might have been negative, had its attention been drawn to the connection between this science and politics:

- Those workers who are convinced that the influence of psychoanalysis is *positive* are also convinced that it can help to *improve* social relations (p < 0.05).
- When they think that it can be *exploited for political purposes*, they say that it has either a negative influence or no influence on individuals' moral and physical lives (p < 0.05).

Whatever variations may be found within each population and between populations, psychoanalysis is reputed to have positive effects. That judgement is not unrelated to the way it has penetrated everyday life. We have obviously not looked at the individual experiences that may have influenced these judgements. Our informants' attempts to understand both themselves and others did, nonetheless, stimulate their interest in psychoanalysis and overcome any prejudices they may have had against it.

Whilst psychoanalysis has penetrated everyday life, the extent of its presence should not be overstated. Its presence is of necessity fragmentary and individualized. I accept that one of this study's most serious flaws is that it did not examine with greater care the use that is made of psychoanalytic concepts or of the way that psychoanalysis affects behaviours. Having realized the importance of looking at both these things at a late stage in this study, I listed a few aspects of how psychoanalysis can be rooted in personal experience. Let me illustrate them briefly. Certain people recall that their interest in psychoanalysis was directly related to their adolescence:

'My interest in psychoanalysis? Like many adolescents, I was disoriented, difficult conditions of existence, a lot of wandering, victim of a bourgeois educational system . . . taught abstract notions that did not have an obvious real content – a neurotic search for the "richness" of the unconscious, provoked hallucinations: poor results' (LP). 'When I was 15 or 16, I was interested in Freud's theories, just like everyone else; never taken any interest since' (LP).

This doctor is expressing a widespread feeling: interest in psychoanalysis declines after adolescence, which is often said to be the best age to go into analysis. This comment has to be seen both as an opinion about adolescence and as a memory of an adolescent interest in psychoanalysis. Studies of adolescence reveal conflicts specific to that transitional period: curiosity, a search for an explanation for sexual problems, a desire to understand the behaviour of others and a need for a guide. In an earlier study carried out in a student environment, I noted that psychoanalysis was used at the moment when adolescents underwent an identity crisis and that it was used as a guide during the period in which the ego was reshaped in order (a) to provide a more confident introspection; (b) to give them a rational or rationalizing understanding of the behaviour of others; (c) to provide an answer to the 'mystery' of relations between the sexes; and (d) to explain various factors in 'depression' that arise both from the subject's family and social background and from the subject's attempts to adapt. Psychoanalysis also has a contribution to make to the adolescent's struggle to regain an inner stability in what is perceived as a very turbulent and uncertain environment. This explains why most of the students and technical school pupils who were interviewed knew about psychoanalysis before being taught anything about it. But psychoanalysis does not just allow an 'understanding' of relations between the sexes; it also offers scientific – and therefore unpunished – access to some of our society's 'taboos'. The reason why such a high percentage of informants say that 'between 20 and 30' is the best age to go into analysis is that people of that age are assumed to be malleable and that psychoanalysis is seen as *the objective and socialized completion of an adolescent self-analysis.* Once the ego of the adolescent becomes structured at the age of about 20, he or she gradually begins to react against psychoanalysis which they now try to replace in their set of values or *reject* along with all the other signs of 'youth'. This replacement or rejection goes some way to explaining why intellectuals distance themselves from psychoanalytic theory and therapy.

3.2 Psychoanalytic introspection and inspection

What raw materials did young people use to interpret their uncertainties? Mainly dreams and parapraxes, according to pupils at technical schools (32 per cent). Students appear to have been more systematic about applying Freudian concepts to a whole range of psychical phenomena (37 per cent). The fact that they left school later and know more about it explains why they so frequently used analytic science in this way. At the qualitative level, the story of their 'encounter' with psychoanalysis is always the same:

'I discovered it by myself, out of intellectual curiosity. I began to get interested in it because I thought I would be able to explain myself. I was trying to explain the crises of puberty (wet dreams) and other people. At that age, the chapter on the sexual life of human beings in the *Introductory Lectures on Psychoanalysis* made a profound impression on me. It had something of a negative influence on my religious beliefs. I now think you have to keep it separate from philosophy. It was a mistake to think the opposite. There's actually a certain taboo on psychoanalysis, and people think you're a queer fish. Sometimes, psychoanalysis is mistaken for a venereal disease.'

Whilst the object or effect of this propensity to resort to psychoanalytically inspired models is to clarify individual problems in an intellectual sense, it is not really always just an intellectual game. More intimate or personal events call for self-analysis:

> 'In my case, it was all to do with my complexes, the fact of having lived alone, only daughter, shyness, inferiority complex . . . fear of sexuality. Reasoning with myself helped me to get over all that.' 'I try to analyse myself, and it's helped me to discover things about me that I never suspected, to understand why I hate some things and to get over my shyness to some extent.' 'I was a prisoner for ten years. I began to be interested in psychoanalysis when I came back from captivity. Didn't understand it all.'

The attempt at self-understanding goes hand in hand with an attempt to understand other people. Of the pupils and the students, 22 per cent and 43 per cent, respectively, have tried to use psychoanalysis to interpret other peoples' reactions. There is nothing unusual about this, as 'wild' analysis is often the result of the advice one person gives to another. Here is one example:

> 'As for me, I tried to heighten the self-awareness in a girl who, having lost sight of a boy she loved from afar, went through a very difficult period of dreams (jealousy or disappointment), and then started having olfactory hallucinations (asked St Teresa to give her a sign – a sweet smell – if she was going to see him again. The Saint had already done this for one of her grandmothers. A few days later she smelt the very sweet scent of Virginia tobacco. There was no material explanation. She was quite over-awed and almost fainted). Apart from that, she's very well-balanced and normal, sensitive but not fanatical, not even mystical. She wondered whether: (1) St Teresa really did do something, which she was a little doubtful about; (2) the smell of tobacco came from a real source. When I explained to her that this was all about sexual repression (because she had struggled to stop going on hoping), she looked very surprised, but then she was very satisfied, had no more problems and put off her hopes for a happy ending.'

When we asked the same subject if she wanted to go into analysis, she replied in the affirmative: 'So as to confirm (or invalidate) my own introspection.' This was not the only case of 'therapy' that we encountered. Sometimes, we were told:

> 'I used to know a girl who failed at everything she tried, so I tried to explain her complex to her.'

In a word, a diagnosis is made in psychoanalytic terms, and the 'treatment' consists in explaining the symptoms in the same terms. It is assumed that the effects will disappear when their causes are known. We look for easy answers, and some mothers think they have found them:

> 'I try to find the reasons why I and the people around me behave the way we do. Especially my children. I try to frustrate them as little as possible. After all, psychoanalysis has taught us lots of things about children that we did not know before. When my second daughter was born, for example, my eldest refused to eat. Now I know that it was because she was jealous' (MC).

But not everyone has such a clear conscience. During the same survey of the middle-class sample, we were told:

> 'I've never tried to apply psychoanalysis in order to understand myself or other people . . . People around me do, young people (my sons in particular take something of an interest in it), they've read lots of books on the question and they try to use psychoanalysis to understand the way their little sister behaves. And they criticize me for not bringing them up properly, for giving them complexes. I think all mothers should be given a little handbook explaining the basics of psychoanalysis, if only to stop their children from criticizing them in that way.'

In this mother's view, psychoanalytic notions are required to reduce the gap between her and her children and to put an end to criticisms that might make her feel guilty. To a young man who is under the impression that he has irremediably ruined his life, psychoanalysis looks like a need he has not been able to satisfy. His regrets suggest an implicit reproach against his parents:

> 'Psychoanalysis is a modern science that allows us to set ourselves free and to recover our equilibrium . . . Psychoanalysis can only help adolescents and young adults. In my case – I'm thirty – my life had been ruined for ever because I've always had to fall back on my own resources, when I really needed lots of affection and understanding. I feel unable to adapt and have no self-confidence. I fail at everything I try to do. I think that, if parents could be made aware of their role in future generations, psycho-analysts would just naturally die out because there would be no need for them.'

Students and young people are not the only ones to transform psy-choanalysis into an interpretative system. In the middle-class pop-ulations 78 subjects spontaneously mentioned this problem. Forty-seven of them stated that they had used psychoanalysis as a means of under-standing:

'I don't know enough about psychoanalysis to tell if I'm really using it, but I like to understand people and I ask myself questions about them. I know a girl, for example, who daren't do anything because she immediately says that it won't work and that she is very frightened of other people. I think she has an inferiority complex.' 'A general knowledge of psychoanalytic theory can help people who have not undergone analysis to understand themselves. In my own case, certain psychoanalytic notions have helped me to understand certain of my states of mind as a child, and the impressions they have left. The same notions help me to understand other peoples' reactions, but after the event rather than at the time.'

In all these cases, psychoanalytic concepts make it easier to understand and to give a meaning to what other people do and say. They can also become a weapon, a way of controlling and influencing others:

'In many cases, I use psychoanalytic notions to understand how others are behaving. I sometimes use them to get something out of someone. As we negotiate, I try to break down their resistances. But the technique becomes personal, and it degenerates into a kind of bullfight.' 'I have used psychoanalysis in the pharmacy to comfort certain very sick patients.'

As we are looking at individual cases, it should be noted that intellectuals also try in the same way to use their knowledge of psychoanalysis to shed light on the way they behave:

'Even if it does not cure you it [psychoanalysis] can put you on the right road [leading to a cure]. I've thought about myself, in the psychoanalytic sense of the term, and I've discovered lots of things about myself. Thinking about my childhood, understanding my childhood, my family, influences, what I accepted and what I rejected.' 'I've always psychoanalysed myself . . . no thoughts, no feelings are completely conscious . . .' 'At the age of 24, I realized that I've always reacted in the same way, and I had the impression that I had discovered the unconscious reasons why I behaved as I did. I became interested in psychoanalysis for my own sake. Reading Freud shed light on the things I'd noticed.'

Priests, doctors or teachers can also use psychoanalysis for professional purposes.
A priest:

'Study, and learning by observation and from confessions. Psychoanalysis came in useful for confession because it allowed me to apportion moral responsibility. Personal experience. I think you can psychoanalyse yourself without bothering with a psychoanalyst.'

A teacher:

'Essential for a teacher: you can detect flaws in children that neither their parents nor their doctors can understand (for example, the abnormal way children behave when a brother is born). Psychoanalysis makes it possible to understand why children behave abnormally.'

It has to be said, however, that people do not always use psychoanalysis because they are convinced of its value.

'I've tried to apply certain notions. Not because it works, but because people think it can be done.'

Why? The reasons are not clear. The usual reasons are that we cling to our cultural habits and, in part, want it to teach us things we think we cannot learn about in any other way. The adoption of a psychoanalytically inspired interpretative system we have learned about in the course of our everyday communications becomes almost *automatic*, and some people are aware of this:

'I use it [psychoanalysis] almost unconsciously, but it's more like a mental game and I don't take myself very seriously because, deep down, I think that psychoanalysis should be left to the specialists and that rustics like me can't get much out of it. Used to play at being an analyst. But I no longer have the time to dwell on my problems' (MC). 'Do I use psychoanalytic notions? I've done it unconsciously on a few occasions. It's more a kind of introspection' (MC).

These interviews illustrate the degree to which psychoanalysis has become part of the world of individuals it has penetrated at an 'unconscious' level. Because it sheds light on and includes things they do not know, it helps them, they think, to resolve problems and to structure the world. In that sense, it is part of a subjectified collective experience, a cultural *habitus*.

Psychoanalysis is closely bound up with the history of the individuals concerned; because it allows individuals to understand themselves and to influence others, it is part of their formation; its image is elaborated at the same time as their image of themselves and of their relationship with the environment. In a world in which everyone is also in search of a little clarity, psychoanalysis provides transparency and intelligibility. But France is certainly not the country in which it has the greatest influence and it is possible that, were it to be undertaken at a different moment in time, this study would shed more light on the dynamics of the instrumentalization of this science and its psychosociological substance.

7

A Freud for All Seasons

1 The Need for Psychoanalysis

Being instruments of exchange or interpretative systems, social representations surreptitiously embedded in the social environment affirm themselves as habits, individual or cultural idiosyncrasies. Such habits, and the
illusion that they are common to large sections of the population, can
trigger a 'need for psychoanalysis'. Although I did not see its extent or
urgency in any detail, I did sometimes note the emergence of that need; it
is rather as though psychoanalysis offered some people a possible solution
to concrete problems that was denied to others. When people constantly
come into contact with a social object they have not mastered and do not
fully understand, it becomes fascinating and the desire to get closer to it
grows.

> 'I have great confidence in psychoanalysis. I think that we should talk about
> it more, and explain what it is to the working classes, as it could improve
> their conditions somewhat' (W). 'I think that psychoanalysis is a fascinating
> science and that we should be doing much more to convince people of the
> usefulness of this science, and that it will become a need without becoming
> a drug' (S).

Even when it is not bound up with specific pathological mechanisms, this
demand sounds like a demand for therapy (or an acceptance of the therapeutic situation): 64 per cent of students would agree to being psychoanalysed, whereas 32 per cent would not. Whilst many of them are
prepared to go into analysis, they give different reasons for doing so, and
curiosity is the main one (63 per cent). Of those students who would
agree to being psychoanalysed, 13 per cent say they would do so for personal reasons; 25 per cent also mention curiosity. The high percentage of
respondents who say 'out of curiosity' reveals both the attractions of psychoanalysis and a desire to keep it at a certain distance. The middle classes

Table 7.1 Would you go into psychoanalysis if you were having difficulties?

Attitude	Yes (%)	No (%)	It depends (%)
Sympathetic	88	7	5
Unsympathetic	31	47	22
Neutral	12	66	22

display a tendency to reject psychoanalysis: 44 per cent of those interviewed would not go into psychoanalysis if they were having difficulties; 38 per cent replied 'yes'; and 18 per cent said 'it depends'. The willingness to go into analysis decreases with age ($p < 0.05$). Informants' gender, socio-economic status and general attitude towards psychoanalysis influence them in ways that merit attention.

Women are much more likely to say that they would be prepared to go into psychoanalysis ($p < 0.05$) than men, who tend to adopt a negative stance ($p < 0.05$). Now the very rapid survey I made of analysts does not appear to confirm that most of their patients are women. The stereotypical view that 'it is women who go into analysis' therefore appears to be based solely upon the fact that they are more prepared to do so. Is it possible that all stereotypes are based upon the conflation of a conditional with a *fait accompli*? Nothing could be less certain. It is not true that more people who are in a better economic position than others *want* to go into analysis, but that they do resort to analysis is not in doubt. The perception that 'rich people go into analysis more often' is based upon indices other than statements of intent.

Neither education nor knowledge of psychoanalysis determines individuals' opinions about the possibility of going into therapy. They are, on the other hand, closely related to attitudes towards psychoanalysis (table 7.1).

On the whole, whether individuals would or would not be willing to go into analysis appears to be determined by natural factors such as age, gender and attitude rather than by psychological factors. The representation of psychoanalysis and its action is also closely related to their behavioural intentions. Subjects who say they would not be prepared to go into analysis are much more likely to answer:

'Psychoanalysis can damage the personality' ($p < 0.01$). 'Psychoanalysis does not strengthen the personality' ($p < 0.01$).

They are of course also more likely to think that psychoanalysis is morally offensive ($p < 0.05$). Those who would be ready to go into analysis give positive answers to these questions, and also think that it takes self-confidence to go into analysis ($p < 0.10$), and that psychoanalysis can provide guidance ($p < 0.01$). The need we mentioned is therefore a combination of individual dispositions and the attraction exercised by the object. It is possible that the attitude towards psychoanalysis of those around the subject (or the subject's image of it) is not unrelated to the subject's stated intentions about going into analysis or not. Three questions allow us to shed some light on relations between the two:

(a) What is people's general attitude towards psychoanalysis?
(b) Do many people go into analysis? An average number? Few?
(c) Do you know people who have been analysed?

The answers showed that whether or not people's attitudes towards psychoanalysis are judged to be more positive or more negative is not influenced by the subject's own readiness, or otherwise, to go into analysis. Most subjects do not know if a lot of people go into analysis, but those who say they would be prepared to be analysed do not say that more people go into analysis. The fact of knowing someone who has been analysed plays no role in the wish (or refusal) to be analysed. When they opt for or against analytic therapy, all informants are influenced mainly by their situation. There is, in other words, no conformism in this area.

2 The Extent of Psychoanalysis's Fields of Application

Our description of the situations that make people turn to psychoanalysis and of its associations reveals the extent to which its representations ignore the boundaries that a sound doctrine would set. It is a long time since Freud's teachings were discussed in purely therapeutic terms.

Although it does not claim to offer clear or exhaustive solutions, psychoanalysis does adopt a particular approach to problems such as education and delinquency. This psychoanalytic vision is now widespread and a sympathetic view is usually taken of it in the field of education. When we asked if psychoanalysis could be applied to the education of children, the percentage of positive answers ranged from 54 per cent for the middle classes to 68 per cent for the liberal professions. This approval is obviously dictated by genuine feelings, but it has to be admitted that it is a statement of principle that does not always commit the individual who voices it.

In the middle-class sample, middle-aged individuals (35 to 50 years) had serious reservations about this ($p < 0.01$), as did those who claimed to have no religious convictions ($p < 0.05$; table 7.2).

The positive views expressed by believers are, perhaps, attributable to the great faith they place in education in general, and in techniques pertaining to the psychological and ethical domain in particular. Extreme political beliefs, in contrast, lower the proportion of people who wish to see psychoanalysis being applied for educational purposes (table 7.3).

Table 7.2 Application of psychoanalysis to education: religious convictions

	Yes (%)	No (%)	Do not know (%)
Practising	66	25	15
Believer	53	25	22
Agnostic	44	49	7

Table 7.3 Application of psychoanalysis to education: political beliefs

	Yes (%)	No (%)	Do not know (%)
Communist and left	52	42	6
Centre	79	18	3
Right	65	26	9
Believers	72	18	10

Subjects who say that they are in favour of applying psychoanalysis to education also say that:

- analysis improves the state of those who undergo it ($p < 0.05$);
- psychoanalysis helps individuals ($p < 0.01$);
- it might be possible to apply it to careers guidance ($p < 0.05$);
- its use in the courts is desirable ($p < 0.01$);
- it can contribute to a possible improvement of social relations ($p < 0.05$);
- they would be prepared to go into analysis ($p < 0.05$).

Those who are opposed to extending psychoanalysis to the field of education have, of course, very different views on all these subjects. It is the remarkable consistency of the answers given by both groups that makes these findings so interesting, and it signals that the image of psychoanalysis contains an actual model. Our informants' attitudes towards psychoanalysis also reflect that model, as informants who are sympathetic to it say 'yes' when asked if psychoanalysis should be applied to the education of children, whilst those who are unsympathetic say 'no' ($p < 0.01$). The subjects' knowledge of psychoanalysis has no influence on their opinions. *It is therefore a subject's attitude towards psychoanalysis that determines whether or not he or she believes that it should be used in education, and not objective information about it.*

When subjects in the 'middle-class' sample were asked if they would have their children psychoanalysed, their answers are consistent with their answers to questions about its applicability to education (table 7.4). Their answers are therefore consistent with their behavioural intentions.

Table 7.4 Answers to the question 'Would you have your children psychoanalysed?', correlated with opinions about applicability of psychoanalysis to children

	Yes (%)	No (%)	It depends (%)
Applicable to children	51	20	29
Not applicable to children	4	88	8

A more detailed examination of the table shows that 20 per cent of subjects who are in favour of the application of psychoanalysis to educational problems *would not have their children psychoanalysed*, whilst only 4 per cent of subjects opposed to the extension of psychoanalysis to education would have their children analysed. Subjects who approve of its application are also more likely to say 'it depends'. Which leads me to make an important point about the relationship between opinion and behaviour (or behavioural intentions): *negative opinions are more consistent and decided than positive opinions*. The 'in favour' and 'not in favour' aspects of an opinion are not simply two sides of the same coin, but two different and asymmetrical positions, each with its own content and delimitation. Favourable opinions are in many ways open, receptive and less well-defined. Unfavourable opinions are closed and more clearly structured (Moscovici 1963). In this domain, we can state that 'any negation is a determination'. If we invert Spinoza's old formula, it takes on a heuristic value (Moscovici 1963).

What is the content of these broad reactions to the application of psychoanalysis in the field of education? Three themes emerge from the interviews:

(a) psychoanalysis can be applied either to the education of *normal* children or to that of *abnormal* children;
(b) analytically inspired practices in education can concern children either directly or indirectly, if their parents know about psychoanalysis;
(c) its role can be preventive or curative. Some people think it natural that psychoanalysis should help us to *understand* children.

'To the extent that early childhood is important, psychoanalysis gives parents a better understanding of aspects of their children that we generally do not know about' (LP).

It follows that psychoanalysis can correct the flaws of earlier educational methods:

'It could play a role in education by clarifying educational methods' (LP).

The normal or pathological character of the child is often taken into consideration, as is the therapeutic function of psychoanalysis:

> 'Difficult children can be psychoanalysed' (MC). 'Where abnormal children are concerned, it should allow them to be (1) identified and (2) cured' (LP). 'It should be applied to children with nervous problems, because they are often disturbed by their suffocating family environment. Psychoanalysis is the best way to get the soul of a child to blossom'(LP).

The theme of educating the educators (and parents) is also encountered very frequently:

> 'Psychoanalysis is not a form of treatment; it is just an in-depth knowledge of children that the specialist doctor uses to give advice to mums who do not understand their children, and to mums whose children are behaving strangely' (MC). 'Training teachers, creating a psychoanalytic pedagogy' (LP). 'All teachers could be given a handbook about psychoanalysis; mums can apply it at home' (MC). 'Educating the educators, making them at least aware of the discoveries of psychoanalysis' (LP).

The idea that the child's family background is the source of its difficulties derives from psychoanalysis. When the origin of childhood disorders is examined in the light of psychoanalysis, psychoanalysis is expected to provide guidance for both teachers and parents (which is not consistent with Freud's pessimistic views on the subject). *Once reality has been organized on the basis of a representation, the representation's answer to any given question is determined by its overall organization.*

Some reservations are expressed about the application of psychoanalysis to education:

> 'Psychoanalysis is often abused. They try at all costs to find an unconscious explanation for what children do. It's a bad influence on children; they want them to have complexes, so they do have complexes.' (LP). 'They [psychoanalysis and education] have nothing to do with each other, and they mustn't. It would be too dangerous. You could get children to say anything' (MC). 'You'd end up watching everything the children do and say' (MC).

The freedom implied by strict observance of analytic technique would be dangerous and would undermine parental authority:

> 'Afterwards, the parents make mistakes when educating their children because they are afraid to punish their children' (MC). 'Yes, but it would be easy to go too far, to let their instincts develop without punishing them' (LP).

The notion of caution acts as a mediator between the promise of psycho-analysis and its inherent dangers:

'Yes, but cautiously. Not everything that children do should be seen in psy-choanalytic terms' (LP).

Psychoanalysis can be rejected for various different reasons: fear, the infor-mant's political opinions, the incompatibility between psychoanalysis and child development, etc.:

'No, you have to be of a certain age before psychoanalysis can work' (MC). 'No, psychoanalysis deals with effects and not causes. The most important things for children are a healthy family life and good living conditions' (LP). 'No, because you would have to start all over again in five years' time. Most people think psychoanalysis is all about complexes, and if you warn children about complexes, that's all the more reason for them to have them in later life' (LP).

This worrying and hesitant bundle of opinions betrays the uncertainty that now surrounds relations between parents and children, and an edu-cational system capable of preparing future generations as well as pos-sible. The war, the lowering of barriers within the family, the increasing involvement of children in family life, and the withering away of the myth of a world of childhood that is divorced from the adult world have replaced the rule stating that children should be dependent with a rule stating that they should be independent and that their relations with their parents should be based on reciprocity. Society, meaning adults, has neither understood these worries and questions nor found a satisfactory response to them. Whilst the generous enthusiasm of some educationalists has challenged established procedures, their influence does not extend beyond the model schools, and there are many fewer of them than there are books about them. And how can adult society trace the future, when its convictions and mode of existence have been undermined, and when it cannot fulfil all the responsibilities it has taken on? As the world around it collapses into chaos, the family survives as a cell that can offer individuals the possibility of a protected and affectively satisfying life. Hence the new importance accorded to psychoanalytic theories; because of the role they ascribe to this restricted environment and to an intersubjectivity focused upon relations between parents and children, they fulfil a need, fill a void exacerbated by the religious or political ideologies inherited from a far away, once glorious past that is becoming more and more remote. Given the diversity inherent in a divided and changing society, it is not surpris-ing that we find such disparate opinions.

When asked 'Can psychoanalysis have a salutary influence on criminal or delinquent behaviours?' 70 per cent of informants in all the populations interviewed replied 'yes'.

We asked (cautiously and in concrete terms) middle-class subjects if they approved of the use of psychoanalysis in the courts: 50 per cent did, 40 per cent did not and 10 per cent had no opinion. Those sympathetic to psychoanalysis were optimistic about its potential for use in the courts, and the rest expressed reservations. Subjects' overall views about psycho-analysis also influenced this option, and those who thought that it strengthened the personality ($p < 0.01$), or provided guidance ($p < 0.01$), thought that it should be used in the courts. The following comments, many of them from lawyers, clarify what these positions mean:

> 'Psychoanalysis in penal affairs: it might help to rehabilitate people. Not repression, but the possibility of making a new start' (LP). 'Using psycho-analysis with criminals and delinquents would be a good idea. Because the rehabilitation they do at the moment isn't rehabilitation . . . Leaving aside subconscious factors. And for the protection of society; it makes it possible to distinguish between habitual and incorrigible delinquents and the rest' (LP).

Seventeen of our informants spontaneously raised this problem while being interviewed; eleven of them were lawyers. Psychoanalysis is no stranger to the jurists' renewed interest in the psychological preconditions that lead to criminality and delinquency, and that is why they accept that it can have legal applications. Whilst some non-jurists adopt positions similar to jurists, the same is not true of all of them, and some argue that all psychological considerations should be ignored when justice is being done:

> 'No, there's absolutely no point and it would lead to miscarriages of justice; judges should be men of integrity, not philosophers' (MC).

Those who stress the need to understand criminals' personalities take a different view:

> 'Yes, it might explain the way criminals and judges behave; we have to take a new look at the notion of responsibility' (MC). 'Yes, it would be very helpful to understand what led the guilty to act the way they did' (MC).

Opinions are divided over the notions of justice and responsibility. These are, as we have seen, divergent criteria, and they are difficult to interpret and to apply. Justice is a law that applies to all, no matter why the criminal act was committed. Individuals cannot escape the judgement of society. Responsibility is a very different matter. Delinquents must be literally held responsible for their actions. According to the code of justice, *nul n'est censé ignorer la loi* ['ignorance of the law is no defence' or 'everyone is assumed to know the law'], but who isn't aware of the roots of crime? Individuals in general must take responsibility for their actions, but social justice has to deal with particular cases. What causes criminal behaviour? How can we find out? How can judges apply the same rules to something that takes so many different forms? And given that they have to understand those they are sentencing, what doctrine should they follow?

Psychoanalytic notions can help to clarify motives and to establish the limitations of individual responsibility. It is because it borders on the pathological that crime is a social anomaly, and therapy is therefore one solution:

'Psychoanalysis in the courts? Yes, because it is very difficult to establish the difference between criminality and madness' (MC). 'Some criminals could certainly be psychoanalysed while they are in prison and come out as normal people' (MC). 'Yes, it could open up new horizons in criminology: responsibility and rehabilitations' (MC).

When asked 'Are other domains suitable areas for psychoanalytic interventions?' some middle-class subjects and some from the 'intellectuals' group mention family relationships: [1]

'Family relationships? If we knew more about each other, we would understand each other better' (MC). 'Sexual life: frigidity and problems between husband and wife' (MC).

Psychoanalysis appears, then, to be able to resolve conflicts and especially conflicts over sexuality, which is itself a source of conflict. We can describe as 'semantic' the problems posed by family relations that are disturbed by a plurality of languages: the language of affects, and the language of sexual behaviour:

'Most conflicts within the family arise out of misunderstandings. Psychoanalysis can clear up many misunderstandings by finding the real cause, which is often very different to the apparent cause' (LP). 'Yes, by enlightening people; at bottom, most conflicts within the family are really about complexes and repressions' (LP).

When psychoanalysis is dismissed, it is usually because of one of its specific characteristics or its inability to resolve certain problems:

'The most important thing of all is that couples have a good physical relationship, and psychoanalysis can do nothing about that' (MC). 'It's no use. It's only useful for dealing with nervous cases, but conflicts within the family are always about money, and psychoanalysis is nothing to do with that' (LP).

---

[1] We recorded the opinions of a total of 122 individuals.

Relations with the family are rarely (26 per cent) seen as a field of action for psychoanalysis, but most of those who say that it is are sympathetic towards it. 'Can psychoanalysis be used for career guidance?' This may seem a curious question, but it becomes less curious if we recall that public opinion tends to think that all the techniques used by 'shrinks' are the same, and that, because it is the best known, psychoanalysis tends to subsume them all. The press publishes psychoanalytic texts and market research organizations carry out 'psychoanalytic' surveys. In short, we can say that the 'psychoanalysis' label is prestigious and that it is applied to all sort of products. More people in the middle-class population are in favour of its use in careers guidance (56 per cent) than are against it (32 per cent) or express no opinion (12 per cent). Younger informants (25 to 30), who have a better knowledge of psychoanalysis on the one hand and who are hostile to careers guidance on the other, are more opposed to its being used for that purpose ($p < 0.01$). The profession of subjects is also relevant: significantly more civil servants and people in managerial positions are opposed to that application of psychoanalysis ($p < 0.05$). They reject it mainly because they also reject careers guidance and all other techniques that claim to decide individuals' futures. A very high proportion of subjects who are unsympathetic towards psychoanalysis give the answer 'no'; general attitudes are influential here too.

The applications attributed to psychoanalysis cover, as we have seen, a very wide field. It can be assumed that its extension is not unrelated to opinions as to whether or not it works.

3 Does Psychoanalysis Work?

This is a delicate issue, and it is difficult to give a definite answer. The only domain in which this question has a specific meaning is that of therapy. Most of those interviewed expressed the conviction that psychoanalysis has a positive action. Few took a truly negative position; they were fewer than the 'don't knows', who were expressing a mixture of doubt and a lack of information. Most technical school pupils thought that psychoanalysis worked (63 per cent) , whilst 27 per cent did not know and 10 per cent said that it did not. Of students, 23 per cent stressed the importance of psychoanalytic theory, with 39 per cent saying that it led to a greater self-knowledge and 39 per cent emphasizing its therapeutic (or diagnostic) value. A relatively high proportion (29 per cent) of respondents expressed reservations about when and in which circumstances it should be used ('it depends on the case', or 'it depends on the psychoanalyst'), whilst 78 per cent were not convinced that it had any effect ($p < 0.01$).

The intellectuals express the same concerns and express the same tendencies. Of informants in the middle-class population, 61 per cent believe that psychoanalysis works and that it improves the conditions of those who undergo it, whilst 27 per cent answered in the negative; 12 per cent did not answer the question. The conviction that psychoanalysis works is bound up with a coherent set of opinions.

Subjects who replied that it improves the state of those who undergo it are also more likely to say that:

- it helps individuals in a general sense ($p < 0.01$);
- it strengthens the personality ($p < 0.01$);
- it provides individual guidance ($p < 0.01$);
- they think that it should be used in careers guidance ($p < 0.01$) and in the courts;
- they would have their children psychoanalysed ($p < 0.10$), and they themselves would be prepared to go into psychoanalysis ($p < 0.01$).

We find, however, that they have some reservations about the psychoanalysis of children. Of those who say 'yes, psychoanalysis does improve the state of those who undergo it':

- 22 per cent would have their children analysed, but 52 per cent would themselves be prepared to go into analysis;
- 45per cent adopt a 'wait and see' attitude, and say 'it depends' when asked about their children; only 19 per cent have doubts when asked about their own willingness to go into analysis.

Subjects who expect analytic therapy to have a negative outcome say they would refuse to go into psychoanalysis (29 per cent) or to have their children psychoanalysed. The lack of symmetry we observed between the sympathetic and unsympathetic aspects of opinion now appears at the level of behavioural intentions. In this case, subjects who accept psychoanalysis are more likely to go into analysis than subjects who reject it. As might be expected, fewer of those subjects who adopt a neutral or unfavourable attitude believe that psychoanalysis can give positive results ($p < 0.01$).

The descriptions and comparisons in these pages show that there is a tendency to approve of psychoanalytic intervention into many sectors of private life and social life. For our purposes, however, the interesting thing is that psychoanalytic theory and technique are recognized as being useful and as having become ordinary cognitive tools and action-resources. This instrumental recognition transforms the meaning of certain everyday problems. Criminality, pedagogy and relations within the family are associated with psychoanalytic theory and discussed in psychoanalytic terms.

More so than any other science, psychoanalysis can become a source of applications, raise certain questions and meet certain needs. It must, in short, submit to social norms and give the guarantees demanded of it by various religious, political and family groups. I do not refer to a guarantee that it works (which is both very important and quite secondary), but to an assurance that its foundations will not contradict the various principles that govern collective life. The change in the meaning of 'psychoanalysis' reflects both a tendency to adapt the science to concrete problems and a tendency to extend the group's rules. This appears to be both a way of expanding its potential field of application and a way of mastering the theory and the practice that inspire it. The way psychoanalysis has put down instrumental roots has given rise to significant new connections and new modalities of behaviour, but it has also brought pressure to bear on psychoanalysis.

8

Ideologies and their Discontents

---

1 Psychoanalysis, Religion and Politics

Because it generalizes the use of its representation, anchoring gives society a hold over a science, and its functions come to be determined by the framework within which it is apprehended. And whilst the different orientations it takes still depend upon its content, they obey the collectivity's current preoccupations. Any orientation that the anchoring takes can shed new light on the representation and its structure by enveloping it in a network of meanings; they are part of the act of representing and all that it implies.

A study of the social representation of psychoanalysis is therefore also a study of how our society sees itself in relation to psychoanalysis.

The emergence of a science or philosophical current always results in the adoption of a series of contradictory positions and in imbalances in the affective mobilization; those imbalances typify the way it clashes with the social group.[1] The penetration of psychoanalysis affects such a wide range of beliefs and stereotypes that the responses it provokes have never been simple. In fact it affects almost all sectors of activity, but we will restrict ourselves to an examination of those that play a fundamental role in the elaboration of the signifying system attached to it.

After the war, both Communist Party propaganda and a speech made by Pope Pius XII attempted to influence the way we think about psychoanalysis. The survey coincided with these events.

In general terms, we were able to ascertain that about 65 per cent of those interviewed attached little importance to these messages, even if they did feel that their content concerned them. And although they had been educated in an ideological framework under Party or Church leadership, their opinions about the political or religious pertinence of psychoanalysis owed nothing to the Communist Party's recent propaganda or

---

[1] Where literature and psychology are concerned, see Parsons's thesis (1955).

to the Pope's stance. This phenomenon has to be seen as an effect of the *specialization* of authority and a widescale *involvement* in a social life which, whilst it is diversified, still has a unity. Communists expect their party to give them political directions, whilst Christians expect their Church to issue injunctions about their faith. But when it comes to other questions, the effectiveness of the advice given by the Party and the Church can vary. Communists and Christians also belong to various social groups and the tasks they perform in those groups sometimes lead them to adopt stances close to those of the Party or Church, but they can also be far removed from them. Social heterogeneity is an obstacle to political or religious mono-lithism, especially when, as in the case of psychoanalysis, not all its orders are diffused with the same intensity.

Intellectuals often take the view that psychoanalysis is not compatible with faith (42 interviews):

> 'The emphasis on the libido goes against the Church's commandments; the flesh is blameworthy, and carnal relations must not take place outside mar-riage.' 'A lot of Catholics go into psychoanalysis; you wonder if they've still got their faith. Psychoanalysis often leads to atheism. But it's not secular; it secularizes thought in a scientific way.'

Twenty informants placed faith and psychoanalysis on different planes:

> 'Faith is a different domain to science; there's no conflict.' 'No direct rela-tionship between psychoanalysis and faith. Faith is grace and opens up the soul; certain problems to do with faith may come within the remit of psy-choanalysis, but there's no absolute relationship.'

Fourteen interviews touched upon the theme of positive relations between psychoanalysis and religion:

> 'If psychoanalysis really is liberating, it is, on the contrary, one of faith's aux-iliaries. It purifies it and makes it more conscious.'

All these interviews deal with the non-institutional aspect of relations between psychoanalysis and religion. Now, the conflict of values that we can sense at this level becomes much more pronounced when we move to the institutional level. At this level, it is not personal attitudes that are dis-cussed, but the attitude of the Church itself (43 interviews):

> 'The Church has taken a stand because people (children) are being given advice at a non-religious level. It's taking bread out of priests' mouths.' 'The Church made a mistake when it condemned psychoanalysis; psychoanalysis could create a generation of hygienic Christians.' 'The Church is hostile – it's an obscurantist prejudice; by its very nature, it is opposed to all scientific

progress.' 'The Pope has condemned the exclusively sexual side of it, but he hasn't condemned it irredeemably.'

A striking variety of contents can be observed for the same attitude. Christians who emphasize the Papal ban (which does not actually exist) put psychoanalysis and faith on two different levels, and see no conflict between them. Alternatively, they may emphasize, in the course of the interview, how cautious the head of the Church has been.

Non-believers think that religion keeps minds in a state of obedience that allows it to wield its power; psychoanalysis, which they see as its rival, seems to them to correspond to a secular vision of man, and they put believers' hostility to the libido theory down to religious obscurantism. But some subjects think as badly of psychoanalysis as they do of religion, and regard both as forms of slavery ('Psychoanalysis is as infernal as confession; it's like breaking and entering the soul'). Psychoanalysis can also be seen as something that is simply 'demoralizing', which puts it on the same level as religious belief.

A few informants from the 'middle-class' sample say that psychoanalysis and religion have nothing in common (19 interviews). Others stress that the two are incompatible (12 interviews). The feeling of incompatibility vanishes when our informants look at the therapeutic aspect of psychoanalysis (18 interviews):

> 'There is a problem at the level of doctrine, but not at the therapeutic level. If psychoanalysis is neutral, believers have no reason to fear they will lose their faith. Besides, it's a funny kind of faith that's based on complexes.'

The interviews can throw up worries when psychoanalysis is seen as the enemy of religion or as a substitute for it, either because it does away with guilt

> 'For Catholics, psychoanalysis is the work of the devil insofar as, for psychoanalysis, neither good nor evil exists.' 'Catholics are suspicious of it because psychoanalysis does away with the notion of sin.'

or because it explains the mechanisms of faith and therefore diminishes the power of religion:

> 'Psychoanalysis offends religion, because it would like to overcome the power that religion gives to God by shedding light on certain systems.'

Or even because it is a substitute for religion:

> 'Psychoanalysis is a substitute for religion. It replaces the effort that the soul or spirit makes to control itself, to know itself. Psychoanalysis is a substitute

for mysticism.' 'The priests are losing some of their influence. It used to be the priests who gave families guidance. Now there's a shortage of priests. People are anxious because they feel they have no more leaders, and they are looking for different solutions. It's quite understandable that the Church should regard the spread of psychoanalysis as a defeat.'

No clearly defined attitude emerges from all these comments, and they contain no definite opinion that can be ascribed to any specific group. In general terms, intellectuals appear to be more unsympathetic, and their disapproval seems to have a lot to do with the actual content of analytic theory (they criticize the irrationalism of the drives, or the way psychoanalysis demystifies our most secret motives for behaving as we do). The positive attitude finds its justification in the individual liberation that therapy can offer. Believers who are not sympathetic to psychoanalysis see it as a threat to their faith because it encourages the relaxation of prohibitions. Sympathetic believers hope, in contrast, that the way it lessens their guilt will purify their faith. This debate is a transposition of very different concepts of the basis of the religious spirit. Some believers try to avoid taking sides, either by divorcing science and religion or by attributing different fields to them; this sensible attitude at least has the merit of avoiding all conflict because it does not force anyone to choose. But, in general, believers experience all these problems with great intensity, whilst nonbelievers see psychoanalysis as a powerful agency that can demolish religious myths. When they have been freed from the anxiety of guilt, human beings will no longer need beliefs that make a cult of mental suffering so as to keep them in a state of dependence. By tearing away the veil that conceals the instinctual life, psychoanalysis sheds a crude light on the mechanisms of the personality and takes away the Church's raison d'être.

'Let us return once more to the question of religious doctrines. We can now repeat that all of them are illusions and insusceptible of proof. No one can be compelled to think them true, to believe in them' (Freud 1927: 31). Freud denounces an attempt to reach a compromise in his own school in the following terms: 'All the changes that Jung has proposed to make in psychoanalysis flow from his intention to eliminate what is objectionable in the family complexes, so as not to find it again in religion and ethics (Freud 1914: 62).

Things have, however, changed since Freud's day. We have only to look at a synthetic work like *Trends in Psychoanalysis* (Brierley 1951) to be convinced that psychoanalysis is now much more tolerant of religion.

When, in the course of the interviews, we asked whether psychoanalysis had anything to do with politics, the question was usually taken to be an allusion to its relationship with Communism. In 24 interviews with intellectuals, the view was expressed that no party could take a stance against psychoanalysis. But in 32 interviews, Freud's views were contrasted with those of Marx:

'Psychoanalysis is an *irrational* theory, whereas Marxism is based upon consciousness and rationality.' 'Psychoanalysis can be applied only to individual cases because it sees social life as a source of conflict, whereas Marxists say that society moulds individuals who, in their turn, mould society; psychoanalysis is unaware of this dialectic.' 'Communists are against psychoanalysis because it is an individualist and mystifying method that takes no account of social realities, and because it is decadent.'

The antagonism between an 'individualistic' psychoanalysis and a Marxism that makes a 'critique of society' brings in its wake notions such as rational and irrational, or instinctual and historical.

Twenty-three interviews adopted a political stance:

'Psychoanalysis is bound up with capitalism, with Americanism; it is designed to distract workers from the [class] struggle, seeing that it regards social conflicts as neurotic forms of behaviour.' 'In the past, the bourgeoisie was scandalized by Freud's theories, but now they've been adopted and are perfectly respectable. The Church is no longer hostile. All this goes to prove that it is a weapon in the hands of the bourgeoisie.' 'Because it's on the right in political terms, Communists reject it; it [psychoanalysis] develops in liberal democracies.'

The equation 'psychoanalysis = violation of the personality' is used to argue that there is not much to choose between 'psychoanalysis' and 'Communists':

'In Russia, they use a sort of psychoanalysis: the famous confessions, as in the recent Slansky trial. That was psychoanalysis on a grand scale.' 'Being materialists, the Communists saw all the ways in which they could use it: their propaganda and the techniques they use to get spontaneous confessions are based upon psychoanalytic methods.'

Most of the interviews I have quoted use intellectual or technical criteria to contrast psychoanalysis with Communism. This contrast between two worldviews is less obvious in the middle classes, where 65 per cent of subjects do not associate psychoanalysis with any particular party. In contrast, 62 per cent put it in the religious domain, for either positive or negative reasons. It has to be said that this population contains more believers than the others. Even so, those who are aware of the relationship between psychoanalysis and communism say that it is conflict-ridden:

'Rational communism rebels against this science, which is full of mystery.' 'According to the Communists, you have to change society, and then individuals will change.'

Some respondents find that the two have elements in common, even though they are heteroclite:

> 'The communists can use it [psychoanalysis] to inculcate their doctrines by force and to brainwash the masses.' 'It would be a mistake to oppose Communism because, deep down, what Communism means is making people happy. Psychoanalysis is a tool that can help.'

If we compare the relations we are examining – psychoanalysis and religion, psychoanalysis and politics (Communism) – we find that the former pairing is the more complex of the two but we also find that there is a positive connection between them, whereas relations between psychoanalysis and politics are both vague and simple. Their importance varies, depending on which of the two populations we look at: intellectuals are more likely to emphasize the links with politics:

> 'Is psychoanalysis compatible with an active political life?'

The object of this question was to test the hypothesis that, in a population with an interest in politics, those 'on the left' think that psychoanalysis is incompatible with politics because it makes individuals become introverted in both social and psychological terms. Among intellectuals 46 per cent maintain that psychoanalysis is incompatible with active political involvement; 31 per cent take the opposite view and 23 per cent do not know. Believers and those who are, politically, on the right, tend to answer the question positively ($p < 0.10$). Communist and left-wing informants take the view that psychoanalysis is incompatible with active political involvement ($p < 0.01$).

Can psychoanalysis be exploited for political purposes? The various populations do not understand this question in the same way. Intellectuals, students, technical school pupils and part of the middle class population

Table 8.1 Can psychoanalysis be exploited for political purposes?

Sample	Yes (%)	No (%)	No opinion (%)	Total no. of subjects
Representative	24	43	33	402
Middle class 'A'	24	55	21	161
Middle class 'B'	31	47	22	170
Liberal professions	65	31	4	175
Students	26	74	0	140
Pupils in technical schools	33	45	22	101
Workers	33	45	22	210

understand 'exploitation' in the sense of '*ideological* exploitation of psycho-analysis'. Workers and the middle-class B sample take it to mean using psy-choanalysis for propaganda purposes and for brainwashing:

> 'Yes, in the same way that every element in propaganda can be used' (MC). 'In politics, you use every possible means, speeches, it's all about influencing people! So it is psychoanalysis!' (W). 'Yes, America attempts to do away with the class struggle' (W).

The only population in which the proportion of positive answers exceeds 50 per cent is that of the liberal professions. In all the other popu-lations, most responses are negative (or non-existent). In the two samples that are the largest in numerical terms (workers and middle classes) views on the possible political use of psychoanalysis depend upon the subjects' general attitude towards psychoanalysis. Those who view it in a positive light are significantly more likely to deny that psychoanalysis can be exploited to political ends, with all the pejorative connotations this implies (p < 0.10). Subjects who take a negative view of it assert, in contrast, that psychoanalysis can be exploited to political ends (p < 0.10). Amongst intel-lectuals, political opinions are the only determinant factor. Communists and subjects who describe themselves as being on the left think that psy-choanalysis can be exploited to political ends (p < 0.05). No other factor – profession, age, gender or attitude towards psychoanalysis – appears to determine the direction of their responses. This is a matter of group stereo-typing; it is more pronounced amongst Communists, but it happens in all populations. The majority of students, in contrast, believe that psycho-analysis cannot be exploited for political purposes, and that opinion is shared by all students. If, however, we look at the representative sample, it appears that, in general, the higher the informant's level of education (p < 0.01), or the better their understanding of psychoanalysis (p < 0.05), the more likely they are to be convinced that it can be exploited in this way. The meaning of these findings is clear. In France, educated people with a good understanding of psychoanalysis believe that its ideological aspects mean that it can be used for political purposes.

We also tried to clarify another point. During the Communist Party's propaganda campaigns, which we mentioned earlier, the theme that came in for most criticism was that of the application of psychoanalysis so as to improve social relations. According to the authors of these articles, the bourgeoisie was happy to include Freudian concepts in its ideological arsenal and consciously used them.

The question about psychoanalysis's contribution to improving social relations was not designed to test that hypothesis, which cannot be tested by using survey methods. Our main goal was to take a snapshot of a society in the act of representing an object that can be either valorized or devalorized, but which remains significant.

Table 8.2 Can psychoanalysis help to improve social relations?

Sample	Yes (%)	No (%)	No opinion (%)	Total no. of subjects
Representative	25	40	35	402
Middle classes	24	53	23	331
Liberal professions	34	50	16	175
Workers	44	32	24	210

A high proportion of respondents in all populations said 'yes' to the question 'Can psychoanalysis help to improve social relations?' (table 8.2). Before we attempt to find an overall explanation, we need to take an analytic look at a few significant variations within the representative sample. They are illustrated by a broader tendency.

Individuals who are well-off or reasonably well-off ($p < 0.01$), who are highly educated ($p < 0.01$) and who know more about psychoanalysis ($p < 0.01$) do not think that psychoanalysis can help to improve social relations. France's dominant groups have no faith in psychoanalysis; it is, in their view at best a technique for individual therapy or a science that is worthy of attention. But they certainly do not see it as a tool that can be used for interventions on a large scale. Political loyalties are, as was to be expected, the only things to influence the answers given by intellectuals: no Communist sees any possibility of psychoanalysis being applied for such purposes, whilst the 'right' and the 'centre' accept that it can. In all other populations, sympathetic and unsympathetic attitudes have a lot to do with whether the answer is 'yes' or 'no' ($p < 0.01$).

An examination of the interviews clarifies what the subjects understand by 'improving social relations', and what their positive or negative attitudes are based upon. As different social groups all have their own preoccupations, they have to be clearly distinguished.

For many intellectuals, psychoanalysis is essentially a form of individual therapy (47 interviews) and social problems do not come within its remit because they are political and economic, or in other words, concrete, whereas anything to do with the psychological realm is neither material nor concrete (29 interviews):

'Social problems are not just psychological; they are primarily economic.'
'Nonsense: psychoanalysis cannot alleviate the problems of the class struggle. Psychotherapy is not a universal panacea; that's psychoanalytic eyewash.'

The only thing that can produce better psychological well-being is a change of social climate. Asking psychoanalysis to improve social relations is pernicious and negative:

'Neurotic problems often have a social cause; psychoanalysis should not be applied to social problems, and we should change society so as to make such problems go away.'

A large proportion of members of the 'liberal professions' believe that educational work with individuals can improve society (41 interviews):

'If an individual is better adapted to the society to which he belongs, it is easier for other people to live with him and he is in a position to see problems more clearly.' 'Given that psychoanalysis makes individuals more aware and more responsible, it can obviously help to resolve the problems of criminality and to improve relations between people.'

Others put more stress on psychoanalysis's possible contribution to the fight against certain social scourges such as prostitution, delinquency and alcoholism.

For this population the expression 'social problems' means two things: relations between the individual and society on the one hand, and a vision of society as a whole on the other. In the former context, the individual and society are seen as two specific entities, and as requiring the intervention of specific techniques and conceptions. Marxism provides the appropriate language for discussions of society, with its economic structure and class divisions. Psychoanalysis is also an inadequate and mystifying discipline which inverts cause and effect, or which provides an incidental understanding of the 'psychological', which is a level of reality subordinate to and determined by the social structure.[2]

Still within the framework of the 'society–individual' dichotomy, we also detect a tendency to argue that society can be improved if individuals become better adapted to it and more balanced. In this case, the reference is not to the class struggle but to alcoholism, prostitution or delinquency. Psychoanalysis can prove to be of some use in these domains. Whether we are prepared or not prepared to apply psychoanalysis to improving social relations depends not so much upon our objective characteristics as on how we see society and social problems.

The middle class's categories of reflection and frames of reference are much less formalized. They can, however, merge with the content we have just summarized with reference to the 'liberal professions' group. In 41

---

[2] At the time of the revolution of 1789, it was already believed that overthrowing social structures would have 'curative' effects and would be a desirable substitute for individual therapy: 'The years preceding and immediately following the Revolution saw the birth of two great myths with opposing themes and polarities: the myth of a nationalized medical profession, organized like the clergy, and invested, at the level of man's bodily health, with powers similar to those exercised by the clergy over men's souls; and the myth of a total disappearance in an untroubled dispassionate society restored to its original state of health' (Foucault 1967: 31–2).

interviews, 'middle-class' subjects expressed a certain optimism about applying psychoanalysis to social relations. (No reason is given for this optimism, or if a reason is given it is that the outcome would be a better self-understanding.) Social relations belong, however, to a domain of action that extends far beyond the individual or psychological field (44 interviews). It was also pointed out that psychoanalysis is an imperfect science and that it can be dangerous, ineffective or mystifying when applied to the problems of antagonistic groups (36 interviews):

> 'Psychoanalysis has yet to be perfected.' 'It might be possible in two or three generations' time, when social classes are less closed. As in America, for example.' 'Nothing can bring down the walls surrounding certain social classes. It would take a bloody revolution to bring them down. Only fear can bring down the barriers.' 'Very dangerous; it would lead to Communism.'

Some subjects found our question utopian (56 interviews):

> 'It's utopian', 'it's too complicated'.

The class struggle seems to them to be so radical that psychoanalysis cannot do the slightest thing to remedy it. Only twenty interviewees described this as a possibility, and only within certain limitations:

> 'Psychoanalysis can be of use when it comes to prostitution or delinquency, but we'd also have to improve the state of society: build houses, provide better living and working conditions.' 'It can help the bosses to understand more about the people they employ, so they can give them jobs that are suited to their psyches.'

These comments bring us back to two trends in public opinion, one centred on a radical vision of class conflict, and the other on a more utopian vision and a willingness to support all attempts to improve social relations. The reason why the former trend is more structured is that the basic alterity and the vision of society stand out clearly, whereas the backdrop to the second is less well-defined. That the intellectuals and the middle classes are talking about the same themes is obvious. The difference between them lies in the ways they systematize and conceptualize social relations. Intellectuals think that social relations have more of a political meaning, and see social contradictions as political or ideological contradictions. Because the middle classes do not look at these contradictions in terms of their historical context, they see them in the reified form of a conflict between groups defined by psychological values. The intellectual's attitude towards psychoanalytic interventions at the social level is determined by the way he interprets science and society. For the bourgeoisie, the problem is: 'Is it possible?', 'Is it real?' or 'Why not?'

The primary reason why workers (meaning, of course, those who know something about it) are so open-minded about psychoanalysis is that they see it as part of a non-political world; the secondary reason is that they recognize its power to change 'human nature'.

Some of the workers interviewed stated that psychoanalysis can improve social relations, and thought that that would be a good thing (42 interviews). The means it can use to do so are, they think, self-knowledge, therapy and education.

But, even when they believe that psychoanalytic intervention is possible, they express doubts about the honesty of the different social groups involved, and about their willingness to cooperate:

> 'Yes, to the extent that it does not serve the interests of the ruling class.' 'Yes, perhaps, if everyone acts in good faith.' 'Yes, if everyone goes along with it, bosses and workers alike.'

A large sub-group of workers (57 interviews) does not believe in the social application of psychoanalysis because there is no relationship between psychoanalysis and social relations, and because of our society's class structure:

> 'They've got nothing in common.' 'Good social legislation for the workers would be better still.' 'It's a good way of deceiving the workers.' 'Impossible: the rich and the poor will always be with us.'

Other answers proved more difficult to classify but reveal the same tendencies. Their day-to-day experience leads workers to doubt the good faith of their employers and their desire for a real reform of social relations. When the question of applying psychoanalysis to improving social relations does not arise, it does not have so many meanings.

Comparisons between psychoanalysis and politics or psychoanalysis and religion show only a part of the value-system in which it is enmeshed. The characteristics attributed to the United States often influence the way psychoanalytic science is judged, and if some people are to be believed, it is an American invention. Because it is seen in the context of a stereotypical conception of the 'American Way of Life' that is steeped in political and nationalistic anti-Americanism, the popularity Freud's ideas enjoy in the United States eventually comes to have a powerful influence on the meaning that is ascribed to psychoanalysis. *Homo Americanus* is snobbish, childish and sheepish. The American capitalist is the very worst kind of exploiter. France, of course, is an enlightened and individualist country, and its inhabitants are lucid adults:

> 'People won't go along with it, no need to; in the USA, they are childish and naïve, and easily taken in; but the French are stubborn, and psychoanalysis

is out of keeping with their temperament' (LP). 'Psychoanalysis has turned up at the right moment, because we are living in abnormal times. There are lots of mad people in America; perhaps that's the way it is with countries: they get the medicine they deserve in the same way that they get the politics they deserve' (MC). 'Without wishing to reject the basic principles of psychoanalysis, we have to reject some of its exaggerations. The way certain psychoanalysts really do commit moral rape, and have no respect for the human personality, and especially the conformist politicization of psychoanalysis, as exemplified by the USA' (W). 'Psychoanalysis is a branch of medicine, and it should have remained a purely scientific form of research that could help doctors to treat the body whilst taking the soul into account but, thanks to the Americans who turned it into a fad, it has become a sort of charlatanism, with specialist doctors. Its goal is to satisfy the ridiculous curiosity of certain rich individuals who have time on their hands, and who want to understand their own personalities' (MC). 'You've only got to look at how it has developed in the USA . . . In France, the worse things get, the more talk there is of psychoanalysis, but I think it has yet to penetrate the masses very deeply; fortunately, the people of France have good, healthy reflexes' (MC).

These comments are not really about psychoanalysis. Thanks to psychoanalysis, the image that some categories of French people have about Americans highlights specific features. Some French people see psychoanalysis as part of a way of life that bears within it the seeds of the dissolution of their national character and their traditions. The United States are also a concentrate of the most striking features of capitalist society and, when it is associated with those features, psychoanalysis becomes a *cultural feature* that has to be fought. A critique of Americans becomes a critique of psychoanalysis, and a critique of psychoanalysis becomes a critique of Americans. Either a 'good' society without psychoanalysis is contrasted with a 'bad' society with psychoanalysis, or a 'bad' American psychoanalysis is contrasted with a 'good' French psychoanalysis. One psychoanalyst can therefore write: 'Thanks to Freud we now look at dreams, symptoms and delusions, and ask: *what does that mean? Homo sapiens psychanalyticus* (or at least *americanus*) no doubt thinks he knows the answer and is in a position to clear up all these enigmas once and for all' (Pontalis 1965: 111). American psychoanalysis is credited with having a penchant for accepting easy answers to difficult questions. The stormy atmosphere that once surrounded psychoanalysis turned it into a German science that only the misty and brutal 'Teutonic' spirit could have created. It has now become an American science, and those tormented and snobbish big babies have turned it into an ideological practice that is a dangerous threat to French traditions. It is true that Freud's doctrine now evokes not so much a world of violent drives as the world of the 'family circle' and of disturbed children who are exposed to its 'complexes'. Psychoanalytic preoccupations and psychoanalytic images have changed, together with the representation of the peoples with which they are identified and which served as their support. Psychoanalysis has not just made the United States its country of choice; in the United States, it has, they say, become an essential spiritual 'food':

> 'Americans consult psychoanalysts in the same way that we go to the grocer's' (LP). 'In the USA, people go to see a psychoanalyst in the same way that we go to see a dentist. They find that normal and going to see an analyst is nothing to make a fuss about, whereas it seems that, in France, psycho-analysis is often associated with magic, with witchdoctors and so on' (LP).

It is widely though that psychoanalysis had been reinvented by the Americans to suit their own purposes. Of middle-class subjects, 78 per cent think that psychoanalysis is most common in the United States, as opposed to 6 per cent who think that this is true of Germany and 3 per cent who think it true of England.

Psychoanalysis's entry into the world of conflicts and their discontents is not without its objective basis, and should be the subject of an in-depth historical study. We will merely indicate how the image of a science can be shaped by the selective knowledge that one group has of other groups, taking into account the intersubjective relationship between them. A map of the links that have been established around psychoanalysis reveals the extent to which it touches upon the essential domains of social life.

2 The Values of Private Life

The points of view of churches, parties or nations supply criteria for the evaluation of psychoanalysis's various images. They also give those images a concrete reality. As the number of criteria increases, it becomes possible to reinforce the representation's content and salient features. No matter whether it is accepted or rejected, the representation shapes the organization of social reality because it is part of it. The meanings that emerge as a result are not always perfectly coherent, but they give rise to the tendencies we have described. If they help to give the science a meaning, they do not affect its content. The same could not be said of all the *values* that are offended by the existence of psychoanalysis. Psychoanalysis comes into conflict with existing norms at a relatively deep level, primarily because of the role it ascribed to 'sexuality' in the genesis of the personality.

Although we attempted to do so, we were not able to gather the raw material needed for a full discussion of this problem. When, in the course of the interviews, we attempted to specify the relationship between psychoanalytic concepts and sexuality, the subjects adopted the follow-ing attitudes: (a) they did not recognize the existence of any particular link between psychoanalysis and sexuality; (b) they refused to discuss the problem; (c) the link was simply mentioned, and the interviewee then changed the subject; or (d) the problem was recognised and commented upon.

The first and third attitudes were the most common. The 'failure to recognize' the role of sexuality in analytic theory can be explained by the taboo on sexuality and by the fact that most informants began to learn about sexuality after the war, or at a time when it looked more like a form of pedagogic and therapeutic action to overcome the psychological effects of the war. The violence of the reactions provoked by any reference to sexuality must not, however, be overlooked. The common consensus here is that psychoanalysis 'exaggerates'. Our informants moved very quickly from its 'exaggerations' to the social taboo they offend.

'Whilst a lot of things men do reflect the "beasts" in them, it seems to me that psychoanalysis forgets the "angel" side, and has very little faith in the human potential for good' (LP). 'Freud is famous for reducing everything to sexuality: he caused a scandal, but all that's been forgotten about now' (MC). 'Being a Catholic, I don't trust psychoanalysts because they reduce everything to sex' (MC).

I have already mentioned this antagonism and described how sexuality becomes a sign of / for psychoanalysis. But this is not the only bundle of social forms to come into conflict with psychoanalysis, and the conflict it symbolizes relates to more than sexual norms alone.

'Does psychoanalysis contradict your moral principles?' – 61 per cent of middle-class subjects do not think so. Those who are sympathetic to psychoanalysis think that it does not offend their moral principles ($p < 0.01$). Those who are unsympathetic say the opposite. Those who think that psychoanalysis can provide individuals with guidance ($p < 0.01$) and that it can help to improve social relations ($p < 0.10$), also think that it does not offend their moral principles. When we move to other regions of the normative field, we find that other evaluative criteria appear.

Psychoanalysis touches upon both the values we associate with 'personality' and the relations between the generations. A fairly widespread ethics requires people to be responsible, dignified and perfectly autonomous. Analytic practice seems to frustrate this demand by discharging us from all responsibility:

'Psychoanalysis means turning social and religious values upside down. They despise the family, and parents; they reject them and make the subconscious responsible for everything' (MC). 'We mustn't go too far, and both explain and justify the way people behave. If we do that, there's a threat to society; we'll end up believing that people have the right to do whatever they like because they are never responsible for what they do' (LP).

Those who go into analysis are regarded as weak because they cannot come to terms with themselves, cannot solve their own problems and cannot just get on with their lives:

'It's always a sign of a weak personality, because he cannot manage on his own and because he does not have the will power to fight his bad instincts' (MC). 'Psychoanalysis traps people into their obsessions, and the lucidity it gives them does not help them make any progress (I am thinking of specific cases); a sort of moral comfort that denies the possibility of making a personal effort to improve, that contradicts religion, and is an obstacle to personal progress' (LP).

Analytic therapy is then described as a negation of personal integrity and autonomy:

'I hate it when they search people . . . it's an assault on freedom' (MC). It frightens me, because they can do whatever they like to people' (MC).

The content of what psychoanalysis uncovers is also immoral, and psychoanalysis is associated with that immorality:

'It's become a dubious exhibition of all the pathetic little stories people tell to a man they're paying to listen to them. All those women who are a bit hysterical rush off to see a psychoanalyst so as to wallow in that sordid, grubby atmosphere; it's a bit like a pornographic confession' (MC).

Psychoanalysis can, however, also be a positive factor to the extent that, according to some respondents, it promotes individual development:

'The analysis of the psyche comes to the help of modern man by revealing him to himself' (MC). 'Anything that studies the individual is interesting because, the more we know about ourselves, the better we are, both from the ethical point of view and where our understanding is concerned' (MC).

The impression that we are living in troubled times in which all values are being called into question places a particular emphasis on psychoanalysis, which becomes a sign of the collapse of those values. Witness this long diatribe:

'They despise the family, parents and they reject them. To say that religion is an old wives' superstition is all very well, but we humans can't reject it completely without feeling both remorse and emptiness; so they've popularized a science that is not yet in a position to justify all that. The reason why you don't get on with your parents is that they've given you complexes, including the famous Oedipus complex that makes you reject your parents. It's not your fault. It's your complexes that are to blame . . . When you cheat on your wife, your subconscious is to blame, if your children aren't learning anything at school, and if you're not making a success of your life, the subconscious lets you off the hook' (MC).

The generation gap is also refracted through psychoanalysis:

'Ever since the war, young people have been looking for what happens in the beyond, and inside themselves, and that makes them feel important. We had the Charleston. It was less intellectual, but that was a post-war reaction too' (MC). 'There used to be lots of young people who wanted to write poetry or to die for love, and now, some of them want to have complexes' (MC).

Depending on which values[3] are associated with personality, will power and relations between the generations, two clear perspectives can be identified: if individual or collective disorders result from a normal situation, analytic therapy looks like an acceptable solution; if the problem seems to result from a psychological structure, analysis is rejected because it is a facile solution and because greater will power would be more appropriate. Psychoanalysis is an acceptable solution in time of war because people do not feel responsible for their psychological failings:

'Psychoanalysis? Yes. It makes us very aware of people's mental deficiencies and imbalances. In my neck of the woods, there are lots of children who were traumatized by the bombing and by losing their parents' (LP). 'But these wars, this instability, the uncertainties that are due to our epoch have brought down the walls; everyone is discovering unheard-of possibilities within themselves and they no longer know how to channel them so as to live in harmony with themselves' (LP). 'A troubled period in which individual conflicts and complexes are more frequent and more aggressive' (MC).

If great importance is attached to will power, a different conclusion is reached:

'No one can do anything for anyone. You need will power, faith' (MC). 'When people want to get better, they can do it by themselves, through self-criticism and will power' (MC).

Thanks to this dichotomy between activity and knowledge, or the replacement of one by the other, the celebration of will power goes hand in hand, paradoxically enough, with a negation of the individual. Having a sense of where one's interests lie is viewed as a sign of weakness and as a factor

---

[3] The problem of the relations between values and psychoanalysis was addressed in 150 interviews.

that causes illness; asking for help is a form of weakness and dependency. We can recognize here one of the elements that determined the image of people who go into analysis. We will not discuss the implications of these different ethical options, but will look in a moment at how they influence values.

To go back to more general considerations, public opinion does not see psychoanalysis simply as the objectified content we have spent so much time discussing. It is also a whole, and the centre of an organized network of meanings; those meanings also link it to society. Psychoanalysis is some-times the object of these links, and sometimes the criterion by which they are judged. Such a network could not have come into existence had psy-choanalysis been seen solely as a science. As it put down social roots, it came into contact with political, literary, philosophical or religious cur-rents, and became inscribed in very different frameworks, and this means that its real situation is both very complex and fluid. A few major tenden-cies can, however, be identified.

(a) *Psychoanalysis is seen as an attribute of a group.* This observation is a constant: analysis is associated with a social class (the rich) or a category of people (women, the younger generation, etc.).

(b) *Psychoanalysis expresses a relationship between social groups.* We have seen how psychoanalysis can take on national or political connotations, and how it can even look like a weapon to be used in the class struggle or one of the signs of Franco-American antagonism. It has to be noted that, from a certain point onwards, psychoanalysis was popular with some left-wing groups, and that it has been regarded at other times as a pure product of a 'Teutonic' culture. These descriptions follow a historical pattern; whereas Freud's theories once symbolized the quintessence of atheism, they are now described as 'mystical' doctrines. These changes of meaning coincide with and reflect changes in its real situation, but they do not overlap completely.

(c) *Psychoanalysis embodies a system of moral values.* This view was often expressed during the interviews. I cannot do justice to the contours of this psychoanalytic ethics, which is usually described as being sexually per-missive. There is in any group a hierarchy or order of preferences deter-mined by the degree to which its members are attached to psychoanalysis, and this influences the ethical framework within which it is seen. This is another way of saying that a subject's representation of psychoanalysis will depend upon the system of values that orients that subject's percep-tion of why people go into analysis. When, in etiological terms, the histor-ical situation of the individual who goes into analysis is thought to require external help, analysis takes on an instrumental function and its ethical aspect becomes secondary. If that is not the case, the problem is not seen as a state, but as a choice, a form of weakness or a lack of will power. This is why respondents can say both that psychoanalysis frees individuals and gives them back their identities, and that it is a source of demoralization

because it takes away all individual responsibility, encourages licentious-
ness, threatens the social bond . . . and, in a word, authorizes deviance. In
most cases of neurosis, the individual continues to lead a normal life. There
are no material signs, and material signs are the only ones that a positivist
culture recognizes. Mental illnesses can therefore be easily defined by the
social rules that define illness. But the erasure of the borders between the
normal and the pathological creates uncertainties. To put an end to those
doubts, we say that the power of the will can turn seeming [*paraître*] into
being [*être*], and that the individual's profession, work or social role can
erase all traces of the difficulties. Life is, they say, the best therapist, for-
getting that it can also be a source of conflict.

I have, perhaps, strayed away from the original point I wanted to make.
But it was no doubt necessary to recall that, when psychoanalysis penetrates our society, it inevitably either comes into conflict with the values of
the groups that make it up or reconciles itself to them. Those values either
mould its representation or absorb it; the way the representation is organized reveals the influence of those values and their constellation in a given
environment. Converting the elements of a specific scientific conception
with respect to the specific values associated with the image of its representation is one way of anchoring that representation in social reality.
  The social image of psychoanalysis emerged at a time when French
society was experiencing major changes. It suffered the repercussions of
the history of that society, and its presence at the centre of all debates is
due to the fact that no fragment of culture can remain unaffected by its evolution, except through its insignificance. The representation of psychoanalysis, the result of this adventure which the specialist of this science
sometimes ignores, even though their knowledge becomes the object,
expresses accidents and encounters – essential or contingent magnifica-
tions of history – but it is, for the moment, neither stable nor complete.

9

On Jargon in General and
Franco-analytic Jargon in Particular

1 Language and Languages in Conflict

A pidgin is defined as a stable form of speech that is not learned as a first language (mother tongue) by any of its users, but as an auxiliary language by
all; whose functions are sharply restricted (e.g. to trade, supervision of work,
administration, communication with visitors) and whose vocabulary and
overt structure are sharply reduced, in comparison with those of languages
from which they are derived. (Hymes 1968: 14)

The language in question is the product of a conflict: the conflict between
one particular group which spreads it by using it spontaneously and a
society which, because it has its own discourse, resists it and unconsciously assimilates it. Its vocabulary tends to assimilate the new vocabulary, which implies both the replacement and the dismantling of existing
linguistic chains. Although this structure is dominated by contradictory
tendencies, it is inherent in the way language mediates between a science
and its representation, or between the world of concepts and that of individuals or collectivities. It becomes imprinted with meanings which, as we
have seen, constitute a network. Using this language is indicative of the
fact that we are using a scientific system of notation as a referential tool in
order to interpret events and behaviours. The process of anchoring is a
process of elaborating this verbal mediator, without which it can neither
develop nor survive. The study of a social representation of a science
involves, in addition to an analysis of its content, an analysis of how its
language penetrates society.

The extension of psychoanalysis and its concepts through the communications and practices that socially institute its reality works towards
imposing a particular system of a linguistic character. Our current vocabulary becomes more diverse and adopts new terms that closely follow the
contours of the social representation and the forms in which it is diffused.
The plurality of representations attached to a single word makes them at

the same time both transparent and opaque. They are transparent to the extent that, through the expression of other meanings by the same term, they can find their way into existing forms of comprehension; they are opaque because the imperialism characteristic of any structured organization isolates and transforms them by conferring all the properties of a specific sign upon a word whose particularity was not previously perceived We might consider such examples as repression, unconscious and complex, once common words of our linguistic baggage and today bearing such characteristics of psychoanalysis. The interweaving of knowledge and language [*langue*] in communications is one of the things we can be most certain about: 'Symbolic formulations cannot be divorced from communications and thought in general' (Lagache 1934: 32). We might say that this is even truer of society: to know something socially is to speak it.

As a result of the formation and generalization of a social representation, notions and linguistic terms specific to a theory, or its scientific 'jargon', therefore interfere with normal linguistic exchanges. This jargon provides them with a socially authorized version of a mode of access to a body of knowledge and phenomena whose nature is normally inaccessible to the community. As this process continues, scientific language loses its specific function and everyday language becomes diversified – it adds another dialect to the list of those that make it up. This encounter helps to create what Bally (1935: 79) suggests we should call a language '*un langage*': 'The heterogeneous and fluctuating matter in which language [*langue*] takes shape; this is the nourishing bath into which it constantly plunges and which, through infiltration, supplies it with the means to renew itself and to endure.' And yet, there are organized currents in the bath – and the linguist does not take sufficient account of this. These are expressions of the representations that dominate the human mind in any given society at any given moment. There is a unity between *langue* and *langage* as the preferential forms of one are echoed in the other. The existence of these themes, which supply the leitmotivs around which *langue and langage* unite, are also channels that allow concepts to become everyday expressions, which means that *langage* has a preference for certain concepts. The concept of a complex and the frequently used word 'complex' correspond, in the same historical period, to the same way of looking at certain psychoanalytic problems, but they do not have the same content. The term 'complex' is borrowed from the Zurich school (Freud 1906: 104), but Freud uses it to describe any group of representational elements that are bound together and charged with affects. As we know, the term became popular with both psychoanalysts and the public. But, by the creator of psychoanalysis's own admission, its popularity did nothing to clarify its meaning: 'None of the other terms coined by psychoanalysis for its own needs has achieved such widespread popularity or been so

Table 9.1 Ratio of terms known to terms recognized

	Terms known: terms recognized				
	1½ (%)	1 (%)	¾ (%)	½ (%)	¼ (%)
Students	7	13	20	20	40
Liberal professions	5	8	13	25	49

misinterpreted to the detriment of the construction of clearer concepts' (Freud 1914: 29–30).

The fact that its technical terms enter our vocabulary is not the only effect of the ascendancy of a science and its representation. It also colours other terms that are already in circulation, as communication does not tolerate the mere juxtaposition of lexicons. By blending them together in an appropriate way, it establishes correlations and solders verbal chains.

To facilitate the exposition, we will use the expression *thematic language* to describe all the lexical units that attach themselves to a social representation or that become imbued with it. This language plays the same role in everyday communication that theoretical language plays in scientific language; it introduces images derived from a scientific conception.

We can say that a subject's knowledge of psychoanalysis is proportional to that subject's knowledge of the terms that express it, but it is difficult to prove that this is the case. It would be ludicrous to construct a verbal index for the 'middle-class', 'worker' or 'technical school pupils' populations, as 'complex' is the only word that almost 30 per cent of their subjects know. The words 'repression' and 'unconscious' are encountered still less frequently. I did, on the other hand, devise a verbal index for the student and liberal professions populations by comparing the number of psychoanalytic terms in the list we showed them that were known [*connus*] with the number of terms they identified as such (table 9.1).[1] The distribution of the terms is very similar in both categories, but the students came up with a greater number of psychoanalytic terms.

Most of the high indices (60 per cent of the proportions 1½ and 1) are found in the group of philosophy and arts students, and they have the best knowledge of psychoanalysis. The lowest indices are found amongst science students. There is a clear relationship between verbal indices and levels of knowledge (table 9.2).

[1] The purpose of constructing such an index is (a) to estimate the extent of subjects' vocabulary by asking them to say spontaneously which psychoanalytic terms they recognize; and (b) to arrive at a quantitative estimate of their knowledge, and its accuracy, by comparing these answers with those given by all interviewees when they are listed in the same order.

Table 9.2 Ratio of verbal index to level of knowledge

	Terms known: terms recognized			
Level of knowledge	1½+1 (%)	¾ (%)	½ (%)	¼ (%)
A (highest)	37	33	20	10
B	4	9	39	48
C	6	0	12	82

Other findings are also of relevance to our investigation, especially those concerning the number of *different* psychoanalytic terms that were mentioned. The following figures give an idea of the number of terms

Students	157 psychoanalytic terms
Liberal professions	117
Middle classes	80
Technical schools	33
Workers	10

The frequency with which each word appears obviously varies, but we see here a paradoxical phenomenon: *the more a group knows about a science, the greater the temptation for it to expand the list of words it attributes to it.* An increase in the accuracy of the information at its disposal has an *extensive* effect at the level of language and not a *selective* effect.

The list of different 'psychoanalytic' terms depends upon the subject's degree of knowledge, and so too does their frequency. The greater the subjects' understanding of psychoanalytically derived notions, the more words they use to describe them.

We should immediately notice a relationship between the extent of vocabulary and frequency in the 'common' language of psychoanalysis. This language is the scientific *langue*'s alter ego. In it, we found two classes of words: (a) a class of 'specific' words and (b) one of 'assimilated' words. The latter included 'recreated', 'associated' and 'derivative' words.

(a)   *Specific* words are words that are actually part of the vocabulary of psychoanalysis: complex, id, defence mechanism, etc.

(b-1)   *Recreated* words are words coined on the basis of specific words. Many refer to a series of novel complexes: Sardanapalus complex, reaction complex, etc.

(b-2)   *Associated* words are borrowed from neighbouring domains and then attributed to psychoanalysis: taboo, obsession, neurosis, trauma, etc.

Table 9.3 Use of words

	Students	Liberal professions	Middle classes	Technical schools
Specific words:				
Number	56	40	26	12
Frequency	479	356	176	69
Recreated words				
Number	64	49	28	14
Frequency	145	100	40	27
Associated words				
Number	8	9	4	4
Frequency	26	23	7	4
Derived words				
Number	29	17	19	3
Frequency	34	24	20	3

(b-3) *Derivative* words are not directly related to psychoanalysis, but display a vague semantic kinship which is reinforced by linguistic usage: relaxation, rejection of virility, etc.

A quantitative examination shows that, as might be expected, the number of *different* terms is lower in the 'specific words' group than in the 'assimilated' group, but the *frequency* of specific terms is higher than that of assimilated terms (table 9.3). It follows that, whilst the spread of this language is proportional to that of the social representation, the use of relatively adequate words still predominates. Socialized *language* is imaginative, but it is not delirious.

The meaning of this assimilation of words is immediately obvious. Public awareness of psychoanalysis is now so great that the science can determine a new context for words such as dream, instinct, symbol, timidity, if only because of the particular emphasis that is placed on them.

The language that emerges from these findings can be looked at in a variety of ways. On the one hand, a symbol and a set of symbols derived from a science or a group are introduced into the circuit of social interlocutors. It is known to be the language *of psychoanalysis and psychoanalysts*, or that of a particularly marked domain, and that is why it is used. Everyone is aware that they are using the language of a *different* group with a specific place in society or knowledge. On the other hand and to the extent that it is a *thematic language*, it is used as though it were a system of indices about a specific reality. But the 'dictionary' it makes available to all is articulated with a shared *langue* and words like 'complex' and 'repression' are now part of everyday vocabulary.

Table 9.4 Word frequency

Sample	Vocabulary			
	1	2	3	4
Students	Complex	Repression	Unconscious/ Subconscious	Libido
Liberal professions	Complex	Repression	Unconscious/ Subconscious	Libido
Middle classes	Complex	Repression	Unconscious/ Subconscious	Libido
Pupils in technical schools	Complex	Unconscious/	Libido	Repression

At the beginning of this study, I noted that psychoanalysis was associated with a particular figurative model in which the relationship between the 'conscious mind' and 'the unconscious', which is determined by repression, produces 'complexes'. I also noted that sexual phenomena hardly ever appeared in that schema.

Now there is a correlation between the most frequent words in the figurative language and the essential themes of the figurative model and, therefore, between social representation and thematic language. This language borrows its *themes* from the science and its representation, but there is also a nuance of difference: 'conscious mind' does not figure in it, whereas 'libido' has a fairly high frequency. The expression 'conscious mind' is rarely mentioned by our informants, perhaps because they have sufficient knowledge of psychoanalysis to recognize the non-specificity of the term, which is therefore alluded to by notions such as 'the unconscious' (which negates it) or 'repression' (which is one of its modes of action).

That the term 'libido' should appear so frequently is surprising, given that most subjects do not mention the relationship between psychoanalysis and sexuality in their descriptions of the psychical mechanism and that, when they do so, it is in order to call it into question. The resistance to the psychoanalysis-sexuality link is also apparent from the fact that the word 'libido' tends to be *recognized*, but is not *used spontaneously*. When, for example, the students list analytic words, the word *libido* ranks fourth, but the frequency with which they recognize it on a list means it ranks as second, immediately after the word 'complex'. The difference in ranks according to whether the word is listed or recognized expresses the opposition to what is the symbol of sexuality in the theory of psychoanalysis.

2 Speech Becomes a Reality

This thematic *langage* is not just a reflection of how psychoanalytic concepts and the figurative model have penetrated society. Word-frequencies are a measure of how the concepts have penetrated it, and the order or ranking of those word-frequencies provides concrete evidence of how far the figurative model has contributed to the elaboration of a representation of reality. At a deeper level, this *langage* is also an expression of how the model helps to elaborate a representation of reality. One might think, quite rightly, that the words 'complex' and 'unconscious', which appear so frequently in speech, are being used in a purely nominal sense. Playing with words is one of our most stubborn habits. Its effects should not be underestimated. To name is to name *something*, or in short to objectify *something*. What is more, the object of this verbal-intellectual act is not an independent thing or phenomenon that already existed. On the contrary: when we name something, we impose limits and properties, and in a sense play a part in the structuration of the object or phenomenon. In a very lucid article, Cassirer (1933: 23, 33) develops a thesis that corresponds quite closely to my observations:

> Objective representation – which is what I am trying to explain – is not the starting point of the formation of language, but the goal to which the process leads. It is not its terminus *a quo* but its terminus *ad quem*. Language does not enter a world of complete objective perceptions simply in order to add to it more individual given and clearly delineated objects, or 'names', as though they were purely external and arbitrary signs; it is, in a sense, the mediator par excellence, the most important and most precious tool we can use to conquer and construct a true world of objects. . . . But language must also gradually conquer the *social* world that has to be talked about openly, as well as the world of 'external' objects and the world of the personal ego.

In that way the extension of this language, the use of its terms to describe behaviours or people, is also an extension of the entities that are supposed to accompany it and of the research into the common reality of phenomena which correspond to it. Jointly, we link and organize within these objectified realities a whole series of manifestations which do not necessarily belong to them, organize them in their terms. When we speak, for example, of a 'reaction complex', or of the 'Sardanapalus complex' or the 'reactive' behaviour of historical figures, we integrate them into a worldview that we attribute to psychoanalysis. The combinations of words we find there are a testimony to the presence of what might be called 'semantic genotypes', or key propositions that allow us to determine a certain figure of the real, and to locate individuals and events within it. Expressions such as 'repressed complex' or 'unconscious repression' are semantic genotypes, and we can use them to produce a whole chain of variants that allow us to explain the unknown and to divide the known into socially accepted categories. Concepts cease to be established images or habitual abstractions and become both true linguistic categories and categories of the understanding – though they are, of course, *collective categories*. We can use them to isolate 'facts' and to control the observation of concrete events. As it is used, each category is consolidated into a 'natural' instrument of comprehension or reflection within the group that uses it for these purposes.

All this suggests that we need to look more closely at certain mechanisms pertaining to this thematic language.

The first of these mechanisms is *normalization*: scientific concepts become part of everyday language and are used without any specific relationship being established with other terms in the vocabulary. When they are detached from their previous lexicon, they appear to be new. The words 'complex', 'repression' and 'unconscious' have an indicative value but no very specific meaning. None of the individuals interviewed could tell us what they understood the word 'complex' to mean. It is its role in communication that gives the word its value and there is certainly a link between a word's ranking and its adoption by everyday language.

The second mechanism is a process of *motivation*. The scientific concept becomes part of everyday language without losing its initial function of designation, but its structure may change and more common meanings may be added to its original meaning. It is thus reduced to immediate experience, and the original term merges with the socially accepted term. The expressions 'reaction complex' or 'timidity complex' illustrate these articulations. on the one hand, the signifier 'complex' becomes conventional and non-specific because it is not associated with any particular content (though it retains a symbolic resonance referring to a particular system of knowledge); on the other hand, it gives a certain motivation to terms in ordinary language. A linguistic sign is motivated by a word when that word evokes the parts that make it up and other parts associated with it. 'Nineteen', for example, is a motivated sign and 'twenty' is not. 'Complex' is not motivated, but 'reaction complex' is. We can speak of motivation when we find that *langue* is being combined with a new borrowing; this can lend a 'scientific' colouration to words in common use and can superimpose an 'everyday' version on words used by a scientific terminology. The extension of the social representation supplies the backdrop that facilitates this motivation, which is linguistic only to the extent that it is based upon a thematic unification of implicit contexts. So far as psychoanalysis is concerned, 'complex' has a much greater motivating force than other concepts. Like the radioactive bodies used in biology, it can act as a veritable 'tracer' that detects the circulation of psychoanalytically derived language or its volume.

'Complex' is also perceived as a *supra-concept*, or as the emblem of Freud's theory, as attraction was for Newton's theory. The entire social representation of psychoanalysis is, as it were, concentrated in this notion and assimilated to it. Some subjects define psychoanalysis as a 'science of complexes'. The complex is both an *organ* and the principle behind the structure of the psyche. We can 'take away' complexes and we can 'catch' them.

The goals of psychoanalysis can therefore be defined as 'avoiding the acquisition of complexes' (LP) or *'analysing, locating* and *neutralizing* tendencies in which complexes take on a pathological aspect by bringing them into the conscious realm or by inducing healthier behaviour' (S).

The substantialized use of the word is a fairly widespread cultural fact that is imbued with a vision specific to the Western world and its verbal constructs:

> The Standard Average European microcosm has analysed reality largely in terms of what it calls 'things' (bodies and quasibodies) plus modes of extensional but formless existence it calls 'substances' or 'matter'. It tends to see existence through a binomial formula that expresses any existent as a spatial form plus a spatial formless continuum related to the form, as content is related to the outlines of its container. Nonspatial existents are imaginatively spatialized and charged with similar implications of form and continuum. (Whorf 1956: 147)

Whorf's propositions are not as generally applicable as he might wish them to be, but they are pertinent to our subject. The thematic language of psychoanalysis is, like that of any other discipline, substantialized and objectifying. 'Complex' takes pride of place amongst these objectified and objectifying notions. Being a principal concept, it is prolific and synthesizes a whole *class* of concepts: the Oedipus complex, the Baucis complex, the Sardanapalus complex, the old-age complex and so on. It generates a whole series of 'satellite myths' about psychoanalysis, as every situation is capable of creating its own complex: we have a sort of proliferation of structures and 'virtues'. The philosophy of the scholastics supplies the prototype.

We also find that 'complex' can take on different grammatical forms and be either a noun, an adjective or a verb. One subject said, for example: 'I don't know anyone who is complexed [*complexé*].' 'To be complexed' and 'to complex someone' are common expressions. These grammatical mutations can be found in a single sentence: 'There is something facile about psychoanalytic explanations; everything is explained in terms of complexes, whereas things are simple and not complex.'

As we can see from the unintentional non-sequitur, 'complexes' can be invoked to explain anything that is difficult, mysterious or complicated. The obscurity of the term's meaning does not prevent 'complex' from playing a dual role in ordinary communication:[2]

- For people who know about psychoanalysis, it saves time because it contains all the information they need and sums up a series of notions.

---

[2] By Freud's own admission, the same obscurity is present in psychoanalytic usage.

- For people who know less about it, the term indicates 'what we are talking about' and makes communication possible despite the lack of essential information; for these people, the relationship between the sign 'complex' and the signified 'psychoanalysis', is, within this frame of reference, not arbitrary but necessary, insofar as it is representative of a wider system.

In the first case, 'complex' is a sign that facilitates both cognition [*connaissance*] and recognition [*reconnaissance*]; in the second, it is a true symbol. In social terms, 'complex' is the symbol of psychoanalysis, or the one thing that distinguishes it from all other social representations. A scientific sign has become a social symbol. Its lack of definition is no obstacle to its motivation or to the plurality of meanings that can be given to it. Ultimately, it can be no more than pure sonic form. A painter calls his objects 'chromplexes' and shows them in an exhibition. Any art-lover can understand the psychoanalytic reference and knows which verbal mould has been used. If, however, we break down the word, its content is not what we expected, as it is produced by the following combination: chrome + Plexiglas = chromplexes.

Because it is so non-specific, 'complex' is a source of symbolic exactitude: it transposes one imaginary into another, and breathes so much life into it that it fades away. Although we did not have the opportunity to prove the point, common sense obviously tells us that all social representations can be concentrated into such symbols, which reify them and make them stand out in the eyes of the social group. 'Atom' plays the same role in modern physics, and 'force' played it in classical physics. The connection that such symbols establish between a certain body of knowledge and a social representation is also an expression of the time-lag that allows the extraction from the real of, first, a *meaning* and, second, a cognitive classification. A social representation of a science emerges from both a search for a meaning and a search for satisfactory information. Its major symbol is the mark of the presence of that meaning, as elucidated by a concept; the lack of specific information leaves the field open to all the combinations that society can come up with. We can find equivalent notions in the representations of other elementary societies. By looking at certain analyses of notions such as *mana* and *orenda*, Claude Lévi-Strauss demonstrates that they have no particular determinate content, and have an indicative function similar to that of our 'thing' or 'whatsit':

> . . . those types of notions, somewhat like algebraic symbols, occur to represent an indeterminate value of signification, in itself devoid of meaning and thus susceptible of receiving any meaning at all; their sole function is to fill a gap between signifier and signified, or, more exactly, to signal the fact that in such a circumstance, on such an occasion, or in such a one of their manifestations, a relationship of non-equivalence becomes established between

signifier and signified, to the detriment of the prior complementary relationship. ([1950] 1987: 55–6)

'Complex' is certainly the 'whatsit' or 'mana' that is identified by psychoanalysis. Such symbols provide the link between scientific language and thematic language, and they allow the group to name and interpret its own experiences. They allow new themes to flourish in oral communications, not so as to clarify ideas but so as to indicate how individuals or situations are to be judged and evaluated. When we say 'so and so has a complex', the expression locates the conversation within a field of representation – psychoanalysis and not Marxism – but the absence of specific knowledge sometimes makes these experiences indistinguishable from others. Similarly, informants who give a psychoanalytic status to words like 'adaptation', 'trauma', 'fetishism', 'phallic power', 'deep ego', 'Eros' or 'killing the father' are introducing a whole series of themes belonging to a multiplicity of theories in a world that has been semantically expanded. As a result of this shift, 'complex' is a matrix-word, referring primarily to an objectified reality, then symbolizing a social representation and an identifiable science, and, finally, being a sign that generates semantic motivations, verbal forms and so on.

The language whose links with the representation of psychoanalysis we have just been looking at is based upon such terms, which are the most active agents of its extension.

10

Natural Thought: Observations Made in the Course of the Interviews

1 Phenomenological Remarks

In the course of this study, I approached social representations as though they were autonomous modes of knowledge. The fact that they generate specific languages is one of the signs of their specificity. Taking the interviews as a starting point, we can now look for others. I am well aware that such a digression cannot lead to definite or precise conclusions. But nor is it completely futile. A phenomenological exploration of the discourse of the people who reflected upon psychoanalysis in my presence may shed light on the almost unknown domain of the concrete or actual way in which individuals think about social objects. I do not intend here to draw up a catalogue of distortions, departures from formal logic and major inconsistencies. Many experiments have been devoted to such deviations, and they have helped to fuel prejudices about the 'illogical' or 'irrational' character of everyday reasoning. Yet if we look at them more closely, both elaborate systematizations and compulsive quests for coherence may be individual signs – and why not group signs? – of serious epistemological or pathological deficiencies.

> Thought which is totally unscientific, and even which contradicts entirely experience may be entirely coherent provided that there is a reciprocal dependence between its ideas. Thus I may instance the writings of medieval divines and political controversialists as examples of mystical thought which, far from being chaotic, suffers from a too rigid application of syllogistic rules. Also the thoughts of many insane persons (monomaniacs, paranoiacs) present a perfectly organized system of interdependent ideas. (Evans-Pritchard 1934: 51)

Neither the rigid application of syllogistic rules nor their non-observance in conversation, newspapers or interviews is, as we have been led to believe, an indication that thought has been debased or that these modes of thought have no value when it comes to knowledge and objectivity. This non-observance at least reminds us that logicians have neither seriously studied nor discovered the laws of the workings of most cognitive systems. If we compare natural thought, which is social, with scientific thought, which is individual, and find that the former may be pseudo-logical because it does not conform to a logic that is foreign to it, that proves only that we regard science and syllogistic thinking as ideal models of intellectual organization. There is obviously no justification for doing so, as it is tantamount to transforming a gap in our understanding of cognitive processes into a gap in reality. Astronomers did not take the view that the planet Mercury was at fault because its orbit deviated from the path it should have taken according to Newton's laws. On the contrary, they saw the orbit of Mercury as a sign that the laws were imperfect. That example indicates that it would be a mistake to dwell for too long on the distortions and inconsistencies of the usual or ordinary intellectual processes so as to devalue them on the grounds that they deviate from principles which we value more highly. We should, rather, be stressing their obvious inadequacy. After all, logic establishes the laws of thought, but its vocation is not to force its own laws on thinkers. Nor is social psychology the guardian of the rules – even those of thought. It has to study phenomena that have been observed and identify regularities specific to them. From that perspective, we must abandon the dichotomy between logical and non-logical, rational and affective and social and non-social, which has given rise to so many famous controversies and with which we are still obsessed.[1] We therefore find ourselves dealing with a plurality of cognitive systems and social situations between which there is a relationship of balance. The frameworks in which the sciences are elaborated – homogeneous data, specialized groups, a search for originality and so on – combine to demonstrate that their intellectual methods correspond to definite collective imperatives. All logic or thought is social in one sense, but not always in the same way or for the same purposes. Where social representations are concerned, we can see that several factors determine the conditions under which they are thought and constituted. We can at least infer what those factors are on the basis of our observations.

We noted, first, the role the *dispersal of information* plays in the genesis and ordering of thought processes. The information most people have at their disposal when they come to answer a question or to express an opinion about a specific object is usually both inadequate and superabundant. They are, for instance, likely to know little about psychoanalytic theory, and a lot about its political implications. This does not allow them to make a fair evaluation of phenomena, relations or implications. The

---

[1] The value of these dichotomies was discussed in the first edition, where it was demonstrated that they result from faulty reasoning and long-standing prejudices. See also Werner (1948) and Brown (1954).

discontinuity between the information that is actually available and the need to grasp all the elements upon which an argument is based is – except in limited domains – a *constitutive* discrepancy. We are not dealing with a quantitative variation in the amount of available data, but with the existence of zones of interest and behaviour where the knowledge we need to acquire can be neither identified nor acquired. For one group, psychoanalysis may represent a region where it is difficult to isolate and assimilate data that might be truly useful; for other groups, the equivalent region might be physics or automation. The obstacles to transmission, the lack of time, the educational barriers (Goblot 1930) reinforce, through their diversity or their fluctuation, the uncertainty in which we find ourselves in relation to the real dimensions and import of any given problem. The indirect nature of the knowledge we possess and of the available accounts are a further source of difficulty, as is the fact that there is no way of verifying what we hear. How can we be sure that the radio's account of something is more credible than that given in a newspaper, and how do we know that one commentator's opinion is more authoritative than another's? Why should we trust the opinion of a priest or philosopher rather than that of a politician when we are dealing with a social or psychological issue? In these circumstances, we make a choice. Comparing, measuring and acquiring hard evidence is out of the question. The vast majority of the subjects we interviewed had no chance of formulating any clear idea of the effects of psychoanalysis, and it is by no means certain that psychoanalysts can do so either.

The multiplicity and qualitative unevenness of sources of information, as compared with the number of fields of interests that an individual must apprehend if he or she is to communicate or behave, make the links between judgements precarious. In the light of this diversity, the distinction between the uneducated and the educated, who use more scientific modes of argument, loses its value. Indeed, in the face of some problems, we are all uneducated. The education we receive at school and university gives us a greater ability to understand the knowledge that circulates in society. It is, however, very common for differences to become blurred and, no matter what level of education they have achieved, individuals are all in the same position when it comes to communicating or expressing an opinion. While carrying out this survey, we noted on several occasions that, despite some lexical variations, the style of reflection was the same, regardless of the informant's social group or level of education.

Second, the way subjects *focus on* social relations or particular viewpoints has an undeniable effect on the style in question. This state – or variable – is the expressive aspect of the relationship between the individual or group and the social object. Individuals or groups spontaneously pay specific attention to a few very particular zones in the environment and distance themselves from other zones in the same environment. Their distance from or degree of involvement with the social object is by definition variable (Sherif and Cantril 1947). Students, teachers and workers locate psychoanalysis in different parts of their worlds. The subject's main efforts are devoted not to understanding that theory in terms of its specific framework, but to emphasizing those perspectives that are in keeping with his or her basic orientation. That orientation leaves its mark on the meaning, content and the positive and negative attributes of the classes that are organized and handled by the subject's thought processes. Historical traditions and the stratification of values – some of them outdated – have the same effects because they commit the thinking subject to a determinate path. An individual or a collective is, in a word, focused because, in the course of social interaction, they are implicated or engaged in the substance and effects of their judgements or opinions.

The third feature of the situation we are describing is the presence of a *pressure to infer* (Moscovici 1967) that influences the workings of intellectual operations. What does that mean? In everyday life, circumstances and social relations require individuals and social groups to be able, at any moment, to act, to take up a position and so on. They must, in a word, be able to *respond*. In order to do so, they must choose between the terms of an alternative, form stable or permanent opinions characterized by a high degree of uncertainty, keep digressions to a minimum and link premises to conclusions that are not, as it happens, obvious. But all this is the result of the observable pressures that require participants to elaborate a shared and stable code and to become involved in a dialogue or exchange of ideas in order to adapt their messages to that code. The time gap between question and answer, between reflex and action and between the accumulation and use of knowledge is governed by constraints that do not correspond to their internal laws. Constant preparation for the reworking of information, and taking that eventuality into account, speeds up transition from observation to inference. In a series of experiments, Zajonc (1960) has demonstrated that individuals who expect to retransmit the messages they have received immediately reduce the number of judgemental categories they use to interpret them and to unify their intellectual field – prematurely in some cases. Jumping to conclusions and a strict adherence to a consensus or code are responses to the social group's members' obligation to stabilize their world, and to re-establish a meaning that has been threatened or challenged. The high number of stereotypical answers and clichés testify to the existence of a capital of pre-shaped conclusions that rapidly determines responses and filters information. Besides, an understanding of the attitudes of various interlocutors or groups ensures that everyone will prefer the 'dominant' answers, or those that are most widely shared, most expected and most likely to be understood and approved by all,[2]

---

[2] 'When set to transmit his impression to others, the person should tend to *polarize*, i.e. he should tend to exclude or suppress or minimize one polarity of the contradiction and order the relevant cognitions around the other extreme' (Cohen 1961: 236).

because they can be both exchanged and validated. This explains how the logic of social representations leads to the use of widely accepted formulae and, as we shall see, why conclusions are so significant. The influence of this pressure to infer in the course of intellectual exchanges is certainly due to the fact that, in our everyday lives, we are 'interested' receivers and see ourselves as senders with a familiar audience of colleagues, friends, co-religionists and so on. The activities that concern us here are inscribed within the framework of communication. From the viewpoint of scientific analysis, taking them into consideration may have positive effects because, as Rapaport notes 'the role of communication in psychic life may have been underestimated, or at least given too little systematic attention' (1951: 727).

Too much attention has, on the other hand, been paid to dichotomies derived from the contrast between the logical and the non-logical. If we abandon them, we arrive at the propositions we have just expounded. Intellectual forms correspond to hierarchical modalities of interaction and subdivisions of the social whole. This is not a new hypothesis, but it must be taken seriously. It implies that we have to study these correspondences and discover the principle that explains relations between intellectual forms and social situations. Restricting myself to a more modest task, I attempted to establish the dimensions of the social reality associated with the production of a social representation. Those dimensions are the dispersal of data, the focus of the individual or collective subject, and the pressure to make inferences about a socially defined object. I have described them with all the reserves of rigour in the face of the results of an observation which sought to be phenomenal and nothing more.[3]

2 The Style of Natural Thought

2.1 *Logical system and normative metasystem*

We can now outline the style of thought that develops in the situation whose features we have just described.

We can characterize this style and the contours of the judgements made by the informants during the survey with greater clarity if we make

---

[3] The dimensions we are describing are very similar to the conditions that Abelson and Rosenberg (1958) assign to their *psycho-logic*. I think, however, that the idea that there is a logic specific to psychological phenomena is dangerous because it presupposes that the logic of science does not concern these phenomena at all. I do not see the rationale behind this *psycho-logic*, and nor do I see why scientific logic should not conform to certain social or psychological situations. The important point is to determine their dimensions and the differences between situations and, therefore, to define them.

a distinction between 'formal', 'written' thought and 'natural', 'oral' thought, and between thought centred upon the 'apprehension of categories' and thought centred upon the 'communication of ideas'. To be more specific, this is a way of thinking that is commonplace in face-to-face interaction in which the interlocutors express and shape their opinions for each other's benefit.[4] At the same time, its purpose is to influence someone or to win their approval. No other outcome is expected, as is the case with the intellectual activity that characterizes science, art, philosophy or journalism. Given that that is the case, this kind of thought is an end in itself and, whilst it does seek influence or approval, it also simply seeks to give individuals or groups the ability to orient themselves, and to understand, rather than to constitute a discourse that can last and be transmitted in the form of something as complete as a book or article. Communication is, then, on one side, direct, and on the other, transitory, limited by time. It is as though the human body and soul were the only things that could record intellectual opinions or products. What is more, the cognitive process at work here displays specific characteristics because it presupposes dialogue and because it is dominated by the play of questions and answers, and of opinions that are registered and then immediately transmitted. This means that we are constantly thinking 'for' or 'against'; we accept or reject what is said and, unless we avoid dialogue, we shape our opinions in and through controversy. It is difficult to see how we could remain neutral, take into consideration the arguments for and against, or keep our distance from ourselves or others. This has major implications at the level of the workings of the intellect. We can see that two cognitive systems are at work in the reflexive effort characteristic of science, philosophy or any form of thought whose goal is the 'apprehension' of categories. The first is an operational system that works with associations, inclusions, discriminations and deductions; the second is a sort of metasystem that reworks the material produced by the first. The same is true of natural thought, but there is one difference. The metasystem or the relations that constitute it are usually and primordially normative relations. We have, in other words, ordinary operational relations on the one hand, and normative relations that check, test and direct them on the other. Normative values and principles are, by definition, organized. This means that relations between the logical terms are directional, and that the relationship between A and B is not the same as that between B and A.

We are very familiar with this in our everyday lives, as what a Communist says about a Catholic does not imply that his words are applicable to him, or that the Catholic could say the same of the Communist. It follows that they both think within a hierarchical world in which there are preferential regions (De Soto, London and Handel 1965), tendencies

---

[4] The face-to-face dimension can be either real or psychological; I have demonstrated (Moscovici 1967) that the implications are the same at the level of linguistic activity.

towards one mode of reflection rather than another and particularly significant meanings. These state which combinations of available propositions are permissible and which are forbidden. If we look for the criteria
defining permitted combinations and forbidden combinations, we find that
the former are associated, either directly or indirectly, with the subject's
group, whilst the latter are associated with another group. The more well-
defined the group, the more explicit the permissions and taboos. A Catholic
will refuse to entertain a certain number of the judgements he succeeds in
formulating for himself if he also knows that they are approved of or voiced
by a Communist. *In this context, like poles repel and opposite poles attract.* In
more general terms, we observe that implicit representations of the values
of the social space and of human relations (Zajonc and Burnstein 1965;
Burnstein 1967) do a great deal to determine how thought processes work.
To sum up: (a) natural thought is communication-centred, directional and
'controversial'; (b) natural thought, like any form of thought, implies a
system of operational relations and a metasystem of relations that provides
checks and validations and that maintains the system's coherence. In this
case, however, those relations are normative. That is sufficient to explain
why this system uses logical rules but does not consciously apply them.
The only conscious attempt to apply them concerns, as it happens, values.
Taking all this into account, we can now define the attributes of the style of
this kind of thought.

2.2 Informal repetition

The most obvious characteristic of natural thought can, paradoxically, be
termed *'spontaneous formalism'*. The existence and use of a stock of clichés,
judgements and expressions that betray a trust in set phrases, or simply
the permeation of language and of reflection, often contrasts with their
organization, which is highly individualistic. Dominant and imperious
expressions encourage short cuts and explosive haste, which converge in
approximate propositions whose meaning can be isolated only when we
revise their terms. Psychoanalysis is defined by one doctor as 'a therapeutic way of ridding the mind of ideas that cause psychosomatic troubles'.
The fragment about 'ridding the mind of ideas' is, in this context, comprehensible if we replace 'mind' with 'psyche' or 'personality'. 'Ridding . . . of
ideas that cause psychosomatic illness' is a synthesis of an old but persistent notion of 'obsessions', which was a key formula in psychiatry, and
'psychosomatic illness', which is a much more modern expression borrowed from psychoanalysis. It is obvious that our informant wished to
stress the concept of 'ridding of conflict'. In order to do so, he uses
eminently commonplace expressions that come to mind automatically.
Conventional formulae facilitate communication or, in the absence of any
information or any desire to explain, spare us the need to make an effort to

integrate our notions into a coherent whole. The argument becomes a sort of translation that reduces everything to a common schema. The proposition 'psychoanalysis is an analysis of the soul' is the shortest illustration of the mechanism. There is sometimes a tendency to use stronger expressions: 'psychoanalysis lightens a person's psyche by using an analytic method'. The informant is trying to define psychoanalysis and to make up his mind about it. Yet once the initial moment – the asking of the question – has passed, he finds himself caught up in a series of loosely connected solutions and fragments of models. What is more, there is nothing to force him to clarify their sequence. All he has to do is to supply a few indices of those models because he can assume that an interlocutor will be able to reconstruct for himself the necessary contexts and connections. Both thought and communication are *economical*. They are economical because the words belong to a language that is accepted by the group and because their connotations are conventional. There is no attempt at adequacy. Organizing and linking the propositions is not indispensable. They are full of indices, shared references and discontinuities that testify to the existence of whole 'fields of pseudo-thought', and of references to a code that is assumed to be present. In this infra-communication, which is a form of communication based upon hints and insinuations, the slippage from thought to language is blatant, and there is almost no distinction between the two. *Repetition*, in all its lexical and synthetic forms, plays an important role. It is no exaggeration to say that reiteration and redundancy are the distinguishing features of natural thought. Here is an example:

> 'I think that the Communist Party regards psychoanalysis as a clinical method like any other, and believes that its goal is to cure the patient. In the USA, the moneyed classes want to use psychoanalysis to distract the working classes from the struggle to improve their living conditions . . . The extra-medical development of psychoanalysis is due to the fact that the wealthy have to find something to counteract the tendency for all men to want to see a quantitative and qualitative change in their lives.'

The content is clear: psychoanalytic therapy is acceptable, but its philosophical and political extrapolations are to be rejected. The subject is mistaken when he or she attributes this attitude to the Communist Party. The last two sentences are specific to the vocabulary of Marxism and reproduce, almost word for word, the same idea, which has, as it happens, a specific meaning: 'a quantitative and qualitative change in their lives' and 'distracting the working classes from the struggle to improve their living conditions' lead to the incontinent and repetitive use of propositions that circulate widely in society. The automatic or formal way they are inserted into the interview is all the more obvious since they are linked by information that is in part erroneous and their succession is not motivated.

The repeated use of commonplace statements is not simply a matter of economy that does away with the need to demonstrate each idea yet again; it also helps to *organize* value-judgements. We can thus see that it is possible for there to be a sort of substratum that is, in some sense, both material and mnemonic, and which lets individuals know where they stand. Someone who is writing has in front of them the text of what he or she has written, and can read through it several times before summarizing the argument and moving on to the next point. A speaker does not have the 'support' of a sheet of paper, cannot re-examine what has already been said, and is obliged to go over it again, and to repeat it in order to develop it. Hence the constant repetition of a few segments of propositions or a few themes. For a speaker who wishes to be understood and who wishes to make what he is saying more predictable, it is important to restrict the meaning of what is being said by repeating it. In the interview cited, the subject's orientation is focused on a group – the Communist group – and this means that he sees psychoanalysis in a particular light: in the light of political relations. Every judgement is brought back to the same point of view, which is reiterated again and again. And the text cited is indeed full of secondary implications, which make it difficult to compare the formal interpretation with the links that are actually being made.

Strictly speaking, we have two arguments here: one which contrasts analytic practice with the use the American ruling classes are making of it, and the other demonstrating that there are, within psychoanalysis, developments that are harmful to humanity as a whole and its desire for 'quantitative and qualitative change'. And yet, for an informed interlocutor – and the informant tries at several points to inform the interlocutor – this is not the case. The two arguments are similar, if not identical. In the light of the ideological framework to which the whole dialogue relates, the class struggle and the transformation of the human condition in general are one and the same thing. This form of thought is rarely retrospective; *the argument is essentially constructive and rarely corrective.* The iterative element is practically never eliminated in such a way as to bind together or organize the two value-judgements. On the contrary, the iterative element is in a sense the one thing that holds the argument together, and its regular reappearance allows the argument to proceed because it is a mark of continuity. Besides, the only checks in operation are, as we have seen, of a normative nature. What has been said has been said and the underlying intellectual approach does not allow any turning back. Besides, the use of stereotypical formulations is also a way of bringing pressure to bear to the extent that the stability and presence of linguistic models corresponding to the subject's representation (and his environments) prevent the subject from paying enough attention to the *alternatives* that are always associated with a proposition. Communication is facilitated as a result, and so too is the process of the elaboration of the representations it conveys. This explains the existence and extension of spontaneous formalism.

2.3 Mixed causality

Let us now look at another aspect of the style of natural thought: the way arguments are linked by implication. The links between them are influenced by a specific conception of the nature of causal relations. Scientific thought only takes into account connections between established causes and their effects. The same is simply not true of social representations: alongside this efficient causality, a *phenomenal or anthropomorphic causality* influences the way judgements are made. We will not make a distinction between the two forms of causality, as they rely upon the same mechanism. If two events are perceived together, one is assumed for various reasons – proximity, the intention of a subject, membership of the same category – to be the cause, and the other is assumed to be the effect.

A Christian who was sympathetic to psychoanalysis told us:

'Psychoanalysis could be one of the religious factors behind a major moral revival. It has to be noted that, since psychoanalysis came into existence, Catholic movements such as the worker-priests have developed.'

It is quite obvious that there is no link between psychoanalysis, the spread of Catholic movements and the appearance of worker-priests. The latter were, rather, a response to the dechristianization of the proletariat and to the influence of Marxism. However, a simple temporal 'coincidence', a favourable attitude sufficed to transform psychoanalysis into a cause and the institution of worker-priests into an effect.

The attribution of 'bad causes' to 'bad effects' relies upon the same intellectual mechanism. A few dialogues illustrate this clearly enough.

> Q: What do you think of the relationship between psychoanalysis and religion?
> A: 'There must be no opposition to the Church. Anything that puts people to sleep suits its purposes.'
> Q: 'Do you see any connection between psychoanalysis and politics?'
> A: 'The Communists can use it to inculcate their doctrines by force and to brainwash the masses.'

The role played by intentionality in the structuring of the world, and therefore of the subject's representation, finds expression in a phenomenal causality.

The continued survival of phenomenal causality should come as no surprise, even though education focuses upon science, philosophy and rationalism. A social object is always seen as belonging to a group and its finality. It is therefore impossible for it to be seen as neutral, or as not corresponding to some overt or calculated intention. The lack of the requisite information and loyalty to certain values determine the meaning of the causal relationship. A doctor who argued that psychoanalysis and the French spirit were incompatible also said:

> 'The political groups have certainly adopted a position on psychoanalysis. Especially the Communists. In Communism, certain principles – I forget which, but I read it somewhere – are identical to those of psychoanalysis. In practice, you just have to look at what goes on. In Russia, they use a sort of forced psychoanalysis to vary and change peoples' convictions.'

The 'psychoanalysis–Communist principles' comparison is not based upon reliable information. The individual concerned has no more than an impression, or a vague memory of having read something about this. His conception of the French nation, and the claim that psychoanalysis and Communism are foreign doctrines, reveals how his judgement has been oriented. Because they both belong to the same category – 'not-French' – psychoanalytic theory and the political movement 'have identical principles' and equally harmful effects. We will not give specific examples of efficient causality because this book is full of them.

The striking thing, – and the thing we really remember – about the mode of thought that elaborates social representations is the reliance on *dual causality*, or on two orders of causality that relate the argument to a context of intentions on the one hand (Heider 1944) and to a context of successive events on the other. The roads it travels in its search for coherence are as disparate as they are surprising. Our analysis must constantly try to reconstruct this shifting logical frame of reference.

2.4 The primacy of the conclusion

The subject's reference to rules or crystallized social representations goes hand in hand with an awareness of the limits within which an argument can be developed. Once the field of judgement has been defined, the outcome of an action or the meaning of a communication or logical sequence can be predicted. The pressure brought to bear by society and the limitations it attempts to impose on its members make the inferences more significant than the other statements put forward in the course of the argument. Tarde put it very nicely when he noted that 'The conclusion is known before the premises' (1895: 35). Indeed, the logical sequence does not coincide with or determine the way the judgement is oriented; it is the orientation that determines the sequence (McGuire 1960b). Because it is given *from the outset*, the conclusion defines the zone from which the other parts of the argument are selected. It is the conclusion that isolates them. This regulatory action gives what should be the final stage in the logical process a dominant position and makes it a symbol or index of the whole. We can attribute this privilege to the fact that, on the one hand, the norms, or social or individual preferences are present in the conclusion and, on the other, to the more general tendency to look for meanings. Premises have a meaning, an import and a value only insofar as they relate to the final judgement.[5] In this case, the conclusion precedes all other propositions, which become so many arguments that can make it all the more significant. The link between the statements is not so much one of mediation as one of *co-inference*. Each statement strives to be a partial expression and clarification of an idea. Because the conclusion is already known, there is an impression of repetition in which particular inferences are no more than variants on the same leitmotivs. When this is the case, the purpose of the sequence of judgements is both to translate and to demonstrate what has already been postulated. This comes down to a constant definition of an opinion or prejudice:

> 'I learned about psychoanalysis when I was studying medicine. I read some passages of Freud . . . that's saying a lot for a Frenchman. Freud catalogues a state of psychology that is highly developed in our country, because the French are heirs to a culture of self-analysis that is much more highly developed than it is in other countries. The average Frenchman can think clearly and logically, and that allows him to manage without psychoanalysis. But it is helpful to people who aren't capable of making a personal self-criticism, or of getting to the bottom of their problems. Weak people might resort to it.'

The subject's perspective is expressed right from the start: psychoanalysis is not adapted to France. The propositions that follow do no more than repeat that leitmotiv, and do not add any arguments that are really new. As the representation is stable, we can predict the subject's every answer. The presence of an accompanying inference or co-inference that takes away the specific role of each stage in the arguments means that we can say that there is no conclusion in any formal sense. Or, which comes down to the same thing, that the conclusion was always there. The logical die was cast before any thought was given to any particular point, and the basic argument imprints its essential features on every solution. The solution merely reproduces it. The fact that the conclusion has penetrated every level – the argument comes ready-made – and that we know the answers before the questions have been asked means that the propositions are linked to their common normative framework rather than to one another. The intellectual style is one of *assertion* rather than proof or progression:

> 'I got to know about psychoanalysis from discussions. My doctor is no great fan. There doesn't seem to be much to it. You more or less put the patient to sleep so as to awaken the subconscious and to isolate his complexes.

---

[5] 'Our evidence will indicate that the only circumstances under which we can be relatively sure that the inferences of a person will be logical is when they lead to a conclusion he has already accepted' (Morgan and Morton 1944: 39).

I wouldn't dare. I couldn't trust anyone. But I might change my mind. It's all a question of the glands. In my case, it's the thyroid. They wanted to have me psychoanalysed. I didn't want to. My doctor told me that in my case it wasn't the thyroid, but I don't believe him . . . I think it's just the glands . . . My sister-in-law is jealous. They psychoanalysed her. Nothing happened. They made an incision and applied a placental extract. She was transformed. If there is no obvious physical, medical or affective explanation for why someone is unhinged, and if medical examinations cannot make any diagnosis, then they can try psychoanalysis. They'll find his complexes and obsessions.'

In this interview, the informant rules out psychoanalysis from the start. His conviction that there is a physiological explanation for his illness resists all the doctor's denials. The representation of psychoanalysis – which he confuses with narco-analysis – is enough to make him all the more reluctant. When psychoanalysis is accepted, the very basis of its intervention has no content. The disequilibrium that might justify psychoanalysis is not physical, but nor is it really affective. Psychoanalysis appears to be a complete impossibility.

We have provided a few samples of natural thought. Whilst we have overlooked a lot of detailed observations, and looked only at characteristics pertaining to spontaneous formalism, causal dualism and the predominance of the conclusion (or co-inference), we can clearly see the broad outlines of its specificity.

3 Two Principles of Intellectual Organization

3.1 Analogy and economy of thought

The intellectual regularities we have just described are based upon two principles: analogy and compensation. Analogy groups notions into categories and generates a new content, whilst compensation organizes relations between judgements. The principle of analogy helps to establish the *characteristics of the object represented*, whilst the principle of compensation establishes *meanings and links* relevant to it. The former focuses on the object, and the latter on the framework of reference that controls and directs the thought processes. The distinction between the two is approximate. Primarily it expresses the dominant function of each principle.

Most of the connections that are established between the essential notions of a representation can be explained in terms of analogy, which is a semantic rather than a formal principle. It marks the type of knowledge produced by a representation and it is an essential feature of cognitive and linguistic activity. We initially see it as a mechanism that *generalizes* on the basis of an old concept or response to a response or a new concept by decanting its content. The underlying realities are grouped together under the same rubric and one is used to explain the other. When, for example, someone says 'Confession is a psychoanalysis, provided that it is not distorted', 'confession' and 'psychoanalysis' enter each other's world. The idea of confession is associated with and extended to a domain external to it. The religious act is understood to be a profane act in which the only thing which remains of importance is the interpersonal relationship. Because they exclude all other connotations, the material setting and the specific roles of those involved become blurred and the encounter comes to resemble a simplified and purely human exchange. The psychoanalytic dialogue, in its turn, takes on a 'banal', concrete appearance, as the image of confession plunges it into a familiar perceived reality. The converse proposition 'Psychoanalysis is a confession' establishes a direct link. Psychoanalytic therapy is *like* confession: the customary representation is immediately transferred to another object, which is now more easily apprehended.

Analogical generalization is specific: notions are neither assimilated to one another nor confused. Up to a point, analogy is no more than an instrumental substitution, but the way it is used can turn it into a constitutive substitution. As a result, we do not reach a higher level of abstraction, but we do *group* terms together by overlooking some of their specific properties. But the fact that we overlook them tells us something about the kind of inference that is being made. If, for example, we start out from class A, enumerate its properties p_1, p_2, p_3, and p_x, and compare it with class B, where we recognize properties p_1, p_2, p_3, we conclude that B also has the property p_x. Similarly, whilst we recognize psychoanalytic practice for what it is – two people alone in a determinate space, the possibility of saying everything, transference neurosis, acting out and so on – we attribute features specific to the transference neurosis or acting out to confession. In this process of inference we look, in a word, at *either* the similarities *or* the differences, rather than emphasizing the similarities *and* the differences. We know why: the goal is to define a class of objects and events, and to differentiate that class from others. Analogy thus frees us from the constraints of the given, but the overall categories it elaborates are imperfect. Despite these limitations, the principle of analogy is a principle that *mediates* between two or more worlds by ensuring that they are permeable. This mediation makes it possible to assimilate something external by adjusting that which already exists. The passage from a scientific theory to a social representation would otherwise be unthinkable. The unconscious of psychoanalysis becomes the unconscious of its representation as it is integrated with more commonplace notions: it is involuntary, hidden and unknown. The complex acquires concrete *and* general characteristics that subsume other terms such as old age, shyness or inferiority.

This brings us to another aspect of the use of analogies: economizing on information. The demands of communication justify this economizing. The pressure to formulate an opinion on the one hand, and a variable ability to receive one on the other both suggest that the body of knowledge has to be reduced. Before accumulating the data needed to answer each question, the subject must be capable of forming an opinion and getting others to share that opinion. As in a democracy, in which every citizen is supposed to have an informed opinion about political problems, even though democratic governments are the first to define data as confidential, we are asked in our social life to exchange views about objects, ideas or facts that are the exclusive property of groups divided from one another by impermeable barriers. The concepts and models that individuals have at their disposal allow them to get around this difficulty, and mean that they do not have to worry about all the details that might support an argument and give it the dignity of an established truth. If we address an interlocutor who has a greater or lesser intellectual capacity than that required to solve a particular problem, the intervention of analogies ensure that he or she can understand it by eliminating what is, for the moment, superfluous data. They also help us to transgress the over-strict rules of communication by simply indicating the domain where the communication is taking place. 'Complex', 'unconscious' and 'psychoanalysis' are terms that convey specific images and contexts, but they can also become part of everyday conversation, provided that they are relocated in a familiar world. In the course of one interview, we asked a worker if psychoanalysis had anything to do with politics. He found the question difficult. The dialogue seemed to have broken down. All at once, the interlocutor found a vital lead: psychoanalysis is a particular kind of conversation that induces behaviours. Politicians address citizens in speeches that are intended to influence their opinions. Our informant began to outline an answer: 'In politics, you use every possible means. Speech means influence, so it's a form of psychoanalysis.' The dialogue picked up again. Now that it had a direction, it was possible to retranscribe our question in the subject's language and to define his point of view. The survey was full of similar examples. When we asked people who had only a rudimentary knowledge of psychoanalysis, and who had never seen a psychoanalyst, to describe one, they inevitably fell back upon comparisons with familiar figures and attributes. The same thing happened when they were asked to describe analytic practice. Most informants had only a vague idea of what happens in analysis or of the concrete situation in which it takes place. Borrowing significant points of reference, they tended to stray beyond the strict limits of the data in their possession. When, for example, psychoanalysis is placed under the sign of sexuality, the analysis is assumed to take place in a *dark* room, with the *woman patient* lying on a couch. The role of the psychoanalyst is somewhat dubious:

'The patient lies on a couch in a dark room and tells her story. Women like having someone to listen to them. Sometimes they fall in love with the psychoanalyst.'

The constructive action of analogy does indeed allow us to transcend the given with limited means, to construct a whole on the basis of the inadequate experience we have acquired, and without restricting ourselves to a search for statistical similarities. By using the same methods, social representations can go beyond the accepted social schemata, and scientific theory itself. Theoretical notions shatter our usual moulds. When transposed to the level of everyday observation, notions such as that of the unconscious or the complex inevitably take us beyond the behaviour we actually see. The introduction of chains of complexes has, in its turn, an analogical effect. The repeated use of these devices results in a crystallization as representations stabilize around certain symbols and certain themes.

Analogical reasoning thus achieves two objectives: the first is to integrate autonomous and disjointed elements into a greater whole, and the second is to master the development of the image of a fact or concept that appears on the horizon of a group or individual by imposing a model.[6]

Although this form of reasoning is described as an inferior form of thought or linguistic creation, that is not really the case. It is the way that one part of society forces the other to use it that takes away all its dignity.[7] Analogy is no more than one *moment* in the work of thought. It is not a permanent state. And whilst the imaginary, which constantly repeats that moment, is an exciting moment in human life, it exists in order to be transcended.

3.2 Preserving identity and difference

Social representations are dramatic and constraining. We perceive objects in terms of the actions they perform and the intentions they express. Scientific concepts and statements are borderline forms whose univocity seems to be guaranteed; they do give rise to controversies between individual or social subjects. The series of propositions that is intended to translate the content of a social representation tends towards an analogous state, stable and complete, where invariance is reached. This state is no more than something which is aimed for, a tendency, and discrepancies with invariance are the rule. The coherence of our judgements suffers as a result, and the ways in which we try to achieve coherence vary from one

---

[6] I will not dwell here upon the link between analogical reasoning and linguistic creation – and especially the creation of metaphors – or their nominal techniques. Any reader interested in this topic is referred to the discussion in the first edition of this work.

[7] Popular wisdom is not, as some rather hasty commentators have claimed, congenitally and exclusively analogical. See Stern (1893).

order of knowledge to another. We will look here at the path taken by the principle of *compensation*. But as it is not the only principle envisaged, we will begin by discussing the principle that is habitually considered.

Formal or scientific knowledge advances the hypothesis that judgements can be linked together in such a way as to constitute a univocal theoretical structure. The intermediary links are defined by the principle of non-contradiction. The normative repercussions of that principle go far beyond the framework of the disciplines of logic and force us to obey an imperative that is at once ethical and discursive. 'The ultimate basis of the principle of non-contradiction is the need for social agreement.' This sociological explanation makes a collective consensus the precondition for coherent thought. Despite its disadvantages, which are probably inherent in collective life, no individual and no group can break the social bond for any length of time. Unity is more important and more real than the consensus itself, which is no more than one phase in the evolution of social systems: the phase in which the parties involved agree not to contradict one another. The social contract is an effective human creation, but it does not guarantee that we can coexist. Constraint, the exercise of power and the use, legitimate or otherwise, of violence makes at least an equal contribution. For the sake of the spirit or of communication, unity has to be respected, beyond or through the contradictions of judgements (Halbwachs 1938: 357). We can therefore take the view that the need to reach agreement at all costs is a basic characteristic of intellectual and social life; it is used to shape and bring together the elements that the external world supplies us with and forces us to take into account. Non-contradiction is one of the criteria that makes the links between them credible. Our culture has, quite rightly, adopted the principle of non-contradiction, and it urges us to apply it too. We therefore find it is used even at the intra-individual level when we attempt to find a balance or to achieve cognitive consistency (Giese 1967). The principle of equilibrium or cognitive consistency assumes that individuals avoid states of cognitive tension and that they prefer states in which cognitions and perceptions are all in agreement (Mill [1843] 1970; Heider 1946). If conflict does occur, individuals modify their cognitions in such a way as to make them consonant or to restore equilibrium. Thus, the fact that Jean likes Pierre and that Jean likes rugby implies a state of equilibrium if Pierre likes rugby too, and a state of disequilibrium if Pierre hates rugby. It is indeed contradictory for Jean to be so powerfully drawn to both rugby and Pierre, because the latter rejects the sport he loves. The only way for him to find any peace of mind is to detest Pierre or detest rugby, in order to be able peacefully to enjoy either his friend or his favourite sport.

In the case of non-contradiction, as in that of equilibrium or consistency, we find that the principle's finality and precondition have to be made explicit. Its finality is, as we have seen, the desire for intra-group unity or intra-individual harmony. Its goal is the avoidance of social or individual conflict, and the preservation of uniformity and integrity is the desired outcome. This is another way of saying that, in both social and personal life, it is desirable to ensure that opinions and judgements converge around a point of equilibrium, and to establish a consensus between antagonistic elements. The precondition of which we were speaking is of a cognitive nature. This striving after non-contradiction and equilibrium (or consistency) appears to result from the use of a bipolar logic, and the goal can be achieved only if such a logic is at work. On the one hand, it is essential that the objects or beings we are required to judge are associated, both perceptually and intellectually, in only two classes. If several classes are involved, it becomes more difficult to determine the meaning of the contradiction or disequilibrium and the terms relating to them. On the other hand, relations between the two classes must be relations of equilibrium; it must, in other words, be the case that what can be said of one cannot be said of the other. If this is not the case, it is difficult to see why there should be any conflict or contradiction, as we are establishing a link between equivalent objects or beings. This point is expressly made by Cartwright and Harary (1956: 286) in a study of mathematical formalization. They contend that the necessary and sufficient condition for an S graph to be in equilibrium is that its points can be placed in two mutually exclusive sub-sets in such a way that every positive line joins the points of the same sub-set and that every negative line joins the points of the different sub-sets.

If we look at it more closely, non-contradiction or equilibrium may, at a certain level, be an expression of deeper, and perhaps more general, phenomena. I suspect that this may be the case because it requires the presence of clear-cut dichotomies and relations of exclusion between them. To be more specific, we are dealing with a closed intellectual world in which every element is deemed to be either black or white, and in which no element can simultaneously be both black and white (Abelson and Rosenberg 1958). Indeed, every object is perceived one-dimensionally and in only one context. Jean is uncomfortable with the idea that Pierre does not like rugby mainly because he does not realize that, like him, Pierre likes some other things such as politics or chess, or that he has other qualities, such as intelligence and generosity. In a word, the tension arises because one of the partners assumes that they cannot be friends *and* remain different. We conclude that these principles of equilibrium are no more than *a particular variant on or the reverse side of cognitive polarization* and that the latter is, up to a point, a necessary precondition for them. We can understand why this should be the case, as the establishment of distinct and mutually exclusive classes is a precondition for any reduction of incongruence.[8] If any doubts remain, we have only to remember that the proverbial 'My enemy's enemies are my friends' – the golden rule of intellectual consistency – implies that anyone who is not my friend is my

---

[8] The reduction of the intellectual complexity of the problems that are to be solved is a second precondition for cognitive equilibrium.

enemy. The maxim obeys a bipolar logic. It follows that the goal of this process of modifying and organizing judgements is:

- the constitution of homogeneous classes of objects, individuals or behaviours that relate to one another positively or have identical attributes; their relations with members of other classes must therefore be negative, or based upon the presence of different attributes;
- the allocation of objects, individuals or behaviours to definite classes in order to achieve cognitive clarity as to their meanings and liaisons.

The principle of compensation relates to operations that are performed on real or logical beings, by maximizing their similarities or differences so as to insert them into a class or to distribute them between existing classes by reducing or increasing the pertinent dimensions. It helps, in other words, to *identify* the classes to which these beings belong and with which they identify. Ultimately, its function is to determine what belongs to me and what belongs to the other, what belongs to the internal group and what belongs to the external group. In bipolar cases, the outcome is the assertion of a difference or specificity: it reveals the social or individual identity of the individual or group who invokes the principle of compensation. Its goal is not to lessen the conflict between the two terms of an alternative, but to eliminate one of them and to defend a preference, or the dominance of one truth or belief. To go back to the example we used earlier: the tendency to re-establish an equilibrium or state of non-contradiction requires Jean, a thinking individual who likes both rugby and Pierre – his friend who does not like rugby – to change and to find that rugby is not a good sport or that Pierre is really not worth liking. From the compensation point of view, the problem looks different. Jean, who wants to have a clear vision of things that fits in with his system of categories, must at some point put either Pierre or rugby into either the class of 'things I like' or that of 'things I hate', just as he has done with Blacks, Catholics, technology, the mass media and so on. Now it is difficult for him to put 'objects' that display no equivalence or reciprocity into the same class; he cannot put Pierre and rugby into the same class, because one excludes the other. If he is to achieve his goal, he must separate them and put them in different categories, just as he is forced to put people who are not his friends into the 'enemy' class. This technique is very widely used, especially in the domain of social representations, as in that of stereotypes, propaganda and so on. My observations show that this is scarcely surprising, as natural thought is the classificatory mode of thinking par excellence (Durkheim and Mauss 1963; Granet 1950); it makes every possible effort to do all it can to group or divide the elements it is dealing with into regions with clear boundaries.[9]

---

[9] The phenomena of assimilation and contrast, like that of extremization, are remarkable but special examples of this broader principle (Moscovici and Zavalloni 1968).

What is more, some of these regions or classes are privileged in normative terms and represent the positions, perspectives or preferences of the social or individual subject. A subject who believes that A implies B and that B implies C also believes that B is 'higher' or 'more positive' than C. It follows that relations of implication between the propositions are subordinated to a series of corrections or a set of evaluations. Logical difficulties and 'deviations' arise because each proposition is always considered both *in relation to the totality and to its place in a series of arguments*. The sequence in which they are considered – in terms of the influence exerted by a powerful field of values – must be viewed as a way of transforming and linking parts *within a whole*. Note the contrast between this way of thinking and the mode which presupposes non-contradiction. Every proposition is related to two things: the overall system of norms or categories, and the proposition that precedes or follows it. The principle of equilibrium or non-contradiction presupposes that propositions are autonomous and that the links that articulate them are also links in a necessary association with the general system. The principle of compensation, which makes a distinction between the scale of categories and their application, does not postulate that fusion. How, then, is coherence to be established? *Every term in the judgement is so changed or chosen that it can belong to the class (or category) that corresponds most closely to the main frame of references of the thinking subject.*

The mechanisms that govern this intellectual work and the unification that results from it are the subordination of the parts to the whole, the existence of a hierarchical scale of attitudes that influence judgement (Thistlewaite 1950; de Soto 1961) and a propensity to identify. Specific operations take place without taking into account partial contradictions (McGuire 1960a). Such contradictions may arise with respect to either the logical framework or privileged normative relations. The subject's task is to modify them on the basis of the overall schema he or she adopts.[10] This can be done in one of two ways:

- justification, which consists essentially in maintaining or changing the relationship with the object, and
- conversion (Asch 1940), or trying to maintain or change the object of the relationship.

Whilst these are the major forms of compensation, there are variants on and derivatives of these modalities, but they will not be discussed here. We will simply give a few examples taken from the interviews to demonstrate how they work.

---

[10] The formation of distinct classes and the predominance of the whole over the parts in intellectual processes may explain the 'rigid' character of the intellectual system and the need for very strong external pressure if it is to change.

We will look first at an example of how the exclusion of psychoanalysis from the subject's world is justified. The transition from one judgement to the next is guaranteed by conjunctions and disjunctions of unequal perfection. A few extreme cases will give us an idea of how this works. In the type of knowledge we are studying, the sequence, unity and coherence of the arguments are often signalled by the underlying iteration of a proposition that holds everything together:

'I know about psychoanalysis because I've read extracts from Freud and some articles in *Psyché*. I spent some time in a special school. And the radio popularizes all sorts of things. And I learned about it from a woman friend who had a very bad experience. Psychoanalysis is interesting, but it is incomplete from the diagnostic point of view. It has no therapeutic value because it shows the individual what's morbid about him without showing him all the good things the future may hold. There's a methodological error, first because it is too oriented towards sexuality, and second because it is too narrow. It traces individual development back to relations within the family without taking into account all the other factors that contribute to individual growth (social environment etc.). And above all, it should not be applied to children. It is negative and leads to mysticism. We should be doing more to develop children's intelligence and activity: that's the best way to cure them of their complexes. Psychoanalysis produces introverted people who are not life-oriented.'

As the discussion turns to the positions adopted by political groups, the subject adds:

'Communists are against psychoanalysis because it is an individualist and mystifying method that does not take social realities into account. It is also decadent: it decomposes individuals. The Pope has condemned psychoanalysis, but I don't know much about that. It really cannot be applied to social problems. Social problems are group problems. Psychoanalysis is therapy for individuals. Applying individual discoveries to groups is a swindle. You can apply it in order to destroy the personality of people who get in the way. Imperialist rule over consciousness. You can compare it with the Nazis' methods. Is there a lot of talk about it? There is in France, in bourgeois and petty bourgeois circles. Not amongst the workers. It is being systematically popularized by the press and the papers, with the backing of the United States. In a word, psychoanalysis has made real discoveries about human behaviour: complexes, for example. But when it comes to treatment, its whole approach has to change. You can't cure people by getting them to tell their dirty little secrets. That's charlatanism. We would be better off giving the unhinged good living conditions rather than psychoanalysing them.'

The subject's basic attitude is clear: he wants to locate psychoanalysis outside the region of acceptable specific forms of knowledge. His ideological frame of reference, which is obviously Communist, leaves him no choice. In order to locate psychoanalysis, he lists its negative attributes because they justify his choice and prove that he has to take this line. But because psychoanalysis is widely accepted and is such a significant social object, the list of negative attributes must be long enough to justify the position that has been adopted. Every proposition recalls and reinforces the initial argument. The representation of human beings centres on a radical dichotomy between the future and the past, between life-orientation and the tendency to become introverted, and between the division of society into classes and the specificity of the social and the individual. A change in social conditions is the only thing that can solve individual problems. Analytic therapy and the extension of its principles are constantly associated with the negative terms of the interviewee's professed conception. Once that choice has definitely been made, the overall direction of the argument is set and it gives the impression that there is no incompatibility between the individual judgements or between them and the totality to which they belong. In order to consolidate this impression still further, negative-sounding propositions pile up. For example 'Decadent, too; it decomposes individuals'; 'You can use it to destroy the personality of people who get in the way.' Psychoanalysis is, in other words, effective but its effects are essentially destructive. Cracks appear here and there, but they are soon smoothed over. It is unlikely that our subject will accept psychoanalysis. If he does so, it will be in order to give even greater force to the negation. The 'enemies of my enemies are my friends', the Pope himself is called to the rescue. Freud's conceptions are too socially acceptable to be refuted with the degree of knowledge that is at this interviewee's disposal. Whilst he accepts that 'complexes' have their value, he does not bother to discuss psychoanalysis as a whole and stresses the theory/practice dichotomy. Whilst a combination of acceptance and rejection helps to consolidate the discourse's coherence, a transitional formula is used when a conclusion has to be reached: 'a change of orientation'. The transitional formula is then demolished in its turn: 'we'd be better off giving the unhinged good living conditions, rather than psychoanalysing them'. This might be a profound insight, were it not that psychoanalysis is one of the things that can sometimes change the living conditions of people who are unbalanced. We need not dwell upon the function of these clichés or the categories of argument that are being used to vigorously express a point of view whose unity is obvious and whose coherence is based upon several uncertainties. How could we associate psychoanalysis with the subject's class of positive 'social objects'? The only possible way to do so is to convert it and to modify its usual attributes:

> 'I've read things by Freud. Conversations and films . . . It's disgusting. I don't hold with this American-style psychoanalysis. Listen, I've taken part in broadcasts about psychoanalytically inspired techniques. Radio's a living unconscious; it's an expression of what psychoanalysis is. We live in such

worried times – worried about life . . . death . . . we have to be worried . . . the unconscious is worried . . . dreams . . . Psychoanalysis isn't human, it isn't based on anything human. Psychoanalysis defies common sense . . . The fact of living means that we are conscious.'

Q: 'What, in your opinion, is psychoanalysis?'
R: 'A search for the soul . . . the hidden soul, everything in us that is hidden . . . a search for the unconscious, unconscious games. Crosschecking the conscious mind's moment of forgetfulness is a way of searching for the soul. Psychoanalysis is a bad thing. Looking at yourself – surely that's no way to get to know yourself.'
Q: 'Do you see any other aspects?'
A: 'Childhood. We can do anything there. That's the first thing we should study. Everything depends on psychoanalysis. A lot of progress has been made in education since psychoanalysis came into being. It's a fashionable science that will disappear; no it won't disappear, but it will be called something else.'

Our interlocutor proceeds by enumeration. The disjointed impression this produces and the fact that the parts of his discourse are so dispersed may be the effect of the instability of the subject's normative orientation, or of the fact that he does not have enough information to specify the meaning of the problems that are being raised. The interviewee is undeniably drawn to psychoanalysis, but also finds it hard to locate it. Commercialization and Americanism are part of a world that worries this subject, and it is not the world of science and humankind. In order to avoid having to consider the 'psychoanalytic problem' in general, the subject picks up and stresses the same few points: the unconscious, America, childhood and so on. Finally, we see him come to a decision: psychoanalysis is positive. Hence his solution: the emergence of a psychoanalysis that no longer has the same *name*, that is called something different. It is only at this point that the subject can freely admit that he is drawn to the science.

In the previous example, we saw how a change of 'label' could facilitate the transition from a subject's 'negative' class to a 'positive' class, from 'outside' to 'inside'. The creation of 'arbitrary' notions or sub-classes makes it possible to safeguard the unity of the categorical system, and to move from one part of the discourse to another.

'No specialist knowledge of the subject. I just know that it can be put to bad use, in political ways that work to the disadvantage of the workers. In the USA, for instance, they use it to adapt people to the American way of life. I disapprove of that completely. But I still think it can be useful for people who have mental problems and difficulties. It all depends on how honest the psychoanalyst is. If the analyst is progressive, he can only do good. There must be some truth in the idea that many of our actions come from unconscious forces. I can see that with some of my pupils, who have strange jealous reactions to others.'

The interlocutor begins by establishing the 'premises' of a vision to which she is very loyal. She then notes that there is a political obstacle that affects the characteristics of psychoanalysis. It becomes more acceptable if it is practised by a *progressive psychoanalyst* or in other words a psychoanalyst who shares her representation of both the world and a domain she wants to distance herself from to some extent. It is only when she has transformed the psychoanalyst into a 'progressive psychoanalyst' that she can accept the possible 'truth' of psychoanalysis. The meaning of such a transformation is not clear. Is it a way of giving the psychoanalyst a further attribute that makes him compatible with the category of people who are acceptable in the subject's ideological context? Is it a way of using exceptions to the rule – like Hitler's 'honorary Aryans' – to create an arbitrary categorical system that leaves the existing conceptual order intact? The interview reproduced here does not allow us to choose between the two interpretations.

The extracts from the interviews that we have commented on demonstrate that analogy and compensation are the solid foundations of a rationality which, in social representations, continues to assert itself in new ways. Analogy increases the power of the imaginary, whilst compensation strengthens the hold of the symbolic order.

4 The Collective Intellect: Tower of Babel or Well-ordered Diversity?

4.1 *Three disturbing observations*

The dimensions of the social situation, and the cognitive style and principles described above are not unknown to the psychologist or the attentive observer of social facts. Detailed studies and fertile situations have clarified various points. Three observations suggest that we should dwell on them for a while longer so as to suggest some useful extensions to a social psychology of knowledge. The first, which cannot fail to have struck any reader who is familiar with the research that has been carried out on the structure of intellectual processes, is the similarity between the form of thought we have described and that of a concrete intelligence (Harvey, Hunt and Schroder 1961). The second deals with the kinship between analogy, compensation and the syncretism of children. The last observation concerns the fact that a plurality of modes of thought can often coexist within the same individual. Even educated people think in specific ways with respect to particular domains or functions. A doctor, a physicist, an industrialist, a student or a worker will certainly approach the analysis of a situation, a phenomenon or an event in different ways when they do so in a professional capacity, and when they are asked to give their opinion of psychoanalysis. These observations are disturbing and, ultimately, contradictory. The first should lead us to conclude that most of the people who responded to our survey have a concrete intelligence. There is an old tradition in our science of endeavouring to establish a close relationship between the organization of the personality and the organization of the corresponding intellectual elements. It has, for instance, been demonstrated that authoritarian individuals are intolerant, dogmatic and rigid, or that they use a closed cognitive system (Adorno et al. 1950; Rokeach 1960). Other classifications could be used, and have been used. We cannot accept this point of view, as it corresponds neither to reality nor to the needs of social psychology. Indeed, it is perfectly conceivable that a dogmatic and rigid individual who uses what might be described as a closed cognitive system in the political or racial domain may be tolerant and open in his role as artist, scientist or student. Perhaps, again, the 'closure' of the cognitive system fits some objective facts, or some properties of the intellectual activities being considered. An eighteenth-century mechanist who was a follower of Newton was by definition a dogmatist because there was no scientific paradigm other than that created by the great English scientist. We therefore suspect that psychologists who liken an organization of the personality to an intellectual ambience have neglected to take into consideration all the aspects of this personality and its intellectual ambience. Further, they do not pay any attention to the factors which define a situation or a social milieu as historically marked. If the method is debatable,[11] so too is the spirit. Dominated by this taxonomic attitude, the study of cognitive phenomena is transformed into a study of cognitive personality, and social psychology is reduced to a differential psychology. The problem is no longer how to establish relationships between a form of knowledge and collective phenomena, but of mapping out the distribution of individuals embodying one form or another.

The confrontation with genetic psychology is more fruitful, if only because it recognizes the explicatory role of social factors. For genetic psychology the presence in the adults we interviewed of the cognitive style and principles we described would be considered as the survival of cognitive style and principles acquired earlier in life and reactivated by the particular conditions of interaction. The thesis of the survival of intellectual organizations belongs to a theoretical framework which presupposes an order in the succession of intellectual organizations. If human development presupposes that certain stages will be overcome, in particular the logic of children, how is it possible that this logic will be found again in the

---

[11] I say 'method' and not 'techniques' because there is always a wealth and abundance of techniques – scales, tests, etc.

representations elaborated by the society of adults? At first sight the response would be simple: in adults, especially less well-educated adults, there persist elements 'conserved' from earlier stages of an intellectual development that has been interupted by causes whose nature it is possible to define. We need to note, however, some attenuations which ought to be made to such a response. From the observations which we have been able to make, the hypothesis of an assimilation of the style and principles described to the reminiscences of a childish system with the consequences which that entails does not appear to correspond to the phenomena. The reason is clear from the facts. If the material presented earlier is re-examined carefully it will be clear that only *partial* elements find their equivalent at certain stages of children's intellectual development. As a whole the cognitive system has its own and different structure. The *fragmentary* study of what is called 'social thought' can give rise to the relations described and the confusions which follow from them.[12] If one refers to the totality, one sees that the link with childhood syncretism, however interesting it may be, is relatively incomplete. But all this only indirectly concerns the idea of a discontinuity (*décalage*) between the laws of intellectual development and the nature of the judgements actually employed in social representation. And perhaps one needs to insist more clearly on the significance of the notion of development. In genetic psychology there is a strict parallelism between the sense of socialization and chronological succession (Piaget 1928). From autism to constraint, and from constraint to cooperation, the stages of sociability have been precisely established. One can say that a child at a particular stage is more socialized than in another stage, in the same way as one can say that one intellectual structure is superior to another. These affirmations are justified and remain univocal in the case of the child, because we can define what we mean by socialization. These criteria become clearly insufficient when one analyses global social situations. One can certainly not say, for example, that 'primitive' societies are less socialized than our own because cooperation has less of a role to play in them.[13] This last proposition makes it seem that the criteria have

---

[12] We can note simply that the wish to explain in this way the existence of modalities of knowledge 'overcome', also found among adults, carries the risk of resuscitating and encouraging inexact, if not false, opinions. We have in mind above all those who establish an equivalence between the thought of social groups and infantile (or pathological) thought. From the partial resemblance of forms one leaps straight to their identity, completely overlooking all the real differences. This step has been taken many times. The study by Martin (1949) is an example.

[13] 'With Lévy-Bruhl we prefer to distinguish a prelogic and a logic according to the social processes which predominate in a particular collective setting. But, as paradoxical as this may seem, primitive mentality seems to us to be less socialized than ours. Social constraint is only a step towards socialization. Only cooperation ensures mental equilibrium, which allows one to distinguish the *de facto* state of psychological operations from the *de jure* state of the rational ideal' (Piaget [1928] 1995: 210).

not been explicated unambiguously, since cooperation can be defined in different ways according to the cultures studied. Even if one accepts the hypothesis of a relation between intellectual operations and forms of sociability one would still need to take account of the fact that the latter (their order, their connections) remain less clearly understood. Starting from a parallelism between chronological succession and socialization one can make better use of the first criteria, which is more assured, than the second, which has not been explored. One can add that the interpretation of the idea of evolution in genetic psychology has constantly oscillated between a historical model and a linear, biological model. The latter has been more prolific, the former is not without foundation.

Social psychology has no possibility of referring to a parallelism analogous to that in genetic psychology, even if it were rigorous. It adopts the same underlying theory of a relation between cognitive systems and social situations, in trying to clarify their functional and structural extensions. At the limit of this common attitude and in the absence of any hierarchy of collective interactions, the notion of the persistence of earlier organizations of judgements loses its consistency. Certainly one could say that one finds traces of childish thinking in adults. But if one reverses the proposition – one finds traces of adult thinking in children – one can see that the essential question remains: what is the relation between this thought and the collective circumstances which sustain it? This leads back to the search for a dynamic within society and its set of mental tools without making any appeal to a biological frame of reference. For, if the child successively acquires the constitutive elements of reason – and genetic psychology describes this acquisition – social psychology is interested in the ordering of these elements once reason has been constituted. The comparison which would allow this ordering to be clarified would be particularly difficult, since the point of departure chosen would inflect the sense of the response.

An example will enable us to understand this difficulty. One knows that there are many resemblances between the child's vision of the world and the vision elaborated by the Greek philosophers – animism, causality, anthropomorphism, etc. One could say, with certain reservations, that the ancient theories owe something to the enhanced influence of a childish mode of thought (Piaget 1951). But the history which allows us to make so many comparisons also provides the counter-proofs. The study of the formation of scientific thought and the discussions which, in the sixteenth and seventeenth centuries, brought together modern science and Aristotelian philosophy produces surprising conclusions. In effect, it became clear that the philosophical 'explanations' were 'true' at the level of an individual observing the movement of bodies and the universe without the aid of mathematics or experimental instruments.[14] Scientific

---

[14] 'This dynamic (prescientific), in effect, seems to adapt itself happily to the current observations which could not fail to compel complete acceptance of the first people

propositions were more adequate and justified in another universe, discovered by mechanics and experimentation (Moscovici 1968). One would, then, be entitled to see in these out of date conceptions their strict adequation to a given physical environment rather than any deficiency of reason. In that case it would not be necessary to have recourse to some appreciation or comparison that might exist with the judgement of children. If we substitute in this example a social universe for the physical universe the embarrassment of psychosociology is evident. How should we understand the observations which have provoked these remarks? Is the cognitive system of social representations as we have described it because our reason conceals intellectual organizations belonging to a younger age? Or is it because it corresponds to a situation and a collective interaction to which it is adapted? At bottom one could show that there is no contradiction here. Nevertheless, for social psychology only the second response is productive. Child psychology and its epistemological extensions are of the greatest importance for our argument. One must recall that it has studied, on a defined material, the way in which logical operations are formed. The necessities of generalization do not oblige us to believe that these operations will be applied to any and every content. Once they have mastered their physical and ideological universe the child and adolescents are far from arriving at a general use of their intellectual tools. Society does not demand it of them. The capacity to do so is not ensured. The acquisition of intellectual mechanisms is not accomplished without reference to a reality, a precise content. The change of environment and its complexity – as well as the complexity of the subject – can reverse the order of these mechanisms. The objective conditions for the insertion of a group or an individual in their physical or social milieu is not always realized at the same level of intellectual development, supposing that we had a universally valid scheme for it. The analysis of this milieu may even reveal the unequal ways in which its most salient aspects have been mastered. The logical possibilities of execution acknowledge, already there, differences of levels. The *coexistence* of cognitive systems should be the rule rather than the exception. Scientific thought has allowed a greater mastery of physical phenomena than biological phenomena, and biological phenomena more than the social or psychological phenomena constitutive of reality. Nevertheless we confront this in its unity. If the procedures of thought contribute to the establishment of solid relations between the being in question – individual or collective – and the external world, they must at the

who speculated about forces and movements . . . For physicists to come to reject the dynamic of Aristotle and to construct the modern dynamics they had to learn that the facts which they witnessed each day are in no way simple, elementary facts to which the fundamental laws of dynamics could be immediately applied' (Duhem 1913, vol. 1: 194). Most of the great historians of science have accepted this point of view, A. Koyré ([1939] 1978) among others.

same time adjust to particular interactions and ponder upon them. In any case, in our study of social representations of psychoanalysis we have frequently called attention to judgements which do not respond to operational criteria of 'correctness'. It is possible to enumerate various categories of subjects using such judgements:

- subjects who have only a very partial knowledge of psychoanalysis;
- subjects who for various reasons (group membership or personal experience) have settled attitudes towards psychoanalysis;
- subjects who gave an opinion without any prolonged reflection about it;
- subjects for whom psychoanalysis is a familiar instrument of interpretation, so that it becomes personalized in some way.

Lastly, one could add, as I have already remarked several times, that the theory and concepts of psychoanalysis are not 'formal' or 'scientific' in the current sense. Judgements are sometimes made without there being evidence of great prudence. Thus, educated people have estimated that this mode of thought, somewhat 'relaxed', was adapted to its object. By extrapolation one can consider that the expansion or retraction of the field of reflection, the 'quality' of its organization – from what can be classed as a lower to a higher level – depends on the attitude which the subject takes in relation to the object.

In other words the same group and, *mutatis mutandis*, the same individual are capable of employing different logical registers in the domains which they approach with different perspectives, information and values. The use of the terms of this register depends ultimately:

- on the degree of depth and mastery of the particular environmental object;
- on the nature of the communications, actions and visible results (influencing conduct, discovering the truth, etc.);
- on the interaction between the actual organization of the collective or individual subject and the degree of differentiation of the social or physical milieu.

With the growth of knowledge and social division we have all become polyglots. Besides French, English or Russian we speak medical, psychological, technical, political languages, etc. We are probably witnessing an analagous phenomenon in regard to thought. In a global manner one can say that the dynamic coexistence – interference or specialization – of the distinct modalities of knowledge, corresponding to definite relations between man and his environment, *determines a state of cognitive polyphasia*. This hypothesis prompts us to broaden our perspectives. Cognitive systems should be construed as developing systems and not uniquely as systems tending to equilibrium. Operative or formal judgements habitually represent one of these *dominant* terms in a field of personal or group preoccupations, while playing a subordinate role elsewhere. In so far as groups or individuals are called upon to confront and resolve more and more complex problems, of a social as much as a natural order, the variability of mental tools adopted is an ineluctable consequence. One mode of reasoning is more apt in response to the exigencies of propaganda, a second to those of economic decisions, a third to the imperatives of science and so on. There is always liaison and communication between these modes, but also specialization. This justifies the connection to a genetic and dynamic point of view in the study of cognitive structures, with a complementary nuance: here genesis and chronological evolution are not to be confused.

These remarks open two avenues of study for us. The first is that of an analysis of correspondences between social situations and modalities of knowledge. Researches on the authoritarian or dogmatic personalities spring from a similar theoretical preoccupation. They seek to establish a link between collectivities dominated by dictatorship, bureaucracy or traditional forms of power and intellectual structures. Unfortunately they have originated in observations of differential psychology which does not have much to teach us about either society or thought. The second avenue, which starts from the hypothesis of cognitive polyphasia, will proceed to the analysis of transformations – equilibrium and evolution – of these modalities of knowledge, of the relations which are established between them and their adaptation.

If the problem which we come to expose is important for social psychology, it is so in a particular way. It is not so much the study of a specialized thought – social, scientific, 'psycho-logic' – or of a cognitive style which is essential. On this last point there is no doubt that descriptions can be extremely extensive and excessive. Social psychology must above all take an interest in the movement of forms of reflection and their order, compared with those of events and factors of *interaction and culture*.[15]

'Natural' thought, conceived in broad terms, is the basis for the divisions which one makes and the intention of treating each of the phenomena which manifest it with equal dignity. Not that there are not survivals in the mind, nor that these always concern elevated ideals. But first we must further deepen the study of the whole to be able to decide by well-informed judgements the value of these propositions. They have very often led us astray as the announcements of a departure, for one does not wish to see them now appearing as a term in the development of a theory.

---

[15] 'The hypothesis of cognitive polyphasia is a way of combating their fragmentation or reduction' of logics, which become social or non-social, and the exclusive attribution of a type of egocentric or paranoiac knowledge to the group. I emphasize, however, that cognitive polyphasia is a hypothesis.

The theoretical examination of social representations has enabled us to distinguish two essential aspects: the description of processes of formation and the study of the cognitive system appropriate to social representation.

Before describing the processes of formation of a social representation we had to show that this was a particular psychological phenomenon, having a clearly defined role: contributing to the genesis of social behaviours and communications. This enabled us to situate it in relation to related notions: ideology, worldviews or science. The conceptual task has been facilitated by the concrete description of the transformation of a scientific theory into a social representation. In the account of this transformation we have been particularly struck by two things: (a) the exclusion of the explanatory principle of psychoanalysis, the libido – with the consequent weakening of its internal coherence; and (b) the appearance of this same principle as the symbol or emblem of psychoanalysis.

After these preliminary clarifications, all our attention has been devoted to an account of the formative processes of social representation: objectification and anchoring. The first concerns the passage of concepts and ideas into schemas or concrete images. We have been able to show how a figurative model of psychical activity is born out of a partial and selected series of information. The generality of its use, like these psychoanalytical notions, changes them into actual doubles, supposed reflections of the real. The examples we have given allow us to see how the complex and the unconscious acquire a sense and organic connotation. In this regard it has been possible to speak of the creation of collective beings and the naturalization of abstract terms. Reality is thus socially inflected to the extent that the conceptual apparatus of psychoanalysis appears to be an immediate translation of phenomena. Objectification, therefore, contributes to the construction at the same time of both the figurative image (the kernel) of the representation and what one calls social reality. The second process takes account of a network of significations around psychoanalysis and the orientation of the connections between this network and the social milieu. Psychoanalysis thus becomes a mediator and a criterion of relations between groups and common values. But, at another level, it facilitates the interpretation of interpersonal relations and conduct. The social representation is elaborated to this end as a polyvalent social instrument, much more general than its intended, strictly scientific purpose would allow it to foresee. It thus becomes a partially automatic system of interpretation and, in the same way, partially integrated into real and symbolic behaviour. In a more succinct manner we have shown the importance of, and the general lines following which a thematic language is constituted. In a parallel direction we have established how it permeates and subtends the social representation of a scientific theory.

Lastly, our attention has been devoted to the description and analysis of the social representation as a purely cognitive system. We began with a critique of the traditional dichotomies, individual–society, rational–irrational etc., to establish the sterility of an opposition between scientific thought and non-scientific thought. Our principal objective has been research into the correspondence between social situation and cognitive system. The situation is defined by (a) the dispersion of information; (b) the pressure to inference; and (c) the focalization of groups and individuals in relation to a centre of interest. The attributes of the cognitive system we have discerned are the following: spontaneous formalism, causal dualism, the pre-eminence of the conclusion and the plurality of types of reasoning. The underlying intellectual principles are analogy and compensation.

The study as a whole has shown us that an individual (or collective) subject can use a plurality of modes of reflection as a function of their mastery of the external milieu and the aims they have in mind. The resulting inferences and specialization constitute a real phenomenon of cognitive polyphasia. It is this phenomenon which social psychology ought to study, and not a social thought heterogenous to individual thought. It remains to clarify the relations and the frontiers of the field explored. The faults of the analysis are visible here and there. The study of behaviour would have reduced them. A theory never recovers the empirical givens. The givens overflow the theory and the theory overflows the givens. The necessity of modifying and amplifying the methods of studying social representations follows from a better adequation of theory and observation. The study of psychoanalysis has given us the possibility of arranging in a series the problems posed in respect of these representations and of sketching some hypotheses. The phenomena with which we are concerned are very important for understanding the functioning of societies. Aware of this importance we have gone beyond the realm of description with the hope that every contribution can be useful and fruitful.

Beyond these very general aims the immediate role of the concepts and interpretations which we have expressed was to take account of the material collected, to give it order and to clarify it.

Part II

Psychoanalysis in the French Press

*Content Analysis and Analysis of Systems
of Communication*

The chapters that follow are devoted to the diffusion of psychoanalytic concepts and language in and by the French press. What can we expect to gain from an examination of a science's presence in these channels of communication? We can, first of all, identify its social representation in a different way. We can also arrive at a better understanding of the most significant regularities in the exchanges that take place around it. Within the framework supplied by these regularities, we see the emergence of three systems of communication which determine the *content* and the *form* of the messages that are sent and received: *diffusion, propagation* and *propaganda*. The last, to give an example, is the doing of the French Communist Party, which rejects psychoanalysis. The *content* of the propaganda is conditioned by the ideology of that party, whilst its *form* and the circumstances of its appearance are determined by relations between the Communist Party and other political groups. In every case, communications are marked by linguistic models and very general beliefs, which also orient the way in which the communicators seek to achieve their goals. The main objective of this section of my work is to make an analysis of forms of communication – diffusion, propagation and propaganda – that correspond to a variety of relations and situations in our society.

A broad outline of the method used to study the materials collected is given here. The tendencies described were identified by examining the *manifest* aspect of the articles published in the light of the judgements and categories that were *isolated* and *defined*. All the publications were studied in an attempt to quantify the number of times the idea of 'sexuality', 'affectivity' or 'moderation' appeared. A number of criteria were chosen to make it possible to determine whether a given article is 'sympathetic', 'interested' or 'external to its author's world'. The goals of the authors can be identified in the same way. Once the categories had been specified, they were used to establish a *grid* that provides the basis for a description of the term's frequency. I will from time to time come back to these data in the following chapters, but I will try to come to closer grips with the same content by adopting a different approach that can bring out its organization and meaning. I will, in other words, resort to a more analytic technique.

The point of departure is provided by grasping the units of analysis, namely *themes* and *links* (or relations). A theme is usually a typical proposition which expresses a whole family of propositions relating to a single content that is formulated in various different ways. To take an example. The theme of the 'need for objective information and to reveal the esoterism of psychoanalysis' takes many different forms: 'There is more and more talk of psychoanalysis, but the general public knows little about it',[1] 'This report will unveil the hidden side of this secret therapy',[2] 'Every day, you hear talk of the Diana complex, the Oedipus complex or just the inferiority complex. Today, J.E. tells you what keys psychoanalysts use to penetrate the mystery of these complexes.'[3] The theme takes, then, the form of a composite assertion that does all it can to give an account of a variable content. At the same time, it establishes a link to the extent that it acts as a mediator between one part of the whole and another. In the model used by the newspaper *France-Soir*,[4] for example, the theme I have just expounded – 'Need for objective information and to reveal the esoterism of psychoanalysis' – establishes a mediating link with the theme: 'In France, psychoanalysis is widely talked about in everyday language but there is less talk of its practice.'

Links express the nature of the relations that exist between two themes within the message that is being communicated. The themes may be equivalent and therefore interchangeable in positional terms. The role of these links is to allow us to identify the order that determines how one proposition implies another. The units of analysis – themes and links – are, however, no more than a *sample* and not a *complete list*, which would naturally be repetitious.

We are, however, in possession of few sufficiently rigorous criteria to sample and select these themes on a strict basis. The only basis for a starting point is a global apprehension of a set of articles, on the basis of which verifiable hypotheses can be formulated, either through a quantitative study or by reason of their coherence. The quest for unity, economy and the greatest possible amount of information orients the study in such a way as to indicate the limitations of the sample and the implications of the themes and links. Once the latter had been identified, they were sorted into columns and lines. Each column and each line constitutes a *dimension*. In the model under consideration, the 'information' dimension appears, for example, as follows:

---

[1] *France-Soir*, 1 October 1952.
[2] Ibid.
[3] *France-Soir*, 9 October 1952.
[4] See Chapter 12 below.

- We do not, in general, have enough information.
- Little is known about psychoanalysis. It is not used sufficiently and lays itself open to possible exploitation.
- There is a need for objective information and to reveal the esoterism of psychoanalysis.
- In France, psychoanalysis is widely talked about in everyday language, but there is less talk of its practice.

The function of the theme is to sum up the content. The function of a link is, first, to express its organization. Themes and links that are organized in dimensional terms constitute a *grouping*. Groupings differ from one another because of their differential nature. We find that in *France-Soir*, for example, one grouping represents *moderation* whilst another represents *excess* in matters psychoanalytic. Several groupings of this kind constitute a *message schema*, or in other words an organized collection of all the messages that appear in any given source of information. The alternation between these analytic and synthetic operations results in the formation of a schema that facilitates our understanding of the real movement of the content and of essential aspects of its role in communication, either as a means of expression or as an instrument.

There is undeniably something arbitrary about the analysis, but because it is an accurate reflection of the element of uncertainty that is inherent in any examination of this kind, it encourages continuous testing. A prior knowledge of the quantified regularities and of how they relate to the elements of the schema limits the arbitrary element and facilitates the introduction of stricter selection criteria.

When dealing with topics like this, it is pointless to *contrast* the qualitative with the quantitative, or vice versa. A qualitative analysis reflects the structure of the content that is being expressed, and a quantitative analysis allows us to weight the terms and parameters of everything that is transmitted, by the press in this case. A combination of the two techniques makes it possible to study relatively complex processes of communication. It also opens up the possibility of constructing hypotheses and verifying them. The goal of future research will be to increase our chances of contributing to the constitution of an autonomous theory of the phenomena of the transmission and action of social signs and symbols.[5]

The content analysis relates to articles published in 241 newspapers and magazines. In the period between 1 January 1952 and 1 March 1953, we *systematically* went through all the publications to which we had access. From that date onwards, a cuttings agency passed on all press cuttings dealing with psychoanalysis (table 2.0.1).

---

[5] The conclusions we have reached are, at least in part, confirmed by M. David in two excellent studies (David 1966; 1967).

Table 2.0.1 The nature of the publications from which texts were taken

Daily (%)	Weekly (%)	Monthly (%)	Unspecified (%)	Total no. of articles
45	30	22	3	1,451

Articles published in specialist journals were excluded from the count, as the object of the present analysis is not scientific communication in the strict sense of the term.

Allow me to make one further remark about how the collected documents were used.

It was never my intention to take sides, or to approve or disapprove of any opinion, judgement or action. This was not a matter of cautious objectivity, but of adopting a lucid approach, as the goal was not so much to reveal the face of this or that group as to establish the internal reasons that explain the way it behaves. I pass no judgement on the truth or falsity of the assertions cited and I do not take the view that the use of certain arguments in, for example, propaganda means that they have no objective content. Is this another way of saying that it is easy to arrive at an objective understanding of the meaning of any assertion or of every change that takes place within a group and is reflected in the press? Not at all. Sometimes, the full meaning of subtle distinctions can be understood only by a limited number of initiates. How are we to understand the distinction a Christian makes between sin and a feeling of guilt, or the distinction between Freud's free association and a form of free association in which, in accordance with the Pope's injunction, secrets must not be divulged? We must not underestimate these pitfalls, or the possibility that our analysis might be superficial. That is a risk we have to take. I have at least attempted to do all I can to minimize that risk by presenting the quotations within a context that explains them, and by placing them in the framework of the circumstances that gave rise to them.

11

The Press: An Overview

1 Who Talks About Psychoanalysis?

The first question I asked myself was: in which publications do articles or statements about psychoanalysis appear? I found 654 in the daily press (*France-Soir, Paris-Presse, L'Humanité*, etc.), 322 in monthly journals (*Ecclesia, La Table ronde, Les Temps modernes*, etc.) and 425 in weeklies (*Les Lettres françaises, France-Observateur, Les Nouvelles littéraires*, etc.). In order to estimate the size of the audiences that can be reached by psychoanalytically inspired texts, the newspapers and magazine were classified on the basis of their print runs.[1] The articles analysed break down as follows: 58 per cent in dailies and periodicals with a *small* print run; 13 per cent in publications with a *large* print-run; and 13 per cent in publications with an *average* print run. Lack of information means that some articles (22 per cent) could not be fitted into this classification. Approaching the same problem from a different angle, I attempted to estimate the influence each publication has on a defined group. A newspaper's print run does not coincide with its influence. *L'Humanité*, for instance, has an average print run, but is of relatively great importance within the Communist press. The only way to estimate its influence was to compare the opinions of several people. To give an example: I regard *La France catholique* as having a major influence on Catholics, and *Témoignage Chrétien* as having an average influence. The criteria are not always as simple as this, and the findings obtained are no more than indicative. Most of the texts (53 per cent) were found in newspapers and periodicals with an 'average' position, and 27 per cent in newspapers and periodicals with an important or 'strong' position within the hierarchy of particular groups.

In general terms, it seems that it is not papers with a big print run that do most to propagate psychoanalysis, but psychoanalysis does appear to

---

[1] Small print run = fewer than 200,000 copies; average = from 200,000 to 400,000 copies; large print run = over 400,000 copies.

Table 11.1 Political and religious orientation of newspapers

Political orientation of paper					Religious orientation of paper		
Communist (%)	Left (%)	Centre (%)	Right (%)	Apolitical (%)	Not stated (%)	Catholic (%)	Protestant (%)
12	18	19	20	24	7	9	2

intervene at the higher levels, where groups' models and directives are 'manufactured' by the questions that are raised by the constantly changing content of science, representations and social relations. This observation is supported by the fact that many of the texts examined came from papers or magazines with a political or religious line (table 11.1).[2]

What are the general characteristics of the articles in which psychoanalysis is discussed in one way or another?

They are *concrete* in style (61 per cent) and usually (66 per cent) do not have a *title* indicating their psychoanalytic content.

I began by examining the content in the strict sense, by making a distinction between those articles that *centred* upon psychoanalysis and those that did not. The latter can, in their turn, be subdivided into (a) a first category of texts containing only psychoanalytic words; (b) a second category in which psychoanalytic concepts are used and in which the theory is *by name*; (c) a third category making the same use of the concepts, but *without* any mention of the theory; and (d) a fourth category which mentions the theory without evoking any of the concepts (table 11.2).

The titles of the articles do not always coincide with the content. A psychoanalytically centred article in *Le Dauphiné libéré*,[3] for example, is entitled: 'When the engineer of souls registers with the Social Security'. It is in fact an interview – half imaginary and half real – with a psychoanalyst and deals with the opening of the Institut de psychanalyse.

A second category of articles uses the term 'psychoanalysis' but not its concepts. An article entitled 'Psychanalyse et prophylaxie mentale' ['Psychoanalysis and mental prophylaxis'],[4] stresses the importance of mental health, the problem of the lack of practitioners and the role of therapy, but makes no attempt to explain psychoanalytic concepts. That was not its aim. Elsewhere, both the word 'psychoanalysis' and its content are present. 'In order to turn you into a purchaser, advertising explores

---

[2] As Catholic or protestant papers also have political tendencies, they sometimes appear in both categories.

[3] 1 December 1954.

[4] *La Vie intellectuelle*, May 1956.

Table 11.2 Content of articles

Centred on psycho-analysis (%)	Terms only (%)	Use of concepts; psychoanalysis not named (%)	Use of concepts; psychoanalysis named (%)	No use of concepts (%)	Terms misused (%)	Total no. of articles
22	28	8	30	7	5	1,451

your unconscious.'[5] The author goes on: 'Psychoanalysis is not just medicine's auxiliary. It also inspires advertising. In order to launch a product, specialists now explore their customers' unconscious and take into account their most secret reflexes.' In this case, the use of psychoanalytic concepts helps to launch French research into what makes consumers buy certain products.

I have given a few quick examples illustrating the classifications I used. Both psychoanalytic concepts and the theory of psychoanalysis are cited in a significant number of articles, but the frequency of 'mere terms' (32 per cent) – *the presence of psychoanalytic terminology as pure language* – is higher than that of articles centred upon psychoanalysis (12 per cent). The latter are published mainly in monthly journals (*Les Temps modernes*, *La Nouvelle Critique* and *La Pensée catholique*), whereas the dailies carry out surveys of subjects likely to interest their readers. Such surveys are published mainly in *France-Soir*, *Le Franc-Tireur* and other dailies. The way the content of the press is distributed across the categories we have defined appears to be influenced by the ideological orientation of the publication in question. The proportion of articles centred upon psychoanalysis is significantly higher in the Catholic ($p < 0.01$), left, centre and centre-left press ($p < 0.05$). The right-wing and Communist press tends, rather, to use terms that simply allude to the theory ($p < 0.01$), and publishes far fewer texts centred upon psychoanalysis ($p < 0.05$).

The data I have just reviewed reveals the existence of a relationship between the type of article and the nature (daily or monthly) and the political orientation of the publication in which it appears.

Who writes the articles? Two per cent are written by psychoanalysts (such as Madame Marie Bonaparte), 16 per cent by individuals recognized as being authoritative in various fields (mainly writers), 52 per cent by authors who do not appear to have any particular competence, whilst 30 per cent are unsigned. As we can draw no conclusions from this, let us simply note that some information about psychoanalysis is supplied by autonomous journalists with no specialist training.

---

[5] *Science et vie*, May 1955.

What role does psychoanalysis play in the press? Because they appeal to psychoanalytic notions without explaining their context, some articles use psychoanalysis as a *mode* of understanding. The theory is used, that is, as a source of explanatory *models* in very different domains: the study of the human personality, of education, of art or of interpersonal relations. The intentions of the author of an article entitled 'Psychanalyse de la belle-mère' ['Psychoanalysing the mother-in-law'] are quite clear:

> Mother-in-law jokes are as old as the hills. But the scientific methods of psychoanalysts now make it easier to explore the recesses of the heart and the soul. And so the old conflicts are seen in a new light, and we can hope to resolve them as a result.[6]

Psychoanalysis is, however, also a language, a thematic language whose extension has already been described. A first index is supplied by the fact that 75 per cent of the articles in which we find psychoanalytic 'words' and 76 per cent of those which contain psychoanalytic concepts but do not mention psychoanalysis, have no clear aim *related to this discipline*. The conceptual model and psychoanalytic terminology circulate in the press, without any direct link with the concepts themselves. In contrast, articles centred upon psychoanalysis or which both give an account of its concepts and mention it by name do have a definite purpose in 87 per cent and 76 per cent of cases respectively. There is nothing surprising about the presence of this preferential language in the dailies (32 per cent) and weeklies (49 per cent). The articles in which it appears obviously do not have psychoanalytic titles (46 per cent) and often have no titles at all (49 per cent). On the other hand, 71 per cent of the titles of articles centred upon the theory do have a psychoanalytic content; nonetheless, 29 per cent of articles in which the use of the word 'psychoanalysis' and psychoanalytic ideas seems to be obligatory in fact focus on problems that have little to do with it. In these cases, the purpose of the article is to *name* names, to *capture* the reader's attention or to give the impression that the author is following a specific theoretical schema. 'Essai de psychanalyse d'une élection' ['Psychoanalysing an election'] (*Ecrits de Paris*), 'Psychanalyse du lecteur' ['Psychoanalysis of the reader'] (*Dimanche-Matin*) are nothing more than critical articles whose content could have appeared under any title.

Information is also important. The purpose of most psychoanalytically centred articles is to provide information about psychoanalysis. They appear under specific headings: news (34 per cent), science columns and investigations (32 per cent). The information they give treats psychoanalysis as something that exists *sui generis*; it is unusual to find texts dealing with psychoanalysis in medical columns (2.5 per cent, an

---

[6] *Marie-Claire*, April 1956.

insignificant percentage), whilst it is often mentioned in literary columns (17 per cent) and even the political column (3 per cent). The discrepancy between these proportions further specifies the meaning given it by the press: it is a representation of the human personality, the worldview of a particular group, an interpretative framework and, incidentally, a specialized form of therapy.

Now that a few markers have been put down, we can complete the map of texts dealing with psychoanalysis. We can now trace the broad outline of the content of these articles.

2 The Many Faces of Psychoanalysis

What image of psychoanalysis does the press give? How is it defined? Of the 1,288 articles that give a definition of psychoanalysis:

- 30 per cent see it as a therapeutic method;
- 30 per cent as a theory of the personality and personality disorders;
- 22 per cent as a general psychological theory;
- 5 per cent a method that explains phenomena in general;
- 5 per cent a philosophy or conception of humanity;
- 4 per cent a theory of sexuality.

The definition of psychoanalysis relates to the type of article, the attitude it expresses, and to the ideological orientation and the category of the publications in which the texts appear. Articles focused upon psychoanalysis emphasize its therapeutic implications ($p < 0.05$), whilst its theory of the personality and its disorders is mentioned more discretely.

When, in contrast, it is a matter of using a specialist vocabulary, or of specialist terms that have been organized into a conceptual model – whether psychoanalysis is mentioned or not – the accompanying image is one of a conception of the personality and its disorders.

We can see a sort of specialization developing: articles that focus on psychoanalysis are usually concerned with practical issues, whilst the conceptual or linguistic usage dominates other texts.

When an article adopts a sympathetic attitude towards psychoanalysis or has reservations about it, it is usually defined as a form of therapy ($p < 0.01$) or as a psychological theory ($p < 0.01$). When the attitude is unsympathetic or ironic, psychoanalysis is described as a pseudo-science or as a mystification ($p < 0.05$). *Attitude aside, psychoanalysis is described as a theory of sexuality, of the personality and its disorders.* Only Communists describe it as a pseudo-science, and they are less likely to admit that it is of any relevance to psychology. Centre, centre-right, right and apolitical papers are almost the only ones to point out that psychoanalysis is a theory of sexuality.

Table 11.3 Roles assigned to psychoanalysis

Theory (%)[a]	Therapy (%)	Theory and Therapy (%)	Ideology (%)	Practice (%)	Education (%)	N/A (%)	Total no. of articles
62	34	16	5	5	5	21	1,451

[a] Totals exceed 100% because the same articles can give psychoanalysis more than one role.

As in our survey, psychoanalysis is understood in many different ways in the press. There is, as we have seen, nothing random about this diversity of views. When we look more closely at how psychoanalysis is described, the tendencies we have described become more pronounced. The different roles assigned to psychoanalysis (table 11.3) correlate with the ideological line of the publication in which the texts appear.

Periodicals that are apolitical or on the left are more likely to give psychoanalysis a theoretical role (p < 0.01). Communist papers and magazines and those that are progressive or on the right are less likely to emphasize its therapeutic functions (p < 0.10), whilst Catholic papers and magazines are more often inclined to emphasize that application (p < 0.01).

If we add that it is sympathetic or reserved articles that show an interest in the therapeutic role of psychoanalysis (p < 0.01), we can conclude that there is a link between the doubts about a discipline's practical implications and hostility towards it. It is likely that there is a correlation between distrust of analytic practice and the focus on its theory that avoids examining or overlooks its practical implications. *That likelihood is reinforced by the fact that authors who are interested in psychoanalysis often instance either its therapeutic role or its therapeutic and theoretical role (p < 0.01). Authors who show less interest tend, rather, to draw attention to its theoretical (63 per cent) or ideological (16 per cent) implications.*

An examination of the themes associated with psychoanalysis – and no fewer than thirty can be identified – shows that the points around which its representation crystallizes form a very extensive network.

The fact that its content is conceived in such a protean way has more to do with the use made of it by the press – which is in keeping with its goals – than with any recognition that it has its own field of action. That field is relatively neglected, as we find mention of it in only 27 per cent of the texts collected. When they do deign to mention it, education, intellectual life, the cinema and, more rarely, the human sciences are seen as psychoanalysis's field of action (table 11.4).

The press's interest in Freud's discoveries has nothing to with the field of pathology, and we can, up to a point, see it as natural that the press should define their practical implications in the way that it does. *To put it in slightly different terms, the press prioritizes those modalities of action which*

Table 11.4 Fields of action attributed to psychoanalysis

Education (%)	Psychosomatic disorders (%)	Self-knowledge (%)	Cultural (%)	Human science (%)	Misused in films (%)	All (%)	Various (%)	Total[a]
22	5	7	20	8	14	7	17	400

[a] Total number of articles ascribing a field to psychoanalysis.

are most familiar to its readers. This observation, which is still superficial, can be completed by a further observation. The choice of education or intellectual life as a field of application betrays a desire to accord *normality* a primacy that masks the anxiogenic image of neurosis or psychotherapy. With the exception of a political and religious minority, everyone can look at psychoanalysis from the outside, and the press tries, on the whole, to express not so much a real world as an acceptable world.

All these findings lead us to the same general conclusion: newspapers and magazines represent psychoanalysis mainly as an *interpretative system* and only incidentally as a specialized discipline (i.e. one with a theory and a technique).

What is the interpretation based upon? Sexuality takes pride of place (25 per cent). The unconscious (20 per cent) and affectivity (16 per cent) are two other agencies or forces that are frequently associated with psychoanalysis and its social model. 'Explaining things with reference to childhood' predominates mainly when it is a question of giving practical advice or understanding the genesis of a literary work. Psychoanalysis thus becomes a science that stresses that the past or childhood is an important aspect of our history.[7]

The attitude of the authors concerned and the rubrics in which their articles appear determine the use of the explanatory themes attributed to psychoanalysis (table 11.5). Authors whose attitude is sympathetic or reserved talk more about 'childhood', affectivity or the unconscious ($p < 0.01$), whereas those whose attitude is unsympathetic stress the theme of sexuality ($p < 0.01$). *We therefore cannot avoid seeing the insistence on the role of sexuality as central to psychoanalytic explanations as an expression of hostility towards psychoanalysis.*

The rubric in which a text appears also conditions the choice of dynamic principle or mode of interpretation. It is mainly articles on education (30 per cent), surveys of psychoanalysis (32 per cent) and book reviews (25 per cent) that invoke the past or childhood as explanatory principles. *Sexuality* is mentioned less frequently in articles on education and in expository accounts of psychoanalysis ($p < 0.01$), but affectivity, in contrast, is more frequently mentioned as an explanatory theme ($p < 0.01$).

---

[7] The other explanatory principles are less important (22 per cent).

Table 11.5 Psychoanalysis's explanatory themes, by attitude

Attitude	Childhood (%)	Affectivity (%)	Sexuality (%)	Unconscious (%)	Symbolism (%)	Dreams (%)	Aggress-ivity (%)
Sympathetic	16	22	18	26	7	8	3
Unsympathetic	10	11	43	14	9	3	10
Reservations	16	14	35	22	3	4	6
None	17	13	27	11	14	14	4

The attempt to moralize psychoanalysis – which goes hand in hand with the implicit use of its concepts – leads to sexuality being replaced by affectivity. The link and explanations are none the clearer for that. Interpretations based upon the unconscious are widespread in background articles (32 per cent), articles on popular science and investigative articles (25 per cent).[8]

Whilst psychoanalysis is seen primarily as an interpretative system, we can see that its principle varies in accordance with the rubric, or in other words the newspaper or magazine's interests. The variety of explanatory themes, the relative abundance of exposés about psychoanalysis and the passions it arouses are rarely complemented by any judgement as to its value. Only 9 per cent of articles pass any judgement on its value as a therapy, and only 12 per cent on its value as a theory. The discrepancy is not great enough to allow us to draw any firm conclusions. A more detailed examination of these value-judgements shows that they are *more sympathetic to the therapy than the theory*. Thirty-four per cent of statements about analytic practice describe it as 'effective and having proved itself', whilst 28 per cent describe it as 'useful but limited', 10 per cent as 'inadequate', 21 per cent as 'dangerous' and 6 per cent as 'ineffective'. Value-judgements about psychoanalytic theory break down as follows: 'arbitrary and exaggerated', 39 per cent, 'inadequate and limited', 21 per cent, 'interesting and fertile', 19 per cent, and 'interesting but exaggerated', 16 per cent. *If we recall that it is mainly authors who are sympathetic to psychoanalysis that ascribe a therapeutic role to it, we can conclude that its practice is less controversial.*

3 Attitudes, Groups and Ideological Orientations

The goal of psychoanalysis is seen as both very general and very vague (table 11.6).

The term 'explaining' both sums up the generality and captures the vagueness. Its various meanings – clearing up a problem, providing a

---

[8] The number of articles in which aggressivity is given an explanatory role is very small. I simply point out that polemical and political articles are more likely to mention it.

Table 11.6 Goals assigned to psychoanalysis[a]

None (%)	Explaining (%)	Curing (%)	Explaining and curing (%)	Educating (%)	Re-adapting (%)	Masking problems (%)
29	50	29	15	4	5	4

[a] Totals exceed 100% because articles mention several goals.

Table 11.7 Dimensions of attitude towards psychoanalysis

1	Sympathetic 31%	Unsympathetic 14%	Reservations 13%	Ironic 5%	None expressed 37%
2	Interested 49%		No interest 12%		None expressed 39%
3	Internal 32%		External 23%		None expressed 45%

framework that introduces order into the real world, relating things to one another – do not exhaust its cultural connotations: self-understanding, providing a key. Periodicals that are sympathetic or have reservations describe the goals of psychoanalysis as positive; those that are unsympathetic are less likely to ascribe it any goal (p < 0.01). When they do so, it tends to be negative.

Let us now look at attitudes. The need to understand in concrete terms the positions adopted by newspapers leads us to identify three attitudinal dimensions (table 11.7):

- the first dimension indicates support or hostility, or the sympathy or lack of sympathy enjoyed by psychoanalysis;
- the second, which is an expression of intensity, marks the existence of an interest or its absence;
- the third indicates the communicator's distance from the object, or its characterization as internal or external to the world of the communicator.

We note, first, that 38 per cent of the texts examined do not display any attitude, either because they carefully avoid mentioning their attitude or because psychoanalysis is described as a mere language. The press tends, however, to be quite sympathetic (31 per cent) or to have reservations (13 per cent). Unsympathetic (13 per cent) or ironic (5 per cent) attitudes are encountered more rarely. Magazines are more likely to mention their support or hostility (p < 0.01), and newspapers are less likely to do so. The difference arises because of the role these publications play and because, for the daily press, psychoanalysis is a convenient modality of communication rather than an object it should be concerned about. Monthly publications are also more sympathetic towards it (p < 0.01).

Articles published in the education, science and medical pages, and surveys and investigative articles are generally sympathetic to psycho-analysis (p < 0.10). The proportion of articles expressing reservations is, as might be expected, highest in the 'science reports' (p < 0.01). Hostility towards psychoanalysis is concentrated mainly in political (and polem-ical) columns and film reviews. The essential reason for film critics' unsympathetic attitude is the excessive use made of psychoanalytic themes in American films.

In order to arrive at a better understanding of the context in which psy-choanalysis is invoked, we must also consider the authority of the authors of these articles. 'Authorities on psychoanalysis' are naturally sympathetic, but there is a high proportion of sympathetic attitudes amongst 'general authorities' (p < 0.01). Communications studies demonstrated long ago the extent to which the intervention of a well-known figure into a domain, whatever its nature, helps to influence public opinion in general. *It does seem that, in France, such interventions help to spread quite unsympathetic atti-tudes towards psychoanalysis.* Articles by ecclesiastics or political writers warn the reader, who is either a believer or a supporter, against the dangers posed by psychoanalytic applications of principles and we read in *L'Humanité* that psychoanalysis is a 'vile propaganda weapon', and that analysts are 'trying to stupefy people with complexes'.[9] We will return to these arguments in the chapters that follow, which examine how they are integrated into an overall conception of the world and of man.

The second attitudinal dimension – interest or lack of interest – is related to the first. In sympathetic, reserved and even ironic articles, we find a certain interest in psychoanalysis. A lack of interest goes hand in hand with hostility (table 11.7).

The determinations are the same. Monthly periodicals show a more constant interest in psychoanalysis than weeklies and dailies (p < 0.01). When they ridicule (27 per cent) or refute it (24 per cent), authors show less interest in it. They display more interest in it when they are trying to defend or discuss it, to introduce Freud or to study a particular question (p < 0.01).

We find the same relationship between the goal and the third attitudi-nal dimension: the discussion of psychoanalysis within and outside its own frame of reference (table 11.7).

If we examine the links between these dimensions, we note that the pro-portion of articles in which psychoanalysis is seen as something external to the world of the group or author is greater than the proportion of arti-cles in which the position adopted reveals a lack of interest or sympathy.

---

[9] *L'Humanité*, 17 February 1949.

The meaning of the extreme positions is clear: a positive orientation implies a certain interest in psychoanalytic theory and allows it to play a role in the formation of a vision of the personality, or of behaviour or education. Negative attitudes are associated with a lack of interest and externality. Reserved or ironic attitudes are an index of both interest and externality with respect to psychoanalysis.

Whilst there is, as we have demonstrated, a link between the stated goal of an article and the author's attitude, we also find a link between the article's goal and the author's religious or political orientation. There is a fairly close link between the paper or magazine's doctrinal framework, its general conception of science, its hierarchy of values and its representation of or attitude towards psychoanalysis. Let us examine each group in turn.

(a) The Catholic press is undoubtedly sympathetic and interested, and it discusses psychoanalysis as a discipline whose notions can find a place within its conception of the psychical organization of the personality. Discussions and expository accounts of psychoanalysis are always characterized by a certain level of abstraction. This is the only group in which the proportion of articles written in an abstract style (46 per cent) exceeds the proportion of articles written in a concrete style (31 per cent). The authors' primary goal is to discuss psychoanalysis (30 per cent), to justify it (30 per cent) and to demonstrate its interest (34 per cent). Catholic publications do this more often than other papers or magazines ($p < 0.01$). This finding is a fairly faithful reflection of the fact that this period was, for Catholics, one in which psychoanalytic conceptions were being adapted to their own conceptions, making numerous articles, both critical and apologetic, necessary. The resistance was not negligible: the proportion of theoretical critiques of psychoanalysis in the Catholic press is relatively high (17 per cent), and neither interest in the subject nor a sympathetic attitude towards it encourage Catholic authors to use its models for the study of a personality or the resolution of a problem. The percentage of articles using psychoanalysis in that way is relatively low (12 per cent). The texts in question came mainly from the following rubrics: scientific and cultural columns (33 per cent), book reviews (17 per cent) and education (11 per cent).

(b) The most negative positions are those published in the Communist and progressive press. Their attitude is unsympathetic (47 per cent) and takes relatively little interest in psychoanalysis because it is external to the way in which they interpret the real. The style is concrete, but where articles written in an abstract style are concerned, progressive authors lag behind the Catholics. This is a sign that the discussion is taking place at a fairly sophisticated technical level (table 11.8).

The primary goal of the texts analysed is to make a critique of psychoanalysis (43 per cent) or to refute it (11 per cent). Attempts to apply it to the study of certain questions are more rare (11 per cent). We see here the emergence of the meaning of the preoccupations to which the theory gives

Table 11.8 Style of articles, political / religious loyalty

Loyalty	Concrete (%)	Abstract (%)	Concrete and abstract (%)	Ironic / concrete and ironic (%)
Communist	60	25	15	0
Left, centre-left	66	16	15	3
Centre	75	6	19	0
Centre-right, right	68	13	9	10
Catholic	31	46	21	2
Apolitical	53	23	20	4

rise: the goal is to negate its role, whatever the domain of its applications might be. The rubrics in which the texts in question appear are, in order: film reviews (23 per cent), book reviews (21 per cent) and science reports (16 per cent). The order is different to that found in Catholic publications. The film reviews usually take an unsympathetic view of the way psychoanalysis is used in films. Communists see it as a sign of the decadence of a culture: that of the United States.

(c) Daily newspapers on the left or the centre-left tend to be both sympathetic and interested. The articles, which appear mainly in the pages devoted to book and art reviews (28 per cent) to news (20 per cent) or in the science columns, are usually written in a fairly concrete style. The authors' goal is to clarify a problem or to study a personality (21 per cent), to justify psychoanalysis (21 per cent), but also to discuss (12 per cent) or reject it (18 per cent) for specific reasons.

The difference between these publications and the Communist or Catholic press centres on several points: many texts appear under the 'news' rubric, and psychoanalysis is used as a system for the interpretation of certain problems. Although criticisms are made of specific points, they result in neither a rejection nor a synthesis.

(d) Some articles expressing a more sympathetic, interested and 'internal' attitude do appear in right-wing and centre-right newspapers and magazines.

They appear in rubrics intended to expound a theory, an event in the scientific or social world (38 per cent), in book reviews (21 per cent) and even in the 'news in brief' column or readers' letters. The texts are more widely scattered, and the authors' goal is primarily to introduce Freud (22 per cent), to demonstrate the interest of his work (20 per cent) or to use it to explain a personality or problem (19 per cent). We can therefore see that the diffusion of Freudian concepts plays a major role in this group.

(e) Newspapers and magazines on the right of the political spectrum are largely unsympathetic to psychoanalysis (23 per cent). It is regarded

Table 11.9 Goals of author and political loyalty

	Communist (%)	Left (%)	Centre (%)	Right (%)	Catholic (%)
Introduce Freud and psychoanalysis	2	14	22	6	1
Justify psychoanalysis; demonstrate its interest	10	21	20	15	34
Study person or problem	11	23	19	27	12
Discuss psychoanalysis	3	12	16	13	30
Criticize psychoanalysis	43	5	1	7	17
Reject specific points	11	17	14	12	1
Ridicule psycho-analysis or analysts	11	8	6	16	5
Introduce other theories or techniques	9	0	2	4	0

as something that is outside the group's frame of reference. The lack of interest is revealed by the fact that a relatively high proportion of the texts examined appear in 'news in brief' columns, in columns dedicated to leisure or in the women's pages (21 per cent), as well as in book reviews. Their stated goals – studying a personality or problem (27 per cent), ridiculing psychoanalysis and psychoanalysts (16 per cent) – reveal that the coherence of the views expressed leaves much to be desired (table 11.9).

(f) Those publications that are classed as non-political tend to fall into a residual category because they do not reveal any specific orientation and defy all attempts at linear classification. Their attitude is generally sympathetic. Most of the articles appear in rubrics devoted to scientific or cultural news (42 per cent), or in the context of book reviews.

The goal of this rather dry presentation of our quantitative findings, and of collating them in order to establish a typology of ideological groups by examining attitudes towards psychoanalysis was to test our initial hypothesis that there is a link between a publication's general orientation, its representation of a theory, its attitude towards it, and more immediate aspects, such as the rubric in which the article appears or the goals the author sets himself when writing a particular text. The value of this demonstration lies not so much in the nature of the hypothesis as in the fact that it allows us to get a clearer picture of how the press views psychoanalysis, to situate ideological groups with respect to it, and, finally, to trace the simple but basic outline of the social models that take it as a starting point.

A general description is a necessary stage which we must then complete in more qualitative terms, but it is also a stage we have to get beyond if we wish to study communication processes, which are *the essential object of this part of the work.*

12

The Diffusion of Psychoanalysis

1 Initial Descriptions

When we study communication processes, we have to take into account the multiplicity of relations that determine and constitute them: relations between the organization of the content and behaviour, between the frame of reference and the object of the communication, and between sender and receiver. The essential lacuna in this study, which is common to many others, is that it was not possible (with one exception) to discover anything about the way those who write about psychoanalysis in the press interact or about their expressive needs, or to verify what effects their messages have on specific behaviours. But no study can claim to be exhaustive. We have been able to remedy the lack of direct information on certain points by relying on other studies and on observation.

Diffusion, which is the system or form of communication that we have to examine here, must be distinguished from the term's ordinary meaning of 'material operation of distribution'. The most accurate image is that of one or more elements that follow discontinuous trajectories within various interlinked structures, and which can produce modifications, be modified or retain their autonomy. The relationship between those elements and their potential effects on a set of values or behaviours is not entirely predictable. The image remains abstract. The goal of this chapter is to clarify it. In order to do so, we will describe relations between sender and receiver within that system of communication. In diffusion, the sender is really trying to establish a relationship of equality or equivalence between himself and his audience and, as a result, to adapt to his audience. An attempt is made, in other words, to establish a sort of unity between publication and reader, whilst at the same time continuing to differentiate between their roles. This implies, on the part of the newspaper or magazine, an attempt to define and fulfil a specific function. When, for example, publications such as *France-Soir* or *Marie-France* discuss psychoanalysis, they do not set themselves up as sources of information that can or wish to orient their readers, but as organs that can *transmit* a common knowledge they wish to share. The objectives of a paper like *L'Humanité* are more imperious, and it seeks to give its readers a clear and unambiguous orientation. This cannot be described as diffusion. The role this newspaper plays with regard to its readership is that of a *mediator*; this implies that it is also a receiver because the object – in this case, psychoanalysis – is external to it. As a result, it identifies with or is equivalent to the population of readers it is addressing because it finds itself in the same situation. In diffusion, then, the source of communication is always obliged to define itself as an agent for the transmission of messages and, in order to fulfil that function, as an expression of its readers, so that it can attract them and get them to identify with it. In diffusion, the problem of the adaptation of sender to receiver, and the former's dependence on the latter, is fundamental. This is not the case with propaganda, where the source of information or orders enjoys a relatively broad autonomy.

By analysing the question of adaptation, we can bring out the essential features of diffusion. We will begin by noting some of this mode of communication's typical stylistic attributes: it is concrete, attractive and rapid. This is because it attempts to get as close as possible to what is assumed to be the taste and vocabulary of the reader. Striking propositions that can draw the attention are very common. An investigation into psychoanalysis undertaken by *Le Franc-Tireur* is, for example, entitled 'Les scaphandriers de 'inconscient' ['The frogmen of the unconscious']. The second article in the series is entitled: 'Thanks to the phenomenon of transference, the psychoanalyst simultaneously becomes his subject's "mum, dad, maid and ego [*moi*]"'.[1] The last section of the sentence alludes to a film whose star was a well-known comic. The reader is thus drawn to a proposition that is at once 'popular' and funny because it refers to a funny film. Taken as a whole, the title is, so to speak, somewhat 'telescoped', as it combines a family situation and a smiling image in the same idea of transference. As a result, no one is put off by the possible aridity of the subject under discussion. The content of the article is, however, fairly accurate, even though it is very short. The following text illustrates this:

> In the first phase of its history, psychoanalysis was primarily an exploration of the individual unconscious. Freud noted the fact that bringing certain repressed impulses into the broad light of day was sometimes enough to resolve conflicts that give rise to disorders. At this stage, transference looked like no more than a very widespread occurrence in any psychoanalytic treatment that was at once relatively secondary and difficult to explain: without any valid reason, the subject either fell in love with the psychoanalyst or, on the contrary, displayed hostility towards him. It was by studying the mechanisms of the transference that psychoanalysis began to make decisive

[1] *Le Franc-Tireur*, 7 January 1952.

progress. This assertion may surprise those who cling to the outdated notion of the *intellectual* exploration of the depths of the unconscious, but not those who understand that the prime mover behind any vital behaviour is of an *affective* nature. Showing someone that he has a potential Oedipus complex or Dupont-Durand complex will no more rid him of it than 'explaining' how a gear box works will teach him to drive a car. Just as we learn to drive a car by educating our reflexes, we learn to live by educating our impulses to love or hate.[2]

The United States are not absent from this text. In a column inserted into the middle of the article, we read:

> The vogue for psychoanalysis in the United States seems to result from an obsessional and collective psychosis. People go to a psychoanalyst in the same way that they go to the dentist or the hairdresser. Some hairdressing salons even employ psychoanalysts who offer to iron out your marital problems or to put an end to your depressions.[3]

The same 'American' paragraph contains two or three jokes to make the reader laugh. The most famous anecdote concerns a conversation between two girls: 'Are you really in love with Johnny?' 'How should I know: my psychoanalyst's on holiday.'

As we shall see later, this way of organizing articles about psychoanalysis is also found in other newspapers, and it corresponds to a desire to please the public and to get it to read. But it also expresses a desire to avoid dishonest compromises or to distance the paper from the object – psychoanalysis – and to win a margin of freedom. Let us first look at how this is achieved, and then examine its role. The methods that are usually used are irony, growing reservations about psychoanalysis, the creation of an aura of humour and references to specialists. The relative non-structuration of the content makes it easier to allude to frames of reference that are familiar to every reader. The distancing effect is achieved more directly by locating psychoanalysis, and especially its so-called exaggerations, in the United States. Non-involvement is another way of demonstrating that one has certain reservations about the theory. The way it is frequently used to interpret everyday behaviours is challenged. We found 63 articles about psychoanalysis in 64 issues of *Elle*. Its use was recommended for a whole range of problems:

> That psychoanalysis or psychotherapy can cure many women of migraine is quite certain.[4]

[2] Ibid.
[3] Ibid.
[4] *Elle*, 16 June 1952.

The same therapy is recommended as a way of curing indigestion.[5] Genital dysfunctionality seems to respond to the same treatment:

> Psychoanalysts believe that most cases of dysmenorrhoea are within the remit of their speciality and can be cured by psychoanalytic treatment.[6]

I am by no means certain about the value of this assertion, which is attributed to psychoanalysts. To say that *psychoanalysts* believe that *most* cases of dysmenorrhoea justify resorting to psychoanalysis is certainly an over-generalization. Definite reservations are, however, then expressed about the way readers use psychoanalytically inspired explanatory models:

> They talk of 'complexes' at the drop of a hat, imagine that they are repressed, and use a terminology that explains your reactions.[7]

A journalist replies to a reader who cited Dr Allendy's comment on 'a boy's neurotic fixation on his mother': ' "Neurotic" provides an answer to everything.' But someone said of the same journalist that:

> After five years of giving advice, consoling people and sometimes even saving their lives, she has acquired an understanding of the hearts of men and women that many a psychologist or psychoanalyst would envy.[8]

Elle tells us that: 'A child is an excellent means of sharing transference.'[9] In the columns of the same weekly, there is no condemnation of the use of psychoanalysis when it comes to combining very different perspectives, such as astrology and modern rationalism. In an article entitled 'What is True About Horoscopes' and subtitled 'Psychoanalysis backs astrology', we read:

> Astrology has found an official ally who will make it easier for it to gain entry to the scientific world, and who will make it acceptable in the salons frequented by university professors: psychoanalysis, which has recently been admitted to the Sorbonne itself. And whilst J. Rostand and P. Couderc refuse to sponsor astrology, the work of Freud does just that. He gave us a set of instructions that do not always respect logic. Astrologers want to create a human language based upon the logical study of the stars. The formulae used by psychoanalysts have evolved since Freud's day. In his *Modern Man in Search of a Soul*, the famous Professor Jung writes: 'The Philistine believed until recently that astrology had been disposed of long ago, and was something that

---

[5] Ibid., 30 June 1952.
[6] Ibid., 31 March 1952.
[7] Ibid., 22 September 1952.
[8] Ibid., 30 January 1952.
[9] Ibid., 22 September 1952.

could be safely laughed at. But today, rising out of the social deeps, it knocks at the doors of the universities.' Astrologers could not ask for anything more. Most 'scientists' are biased when it comes to psychoanalysis. It has gained ground by studying the irrational and dreams. It is knocking at the doors of the unconscious. If it is carried our badly, psychoanalysis can lead to madness. When astrology is poorly understood, it can become an obsession.[10]

Note the oscillation between bold applications and frequent warnings; its meaning will become clear below.

The frequent use of humour reflects an attempt to distance the publication from the message it is transmitting and at the same time to make it look attractive. Many articles on psychoanalysis are accompanied by ironic titles and cartoons. The smiles they attempt to raise, or the way the authors seem to smile as they write, are, as it happens, a sign that the publication is distancing itself from psychoanalysis or certain psychoanalytic ideas. No matter whether it is an interview with Dr Lacan or an article by J.-B. Pontalis or J. Eparvier, the context is always one of non-involvement with the content.

The series of articles by Monsieur Eparvier published in sixteen successive issues of *France-Soir* represents a successful attempt to use techniques that adapt the paper to its readership and emphasize the paper's function as mediator. The ideas expounded in the series of articles are relatively accurate. No essential errors creep in and the author provides a fairly complete account of psychoanalysis. The texts are accompanied by jokes and cartoons. The titles, like those in *Le Franc-Tireur*, are suggestive: 'Marriage is symbolized by a series of bedrooms, and death by a departure or a means of locomotion'; 'Suzanne dreams that she is being handcuffed by nurses in the mountains; this is a sexual dream about self-punishment'. Despite the titles, the articles are not extracts from a dream book, and they provide a fairly sophisticated account of the psychoanalytic theory of dreams. The only problem is that the theory is introduced as though it were a dream book. The articles are scattered, usually at the beginning, with expressions like these: 'This is a specialist speaking' or 'say psychoanalysts'. The prestige of the specialist allows the journalist to appear not to take sides. This is not always the case. The journalist can be a kindly intermediary who can free the reader from some anxiogenic situation. An article about the Oedipus complex begins in dramatic style:

Psychoanalysts assert that between the ages of three and five, children fall in love with the parent of the opposite sex. So even the most adorable children are prone to the two most horrifying of all tendencies: parricide and incest . . . This theory, on which psychoanalysis is based, naturally caused a scandal when it was first expounded. Even those who had serious doubts subsequently came

[10] *Elle*, 18 October 1952, citing Jung (1933: 243).

to terms with it to a greater or lesser extent, and it is now finally accepted not
only that there is such a thing as the Oedipus complex – but also that it is
absolutely normal and that the only things that matter are how it is repressed
and how it evolves.[11]

Having taken certain precautions, the author of the article generalizes
what is in part his own opinion to a universal 'they'. This conclusion allays
all worries by asserting that the Oedipus complex is normal:

> The Oedipus complex should therefore not be regarded as something dan-
> gerous. Like all the other complexes, it only becomes dangerous when it
> becomes hypertrophic.[12]

The latter proposition is so vague as to leave such a wide margin of
freedom that it is open to a huge range of very different interpretations.

The appeal to the authority of a specialist both adds weight to the
propositions contained in the paper and allows the person writing to look
like a mere agent who is comparing authoritative opinions with those
of his or her readers. At the same time, the journalist becomes part of the
readership, as he appears to be doing no more than collating opinions
about any given problem.

At this point, we have to introduce a further qualification. Diffusion is
a form of communication that concerns not a strictly defined group, but
what are often called the masses. I will not attempt to provide a definition
of either the masses or the public (Blumer 1951), as that has been done
many times. The masses or the public can be described as the aggregate of
a large part of the population of a country or town whose heterogeneous
population is widely distributed in spatial terms. Their organization is, in
certain respects, quite loose. It should be added that the individuals
making them up belong to very disparate groups that are, however, linked
together by social relations that sustain both their unity and their diversity.
The multiplicity of points of reference, the shifting links that exist between
them, and the variable quantities of affect that are invested produce unstable equilibriums, and apparently simple possibilities for restructuring,
since they are only established at certain levels and as a function of a
clearly delineated centre of interest. There are many different publics: a
public for horse racing, a population for royal marriages or sport and,
perhaps, one for psychoanalysis. The public cannot be identified with
any one group. The same individual can be a member of several publics.
A newspaper or magazine that sells hundreds of thousands of copies
must 'stick with' its readers and must, therefore, both reproduce their

---

[11] *France-Soir*, 10 October 1952.
[12] Ibid.

oscillations and find a common denominator. Above all, it must be seen, or appear to be seen, to change over time and to have a varied content at the moment it is read.

The discontinuity of the readership is immediately reflected in the discontinuity of the publication's editorial organization, but also in the discontinuity of its opinions. It is this combination of distance and non-involvement on the one hand and diversity on the other that allows the interplay and gives the paper the degree of freedom it requires if it is to be able to adapt. Its ability to do so depends upon the characteristics of the reading masses, but also upon the unevenness of their intellectual formation and their underlying interests. *L'Humanité* addresses Communists and workers, *La Croix*, Catholics, but *France-Soir* or *Elle* address 'Parisians' or 'the French' as well as women. We can immediately recognize the difference between the categories cited. Journalists have to work with an image of their readership; intuition, the tricks of the trade and opinion polls help them to do so. A newspaper editor has to take all this into account. The individual who reads the editorial is not the same as the individual who reads the sports page, the comic strips or the political column, yet the paper has to be read by all of them. The various people who supposedly make up the team therefore enjoy a certain autonomy. This has the immediate effect of making the different contents relatively interdependent.

Le Monde, which is a very prestigious newspaper, has a political line that is, in certain respects, coherent, and a style of its own. Let us look at how it discusses psychoanalysis. In a review of a play by Montherlant, its theatre critic writes:

> . . .Not all diseases require fresh air . . . For some aberrations of the heart and the senses, silence is a better form of therapy than the babble of psychoanalysis. We can see where that will get us: effusiveness on a grand scale, epidemics and the frenzy of, for example, Sartre's *Saint Genet*.[13]

The book reviewer Monsieur C. praises Etiemble for having 'got over' psychoanalysis, and Marxism. In an article on psychiatry, in contrast, psychoanalysis is described in terms that are both concrete and sympathetic; both its fields of action and the importance of Freud's theoretical contribution are described.[14] The film critic assumes that it is possible to explain the personality of Greta Garbo in psychoanalytic terms. Yet the same critic remarks ironically of a film director that:

> After having conformed, like everyone else, to Freudianism on film, he now seems to want to get back to less gratuitous stories.[15]

[13] *Le Monde*, 21 August 1952.
[14] Ibid., 26 July 1956.
[15] Ibid., 22 November 1952.

The music critic Monsieur R.D. sometimes welcomes with interest the possibility of a psychoanalytic interpretation of musical works, and reproduces in detail the way P.-J. Jouve uses events in the composer's life to explain the subject-matter of Mozart's *Don Giovanni*. When he evokes the life and personality of Chopin and the way he compares artistic creativity with physical love, he says that the great composer elaborated a Freudian theory long before Freud. In other rubrics, journalists stress the therapeutic benefits of psychoanalysis, its contribution to modern culture and even to our understanding of characters in novels; elsewhere it serves as a backdrop to attempts to explain certain murders.

The confusion created by these convergent and divergent opinions about psychoanalysis, which results from the clash between multiple and specialized visions, reveals the existence of the variable limits that are placed upon these fluctuating judgements. We can scarcely speak, in this case, of contradictions or dichotomies; we are talking about a non-systematization, about the absence of any need to formalize the representation of psychoanalysis. The most contradictory judgements can be found in the same publication, and sometimes under the byline of the same writer. In *Les Nouvelles littéraires et scientifiques* we find various critics advancing the following propositions:

'The meaning of true melancholia is neither psychoanalytic nor psychiatric, and it can only be revealed by the spiritual.'[16] 'These vulgar psychoanalytic remarks about Stendhal.'[17] 'The most twisted of our psychoanalysts are like gloomy fusspots . . . the muddy curiosities found by the prospectors of the unconscious'.[18]

Elsewhere, we read in a review of a children's book:

I will not say what surprised me in these pages about school and psychoanalysis. One author is terribly sorry about the latter. As a judgement, that is hasty and a little superficial.[19]

Le Monde's film critic, who often mocks psychoanalysis, writes: 'The rich hate the poor, but when they die there is a reversal of opinion which only psychoanalysis can explain.'[20] *Le Monde* is neither anti-American nor hostile to psychoanalysis, but we can find in its pages some very cutting

[16] *Les Nouvelles littéraires*, 24 April 1952.
[17] Ibid., 19 January 1952.
[18] Ibid., 17 April 1952.
[19] Ibid., 24 January 1952.
[20] *Le Monde*, 28 February 1952.

comments about the violation of certain principles, and especially that of art for art's sake or of the autonomy of specific activities:

> M. W.S. is, they say, twenty-seven. His understanding of the human heart is, it appears, astonishing. The book is mainly formulaic and uses the techniques found in baggy novels; there is some padding and an awful lot of tedious nonsense. The world of dreams and all the various frustrations are clichés that have become as inelegant as the word 'hysteria', which was once used to mean the same thing. Characters in a gloomy bed certainly need psychoanalysis; it replaces the religion they are looking for in the wrong place: in barbiturates, whisky and in substitutes for sex.

One can also see that the flowering of disparate and discontinuous directions is due to the coexistence of separate worlds of values. Besides more or less clearly defined positions one often finds allusions or incidents. The journal as a whole, whether it is *Le Monde*, *France-Soir* or *Elle*, avoids taking too visible a stand in relation to psychoanalysis or a related and unitary rule of behaviour. At the same time, it leaves to the public, the receiver, a certain freedom of orientation.

So far, we have examined those properties of diffusion that are constituted during the attempt to adapt publications to their readers. We have found that this form of communication leaves readers some freedom to make up their own minds. We now have to look at its influence on behaviour. In the absence of any direct information, we can turn to observations and information supplied by other studies:

> There is a proverbial saying to the effect that it is the unexpected that happens. Since what happens makes news, it follows, or seems to, that news is always or mainly concerned with the unusual and the unexpected. Even the most trivial happening, it seems, provided it represents a departure from the customary ritual and routine of daily life, is likely to be reported in the press. This conception of news has been confirmed by those editors who, in the competition for circulation and for advertising, have sought to make their papers smart and interesting, where they could not be invariably either informing or thrilling. In their efforts to instil into the minds of reporters and correspondents the importance of looking everywhere and always for something that would excite, amuse or shock its readers, news editor have put into circulation some interesting examples of what the Germans, borrowing an expression from Homer, have called *geflügelte Wörter*, 'winged words'. The epigram describing news which has winged its way over more territory and is repeated more often than any other is this: 'Dog bites man' – that is not news. But 'Man bites dog' – that is. *Nota bene!* It is not the intrinsic importance of an event that makes it newsworthy. It is rather the fact that the event is so unusual that if published it will either startle, amuse or otherwise excite the reader so that it will be remembered and repeated. For news is always

finally, what Charles A. Dana described it to be, 'something that will make
people talk', even when it does not make them act. (Park 1955: 80–1)

As we have just described, the news published in the press has no influence on morals or political actions. It tends to disperse and distract our attention, and therefore to reduce tension, rather than to increase it. The usual function of the news is to keep individuals and societies thinking along certain lines and to keep them in touch with the world and with reality. Making some minor adjustments is a small price to pay. 'It is not its function ordinarily to initiate secular social movements which, when they move too quickly, bring about catastrophic consequence' (Park 1955: 140). Parts of Park's description of the press and the news are applicable to diffusion. They corroborate our observations of relations between behaviour and the messages that are sent out: articles about psychoanalysis are not intended to make everyone react to it in the same way: they want to talk about it, and to get people talking about it.

This mode of exposition tends to bring about a gradual adaptation to psychoanalytic ideas rather than an acceptance of the whole of psychoanalysis. When psychoanalysis is recommended, it is always with very specific goals in mind: migraine, obesity or dysmenorrhoea. A serious weekly advises us that 'Cellulite can be . . . psychoanalysed'. The injunctions are always cautious. Psychoanalysis is never recommended on its own. The reader is 'free' to make up his or her own mind.

One might wonder about the effectiveness of a form of communication that leaves its receivers to draw their own conclusions and to make their own decisions. As we have noted, positive and negative arguments can coexist within the same article. A few experiments suggest some useful answers to the questions we are asking (Hovland, Lumsdaine and Sheffield 1949). During the war, soldiers were shown arguments 'for' and 'against' the same problems. It transpired that, when they were fairly well informed, 'for and against' films were more effective at provoking a favourable reaction than one-sided films. This phenomenon was then explored systematically. It was found that changes of opinion were more marked when the receivers of the messages drew *their own* conclusions on the basis of what had been communicated to them. The apparent non-involvement of the sender – which is the case with diffusion – also has implications at the level of opinions. A text presented by an 'uninvolved' orator is more likely to change opinions than the same text read by an orator who is 'involved' in its content. The findings from these experiments make an important contribution to the understanding of the form of communications we are studying here. We have seen that magazines or newspapers are not or do not appear to be 'involved in' psychoanalysis. On the contrary, they make an obvious attempt to distance themselves from it. What they are communicating can therefore have a major impact on the readership's image of psychoanalysis, irrespective of whether the author of the article is or is not expressing a personal opinion. Although it cannot be demonstrated directly, we can infer that, in the case of *Le Monde*, as in that of other newspapers, articles on this theory have a real influence precisely because the points of view expressed are autonomous, because they change and because they have no obvious intentions or marked preferences for any particular mode of behaviour.

The effectiveness we have just mentioned is of course bound up with the view that objectivity is conditional upon the existence of multiple perspectives. That is the objectivity, or the external appearance of objectivity, that the publications we have studied strive to achieve.

All this presupposes that, whilst it does not, on the whole, seek to promote specific behaviours, diffusion is not without its effects. That is only to be expected, but it is important to make the point specifically. Its effects must be compared with those of other forms of communication. Are they proportional to a newspaper or magazine's *circulation*? The answer to that question is negative. Relatively recent research (Lazarsfeld, Berelson and Gaudet 1944) demonstrates that a local newspaper addressing a specific group – farmers – had more influence on electoral behaviour than a much more widely read paper addressing a broader readership. An earlier study (Lundberg 1926: 712–13) showed that the correlation between the opinions of the paper and those of its readers was fairly weak. The author concluded that a modern commercial paper has little direct influence on its readers' opinions about questions pertaining to the common interest. It probably tries to reflect those opinions, rather than to influence them. The stance a paper adopts with respect to questions pertaining to the common interest has a negligible influence on readers' choice of paper. We have, then, two series of hypotheses: (a) the way the message is presented when it is diffused can have an effect on behaviour; (b) there is no correlation between the circulation of a means of diffusion and its effects on specific problems. In order to arrive at a better understanding of the correlation between diffusion and behaviour, it may be advisable to introduce other considerations of a more specific nature. This form of communication is not highly institutionalized; it appears, that is, to be a reflection of its readership rather than an expression of an organized group.

When an organized group formulates a point of view, it also brings concrete pressure to bear because the press is not its only means of communication. *L'Humanité*, *La Pensée catholique* or *Aspects de la France* are at once newspapers and real organs; they are institutions controlled by parties or religious or political groups. Their verbal content is no more than one aspect of the messages they send out. In a society like ours, individuals belong to several publics and groups simultaneously. Mass-circulation papers – and how 'mass-circulation' is defined depends upon the domain we are looking at – always try to avoid offending religious or political values associated with well-defined groups. There is some interference, but it is more insidious, less direct and less deliberate. As Park notes, they are more concerned with getting people to talk than with getting them to do something. Diffusion in fact has little power to mobilize, and how people behave is of little importance. The discontinuity of the texts published on psychoanalysis and the caution with which advice is given show that they are designed to make suggestions or to hint at behaviours that are possible, but never necessary or imperative.

We are now in a position to describe the essential features of diffusion:

- The source of the communication does not display any clearly defined intentions and has no sustained orientation.
- What is communicated is designed to influence certain *particular* behaviours, but it does not emphasize the link between what is communicated and those behaviours; the relationship between the two is incidental.
- The sender tends to become an expression of the receiver.
- Both sender and receiver are defined in very general and therefore imprecise terms.
- The receiver – the audience – does not constitute a highly structured or oriented group.
- The object of the communication is handled in such a way as to maintain a certain distance between the sender and what is communicated; this apparent non-involvement permits and presupposes a degree of freedom that allows the source that sends the message to adjust it to its audience.
- Different messages from the same source remain relatively autonomous, as we can see from their discontinuity.
- Although it is not a form of communication with the overt aim of producing specific behaviours, diffusion can be effective.

The features we have just outlined provide only a partial explanation for the links that are established, within this system of communication, between a publication and its readership. Whilst we have to note the autonomy of those elements of the content concerning psychoanalysis in the newspapers and magazines studied, it would be a mistake to conclude that the 'relationship' between them is not organized. In order to explain how it is organized, we will take the example of the women's weekly *Elle*, whose goal is to promote a lofty ideal, happiness, by recommending a conventional moderation that takes the uncomplicated form of beauty, health and success. The advisory role the weekly has taken on obliges it to master a whole range of key solutions that are accessible to all levels of society.

One's health can be compromised by persistent and reversible disorders that can be imputed to particular psychological states: hence the recourse to psychotherapy or psychosomatic medicine. Both physical imperfections and inequalities at the level of social success give rise to 'complexes', or arise because of them. Psychoanalysis, or psychotherapy, can provide a remedy. In the United States, the spread of psychoanalysis has led to its abuse. A sense of proportion implies that less should be said about it. In the course of our content analysis of the 64 issues of *Elle* published between 1 January 1952 and 9 April 1953, we found, as we have already seen, 63 references to psychoanalytic concepts, or roughly one reference in each issue. Psychoanalytic theory makes an *explicit* appearance on only twelve occasions. The difference between what is expressed implicitly and explicitly is significant. The implicit use of psychoanalysis is a reflection of the fact that it constitutes an interpretative system for the journalists themselves. At the same time, a good number of ideas and suggestions can be offered without taking into account the attitudes of either the magazine or its readers towards psychoanalysis. Images and notions that derive from psychoanalysis can therefore circulate without being directly related to their theoretical background. Not one in-depth article is devoted to psychoanalysis. It is therefore used mainly as a conceptual underpinning for psychosomatic medicine.

As we have seen, psychoanalysis is usually not mentioned. But psychoanalytic terms and models are to be found in *Elle*, especially in the articles on education. The terms are also used in banal contexts such as the lonely-hearts column, where complexes flourish. This is a linguistic usage. Although psychoanalysis is, for *Elle*, a standard conceptual framework, there is no shortage of irony, warnings and caveats about the abuse of psychoanalysis (especially in the United States) or of allusions to the fashion for psychoanalysis. 'Complexes are in fashion.' Which raises a smile. The most frequently used psychoanalytic words are, in order, complex, unconscious, repression and neurosis. Much the same order of frequency was found in our survey. Whilst psychoanalysis enjoys a certain prestige as a mode of understanding, it remains interchangeable at the level of therapy: 'The diagnosis of skin complaints has improved and, thanks to psychosomatics (treatment through analysis or suggestion), we have a solution for most nervous troubles'.[21]

Despite the adoption of a vision of psychical activity, no specific or definite behaviour is recommended. The use of an *implicit* representation that is shared by both the weekly and its readership makes communication possible. This avoids a potential clash with those factions of the readership that might, for political or religious reasons, have particular views on psychoanalysis. When it is discussed explicitly, a form of 'equilibrium-accountancy' is used. The basic normative principle is the golden mean, moderation. This is, above all, a principle that is widespread amongst the middle classes. It also features in this encounter with diversity, and in the way a readership with multiple orientations compensates for it. This moderation takes the form of a piece of advice: don't overdo it and look

[21] *Elle*, October 1952.

for order. As *France-Soir* notes, attempts are being made to follow this advice:

> It was about thirty years ago that psychoanalysis and Freud's vocabulary (much of which is still with us) began to be talked about outside medical circles. As this third of the century draws to a close and at a time when the young science is being applied to anything and everything, enjoys excessive fame, and is sometimes fashionable, it seems appropriate to take our bearings.[22]

All the techniques appear in a single sentence. An attempt is made to produce a distancing effect by making a distinction between psychoanalysis and Freud's vocabulary. The idea of abuse or of the absence of any controls is expressed by talk of it being 'applied to anything and everything'. A more reasonable approach is required. Its youth means that psychoanalysis can be forgiven for many of its mistakes. The elaboration of a moderate vision of the theory is facilitated by the parallel – and the contrast – drawn between its excesses and the level-headedness of mature reflection.

If we recall the examples cited, we are now in a position to understand the 'accounting' process. One reader is advised not to think in terms of complexes or of psychoanalytic schemata (such as that of neurotic fixation). But *Elle's* writers do not shy away from making a very loose use of similar schemata and the vocabulary of psychoanalysis. They naturally assert that exaggerations about psychoanalysis are commonplace in the United States. Yet the weekly *Elle* still celebrates psychoanalysis's encounter with astrology, and insists that the former gives its official backing to the latter. The twofold nature of the compromise and of the norm of moderation becomes extremely clear. The readership does not really know how to react because the same article gives both the arguments for and the arguments against, and both violates and respects the norm of moderation. It talks about complexes, but the discussion is restricted to the inferiority complex, and no mention is made of the Oedipus complex. Repression is an explanatory concept, but the article goes no further than that: what is repressed? There are no direct allusions to the drives, the libido or sexuality. General morality is never in any danger. Children are said to have affective needs, and early childhood is said to be important. There is no systematic explanation of why this should be the case, and there is no mention of either the different stages or the origins of affective traumas. There is no description of analytic therapy itself. Scattered propositions hint at a particular vision of psychoanalysis,[23] and everyday expressions are used to 'dress up' analytic ideas with

---

[22] *France-Soir*, 13 February 1953.
[23] For reasons of economy in the present work, we will not make an *internal* examination of the content of these figures. I hope to explain the relations, significance and coherence of the text, and to interpret them in non-functional terms, in a subsequent volume.

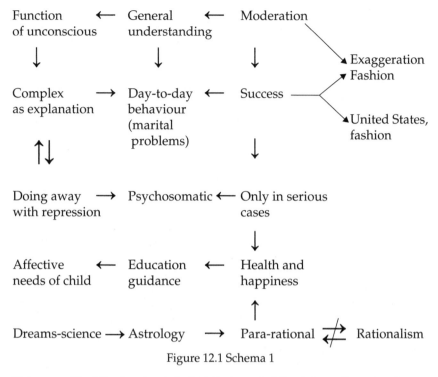

Figure 12.1 Schema 1

We have used the following signs to indicate the type of relation between the various themes:

Π = implication, implies;
= = equivalence of propositions, interchangeability;
⇆ = reciprocal implication, circular relationship;
≠ = opposition.

specific connotations. Nevertheless, there is a characteristic organizing schema of themes and messages in the weekly *Elle*.

An examination of this schema in figure 12.1 tells us a great deal about the structure of the social models specific to diffusion.

Even if the occurrence of the themes presupposes that they are autonomous, indeed even opposed, their links are not absent, simply aleatory.

We find in every line of *Elle*'s model a domain (psychosomatic education etc.) in which one type of explanation predominates (unconscious, complex, repression, etc.). The first column contains 'explanatory' schemata illustrating the content of psychoanalysis. We observe that there is a discontinuity between those assertions based upon a psychoanalytic mechanism and 'the affective needs of childhood'. Questions about education and the applications of psychoanalysis are in fact implicit and distinct from those we find in the other rubrics. The second column deals with instrumental aspects. The third column contains imperatives or values relating to the instrumental use of psychoanalysis. The directional arrow (←) shows that these moral precepts imply that there are limits to the various applications of psychoanalysis, and that they are not inherent in them. The final column deals with 'exaggerations' or notions that come into conflict with the weekly's values. The meaning of the links is not always the same. Explanations that invoke 'the unconscious' or 'overcoming repression' are, for example, effects of the function of the unconscious. But 'explaining in terms of complexes' and 'overcoming repression' do not appear in any particular order.

The links we have just described are *implicit* or latent. Their interweaving and meaning cannot be understood in every particular case. The connection between the themes can be described as *aleatory*, as opposed to other connections and models which are, as we shall see, relatively systematic, explicit and necessary. Such thematic relations can be described as communicational *regularities*; they have a general validity but can also fluctuate to an appreciable extent. This has one remarkable effect: the way the units of analysis (themes and links) are organized in the message-schemata specific to diffusion produces an open set with poorly defined contours. Different versions of the same model cannot be superimposed and they are not congruent, as their elements enjoy the autonomy we have already described. They are therefore *mobile*. It is, on the other hand, possible to understand the features we have described if we recall that, in the communications system that concerns us, the social model is constructed as though it were the *resultant* of heterogeneous trends relating to certain principles – such as moderation – and not a starting point that can regulate the content transmitted by the sender to the receiver as happens in, for instance, propagation and propaganda. Ultimately, information about a socially pertinent object can be diffused without it being possible to detect a schema that organizes the message, or even in the absence of a social model. Despite the high number of articles in which psychoanalysis is mentioned in a newspaper as important as *Le Monde*, it can scarcely be said that either its image, the role that is generally ascribed to it, or the behavioural norms have any coherence. The same applies to *Le Parisien libéré* and *Paris-Presse*. The communication is purely sequential; it is difficult to grasp any context that might allow us to identify with any certainty the function of the themes and links capable of promoting or giving their readership any impression of totality.

2 Rhetoric to the Fore

Psychoanalysis is diffused in various repetitive ways by a non-coordinated multiplicity of sources of information. It is not always directly apparent in them. A content analysis demonstrates that explicit references to its content constitute no more than a small part of the articles that are published.

Articles centred on psychoanalysis	22%
Use of simple psychoanalytic terms	28%
Use of concepts but no mention of psychoanalysis	8%
Use of concepts with mention of psychoanalysis	30%
Description of psychoanalysis, but no use of concepts	7%
Terms misused	5%

The content of the communications tends to be 'segmental' because the message is made up mainly of words (complex, repression, psychoanalysis, unconscious) and propositions which may or may not be 'accidental'. We are therefore dealing with elements, segments and indices rather than texts organized around a psychoanalytically inspired subject. The reiteration of these segments, either in the same form or with some modifications, and their transmission to various rubrics by the most disparate of means, leads to a *latent* learning process that facilitates an understanding of something specific to psychoanalysis, or something that is attributed to it, even in the absence of specific information. The constant appearance of the various themes that an individual comes across in his usual paper or periodical, at the cinema or in the course of a conversation makes it possible to generalize and organize the segments of the content communicated; as a result, they become established in the cognitive and linguistic field. As each of these themes is reinforced, a sort of *sign* becomes established; it belongs both to psychoanalysis and the communication, because it is produced by the latter. The diversity of the sources and their degree of extension help to outline a structure, a halo, a model or a representational kernel that subtends the sign's usage. We could even delineate the domains to which it is attached. Examples might include 'complex' in advertising and 'psychoanalysis' in what might be termed psychoanalytic 'folklore'.

The fusion of a psychoanalytic concept and an advertising slogan presupposes not only that the public can relate the concept to an underlying representation, but also the hope that it can motivate a specific form of behaviour. Advertising must hold our attention, if only so that we can note the effectiveness of its impact. If we look at its effectiveness, we find that its interest lies in the cultural regularities that it reveals rather than in the behaviours it inspires. When repeated in a hundred unexpected ways, the slogan 'X whiteness', for example, has not only the desired effect but also side effects, because it becomes a habitual communicational formula that extends far beyond the circle of people who are truly interested in product X. When its extension reaches this point, the proposition becomes a brand or a sign of the cultural, linguistic and cognitive habits of Paris or France during a certain period. 'No more complexes' is a phrase from the same category, which a chlorophyll toothpaste chose for the adverts it placed in several newspapers, the best known and most widely read being *Le Parisien libéré*.[24] Even the names of products can incorporate psychoanalytic terms. The weekly *Noir et blanc* sings the praises of a beauty cream called 'Libido'.[25] 'Libido de toilette' is a phrase that captures the imagination and cheerfully expands its horizons. 'Complex' has, however, a greater market value and seems to be more suggestive. A 'Complex Cream', for example, promised to provide a remedy for the distressing existence of aesthetic and psychological ailments. All the major women's weeklies carried adverts for it. The copy in *Marie-France* read:

> 'From scientific complex to psychological complex.' 'Complex Cream nourishes the skin. Its ingredients mean that it is a truly scientific complex.'[26]

A slogan does not need to be explicit to have a value, but it should be pointed out that the repetition of 'complex' suggests that the product can remedy a failure to apply a proper cream. On other occasions, 'complex' is mentioned more because it is a point of attraction, or a linguistic formula that has some prestige, a broader representation and connotations that conjure up lots of images:

> 'Martine has got rid of her complexes.' 'Martine was consumed with fears and "complexes", to use the fashionable term. One day, just to see, I bought a packet of X to wash my stockings. Ever since, they've been fine and I've got rid of my complex about having ladders . . . I bought all the X products one after the other . . . and I noticed that my complexes were gradually going away.'[27]

This text appeared in *France-Soir*, a daily that is a major support for French advertising. Product X's therapeutic propensities presuppose a certain – and somewhat threatening – image of psychoanalysis and complexes, and that propensity becomes more pronounced when the discussion turns to 'psychological' institutions. In 1957, *Constellation*'s readers learned that:

> Symptoms do not lie! You probably 'have' complexes . . . if you tend to put everything off until tomorrow and if you lose confidence in yourself too easily and so on. Don't paralyse yourself. Follow the X method of psychological training . . . [you] will quickly become able to pull down the wall of complexes that is blocking your vital impulses. All your inabilities will certainly be swept aside by the flood of the immense resources that slumber inside you, and your complexes will be annihilated. In only a few months,

[24] *Le Parisien libéré*, 14 February 1952.
[25] *Noir et blanc*, 17 November 1952.
[26] *Marie-France*, 10 March 1952.
[27] *France-Soir*, 23 January 1952.

method X will make you a superior man. Your complexes, shyness and hesitations will be rapidly swept away.[28]

We have already encountered this image of psychoanalysis in our description of the findings of our survey: it is viewed as a technique that can set an individual's potential free, and it is indeed this image of the psychical organization that the term 'complex' is associated with. The persistence and widespread nature of this preoccupation, which centres on the release of an inner power and control over one's destiny goes hand in hand with a vision of a conflict in which everyone is damaged, alienated and prevented from developing in accordance with their own lines of force by the major and minor accidents recorded in a biography that is constantly being rewritten. 'Complex' and 'psychoanalysis' have been inscribed in this tradition of preoccupations.

Given the limited number of questions a group or any human group asks itself, the essential characteristic of an answer is its ability to select, from an infinite number of possible solutions, the one that is least dubious, and therefore least likely to change. It is as though, having always been faced with the same difficulties, humanity was constantly mistaken about its ability to find lasting solutions. When humanity begins to fulfil its childhood dreams, a problem, the solution to it and all the elements that cluster around it form, in any given culture and in relation to a specific object, a *synchrasia* to which it constantly returns and which helps to establish the contours of the culture in question. We speak, for example, of the Dionysian nature of the Greek *polis* or of the possibility that any individual can scale the heights of the social hierarchy of the United States. This community of themes and ideals belonging to a collectivity can perhaps be detected at a less global level. The complex, through the way advertising uses it by weaving it into this impulse towards development and freedom, by substituting a liberating product for a liberating therapy, is one of these synchrasia, and its importance should not be underestimated. Its diffusion has given it a meaning and a role, and when we find it being adapted to suit every case, we are no longer surprised to find that it is tailor-made for describing the quality of a personality, or that a cream, a soap or method X can clean it up or, rather, sweep it away. A consensus as to its qualities has been reached, despite the communicational discontinuity or the disparity of the sources. When it is associated with messages that are designed to be effective, psychoanalysis is diffused thanks to the insinuations of a folklore centred upon it. Because it attempts to get as close as possible to the public, diffusion strives to resemble *informal* forms of communication such as rumour and transmission by word of mouth. The function of this 'unverified' news, these 'bits of gossip' and these humorous

---

[28] *Constellation*, November 1957.

items is to create a relaxed mood of intimate contact based upon insinuations whose significance extends far beyond their literal meaning. The representation of the object, or of the world, emerges from this folklore of
stories that are true and stories that are not true. Given that a story is also
a picture or reproduction of a situation or encounter, the psychoanalyst
replaces psychoanalysis. The image becomes personified.

Being both the psychiatrist's heir and the promoter of a theory in which
anything strange is an expression of the inverted world of madness, the
psychoanalyst is a creature with a 'particular' perspective:

> A psychoanalyst tells a lady who has confided that she never quarrelled with
> her husband: 'How strange; in that case, you certainly weren't made for one
> another.'[29]

The Freudian concept of conflict undergoes an expected transformation,
and the psychoanalyst's comments reveal the bewilderment of someone
who spends his life dealing with anomalies and problems that make
harmony look like a distant prospect. This shows in the way he behaves,
and it is not the way most of us behave:

> A psychoanalyst was invited to lunch by friends and welcomed into their
> country house. When his hosts gathered around the table they had set up in
> the grounds, he went into the house, locked the door and watched them
> through the keyhole.[30]

When he goes from the garden into the house, he is not just going in the
opposite direction to his hosts; this is a condensed image of the analyst. He
is someone 'in the house' who avoids fresh air and the garden, and
someone whose curiosity implies not only isolation, but also indiscretion.
The keyhole and his tactlessness complete the picture of a man who is not
so much eccentric as asocial. He is also someone who watches:

> A psychoanalyst is a gentleman who, when he goes to the Folies-Bergères,
> passionately watches the audience.[31]

Anyone who has been in analysis will concretize the findings of psychoanalysis in his or her own way. Because it is a 'talking' therapy, its
effects are restricted to the *meaning* of behaviours and do not affect their
material structure. The concepts gradually change: suggestion and auto-
suggestion remain secondary to this action at the level of meaning.

---

[29] *France-Soir*, 11 October 1952.
[30] *Témoignage Chrétien*, 3 February 1956.
[31] *Images du monde*, 10 December 1955.

Psychoanalytic interpretation becomes a 'question of interpretation', and the importance of the relationship between the symptom and the patient's general behaviour becomes both a caricatural statement of a serious idea and an assertion that psychoanalysis cannot reach any convincing conclusions.

Paris-Presse once gave the title 'Appel de Freud' ['Freud Calling'] to the 'true' story of an actor who could not sleep and who declared:

> Psychoanalysis cured me. Ever since, I have stayed awake all night so as to remind myself of how much I used to suffer from insomnia.[32]

People who go into analysis or who are preparing to do so are not spared these joking criticisms, and the total subjectification of our imperfections is a choice target:

> One day, a man went to consult a psychoanalyst and told him: 'Doctor, I suffer from terrible inferiority complexes. I feel that way when I'm with my boss.' A few weeks later, the psychoanalyst makes his diagnosis: 'You don't have a complex, sir. You're just inferior.'[33]

Incongruous situations are the psychoanalyst's lot, as we see from the joke about the lady who is talking to a psychoanalyst in the consulting room:

> 'Allow me to introduce you to my husband, doctor – he's one of the men I had occasion to talk to you about.'[34]

Does psychoanalysis have to be explicitly present in these jokes? No. It takes only a hint to provide the immediate context and to reveal the meaning. *Paris-Presse* published a short piece entitled 'Freud'. The text can be understood immediately.

> There's a story about an old MP who is dreaming. He dreams that he is making a speech to the House. When he wakes up, he is making a speech to the House.[35]

The thread leading from Freud to the dream is a slender one, but it is that thread that makes us laugh at this overlap between sleep and wakefulness, desire and action, and the real and the symbolic. The hint of irony shifts from the man who falls asleep on his feet and the comic combination of the dream and the real, to the negation of both and to the transmutation that

[32] *Paris-Presse*, 1 November 1952.
[33] *Elle*, 22 September 1952.
[34] *Les Lettres françaises*, 27 June 1952.
[35] *Paris-Presse*, 16 August 1952.

occurs when every term in the joke says something other than what is being said. It is the elliptical transition from one proposition to the next that leaves this room for manoeuvre, as the sequence itself is a fusion. America, which is the adoptive country of psychoanalysis, receives its due. Speaking of the extension of the theory to the United States we are told about:

> The reflection of a woman sitting in front of her mirror who noticed that her tongue was chalky and wondered: 'Should I take a purge, or should I phone my psychoanalyst?'[36]

A cartoonist, finally, mocks some of the ludicrous over-simplifications of the 'drawing room psychoanalysts' who interpret dream symptoms:

> 'Doctor', says the patient, 'In my dreams, I see great sides of bleeding meat.' 'What is your profession?' 'I'm a butcher.'

Certain linguistic associations encourage relaxation. One column is headed 'Freud's corner'. It begins: 'One American in twelve is in danger of going mad, and Freud Boulevard is the busiest in Hollywood.'[37]

The psychoanalyst, the patient and the United States are this folklore's main 'characters'. Meeting them in a world where the unusual has become usual makes us smile. The comedy springs from an unexpected challenge to what was the object of a consensus. Thus constituted, these jokes do no more than take over the schemata used in the countless 'lunatic jokes'. Based upon shared opinions which are limited but tenacious, they follow the lines traced by other synchrasias. It would be a mistake to confuse them with the norms or values of a group. First, because they are not fundamental or directive in nature and, second, because they are partial and concern only particular aspects of the representation of an object, or part of the content that is being diffused. When it addresses its readers, a newspaper uses 'channels' that have been prepared in advance, and paths we already know. A synchrasia can reveal itself in language – 'complex' – or folklore – the pre-existing schema of 'lunatic stories'. As we shall see, it can also be structured around an object, namely psychoanalysis. This facilitates the adaptation of sender to receiver, as both parties can to some extent predict the content of the message and its repercussions. By the same criterion, every element finds a ready-made context, even though it is fragmentary. The exchange that takes place between a 'segmentary' content and a cultural synchrasia is functional. The former sustains the impression of novelty (which may be either real or false), whilst the latter avoids

---

[36] *Franc-Tireur*, 7 January 1954.
[37] *La Tribune de Saint-Etienne*, 4 November 1955.

conflict by integrating the content into a familiar framework. Jokes about psychoanalysts are, it is true, constructed on the basis of relatively well known schemata, but they become 'psychoanalytic' jokes because they reveal unfamiliar connections. When the cure is seen as a stage at which the patient assumes responsibility for his symptoms, a new perspective is adopted: the kernel of the complex now lies in the conflict. The outcome of psychoanalysis is seen as an *internal* modification of the personality. A collective consensus is a form of synchrasia. We find three main examples pertaining to psychoanalysis: (a) the adequacy of psychoanalysis for dealing with the problems posed by children; (b) its therapeutic role; and (c) its relationship with the United States, and with American films in particular. Until a certain point, these consensuses applied to *all* the press. From 1950 onwards, only the third still had a 'universal' value because it was the only one to which all publications, including Communist publications, subscribed. Discussing these problems in one way or another did not raise any difficulties: journalists knew that they would automatically be in agreement with their readers. The stylistic formulae were widely used. There was no need to cite psychoanalysis because the text always contained an idea that was assumed to be acceptable to the reader:

> A child who leaves its mother's breast experiences an emotional shock. This produces a sort of complex between the 'frustrated animal' and the violent desire of a young child looking for some compensation.[38]

> How should you bring up your baby? If you want to get off to a good start, the following are banned: tiredness, 'the dumps', 'excessive' strictness, and 'complexes'.[39]

> Running away is also the result of a complex, but it is often hard to discover . . . You have to look for its antecedents, search your unconscious . . . find the origins of a moral trauma or an obsession that has been forgotten but which is still active.[40]

> The important thing is to allow the child to develop its personality freely; doing away with the sources of the complexes.[41]

It would be pointless to go on giving more examples. They all denote an interest in the problems posed by childhood, and constantly use psychoanalytically inspired schemata and notions. The explanation for this is clear: the Freudian conception of psychical development attributes great

---

[38] *Marie-France*, 21 January 1952.
[39] *Elle*, 8 October 1952.
[40] *Libération*, 21 May 1951.
[41] *Elle*, 15 September 1952.

importance to these problems, and few other theories in this domain have its degree of systematization.

There is, finally, a universal hostility to some aspects of the American lifestyle and to the use of psychoanalytic schemata in American films:

> A madman wants to commit suicide, but waits fourteen hours before doing so. A completely botched film . . . the rubbish talked by the duty psychoanalyst cannot do anything to bring this puppet to life. The film is really about the hysteria and sadism that are fuelled by the press, radio and television in the United States.[42]

> This childish film demonstrates yet again the extent to which Americans are being brain-washed by psychoanalysis.[43]

> Why does the hero want to commit suicide? We never find out, despite the brief explanations which, in the good old American tradition, blame the Oedipus complex and a few other complexes into the bargain.[44]

> The screenplay makes far too much of the vaguely psychoanalytic clichés that have been all the rage in Hollywood since the war. We are not spared the inevitable mention of psychoanalysis and the badly dissolved Oedipus complex. Hollywood really is frightened of mystery.[45]

In 72 per cent of the film reviews that take psychoanalysis into consideration, the theme that is unsympathetically associated with it is 'Americanism'. This is because only the American film industry encourages the making of films with a psychoanalytic theme.

The articles converge around specific points because they are all in the same objective situation with respect to that discipline or another collectivity, or because the various sources of information and the groups that use them share the same opinions. Similarly, there is, as our survey demonstrates, a definite consensus between the press and its readership. The regularities we have observed, and our culture's synchrasias, have, however, a limited impact because, at the level of the transmission and exchange of the propositions that delineate them, they are also the source of the same communication's *opacity* to the extent that they make us forget their contextual diversity. Whilst *Le Monde* or *Le Parisien libéré* uses a film as an excuse to criticize American cinema, *Les Lettres françaises* uses it to criticize the entire American way of life, and its criticisms are no more than one element in a more general rejection of psychoanalysis and the United States.

[42] *Les Lettres françaises*, 24 January 1952.
[43] *Le Monde*, 11 February 1953.
[44] *Marie-France*, 18 February 1952.
[45] *Le Parisien libéré*, 15 February 1952.

Communicability and its opposite emerge spontaneously. When a content is being diffused, the message is often far from being the key to it or a code for it, and the consensus is usually sustained by a *literal* understanding, or by the communicational effectiveness of the literal. The fit between the press and its readership, the adequacy of the image of the one to the image of the other, and to that of the groups that make up the press *and* its readership, presuppose the existence of synchrasias that can initiate a dialogue and hold the attention without immediately giving rise to either agreement or disagreement, which leaves both parties free to either accept or reject the content. As we have already said, diffusion requires both this margin of uncertainty and the ability to make contact with the readerships easily by taking the line of least resistance. At the same time, it strives to make the object that is being diffused familiar, and to ground it in social reality. Psychoanalysis – which is at once a theory, a representation and a noun – takes its place amongst all the other geological strata that will one day reveal what our era looked like. As it must be no more than moderately disturbing, psychoanalysis is described as something déjà vu and, because it is not disturbing, its novelty is purely relative. Ultimately, psychoanalytic models and psychoanalytic language have a *contemporary* style but are impregnated with old notions and images. The contrast between the cultural style and the synchrasia, and between the form and the content that are being communicated, is striking. And journalists are not shy about pointing this out for the benefit of anyone who might be interested:

> Saint-Beuve loved Adèle Hugo. This tenderness makes the opening pages of his *Port-Royal* languid. We would now call it transference. Or perhaps, to put it more simply, an attempt to forget.[46]

> He only uses this pompous term to impress. Had he lived in the last century, he would, like Balzac, have written a 'physiology'. It's just a question of fashion.[47]

These comments from *Aspects de la France* refer to a book that is described as a 'Psychoanalysis of France'. A few lines later, the author offers his own psychoanalytic interpretation of French history:

> I accept that my demand is idiotic: a film that could provide an analysis, I should say a psychoanalysis of a great man in the form of an image. I even admit that such a study is a matter for specialists alone.[48]

> We should psychoanalyse . . . why the jargon? Analyse is quite enough.[49]

[46] *Le Monde*, 15 February 1952.
[47] *Aspects de la France*, 5 August 1955.
[48] Ibid.
[49] *Rivarol*, 8 August 1952.

This is the indeterminacy that hangs over the transmission of segments of a content: we cannot tell if they are names that are meant to return a sparkle to a collective consensus, or parts of a whole which is being referred to. Is this uncertainty accidental, or is it an essential feature of the structure of diffusion?

3 Language, the Fiction of Communication and Impregnation

The elaboration of messages and their adequacy for specific cultural regularities, the effects we have been discussing, imply a recognition of the mediating role of diffusion between social groups and their systems of values, and between them and psychoanalysis. That mediation can, however, take very different forms.

In order to explore those forms in more detail, we can introduce a useful distinction between the *instrumental* and *consumerist* functions of communication. The instrumentality of communication is defined by the existence of a relationship between the behaviour or symptoms it seeks to induce and the sender's image of his objectives. Communication is a means of action whose goals are made clear enough to orient the content of what is being transmitted to others. The act of communicating acquires a particular dignity because a relationship must be established between the sender and the receiver. Consumerism presupposes a form of communication that is an end in itself because it is a self-sufficient activity. Its results and influence have nothing to do with the specificity of its contents, which are, up to a point, of secondary importance. Communication's sole function is to satisfy the need to communicate, which is created socially. Its marginal effects may be significant, but they are not its explicit aim. The resultant 'gratuitousness' has to be understood in a very limited sense, and is explained by part of the press's conditions of existence. A newspaper or magazine can sometimes be no more than a mode of expression, but it can, in other cases, also be a field of financial investment. From this somewhat lucrative perspective, producing texts, buying and selling news, photos or stories, and printing advertisements is the programme of most contemporary publications. The law of the market presides over their destiny like some sovereign. Given the nature of these basic facts, the content itself is of no great importance. The need to make a yield from the sums invested and the search for profit always results in an insensitivity in relation to the means. Whether the paper sells locomotives, guns, fishing rods, news or fabrics is largely irrelevant. Some very powerful consortia sell all those things. The important thing is selling and, therefore, adapting to an ever-expanding readership and keeping it happy.

The appearance of what is known in the United States as the 'yellow press', which is devoted to royal romances, approximate historical reconstructions and murders, signalled the demise of the old papers of record, which were expressions of local, political or religious groups. This question greatly preoccupied sociologists (Park 1955), journalists and politicians, who saw it as a threat to democratic liberties and educational ideals. Although it is, in historical terms, a recent phenomenon, the yellow press's conceptions and techniques soon came to dominate the whole of the press. Most dailies now represent a compromise between the 'record' and 'yellow' styles, and succeed in achieving a balance to a greater or lesser extent. I recall this classification here because it allows us to define in more concrete terms the two functions we have identified. Even so, one type of paper should not be identified with one or the other function, as the two overlap and because the distinction between them applies only in extreme cases. Like any other theory that can, in some ways, fire the imagination, arouse interest and allow the discussion of 'taboo' subjects, psychoanalysis provides the raw material for a lot of articles. It fills space, attracts attention and offers a new terminology, but this does not mean that it is discussed seriously or on its own terms. Psychoanalysis, like 'blood on the front page', 'horoscopes' and 'gossip', is something that sells newspapers. Whether it is discussed in sympathetic or unsympathetic terms does not matter: all that matters is getting people to talk about it. It can be the subject of jokes or the subject of caricatures, but it makes people read.

The notion of instrumental communication is fairly clear, if only because it is this form that is usually taken into consideration by studies in social psychology. In the present case, it relates to exchanges that take psychoanalysis as their centre of attention, and information about it as their goal. A shift between the two functions of diffusion – instrumentality and consumerism – is commonplace, and *bifunctionality* should probably be seen as *characteristic of this system of communication*. The meaning of the duality becomes clear if we look at the thematic language developed by the press. This language is not very different from the language we described in the survey. Complexes play the same basic role in both. We will find that psychoanalytic terms are used to 'baptize' current events, or to give standard expressions a new lease of life. These terms are, however, often used in the press in a playful way and are intended to amuse its readers and to conform to widespread tendencies. Playing with commonplace notions, and an awareness of playing a game, are mere *fictions of communication* typical of part of the content that is being diffused. Although it has its playful side, the fiction of communication does help to introduce and generalize psychoanalytically inspired conceptions and terms.

The playful use of thematic language is quite in keeping with the attempt to achieve the distancing effect we described earlier. Not only does it make psychoanalysis present and uncertain; it also moulds, describes and adds a *phenomenal* density to abstract notions that have been integrated into everyday situations. Metaphors serve the purpose admirably, and the perception of the real becomes imbued with certain Freudian-inspired features:

'[In the Kon-Tiki Islands], they used to hold love feasts in which the prevailing atmosphere was that of a Freudian dream.'[50] 'We spoke in one column about the climate in which "complexes" develop. Sport makes that climate healthier.'[51] 'I felt a loosening of the iron grip of the complexes that had so often made a lucid torturer think he was dispensing justice.'[52] 'A case of neo-Freudian obsession.'[53] 'I am not afraid of flirting with these famous American complexes. I like complexes; they make individuals more interesting. That is part of their mystery.'[54] 'Tristan B has parodied the Bible. The dark psychoanalytic clouds had yet to gather over Sodom and Gomorrah.'[55] '. . . in this Freudian atmosphere.'[56]

These statements are metaphorical but, above all, they represent an attempt to grasp, characterize and designate a form of the real, and this form bears the hallmark of psychoanalysis.

A content analysis of the published articles reveals other perspectives. Their thematic language indicates that psychoanalytic theories have been truly naturalized, and that they have been adopted as a system of understanding and expression. Cognitive schemata derived from them operate, with a greater or lesser degree of felicity, in many of the texts and facilitate the expression of points of view and questions of interest to both reader and author. We constantly see a transition from propositions in which psychoanalytically inspired terms are used to prop up funny stories to rapid descriptions that attempt to shed light on pertinent questions. The fiction of communication[57] and communication succeed, on the one hand, in generalizing linguistic signs and, on the other, in internalizing a vision of individuals and the ways they behave. But psychoanalysis is neither completely accepted nor completely acceptable. From that moment the newspaper or magazine rejects it. The oscillation between the two attitudes, together with the margin of indeterminacy it produces, gives an impression of being outside the theory-object. At times, the paper rebels against its tyrannical presence; at other times, it is only too happy to use it. As a result, psychoanalysis is always there in one form or another. The

---

[50] *France-Soir*, 2 January 1953.
[51] *Guérir*, February 1953.
[52] *Psychanalyse et astrologie*, July 1952.
[53] *Les Nouvelles littéraires*, 28 August 1952.
[54] J.-L. Barrault, *France-Soir*, 16 October 1952.
[55] *Le Monde*, 1 June 1952.
[56] Ibid., 18 July 1952.
[57] Of course this is a fiction of communication in relation to psychoanalysis and not in relation to the sender.

press behaves as though it were fascinated by it, and that term does more than the traditional notions of imitation or suggestion to explain why psychoanalysis has been adopted and why it imbues the vocabulary and the conceptions expounded in so many articles.

The texts that follow illustrate these remarks. The psychoanalytic terms (complex, unconscious, repression) appear in much the same order as they do in the survey, as we saw in the cases in *Elle* and *Guérir*. Even greater emphasis is placed on the role of the complex:

> Complex . . . the word is used in the first things said by women who come to consult a doctor about matters of beauty. The nose, wrinkles . . . anything can give rise to a complex.[58]

The text cited explains why the affects of women who care about their body-image crystallize around the 'complex' theme. We will not dwell on that. The comment added by the doctor tries to emphasize that this is no more than a figure of speech, or a metaphor that other people take seriously. Yet the same weekly advises its readers to avoid the 'ageing complex' and, in this context, the indication refers to something more than a word: it refers to a vision that its readers are assumed to understand. One journalist writing in *Marie-France* advises a reader to take up dancing, and reminds her that it can help 'children who are screwed up by complexes that paralyse their affective lives and that may be a handicap in the future'.[59]

Because they have become so generalized, the psychoanalytic terms have taken on a lot of meanings. Their analogical use allows a change of register and satisfies the need for something new, as well as the need to fight the banality and devaluation of the linguistic signs. We do not need to emphasize the fact that words can become worn out. A 'language policy' is required to keep the readership attentive. This has more to do with transforming expressions than with enriching their meanings. A combination of several 'languages' united around socially pertinent themes is one solution. Because it avoids saturation, the transition from one 'language game' to another satisfies the need communication has to satisfy: establishing a connection with society as a whole. The most typical example is supplied by the 'superiority complex/inferiority complex' doublet. The doublet reproduces the old dichotomy of dominant and subordinate positions. Although it has no particular theoretical implications, it has given birth to a figurative expression with an imprecise content and which, I suspect, has nothing specific to do with Adler's conceptions. In an article in *Le Monde*, for example, a correspondent from the United States

---

[58] *Guérir*, November 1952.
[59] *Marie-France*, 16 March 1953.

writes that American teachers regard their pupils as their equals, whereas French teachers 'complacently give them inferiority complexes'.[60] *Christianisme social* speaks of the 'inferiority complex and grudges of peasants',[61] whilst *France-Soir* claims that 'The disease that most French people suffer from is indeed an inferiority complex, as they are always struck dumb with admiration for foreign inventions.'[62] *Rivarol* describes the reactions of a 'lower' class as manifestations of a 'subjection complex'.[63]

In this context, 'inferiority complex' and 'superiority complex' are no more than convenient expressions that can be used to describe very old conceptions in a different way. There are countless allegorical variants on 'complex', and creating a new complex is easy: 'savings complex', 'timidity complex' or 'fear complex' are so many ways of providing a new frame of reference for commonplace expressions. The purely verbal or consumerist aspect appears more clearly in texts that are lightened by their authors' sense of humour: 'When he said that he thought he was too old to play Romeo, Jean Marais gave Serge Lifar a complex.'[64] Any mention of a head of hair – long or short – recalls the 'Samson complex'.[65] A critic writes in the same weekly that 'Complexes are as light as eider down.'[66] A columnist in *Le Monde* says of a footballer that 'He did not act like that because of some egocentrism complex or some desire to score a goal.'[67] 'His father was so strict that he inflicted a fearful inferiority complex on him at an early age.'[68]

We have cited a few examples of a language that supports a family of metaphors or an expression of cultural synchrasia because it is not only the product of the diffusion of psychoanalysis, but also one of its tools. At a deeper level, this diffusion is also an expansion of models used to interpret the real; they are seen as a 'natural' aspect of a certain way of thinking. The twofold naturalization we have described – the normalized identity of a representation of the real, and the psychological interpretation of mechanisms of a different order – provide a backdrop for many comments on the most disparate phenomena. One of *Elle*'s readers writes to its agony aunt: 'When I am dancing, the boys usually hold me too tight. I find that indecent. Do I have a complex?'[69] And a minister declares: 'Certain statements might reveal the subconscious of allied leaders, or the perspectives they adopt in order to be able to "act".'[70] Both the reader and

[60] *Le Monde*, 16 October 1952.
[61] *Christianisme social*, October–November 1952.
[62] *France-Soir*, 14 March 1952.
[63] *Rivarol*, 6 December 1952.
[64] *France-Soir*, 28 June 1952.
[65] *Les Nouvelles littéraires*, 24 April 1952.
[66] Ibid., 20 March 1952.
[67] *Le Monde*, 3 March 1953.
[68] *Les Nouvelles littéraires*, 12 March 1952.
[69] *Elle*, 26 January 1953.
[70] *Le Monde*, 26 February 1952.

the minister demonstrate that a psychoanalytic schema for understanding and perception of the real has penetrated French society. The press is largely responsible for its popularity. Speaking of see-through clothes, a journalist on *Marie-France* explains: 'People suffering from complexes dress very severely. Repressed emotions and a repressed ability to dress as we like go hand in hand.'[71]

Guérir advises that a baby should not be denied a dummy because

> This will bring it into conflict with its mother's authority long before it is able to tolerate such conflict without being damaged. It will disappear of its own accord at the age of between two and three, if the child develops normally. If it does not, it has to be interpreted as a symptom and the illness it denotes has to be treated. It would be dangerous to use threats to make it go away. It could be the first seeds of a neurosis that a mother, who is herself neurotic, is sowing in the psychical life of her child without realizing it.[72]

Psychoanalysis is not mentioned, but the emphasis is on the importance given to the theory that neuroses have their origins in childhood, even though it is not clear that the author, who presents his or her opinions in partial fashion, is unaware of the other aspects of their origins. The same magazine supports the view that: 'The face is often the seat of the most disparate affections that create so many complexes.'[73] The assertion hints at a causal action and a localization of complexes: this is a form of naturalization, both in the sense that a model is being accepted as something real, and in the sense that a concept is being 'reified'. The magazine *Elle* uses similar formulations:

> This is very probably emotional blackmail. The child is greedy for love; her unconscious is looking for signs of interest, even in reprimands and in the anxiety she can sense.[74]

Mme S. replies to a reader who has written to the agony column:

> This is probably an unfortunate memory, perhaps a very old one, that is buried very deep in your unconscious and which comes back whenever your fiancé comes near you. Recognising it as a memory and reducing it to that should be enough to break the evil spells. That's a job for a doctor and psychotherapist.[75]

---

[71] *Marie-France*, 23 June 1952.
[72] *Guérir*, October 1952.
[73] Ibid., January 1952.
[74] *Elle*, June 1952.
[75] Ibid., October 1952.

The problem raised by the reader is interpreted in psychoanalytic terms, but that conception is not present in any obvious sense, and the fact that psychotherapy is recommended makes it even harder to say just which frame of reference is being used. Another writer on the same magazine remarks:

> A woman who is attracted to authoritarian men will seek to be dominated. She will say 'I always end up with tyrants' and blame her cruel destiny, but it is her *unconscious ego* that provokes these situations.[76]

It would, however, be a mistake to believe that women's weeklies which restrict themselves to discussing childhood and emotional problems have a monopoly on this naturalization. Literary inspiration and political behaviour are not spared. Speaking of the German elections, one of *France-Observateur*'s correspondents remarks: 'Victim complexes and anti-Soviet complexes can be seen as symptoms of new parliamentary democracy.'[77] A speech made by a French general during the visit of a German general contains a judgement that explains international relations: 'We have come into conflict at the military level too often to have any complexes.'[78]

The extension of a language and of representations of certain behaviours and relations, which is promoted by their constant diffusion, tends to create psychoanalysis's social reality. Rather than elaborating a fragmentary representation of a behaviour, this form of communication helps to make a message even more concrete by lending it a certain social validity. The ubiquitous activity of language and the specific orientation of a model that supposedly reflects the real offer a basis for both action and thought. They give analytic concepts the dignity of an unavoidable and imperative presence in all debates, no matter what is at issue and no matter what they are about. Communicating about psychoanalysis becomes a necessity, and the social reality of its representation pressurizes us into communicating about psychoanalysis. It then comes to be seen as a social phenomenon, a belief or part of the normal environment of life.

> We knew that psychoanalysis was one of the pet themes of our day. You hesitate about choosing a job, a wife or a tie: psychoanalysis. You are uptight or relaxed, indecisive or over-decisive, or you feel screwed up or relaxed, or feel that you have fallen prey to what the naïve and the fashionable used to call a vague melancholy: psychoanalysis. Depending on what gender you are, you dream three nights in a row of a black horse or a white mare: psychoanalysis. You obviously have a gift for getting complexes: psychoanalysis, I tell you, psychoanalysis! It is the new key to dreams, therapeutic magic.

---

[76] Ibid., 13 October 1952.
[77] *France-Observateur*, 8 May 1952.
[78] *Le Monde*, 15 January 1956.

It will cure you, and break the spell; it will shed light on the nest of vipers [*noeud de vipères*] that is nestling so dangerously in your bosom and puts a viper in your fist [*vipère au poing*] . . .[79] What is apparently the simplest of minds is nothing more than an unconscious complex.[80]

When we read the laconic phrase 'Psychoanalysis is in fashion' in *Elle*, we rise up against the same tyranny. Monsieur E.H. remarks of a novel that it could be a test case for 'the trial psychoanalysis will have to face one day'.[81] The *Parisien libéré*'s critic congratulates an author for being 'the least complexed of the year. He cheerfully lets off steam in plays that wittily mock our era, in which King Complex is in such good form.'[82]

Psychoanalysis and 'complexes' are treated with contempt at the very time when they are being used on such a wide scale. There is no deplorable contradiction in this. The discontinuity of its diffusion and the autonomy of the message mean that there is no conflict here. At the same time, we see a manifestation of what we predicted: the discrepancy between the generalization produced by consumerist communication, which turns complexes into transient and obsessive social baubles, and the naturalization that moulds the way journalists think and write. The constraints brought to bear by the presence of psychoanalysis in publications, languages and institutions quite naturally provoke reactions. We have cited some of them. They also result in impregnation and lead to the creation of automatisms that cannot always be easily avoided. Monsieur Servin, who was Secretary of the Communist Party and a man who was certainly not sympathetic to Freud's theory, said, at the time when psychoanalysis had been condemned, of a political figure:

> Monsieur B. . . . you are not a Communist: you have an absolute right not to be, and far be it from me to think of converting you. But your ill-repressed anticommunism leads you to take exaggerated liberties with the truth.[83]

The great scientist Joliot-Curie, who was at the time a member of the Central Committee of the Communist Party, stated:

> If capitalist leaders sincerely believed in their ideology, would they try to destroy by force an ideology that makes them feel that they have an *inferiority complex*?[84]

---

[79] The word play alludes to novels by François Mauriac and Hervé Bazin respectively: *Le Noeud de vipères* (1933) and *Vipère au poing* (1948) [Translator].
[80] *Le Monde*, 13 March 1953.
[81] *Le Monde*, 21 May 1952.
[82] *Le Parisien libéré*, 26 March 1952.
[83] *Le Monde*, 25 January 1955.
[84] *L'Humanité*, 21 April 1949.

These examples allow us to emphasize that, despite all the stubborn prejudices, the fact of being part of our culture and of being exposed to the diffusion of certain themes eventually influences our verbal reactions and the way we interpret relationships and people.

The psychoanalysis that is being diffused appears in the fabric of thousands of images of the real and is active in everyday language; it has become not only one of the mirrors of our culture, but also an object of multiple fascination. The need for its intervention is not always logical, and is above all psychological and social. It is not the internal coherence of M. Servin or that of *L'Humanité* that leads them to express themselves or to think in psychoanalytic terms. Monsieur K. does not seem to have any great love for psychoanalysis, but that does not prevent him from summoning it up as though it were a ghost he both loved and loathed; it is as though it was something that people try to ignore, even though they need to be familiar with its interpretations and to be aware of its presence. We can do no more than sample a few texts:

> 'Superfreudian twaddle.'[85] 'The dense audacities of Freudianism.'[86] 'We are only too familiar with Freud's decree: these boys escape the Oedipus complex only to stumble into the Patrocles complex.'[87] 'P. has been subject to his mother's power throughout his life . . . That's how psychoanalysis wants it to be.'[88]

And so on.

Most of the press reacts to the spread of psychoanalysis by issuing warnings against this invasive theory, its 'deviations' and its 'absurdities'. The dream of a golden mean, of a well-behaved psychoanalysis that neither goes beyond nor disturbs the norms established by the author or publication finds expression in these attempts to restrain psychoanalytic concepts; they can perceive its specific value but want to stop it invading every domain of life. The text in *Le Monde* captures the tenor of these reactions perfectly. As we have seen, *France-Soir* mocks the forms taken by psychoanalysis in the United States. Despite these protests, the same publications abound in 'exaggerations' because the 'other' they are trying to master – psychoanalytic concepts – is at the same time the 'other' who envelops and betrays the intentions of the papers or magazines in question. Having deplored the fact that there is so little general information about psychoanalysis and having given a relatively accurate account of its content, Monsieur Eparvier, writing in *France-Soir*, tells us about psychoanalysis's

---

[85] *Le Monde*, 28 March 1952.
[86] *Les Nouvelles littéraires*, 19 June 1952.
[87] *Le Monde*, 24 February 1953.
[88] Ibid., 24 May 1952.

'discoveries': the colour yellow and facing east at work increase productivity. In the same paper, we find an argument about professional entrance exams masquerading as an article about 'psychoanalytic' domination. *Femme* magazine also takes it upon itself to publish a series of articles on the same discipline. The introduction expresses the same wish to be objective and sober, but the way the series of articles is described reveals that psychoanalytic terms are immediately transposed into less purist terms:

> The ambition of our next articles will be to prove that psychoanalysis, when regarded as *the art of living better*, can shed light on women's affective lives, on marriage and on their role as mothers.[89]

The reference to an 'art of living better' is an early indication that the implications or 'exaggerations' are going to be given a free rein. And that proves to be the case. *Marie-France* says it is 'reacting' against invasive 'complexes'. We read in the agony column that:

> There are a few letters about an unacceptable inferiority in my postbag. *Naturally* enough, they deal with the notorious inferiority complex.[90]

In order to shed more light on the question, the weekly publishes an article entitled 'I do not have any complexes'. It is illustrated with a photograph of a girl in a tennis dress. The caption to the photo tells us that 'a good game of tennis drives away all the imaginary complexes in the world'. The journalist begins by informing us that:

> I have learned that there are three main complexes: the jealousy complex, the abandonment complex and the Oedipus complex . . . We have heard so much about complexes, 'complex, this . . . complex, that' that some people end up thinking that they are eminently contagious diseases. At the age of forty, they are afraid of 'catching' one just like that on the street corner, whereas all complexes take shape before the age of seven. Others are firmly convinced that complexes exist only in the imagination of those with too much time on their hands. That's wrong, all wrong. *A complex is actually a mental illness that begins in the very first years of life* and it is possible to cure it by getting the appropriate help. But we hear so much talk about complexes . . . that *we end up seeing them everywhere.* I actually think that we are suffering from a complex about complexes.[91]

The woman who wrote these lines ends by telling us that she is glad that she *has no complexes*. It would be easy to look at an article like this, note the

[89] *Femme*, November 1955, no. 14.
[90] *Marie-France*, 1 September 1952.
[91] Ibid., 31 March 1952.

lack of information, and say that journalists do not know enough about psychoanalysis. But any such comments would be both superficial and inadequate. Why didn't the weekly talk to a specialist? Simply because a specialist would not exactly say what the readership, and perhaps the editorial team, wants to hear. It would be more helpful to go back to the text of the article. The list of complexes betrays the lack of information. How is the relationship between individual (subject) and complex (object) being viewed? The title, the photo and the first propositions tend to deny the existence of complexes, which are basically seen as exaggerations or imaginary excrescences. Their presence is so imperious that it is hard to ward them off. The complexes return, and all at once we see them being transformed into a 'mental illness' that begins 'in the very first years of life', and which can be 'cured' with 'appropriate help'. The complex once more transcends the individual – an illness born of childhood – and becomes a destiny no one can escape. The author cannot deny the existence of complexes, not for scientific reasons but because they are everywhere and because accepting their existence is as embarrassing as denying it. The phrase 'We hear so much talk about complexes . . . that we end up seeing them everywhere' sums up the atmosphere that allows this discussion to take place.

The fascination that the magazine – insofar as it is a subject – communicates via the object that is being represented emphasizes certain aspects of the representation and of their autonomy. These elements are magnified or 'fabricated', and they express attitudes and expectations shaped by a socially active collective imagination. They really are *satellite myths* about psychoanalysis. These satellite myths come into being as partial fictions that exaggerate and emphasize certain aspects of the object. In fiction, the arbitrary coexists with constraints, and the relationship between the two specifies the object's meaning. For our purposes, it is important to stress that the fiction is a product of a form of communication that is both consumerist and instrumental.

4 Overview

It is difficult to give a concise description of diffusion not only because this communication system constantly feeds into others, but also because it is protean. Here, more so than anywhere else, it is dangerous to hypostasize and to draw hasty conclusions, especially about identifying diffusion with a certain section of the press. I stress that the analyses we have outlined are concerned only with psychoanalysis, as the same dailies or weeklies could use other questions to spread, for example, propaganda. When we listed various forms of communication, we emphasized the major role of the structure and evolution of social structures. This presupposes that society is divided and made up of a diversity of groups. At the level of what is known as the public, we find, beneath shifting appearances, an expression of its necessary unity. A few historical remarks may shed light on the question. The dissolution of absolute power and the birth of parties, political clubs and trade union or religious pressure groups resulted in a proliferation of publications designed to propagate ideas within the context of a social organization whose stated ideals were tolerance and equality of rights. In theory, the victorious bourgeoisie, which was both liberal and a believer in competition, granted everyone the right of association and the right to say what they thought about the essential questions facing the collectivity. In contrast with the ideological and religious centralization of the Ancien Régime, the new social relations introduced new forms for the exchange and transmission of ideas. The press, as a cultural tool, had to reach all citizens. Of course financial and political powers always intervened in order to invalidate the rights that the French and English revolutions had won at the cost of so much human sacrifice and to stop them from being used. Even so, the multiplicity of groups and classes that made up society allowed the development and communication of the most disparate opinions. These remarks only provide an in-depth examination of social relations insofar as we have noted that diversity, and its division into groups and classes is inscribed within the structure of French society. Whilst it is real, its hierarchy of groups and classes does not stem from that collectivity's principles. The discontinuities and diversities we have noted in diffusion reflect that hierarchy. A further tendency that must also be taken into account is the constant trend that increasingly concentrates the population in the large urban centres. At the same time, the appearance of new communication technologies provides those who live furthest away from the urban centres with the ability to take part in social life in general. The increasing availability of leisure time and the disappearance of illiteracy allow very broad social strata to keep themselves informed and to take an interest in the news. As has been convincingly demonstrated (Berelson [1949] 1965), reading newspapers has become both a deep-seated need and a social ritual. Social concentration has led to the concentration of the press and radio, and given birth to large companies and real monopolies which, as they merge and remerge, tighten their hold on 'the market for news and information'. What is true of France on a relatively small scale is true of Britain and the United States on a greater scale. A careful study of the French press since the Liberation would demonstrate the accuracy of these remarks. Advertising, the press distribution service and publications are now all controlled by the same major financial groups. Those same groups also have interests in other branches of industrial production. Newspapers and magazines addressing heterogeneous sectors of public opinion have had to look for common denominators. They are not to be found at the highest intellectual levels. As in any business, the goal is to offer a product that can be sold to and consumed by a growing number of people. As it is a private business, the press is therefore dependent on its consumers and has to be very cautious about trying to change their tastes. In this domain, competition does not promote quality. Drawing an audience becomes the main preoccupation of publications, which obviously means that they try not to offend or drive readers away. The current phase in the evolution of the press is a commercial phase. It follows other phases in which papers and magazines made more effort to orient and educate members of the groups and society they were addressing. The question of the unity and diversity of an ever-expanding mass of readers is becoming essential.

There is, in every publication, a consensus about every question that is designed to respect what we have termed a cultural synchrasia. The commercial nature of such a great part of the press, the role played by the 'yellow press' (Nixon 1948: 53) and consumerist communication are becoming more important than instrumental communication. The market values of themes and freedom of expression, the creation of a style, the use of tried and tested techniques and the personality of each writer, the pressure to communicate about particular problems, and particular interests that try to promote their own points of view – it is difficult to establish a stable equilibrium among these contradictory exigences, and the oscillations are expressed through the absence of coherent conceptions of social problems and phenomena, including psychoanalysis. Competition, which takes place between print runs rather than ideas, results in an attempt to identify more and more closely with the readership, and the sender therefore becomes closely dependent on the receiver. 'Keeping the readers happy' is therefore no more than an elegant euphemism for the old adage 'the customer is always right'. In order to orient their readers, papers try in very roundabout ways to modify their representation of the world, whilst ensuring that the transformation cannot be seen and taking care to avoid conflicts that might put the readership off the paper. The fact that society is divided and that there is only one channel of communication explains the discontinuity we have emphasized with respect to psychoanalysis. As psychoanalysis does not have the same importance as, say, political issues, contradictions can emerge more easily. We constantly see journalists who are known to have left-wing opinions writing for papers at the opposite end of the political spectrum, but only when it comes to specific questions about art, films or books.

The hypothesis that there is a connection between social relations and communications systems has, alas, been demonstrated experimentally. Under the fascist dictatorships, propaganda replaced diffusion. But global social relations do not explain everything, because we can observe, in our society, the coexistence of several forms of communication, such as propaganda and diffusion. At this point, we have to introduce the further dimension of types *of relations* between groups. In wartime or when conflict breaks out between nations, for instance, propaganda becomes a privileged way of transmitting ideas. The growing importance of propaganda at the political level is in part due to the conflict between the countries of the West and the East. Economic competition, for its part, stimulates advertising campaigns. The interaction between social relations and types of intergroup relations explains the multiplicity of communications systems that exists in our social organization.

A rapid survey of the links between diffusion and society will allow us to begin to look at more specific questions. It should be recalled in this context that, in diffusion, messages are discontinuous and segmentary, and that relations between them are aleatory. Because they are not strictly hierarchical, the segments and fragments reveal regularities that make up a non-systematic social model. The integration of the text into the context is incomplete. The fact that the opinions and information that are transmitted are not highly structured allows their receiver to organize them freely on the basis of his or her own perspectives and attitudes. This has clear implications at the cognitive level: *there is little involvement in the propositions*. Articles are not constructed as a whole, but as a set of sub-articles, each with its own domain of pertinence. *Marie-France*'s articles about complexes are one example. Complexes are at one time imaginary and at other times something created in childhood. Sometimes they are general, and sometimes they are particular. The sequence of arguments is not contradictory because the different levels are not emphasized or related to one another. The mediocre quality of the information makes the unfolding of the exposition even more unclear. In *Guérir*, for example, narco-analysis is cited as a technique that can speed up analytic therapy. *Marie-France* speaks of a jealousy complex in an attempt to combat the tyranny of complexes. It is in *France-Soir*'s *medical* column that we find an article on 'straw polls' in the United States. In all these cases, the writers and their papers are acting as mediators. They speak of 'specialists' and 'authorities', but it is the journalists who transform all the information so as to present it to their readers. We have seen that, in diffusion, adapting the source of communication for the readership is an essential issue. Insofar as the source is sometimes contradictory, this has the effect not only of creating an aura of indeterminacy around the problem under discussion, but also of giving it a multiplicity of meanings. Their multiplicity makes it easier to adapt the material to suit the audience, and at the same time enhances the sought-after distancing effect. In this case, irony plays a primordial role. Yet the sole purpose of the distancing effect is to give the publication more freedom with respect to its object and its readers.

The formation of a language that specifically addresses psychoanalysis – which is the communicational object – is a better way of ensuring that the two terms – sender and receiver – understand one another better because it uses shared themes and avoids the saturation that can always occur because of repetition by giving new metaphorical meanings to worn out notions.

Participation in a common society and culture relegates the distinction between the source of the communication and the audience to the background, and foregrounds the relationship between the source and the conception that grounds it, at a given point, in the life of that culture. The naturalization of psychoanalysis and its impregnation of language and cognitive attitudes are both products of this social involvement and its most striking expressions. The fact that the representation of psycho-analysis fits the frame of reference of the paper or magazine is considered to be scarcely worth mentioning. On the contrary, the fact that psycho-analysis fits perfectly into social reality and becomes part of it has to be seen as one of the essential effects of its continuous and multilateral diffu-sion. The fascination with psychoanalysis, its concepts and its representa-tions, is the natural result of this effect and of its social investment. Once a social entity has been conceived, it ceases to be a representation and is inte-grated into that class of beings that serve as points of reference for action and dialogue. The discipline that concerns us ceases to provide an oppor-tunity to mediate between a sender and a receiver and becomes a precon-dition for the emergence of both. The content of the press therefore has a documentary interest because it identifies the expressions and constants of a given society, and not just the messages between two groups (publica-tion and public) in which everyone has a defined role.

The moment has come to ask what influence this form of communi-cation can have on symbolic and real behaviours. There is no univocal answer to this question. We therefore have to advance a number of hypotheses corresponding to a series of possible effects. Before doing so, it should be recalled that diffusion does not emphasize any necessary or global behaviour. The relationship between the message and the likely response is *incidental*. The discontinuous way in which the information is transmitted is certainly capable of generating opinions, and even behav-iours, about specific points. Perhaps it should also be stressed that the modifications it seeks to induce come about very slowly. The production of effects, and its rhythm, are, however, relative notions. The explanation for the conventional argument that diffusion and the commercial press are undermining the public's interest in questions pertaining to the collective interest is that this interest is seen as a fundamental criterion. In the present case, it should be noted that opinions and behaviours have been 'priva-tized', or in other words that they centre on the restricted and immediate problems of individuals. The public tries to 'escape' rather than confront the obstacles and complexities of the social situation. In simple and famil-iar contexts, intellectual habits discourage the adoption of over-extended temporal perspectives and make it difficult to look for and accept over-elaborate solutions. The oscillation between the instrumental level and the consumerist level, finally, sheds an ambiguous light and does not permit any consolidation of the behavioural object. Psychoanalysis, for example, alternates between being a language, an amusing topic of conversation, a pretext and, at the same time, an orientation and a therapy we can turn to. Even when it is described as a possible form of therapy, people usually immediately add that other medical applications can produce the same results. This creates a state of quasi-indifference. What is more fundamental is that the new behaviour, namely the recourse to psychoanalysis, is presented as only one of many possibilities. If older forms of treatment can produce the same results, it is difficult to see why the reader should try something new. Ultimately, the new merely reinforces the old or the status quo. Such processes reveal the conservative nature of diffusion via the press: conservative behaviour, but also confused and atomized behaviour. The public therefore finds itself in a state of unstable disequilibrium at the level of action, and no clear directions are given. This is the probable effect of diffusion on behaviour. The privatization of opinions and behaviours, whose importance is emphasized by sociologists, makes it easier to achieve an equilibrium within a limited circle. Social involvement via communication, finally, prevents members of a collectivity from being totally involved. The distanced and ironic attitude the sender adopts towards the object becomes the attitude adopted by the receiver of the information and the social models: both the newspaper or magazine and the reader remain uncommitted. Diffusion does have an influence on behaviour and opinions, but its influence is multiple and indirect. We are entitled to say that it produces effects, but does not try to get results. As Park pertinently observed, its goal is to get people talking, and not to get them to take action. Is there such a great distance between the two? The relations between action and the particular communications system we have been describing trace a frontier between that system and both propaganda and propagation, which we will explore in the following pages.

13

The Encounter between Religious Dogma and Psychoanalytic Principles

1 Propaganda: Its Characteristics and Its Domain

Psychoanalysis was relatively slow to penetrate France. The moral and philosophical hostility it aroused was overcome by its conquest of literary circles. Psychiatrists, doctors and philosophers expressed reservations, whilst the neo-Kantian and positivist and clinical traditions were very slow to surrender. It took a complete change of climate to make possible a more serious, but no less passionate, consideration of psychoanalysis. The revolution in physics, the growing importance of Marxism, the penetration of phenomenology and the revival of interest in Hegel on the one hand, and the institutionalization of analytic practice, social tension and the ideological division of the world on the other, created an atmosphere conducive to a change of perspective. They thus established the preconditions for the expansion of psychoanalysis.

The presence of psychoanalysis in French society forced all groups with practical and ideological responsibilities, and especially the Catholic Church, to adopt a stance with regard to it. Because of its own philosophy, its responsibility for educational matters and the leading role it plays in France, the Church has come to view psychoanalysis not only as a very important theory and form of therapy, but also as a vision of man which, at least in the work of Freud himself, makes a critique of religion. And yet Catholic thinkers, psychiatrists and psychoanalysts did help psychoanalysis to put down roots in France. Even so, they still had to try to reconcile certain of the demands of their beliefs with those of Freudian theory, and that was a slow process.

The Catholics were obviously not innovators. They followed the general tendency to transform certain aspects of psychoanalysis for both theoretical and practical reasons. The influence of Catholicism in our country being what it is, a vaguely sympathetic attitude towards the discipline inevitably had concrete implications. It was by no means easy to reconcile psychoanalysis, and especially Freud's writings, with a religious worldview. Freud was a liberal thinker steeped in nineteenth-century ideas about the social and psychological function of religion. For him, as for the philosophers of the Enlightenment and many rationalist and liberal scientists, religion represented an intellectual deviation, a systematic expression of illusions and prejudices whose finality had to be understood and whose implications had to be fought. As a result, many philosophical and literary currents found in Freud's writings a basis for their critique of religious rites and belief. Freud was as clear and uncompromising about this point as he was about the importance of sexuality for the aetiology of the neuroses. He never really abandoned his ideal of a psychological science resembling physiology. Despite the speculative nature of some of his metapsychological hypotheses, the creator of psychoanalysis was what was then called, with less disapproval than the term now suggests, a mechanistic materialist. Freud constantly reworked his theories and concepts in the light of the facts and the ideas of his disciples and former disciples, but was guided mainly by his own constructive genius. The epistemological and ethical tendencies we have described remained, however, basic and were widely recognized. There were many things for Catholicism and psychoanalysis to fight over. Even though they found it difficult to deal with these delicate questions, it has to be admitted that the men of the Church and the Church itself displayed consummate skill in dealing with scientific discoveries and works that could not have been more contrary to their principles. Bruno and Galileo were episodes from a past that was both glorious and painful to remember; the approach had changed, and rather than rejecting an intellectual tool as powerful as psychoanalysis, the problem was more one of appropriating it and using it to the Church's advantage.

Freud himself, prescient or deeply knowledgeable, suggested the means for expressing the unity of the discipline he thought he had created: the separation between theory and practice. After a period of uncertainty and either obvious or latent hostility, R. Dalbiez's famous book on Freudian doctrine and psychoanalytic method (1941), first published in France in 1936, lent credence to the idea that Freud was a clumsy philosopher and tried to drive a wedge between his doctrine and its applications. Christians could now talk about psychoanalysis as a practice, and either ignore the theory or wait for it to be modified. Dalbiez's book has never satisfied all Christians and especially not the fundamentalists, who still criticize it today. The fact remains that the slow task of assimilation, revision, or the pressure to plan such revision had begun or, rather, was becoming more clearly defined at a time when more and more Christian analysts were beginning to practise.

It might be argued that the task of revising psychoanalysis in such a way as to bring it into line with religious principles had already been begun by Jung. Let us simply note that Jung's revisionism was of no great interest to Catholics, and that Dalbiez himself was not slow to criticize some of his weaknesses in this domain. Even before the Second World War, but especially after it, Catholic psychoanalysts – laymen or not – helped to reconcile psychoanalysis with religious conceptions to the extent that they published purely clinical studies. The reconciliation of the two inevitably led to many splits and sowed so many doubts that the fundamentalist branch of the Catholic Church declared it anathema. Whilst it is well known that this branch influenced the decisions made by the Catholic hierarchy's higher authorities – one psychoanalytically inspired book was put on the Index as a result – we are entitled to assume that there was little unanimity about the appropriateness of expressions of sympathy for Freud and his work. Given this level of tension, the speech made by Pope Pius XII to a gathering of Catholic psychiatrists in 1952 (to which we will return) simply facilitated the spreading of interpretations, without any one tendency being given the imprimatur it expected.

A description of a content analysis of the Catholic press brings us back to the more limited dimensions of our field of investigations but, precisely because they are more limited, they are also clearer. In the previous chapter, we noted that Catholic publications showed considerable interest in psychoanalysis and that they regarded it with some sympathy. The following newspapers and magazines were the object of a systematic analysis: *L'Aube, La Croix, La France catholique, La Pensée catholique, Témoignage Chrétien, L'Anneau d'or, Etudes* and *La Vie spirituelle*. The articles published in them break down as shown in table 13.1. Most of the articles are sympathetic; 25 per cent adopt a hostile or indifferent attitude.

It therefore appears that psychoanalysis is now accepted by most Catholic publications. If, however, we look more closely at their content, we find that religious values are slowly being adapted to psychoanalysis and that even more is being done to adapt psychoanalysis to religious values. In order to understand this process, we must begin with a description, albeit a rapid one, of the situation of the Catholic group, which had to take a stance with respect to a theory with considerable social influence. The Church's means of communication are, at the level of the press, relatively limited because the hierarchy controls few large-circulation papers and magazines. It has never been directly involved in anything but a very limited number of publications. Their role is to orient and prepare messages before they are *explicitly* organized in ways that make them clear enough to be picked up by other Catholics and transmitted as they stand. The transmission of structured and explicit messages based upon a clearly defined frame of reference is one aspect of the form of communication I

Table 13.1 Percentage of articles on psychoanalysis by newspaper

L'Aube, La Croix (%)	La France catholique, La Pensée catholique (%)	L'Anneau d'or, Témoignage Chrétien (%)	Etudes, La Vie spirituelle (%)
27	31	28	14

propose to call *propagation*. It is relatively easy to describe. It should first be noted that the Catholic group is itself divided over what attitude it should adopt towards psychoanalysis. This conflict of ideas cannot, however, be allowed to become too intense, as all believers must accept certain postulates and the same authority. The existence of divergent views does not give rise to discontinuous or contradictory communications. On the contrary, Catholic magazines and dailies *bring pressure to bear in an attempt to achieve unity* by finding a common denominator between all Catholics on the one hand, and between their basic doctrines and psychoanalysis on the other. There is, however, no *demand* for uniformity, as there is in propaganda. Catholic communications are not designed to incite behaviours, but simply to create *norms* or a convergence around an acceptable doctrine. Such a convergence implies that the social object changes in such a way that it can be integrated into an established frame of reference. This change produces a *conceptual system* in which established principles and a theoretical content can be shown to have a mutual adequacy. At the objective level, the integration of new elements introduces new perspectives without creating any tension: new demonstrations of fidelity to the group and individual self-determination help, on the contrary, to avoid the adoption of conflicting positions. To sum up, we can identify the following as features of propagation:

(a) Its field of *direct* action is relatively restricted.
(b) Its goal is to integrate a social object – psychoanalysis – into an existing frame of reference.
(c) It attempts to get the whole group to accept one faction's dominant conception.
(d) Its goal is not to encourage new behaviours or to reinforce existing behaviours, but rather to establish an equivalence between behaviours and the norms in which individuals believe. The goal of communication is, in other words, to give actual or likely behaviours a meaning that they did not previously have.

The cognitive aspects of this form of communication are, at a certain level, no different to those of a normal exchange of views. The dominant emotional implications characteristic of loyalty to the group and respect for authority are triggered, but no attempt is made to give them a high degree of intensity. An account of articles published by part of the Catholic press will demonstrate the point.

2 The Assimilation and Adaptation of Secular Notions

An exhaustive examination of Catholic publications would demonstrate that they use all forms of communication: diffusion, propagation and propaganda. They are not, however, all used to the same extent. Articles displaying the characteristics described in the previous chapter can be found in *Témoignage Chrétien* or *Ecclesia*. Anti-psychoanalytic propaganda is the work of fundamentalist Catholics. As I have already said, I propose only to study propagation, which is the dominant modality of message-transmission in most Catholic magazines, weeklies and monthlies.

The similarity with the 'mainstream' press is sometimes obvious. In a discussion of the causes of the Crusades, for example, *Ecclesia* describes them as a way of reconciling warriors' liking for violence with the prohibition on spilling Christian blood. The article's author, a well-known member of the Académie française, sums up his arguments with a formula that reveals his source of inspiration:

> A psychoanalyst would say that, as the holy war of the Crusades provided an outlet for repressed passions, it could only improve the morality of the West.[1]

In an attempt to answer the question: 'An End to Arguments About Obesity?', *La Vie catholique illustrée* gives pride of place to emotional and affective shocks, and recommends the lifting of repression as a way of curing the 'patient'. Psychoanalysis is not the only therapy to be cited, and the habit has become so ingrained that the author cannot resist scoring a point against it: 'But as we know, psychoanalysis is never short of brilliant explanations.'[2] Writing in *L'Aube*, Monsignor E.B. criticizes *La France catholique*'s silences:

> It has been noted that *Le Monde ouvrier*, which is the paper of the MRP, never uses the word 'communism'; the word 'democracy' is hardly ever mentioned in *La France catholique*. Psychoanalysis teaches us that there is nothing accidental about systematic silence, and that it betrays some vehement passion, such as love or hate. I will merely conclude that Democracy is not a matter of indifference to *La France catholique*.[3]

Catholic papers as different to one another as *Témoignage Chrétien* and *Ecclesia* sometimes use complexes, and especially the guilt complex, as an explanatory pivot. According to *Témoignage Chrétien*, 'Witch Hunts' in the United States can be explained in terms of the need to dissolve a collective guilt complex by putting the blame on a few individuals. In a discussion of a book entitled 'The Religious Development of Adolescents', *Ecclesia*'s

---

[1] *Ecclesia*, June 1952.
[2] *La Vie catholique illustrée*, 11 September 1955.
[3] *L'Aube*, 28 April 1951. MRP = Mouvement Républicain Populaire, a post-war Christian-Democratic party [Translator].

critic notes that: 'Confidences tell us more than confessions, which often reawaken guilt complexes.'[4] The similarities with the non-Catholic press, which we discussed earlier, are, however, superficial: there is no psycho-analytically centred thematic language, and the generalization of its conceptual frame of reference is very limited. Psychoanalytic terms tend to be used in a technical sense; the word 'complex' is not used more frequently than any other, and it is, with some exceptions, quite rare for interpretations of events, people and books to be inspired by the work of Freud or his disciples. The distinguishing feature of Catholic-inspired texts is their obvious desire to examine in some depth the relationship between psychoanalysis and their own philosophical orientations. The advice about the need for 'caution' that we find so often (65 per cent of the articles mention it) captures the tone of the articles. It allows them to remain within the limits of the dialogue. It would, however, be a mistake to confuse this 'caution' with the attempt to find a golden mean that we saw in our analysis of diffusion. 'Caution' indicates the existence of limits defined by principles, whereas a 'golden mean' tends to indicate an oscillation, overt or covert, between extreme options. The twin centres of interest that dominate the Catholic press are relations between psychoanalysis and religion, and relations between psychoanalysis and various concrete problems.

We read in *La Croix* that 'Psychoanalysis makes Christians feel ill at ease.'[5] This is a significant statement. The main reasons for their feeling of unease can be summed up as follows: (a) psychoanalysis reduces human complexity to its elements; (b) Freud has an erroneous conception of man and of the human worldview; (c) psychoanalysis causes confusion at the ethical level because the notions of responsibility and sin are made meaningless; (d) pansexualism does not correspond to the facts; (e) psychoanalysis is, thanks mainly to its applications, an important discovery; and (f) certain of its notions are valid, when understood in a limited sense. Christians may well be perplexed, but they also derive a certain satisfaction from the change of climate that Freud's theories and the work of his followers have helped to bring about. In an article on the Sorbonne, *La Croix*'s reporter finds cause for satisfaction in what he sees as a reaction against nineteenth-century rationalism. In his view, psychoanalysis is playing an important role in that reaction. He can therefore find grounds for a rapprochement between the Catholic conception of man and the conception he sees emerging from courses and lectures at the university. The notions of evil and sin that are being developed there do not have a very Christian ring to them, but there is an underlying similarity. The fact that psychoanalysis and Christianity can reach agreement over these complex

---

[4] *Ecclesia*, February 1953.
[5] 'La Pensée et l'actualité religieuse ('Un point de vue chrétien sur la psychanalyse')', *La Croix*, 12 August 1952.

notions is a good antidote to the unease the discipline inspires in Christians. For other Christians, there is a much wider gulf between psychoanalysis and Catholic doctrine on sexuality, morality and sin. It is therefore not surprising to see the highest Catholic authorities rejecting Freud's theories. Fr. Gemelli, a well-known psychologist and an influential member of the Pontifical Academy, published a radically hostile article on Freud in *Vita e Pensiero*, and it was reprinted in France. In his view, 'psychoanalysis, *like communism*, is one of the sicknesses of our time'. Analytic training and therapy have, in his view, little to recommend them, and are ineffective and dangerous:

> As a means of effecting a cure, psychoanalysis is not only a school that teaches irresponsibility, but also a tool for the dehumanization of man.[6]

Rejecting the view that psychical health can be promoted at the expense of the higher values of life, the Reverend Father also rejects the distinction between method and doctrine, as well as the excessive indulgence shown to Jung:

> For all these reasons, Catholics cannot support the doctrine of psychoanalysis; they cannot accept it, and they cannot submit to psychoanalytic treatment; Catholics must not entrust their sick to psychoanalysts for treatment. Psychoanalysis is a threat because it is the sickly fruit of Freud's crude materialism.

French Catholics are explicitly blamed for their tolerance of and interest in Freudian-inspired theory and therapy. What are the views of French Catholics? An article entitled 'Theology and Depth Psychology' attempts to enlighten a priest on this question.[7] It denies that psychoanalysis is pansexualist and demonstrates that it can shed light on the patient's religious feelings. Therapy does not create new problems and, when it is applied properly, there is no reason to fear the influence of the analyst who, by definition, remains neutral. It is not only desirable but necessary for priests and therapists to work together – at the ethical level. That they should work under Church control is thus accepted both in theory and in practice. The outcome is a recognition of the value of psychoanalysis.

Both supporters and opponents of psychoanalysis discuss the concept of pansexualism (62 per cent of articles), and all are agreed that it has to be rejected. Some reject it as a way of denigrating Freud; others do so in order to demonstrate the 'precise' meaning of the term. Because conflict between Christian morality and the ethics attributed to psychoanalysis has to be

[6] *Revue des revues*, no. 16, 1952.
[7] *La Vie spirituelle*, no. 19, 1951.

avoided, a study undertaken by a number of practitioners and theologians associated with the *Cahiers Laënnec* describes what they believe to be satisfactory pragmatic and conceptual cooperation between the two. An issue of the journal entitled 'Psychoanalysis and the Moral Conscience' devoted to these questions reaches the following conclusions: the discoveries of psychoanalysis do not upset Christian thinking about the moral conscience (Fr. T.); ethics can learn from further study of Freud's contribution (Canon N.); psychoanalysis allows authentic choice, and in that sense it is pre-ethics (Fr. P.); theology must use the understanding of the dynamism of symbolism to its own advantage (Fr. L.B.); and depth psychology must be modified in the light of the (Christian) values of existence.[8] These conclusions are supported by three principles: moral precepts are neither complete nor immutable; they have a psychological basis, and the insights of psychoanalysis can therefore help to clarify them; freeing the individual from childhood conflicts can pave the way for a free and authentic adoption of religious values. These comparisons are not without their practical concerns, and the most important are as follows: is it possible that psychoanalysis will promote moral laxity, and can Christians trust psychoanalysts who are not Christians? The Church has a definite position on these questions, and can scarcely allow someone who is not a priest to give moral guidance. Whilst the Church does not intervene in any technical sense, it does wish to be present:

> First, because it would be desirable for a moral or religious adviser to counsel anyone undergoing psychoanalysis if there is any danger that the treatment might have serious repercussions for the patient at the moral or religious level, or that it might result in a major transformation of his personality . . . Second, it would be advisable to know just what the psychiatrist thinks about activities that infringe the moral law, such as masturbation or homosexual practices. This is neither a moral assessment of his views nor a condemnation or an ironic absolution, but a technical value-judgement. To restrict the discussion to the acts we have mentioned, we can be satisfied if the psychiatrist sees them as signs of a growth defect. And indeed, how can they not be regarded as such, when the patient has come to be cured of a behaviour in which they are a factor? Everything else is a question for a moralist. And the moralist will demonstrate that these actions offend the moral order because they are abnormal.[9]

Is it possible for a moralist (priest) and a psychoanalyst to work together, and would it be in keeping with the principles of therapy? According to Catholic psychoanalysts, the answer is 'yes'. The question of the conceptual and practical frontiers between Catholicism and psychoanalysis raises

---

[8] *Cahiers Laënnec*, no. 2, May 1948.
[9] P.T. 'Description de la conscience morale et incidences psychiatriques', ibid., pp. 20–1.

a lot of subtle distinctions. Confession is obviously not to be confused with psychoanalysis, but the similarity between them means that a parallel has to be drawn. *Témoignage Chrétien* returns to this question more than once,[10] either in order to argue that psychoanalysis is a 'parody of confession', or to demonstrate that both confessors and psychoanalysts have to deal with the same problem: language. Taking as his starting point the novel idea of a need for confession, Monsignor Foliet concludes that in Anglo-Saxon countries, which are protestant, 'psychoanalysis fills the spiritual gap created by the fact that there is no confession'. Psychoanalysts are actually described as the 'priests of a new religion'.

Confession is something holy, but Catholics accept that priests do not have a monopoly on spiritual guidance. Psychoanalysts are knocking at an open door, provided that they do not frustrate religious vocations or attempt to eradicate principles that are basic to faith. The feeling of sin is one such principle.

> A lot could be said about a different identification: the identification of the feeling of guilt with the sense of sin. The feeling of guilt arises because unconscious taboos have been attacked or broken by other tendencies that have also become unconscious. Although the subject, who is unaware of its origins, is capable of seeing it as a real or imaginary sin, his feeling of guilt is no more than an affective reaction, and is no more than a semblance of a value-judgement. Now the feeling that one is morally at fault necessarily implies a real value-judgement and faith alone can give one the feeling of sin, in the Christian sense of the term. For revelation alone can tell us what we are in the sight of God: sinners who have been redeemed. A distinction should therefore be made between the feeling of guilt, or the awareness that anyone, Christian or not, can have of their failure to do what their conscience tells them to do, and the feeling of sin.[11]

Theologians are in a better position than most to appreciate the value of these subtle reflections, but it might be difficult to put them to any practical application. For our part, it is enough to note that Catholics need to be involved in on-going conceptual work because psychoanalysis is present in their cognitive field and their field of action. The fact that the Church is present and active in the world implies choices. Christians are not just the embodiment of an idea or beings who devote themselves to the expectation of eternal life, but men, women, children and members of families who live in a society they have created, even though it is not necessarily based upon Christian principles. Turning psychoanalysis into an ally, as has been done with evolutionism, quantum physics and even Marxism, is

[10] *Témoignage Chrétien*, 11 April 1952.
[11] *Cahiers Laënnec*, no. 2, May 1948 p. 19.

Table 13.2 Political and ideological position of papers

Field of action	Communist (%)	Left, Centre-left (%)	Centre, Centre-right (%)	Apolitical (%)	Right (%)	Catholic (%)
Education	16	25	20	20	11	48
Other	84	75	80	80	89	52

a way of gaining a foothold in that life, taking out a mortgage on the future and acting upon the present. In the name of that present, a 'Christian use' of psychoanalysis is recommended:

> It's the same with psychoanalysis as with existentialism or the language of Aesop. It can be the best of things or the worst of things; and just as atheistic developments in existentialist philosophy in no way contradict the value and quality of Christian existentialism, we can readily accept that the serious risks inherent in a psychoanalytic conception of man by no means preclude a *Christian use of psychoanalysis*. The question is on the agenda in any case and, whilst the hierarchical authorities are anxious to warn Christians against dangerous abuses, it is quite clear that their warnings by no means condemn psychoanalytic methods in principle.[12]

An article from the *Osservatore romano* reprinted in a French Catholic publication points out that there are several different kinds of psychoanalysis and recommends one that respects Christian principles.[13]

Catholics are usually sensitive and sympathetic to analytical therapy, but they are even more sympathetic to its possible theoretical contribution to the understanding of child development, married life and family life. It is in the Catholic press that we find the highest proportion of articles claiming that education should be one of psychoanalysis's fields of action. This signals a fairly characteristic orientation of Catholic interests.

Before looking at some specific examples that illustrate the concerns of the Catholic Church, we should note that the content of what is said about psychoanalysis is determined by (a) that Church's normative principles; and (b) its field of action in France – education, missionary work and confession.

There is no evidence of fascination, but there is evidence of an active response to certain cultural and practical problems in which there are few contradictions but a constant quest for coherence and an attempt to

[12] *Informations catholiques internationales*, 1 October 1955.
[13] *La Croix*, 26 September 1952.

establish a new system. Its crowning achievement would be an outline of a psy-
choanalysis with a meaning that is in keeping with the group's norms and goals.

The relatively abstract style of the articles, their pedagogic tone and their logical organization are immediate reflections of these concerns.

Under the ironic or jocular general title 'The Garden of Complexes', *Témoignage Chrétien* published a series of five articles on the genesis of the affective life of children. Its account of psychoanalytic concepts is very accurate. The journalist's conscientious attempt to make what are, after all, difficult theories intelligible obviates the need to expound a familiar content. *L'Anneau d'or*, which is a specialist magazine, attempts to define a more explicitly Catholic line. Its postulates are simple: the teachings of psychoanalysis are accepted point by point, but care has to be taken to avoid its penchant for the morbid and the traumatic. Children need love, and the influence of conjugal love on relations between parents and chil-dren, and between brothers and sisters, must be seen as essential. A lack of conjugal love will, for example, divide brothers and sisters:

> The father spontaneously directs some of the affectivity he should be giving his wife towards his daughter, and the mother directs some of hers towards her son.[14]

This bare outline of the Oedipus complex paves the way for a psycho-analysis that defines conjugal love as something essential to the greater happiness of the children:

> We ought to take psychoanalysis's observations one by one, not so as to demonstrate the damage that can be done by an unhappy marriage life, but to emphasize the benefits and educational power of a happy one.[15]

The psychoanalysis these authors are looking for is an optimistic and con-ciliatory psychoanalysis that provides an intellectual and practical train-ing for affective comfort. By way of contrast, 'morbid' and 'traumatic' are the adjectives that are usually applied to the Freudian dramas in which the heroes are neither good nor bad, but always good *and* bad, and willing to sacrifice everything to learn the truth or gain their freedom. The price they pay for this rationality is the loss of their own reason.

Analytic concepts are used to elucidate hidden aspects of many domains and are, as result, directly linked to hypotheses that have in one sense very little to do with them. 'Children: Terra incognita': this is the title *L'Anneau d'or* gives to a series of articles organized around the theme of how little we know about heredity. A child's basic characteristics are

[14] *L'Anneau d'or*, May–August 1951.
[15] Ibid.

innate. Even a newborn baby has a rich affective tonality. Its nature appears to be hidden, but there is an answer to that:

> The formidable unconscious discovered by Freud appears to be of growing importance – collective and individual. It is something that dwells in all of us, and it can be enriched or modified in the course of our individual lives, whose essential lines are determined at birth.[16]

This text's original feature is the hypothesis of an almost innate unconscious that rigorously determines a life in which everything is preordained at birth. Is this a sign of Jungian influence? The author seems, however, to be following Freud. In reality, a belief in innate ideas is in fact one of the foundations of a creationism that many Catholics have never abandoned. The unconscious acts here as a link between a basically anti-evolutionist conception and a genetic theory of childhood. It is strange to see Freud's theory of the childhood origins of neuroses becoming a support for creationist thinking.

Parents are unsure as to what they should be doing: 'We are so frightened of harming our children that we no longer dare to do anything good to them'.[17]

In most of these articles, the emphasis is on *affectivity*. Psychoanalysis's great discovery was the importance of affective bonds in early childhood. The role of sexuality (libido) is recognized, but preference is given to the more general, and more accessible, term 'affectivity', perhaps because it is half way between (Christian) love and (psychoanalytic) libido.

> Affectivity, or in other words the mysterious ability to empathize with another person, makes it possible (and necessary) for us to live in harmony. But where there is harmony, there is always the possibility of disharmony. Wherever there is love, there is the possibility of jealousy and hatred.[18]

Pathological symptoms in the life of a child – stealing, running away from home, bed wetting – are affective. Pedagogy can find inspiration in our understanding of affectivity:

> This understanding of the laws of affectivity is, as we can see, of extraordinary importance, and, even now, we are still far from having drawn all the pedagogic conclusions that need to be drawn from modern science . . . It is of utmost importance that parents should take an interest in this affective education, as it is very likely that, in this domain, the general direction of a life is established in the first three or four years of life.[19]

[16] Ibid.
[17] *Témoignage Chrétien*, 15 February 1952.
[18] Ibid., 19 January 1951.
[19] Ibid.

Is psychoanalysis a valid form of therapy? A degree of caution is essential. Preference should be given to psychology:

> When it comes to treating children, use psychology rather than psycho-analysis, because the latter awakens demons that are best left sleeping.[20]

Catholics regard psychoanalysis as an ally or as a foundation wreathed in scientific prestige that can strengthen their cult of the family and of mothers: 'A normal child has a good relationship with its mother or educator.'

The theme of what *France catholique* calls 'Parents: models to imitate' is inspired and supported by the work of Spitz, Bowlby and Mme Roudinesco. The family provides a concrete model for the child, but it is also actual married life, which implies sexual and affective relations. It would be a brave man who tried to expound the subtle and shifting theories that theologians advance in their attempt to reconcile Christian demands with modern practices. There is an abundance of both taboos and advice. Sexuality is an immediate given which, as the magazine *L'Anneau d'or* tells us, is established at the level of the unconscious before it appears at the level of consciousness and the personality. The purpose of this unconscious sexuality is to discover a higher level of reality. Its psychological function is to transcend genitality:

> Not only analytical psychology, but all personalist philosophies have to some extent recognized the relationship between this unconscious sexuality and the values of communion and reciprocity.[21]

Once the authority of psychoanalysis – which knows what sexuality means – has allowed them to transcend genitality, and even to make it secondary, Christians invoke a third order: that of creative vows and the gratuitousness of gifts. Married life must also constantly be kept separate from the restricted context of sexual relations. There is, of course, nothing original about this. Every individual – Catholic or not, married or single – tries to do so. The only difference is that Catholics are positively asked to pay less attention to sexual relations and to subordinate them to more essential aspirations. As we have seen, psychoanalytic theory can be used to elaborate such a theory. It is therefore not surprising to find that the theory is made subordinate to strict moral principles at every stage. Its dangerous nature is never forgotten. 'What contribution can psychoanalysis make to married life?' asks a columnist writing for *La France catholique*. After warning us of the need for caution, he tells us that it makes it possible to

---

[20] *La Croix*, 14 May 1952.
[21] *L'Anneau d'or*, January–February 1952.

'lance wounds' and to see things more clearly, but that it cannot resolve anything. For anyone in analysis, revelations of a sexual nature are a source of doubts and temptation. Knowledge can be dangerous:

> Achieving a more balanced sex life (and therefore a more balanced married life) is not just a natural task, but also a superhuman, supernatural task. The human condition is peccaminous. The sexual instinct is, however, not something that cannot be part of spiritual life; it is one of its elementary components.[22]

Catholic publications usually display a number of different concerns. They try, first of all, to discover whether their religious principles and moral laws are compatible with psychoanalysis. Freud's basic philosophical principles – his materialism – seem to them to be fallacious. Those principles do not, however, affect what Catholics see as the essential feature of psychoanalysis. On the contrary, Freud's writings tell us that, when well conducted, therapy can be the source of an 'authentic' moral life. It will be recalled that reconciling psychoanalysis and Catholicism can take the form of a collaborative effort on the part of priest and psychoanalyst that leaves faith intact. The fields of action of both the analyst and the priest are safe. Once the principles of psychoanalysis have been accepted, they can then be used to inform and to educate. It should not be forgotten that *L'Anneau d'or*, for example, is a magazine that tries to give couples advice about all the delicate questions that may arise in their lives: as we have seen, the advice concerns children, their relations with their parents and their affective environment on the one hand, and relations between husband and wife and their sexual and emotional problems on the other. Psychoanalysis is an interpretative system that is often used to elucidate all problems of this kind. Provided, of course, that the basic rules of the Church are respected.

Whilst most of the papers we examined do not voice it, there is still a stubborn and organized opposition to this theory. *La Pensée catholique* never tires of waging war on it. The terms used are always violent. A few texts chosen at random will give a fairly clear idea of their tenor:

> Hiding behind science and exploiting the prestige enjoyed by anything that can lay claim to that great name, they tear every veil to shreds and trample the most elementary concerns as to modesty underfoot. Thanks to this scientific detour, men have found a way to calmly profane their own mystery and to talk about it in terms that cheapen it because they imply the degradation of their mystery. A collection of ignominious complexes excogitated by those who dig around in the dustbins of the psyche: these are the delightful

[22] *La France catholique*, 18 July 1952.

things we should be talking and writing about; that is what they explain to us in serious articles about the saints; that is what a man in charge of souls, a confessor or a master of novices must, if he is not to look incompetent, look for inside himself and inside the souls the Church has committed to his care ... An idealist and Cartesian conception of the soul and of freedom ('Where there's a will, there's a way', and the soul is reduced to meaning a clear conscience) paved the way for this infatuation with psychoanalysis. For there is indeed something instinctive about human beings, and unconscious impulses are sometimes very perverse. And no idealism can do anything about it. So when Freud reminded us of this, but distorted everything, we can understand why he was hailed as the bearer of the truth.[23]

The editors of *La Pensée catholique* support every attack on psychoanalysis, even when it is made by Communists:

Sadly, we have to conclude that certain reactions against psychoanalysis – and they are on the whole judicious – are the work of Marxist psychiatrists with a real professional competence.[24]

La Raison's attacks on Mme Choisy are discussed in the following terms:

The author attacks Mme Choisy with great energy, and recalls her intellectual curriculum vitae and especially (and in great detail) her origins and secret connections with the AROT foundation (Association pour la renovation de l'occultisme traditionnel) [Association for the Reform of Traditional Occultism].

One individual plays a major role in this campaign. R. Allers is a Christian psychiatrist, but I do not know if he is well known or competent. The nickname 'Rudolf Allers: the anti-Freud' explains why he is so popular with *La Pensée catholique*:

We can therefore follow him [Allers] with a sense of security when he tries to clear the French intellectual sky. Evolutionism . . . Freudianism! Those are the clouds – and they are clouds of poison – that have to be broken up . . . There were, however, other scientists who, like Auguste Marie (sometime consultant at the Sainte-Anne psychiatric hospital and director of the Laboratoire de psychophysiologie at the Ecole des Hautes Etudes in Paris), believed that 'psychoanalysis is an imported commodity . . . there is little demand for it in Paris'.[25]

[23] *La Pensée catholique*, no. 26, 1953.
[24] Ibid., no. 18, 1950.
[25] Ibid.

All these polemical texts refer to Christian psychoanalysts rather than psychoanalysts in general. This is sometimes made explicit:

> There are indeed a number of 'neo-psychoanalysts' who believe that they have 'spiritualized' Freudianism: they have made a few changes, but they no more alter its main 'doctrines' than a nut hurled against a wall can stick to it. Yet they retain the whole of the theory of childhood sexuality and especially the Oedipus complex.[26]

The goal of these Christian fundamentalists is to create a totally negative representation of a psychoanalysis which is pansexual, biased, materialist and modern, and which can scarcely be reconciled with Christian thinking. The group's principles encourage it to oppose anything that might disturb the unity, tradition and authority of a Church that is seen as a monolithic bloc that can never change. This group loathes psychoanalysis, which it sees as a symbol of moral dissolution, in the same way that it loathes evolutionism, idealism and Cartesianism. The fundamentalists' enemy is not really a world that is changing, alien and doomed to damnation, though that does not stop them from worrying. It is the way those changes are being interpreted within the Church, which is one and indivisible in the same way that the first articles of their constitutions define republics and kingdoms. The Church's adversary resembles those Catholics who, by trying to reconcile psychoanalysis with Christian principles, sow discord within a human community that should be built in accordance with the canons of the Middle Ages. The labels 'Christian' and 'Catholic' are the only things they remember about the Middle Ages. They forget the heretics, the atheists, the followers of Averroes and the pagans, and the long centuries during which the Church had two heads, and during which emperors, kings, princes and even Florentine merchants bought or imposed favours. All science – and science is in itself an evil – and all new conceptions pose a threat to this ideal serenity.

The confrontation of two fundamentally opposed Catholic currents called for a clarification which was supplied by Pope Pius XII's address to the Fifth International Congress on Psychotherapy and Clinical Psychology.[27] The address made it quite clear that some of psychoanalysis's general ideas – those dealing with unconscious processes – met with the Pope's approval:

> There is talk of dynamisms, determinisms and mechanisms that lie hidden in the depths of the unconscious, and that have immanent laws that govern certain modes of action. Those modes of action are mobilized in the subconscious or unconscious, but they also enter and determine the conscious realm.

[26] Ibid.
[27] *Etudes*, June 1953.

Catholic doctrine follows the teachings of Aristotle and Thomas Aquinas by giving a special role to the soul. That entity is in some sense different to other forms of psychical life and dominates them:

> It follows from this ontological and psychical given that we would lose sight of the real if we attempted, in theory and in practice, to give one particular factor, such as one of the elementary psychical determinisms, a role that determines everything, and puts a secondary power at the helm. Those dynamisms may well exist in the soul, and in man, but they are not the Soul of Man.

According to the principles of the Catholic religion, human behaviour and all the psychical forces at work in it can be transcended and are subject to imperatives that stand above the banal horizon of nature. Original sin plays a privileged role, not because it gives the Church control over the faithful (this conception is foreign to Christianity), but because it is the constituent basis of transcendental links. In that sense, Catholicism does not recognize any guiltless humanity, and accepts that guilt is an important component in many neurotic illnesses. This makes the encounter between Church and psychoanalysis a particularly delicate affair:

> The feeling of guilt is therefore one of the psyche's transcendental relations. A feeling of guilt is an awareness of having broken a higher law, even though we recognize the obligation to obey it; this awareness can turn into suffering, and even mental illness. Psychotherapy is dealing here with a phenomenon that is not within its exclusive remit because it is also, if not primarily, religious in character. No one can deny its existence, and irrational or even unhealthy feelings of guilt are not uncommon. We can, however, have an awareness of having committed a real sin, and of the fact that it has not been redeemed. Neither psychology nor ethics has any infallible criterion for discussing such cases, because the conscious process that gives rise to guilt has a structure that is too personal and too subtle. What is, however, clear is that purely psychological treatment cannot cure real guilt.

We are later told that only a priest can absolve sins.

Confidentiality is another aspect of psychoanalysis that concerns the Pope – the confidentiality of the patient, and not of the psychoanalyst of course:

> The practical psychotherapeutic point we are outlining concerns one of society's essential interests: keeping the secrets that are threatened by the use of psychoanalysis. It is by no means impossible that a phenomenon or body of knowledge that is secret and buried in the depths of the unconscious could lead to serious psychical problems. If psychoanalysis detects the cause of the problem, it will, in accordance with its own principles, evoke that unconscious

in its entirety in order to make it conscious and to remove the obstacle. But there are secrets that can never, absolutely never, be told, even to a doctor and even if keeping them does have serious personal consequences. The secrets of the confessional must never be made public. Anything that is said in professional confidentiality can never be revealed to a third party, even if that third party is a doctor. The same applies to other secrets.

Fr. B., who is a psychoanalyst and Jesuit father, demonstrates that there is no incompatibility between this discretion and a well-conducted analysis: a Christian is presumably in a better position than most to distinguish between silences that are due to real resistances and those stemming from a legitimate wish to keep secrets that have been confided on a confidential basis. The head of the Church is understandably concerned with appeasing those Christians who fear that the principle of the secret of the confessional might be transgressed. The discourse of the confessional touches, with the usual caveats, upon behaviours and concepts that are usually associated with sexuality and psychoanalysis. In his address to a gathering of clinical psychologists and psychotherapists, the Pope moves rapidly from general psychology to psychoanalysis, rather as though the latter were the basic conceptual armature of any clinical approach. In doing so, he implicitly recognizes the supremacy of psychoanalysis, and he is not mistaken. That generalization notwithstanding, he expresses a preference for indirect therapy:

> The above remarks about ill-considered initiations for therapeutic purposes also apply to certain forms of psychoanalysis. These should not be regarded as the only ways of attenuating or curing psychical sexual disorders. The hackneyed principle according to which sexual disorders of the unconscious, like all other inhibitions of the same origin, can only be removed by their evocation in consciousness, becomes invalid if its generalization is ill-considered. *Indirect treatment can also be effective and is often more than enough.*

The Pope ends his major speech by leaving the decision to the practitioners:

> Leaving that aside, you must believe me when I say that the Church is warmly sympathetic to your research and your medical practice.

This speech, together with an earlier address, was widely distributed and discussed in France. Catholic supporters of psychoanalysis took encouragement from it, but felt at the same time that they had to demonstrate that the discipline and its applications were in keeping with the principles laid down by the Church's highest authority. In a country like France, this was tantamount to saying that it was acceptable to propagate a social model of psychoanalysis that was in keeping with the religious principles of large sections of the population. This was widely reported in the press. Seventeen newspapers and weeklies, which could not be said to represent either the hierarchy or a Catholic movement, published long extracts from this address. The passages that caught their attention dealt with (a) sex education and (b) the partial acceptance of psychoanalysis. *La Dépêche de Toulouse* ran the headline:

> Freud and Vatican sign armistice. Far from putting it on the Index, the Church now accepts psychoanalysis as a psychotherapeutic method for the soul.[28]

The cold war between psychoanalysis and the Catholic Church was mentioned. The author expressed the view that the Pope's speech could be seen as an acceptance of the basic premises of Freud's theory. *Samedi-soir* reported the same event in these terms: 'The Pope did not condemn psychoanalysis, and gave it its "Catholic charter".'[29] According to other newspapers, the Pope *objected to abuses of psychoanalysis* (*Le Figaro*) or 'set limits' that the discipline must not cross. There were few original comments, and most articles did no more than summarize the address we have been discussing.

The Catholic press widely reproduced the words of its guide. Catholic psychoanalysts, notably Fr. B. and Dr E. used the doctrine outlined by Pope Pius XII to demonstrate that their practice was compatible with the directives they had just received. Given that most of the arguments deployed in the address had been widely discussed in the Catholic press, psychoanalysts could breathe relatively easily.

3 In Search of a Catholic Conception of Psychoanalysis

Any analysis of propagation as a system of communication will, of necessity, be brief, as its characteristics are 'banal'. We can, however, bring out its features and attempt to situate it with respect to other systems. The situation that made it necessary to adopt a position with regard to psychoanalysis and to transmit information and opinions about it can be rapidly outlined; it comprises:

- external pressures resulting from the social presence of a new conception of man and from Catholic interest in it;
- internal pressures resulting from the similarity between the concerns of priests and those of psychoanalysts, and from the condition in which the Church must act in domains such as education and the spiritual guidance of adults;

---

[28] *La Dépêche de Toulouse*, June 1953.
[29] *Samedi-soir*, June 1953.

- differences of opinion between Catholics; differences of opinion about psychoanalysis cannot be allowed to go beyond certain limits: all Catholics must share the same beliefs, and respect the Church's hierarchical organization.

The first thing to be said when accounting for the communication genre of the Catholic press is that, unlike diffusion, it is explicitly goal-directed. It does report, it mainly entertains. The motive and style of most newspapers express the position of a clearly defined group, the Christians, towards a socially meaningful object, psychoanalysis. *The relationship between the source of communication and the overall membership of the group does not imply a strict reciprocity, as the source is invested with an authority that may be challenged.* Having lost the power to impose a distinction between right and wrong, orthodoxy and heresy, the way the Catholic press communicates is hierarchical rather than authoritarian. They do the best that can be done: they provide the content of an intellectual and attitudinal consensus towards a social representation of psychoanalysis in the frame of the predominant religion in France. As in propaganda, there is a constant reiteration of the frame of reference. In that sense propagation can be said to be a hierarchical genre of communication, not an authoritarian one.

What social representation is being propagated? Here the risks are that any account will be simplified with some arbitrary omissions. It is difficult to do justice to a body of literature which is so significant owing to its serious-mindedness and its volume without trespassing the limits of the present study. The articles we have analysed are often inspired by attempts to create a spiritual psychoanalysis or depth psychology. And their authors, even if they belong to the Church, or are steeped in the Christian doctrine, do not always speak as its representatives. At times they sound like critics of the Church's standpoint: but unlike those who criticize it from outside, they defend its teaching with clear requirements, shared criteria for establishing what is religious and what is not. Despite these complexities I do, however, hope that the outline of these communications, their themes and liaisons, will do justice to those complexities and to the opinions expressed (figure 13.1).

In the schema I have outlined, themes situated on the same line centre on the same problem and are just the semantic translation of it in different contexts. The first and second columns show the order of assertions about the philosophy of a non-Christian (or Freudian) psychoanalysis and about the principles of that psychoanalysis. The third column outlines Christian principles which challenge both (Freudian) psychoanalysis and its philosophy, and which provide a basis for its reformulation.

The fourth column synthesizes the arguments which eliminate certain philosophical presuppositions from Freud's theory, and which make it possible to reconcile it with the Church's moral and theological rules; the ways in which the two are reconciled can be seen in column five. There is

Philosophical principles of psychoanalysis		Description of 'materialist' (Freudian) psychoanalysis	

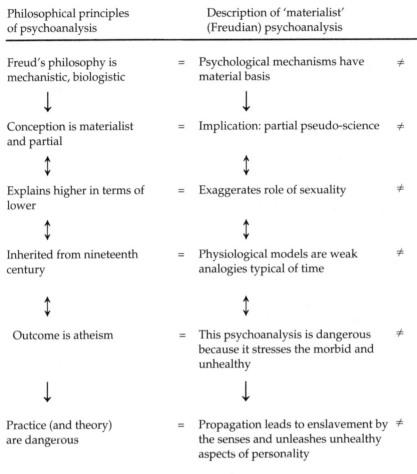

| Freud's philosophy is mechanistic, biologistic | = | Psychological mechanisms have material basis | ≠ |

↓   ↓

| Conception is materialist and partial | = | Implication: partial pseudo-science | ≠ |

↕   ↕

| Explains higher in terms of lower | = | Exaggerates role of sexuality | ≠ |

↕   ↕

| Inherited from nineteenth century | = | Physiological models are weak analogies typical of time | ≠ |

↕   ↕

| Outcome is atheism | = | This psychoanalysis is dangerous because it stresses the morbid and unhealthy | ≠ |

↓   ↓

| Practice (and theory) are dangerous | = | Propagation leads to enslavement by the senses and unleashes unhealthy aspects of personality | ≠ |

Figure 13.1 Schema 2

It will be recalled that the signs are to be read as follows:
→ implication
≠ opposition
= equivalent or interchangeable propositions
⇄ reciprocal implication, circularity

nothing new about the content of these themes, and much of it has already been described. The inclusion of a few more texts is simply a way of clarifying them.

> Not content with sounding the depths of the unconscious and attempting to cure mental illnesses, Freud based a whole anthropology on his findings . . . That is Freud's tragedy. It takes a philosopher and metaphysician to explain

Christian postulates	Christian view of psychoanalysis
Christian principles are basis of everything $\longrightarrow$	Psychoanalysis contains metaphysics existing on different plane $\longrightarrow$
$\downarrow$	$\downarrow$
Conception of man is spiritual and total $\longrightarrow$	Materialist, determinist metaphysics $\longrightarrow$ not necessarily basis of psychoanalysis
$\downarrow$	$\downarrow$
Explains lower in terms of higher $\longrightarrow$	Affective and unconscious are not just obscure forces $\longrightarrow$
$\downarrow$	$\downarrow$
Christian thought contributes to twentieth-century scientific $\longrightarrow$ revival	Modern discoveries allow us to reject nineteenth-century views $\longrightarrow$
$\downarrow$	$\downarrow$
Christian thought a necessary complement to science and $\longrightarrow$ scientific research	Psychoanalysis not bound up with atheism; is a depth psychology $\longrightarrow$
$\downarrow$	$\downarrow$
Conception of man provides possible framework for psychological theory (and therapy) $\longrightarrow$	Limited analytic therapy does not give rise to conflict; does not necessarily affect faith $\longrightarrow$

Figure 13.1 (cont'd)

everything about man. Freud was not and never claimed to be a philosopher. Let us be bold enough to state that in order to explain everything about man, one must be a Christian and know what God has revealed to us about man, his origins, his nature and his destiny. Freud was not a Christian. He came from a Jewish background, but was in fact an agnostic and materialist, as were most people in the medical circles of his day. His initial platform was therefore too narrow to allow him to develop a concept of man. His anthropology – which is the third meaning of the word 'psychoanalysis' is erroneous from a philosophical point of view, and unacceptable to Christians.[30]

---

[30] *Saint Luc*, 3 March 1956.

Possible encounter between psychoanalysis and religion

Church must integrate findings of psychoanalysis

↓

Psychoanalysis allows understanding and integration of relations between body and soul

↓

Elementary determinisms are subordinate to spirit

↓

In this perspective psychoanalysis can identify authentic aspects of faith

↓

Psychoanalysis is compatible with conception of synthetic unity of man

↓

Spiritual director can work with therapist (Christian psychoanalyst)

Figure 13.1 (cont'd)

Freud in fact noticed – quite rightly – that most mental illnesses are sexual in origin. He was therefore struck by the major role played by sexuality in the ego or super-ego. He quickly relegated all affectivity to unconscious sexuality, and all aggressivity to an equally unconscious asexuality. This was this first mistake, and it has attracted too many followers . . . Hence the pansexualism. He obviously rejects the accusation of pansexualism – successfully when he is replying to accusations of immorality, but less successfully when he makes a distinction, which is verbal rather than real, between 'sexual' and genital. 'Pansexualism' is an objective summing up of the whole of his psychology. When we speak of psychoanalysis, we must be careful neither to condemn it as a whole nor to accept all of it uncritically.[31]

Whilst we reject Freud's philosophical generalizations, we have to admit that his experimental clinical system is in many respects rather different to psychoanalysis's socio-ethico-philosophical superstructure . . . If we bear in mind that what Freud means by love is not cohabitation, that the super-ego is not, despite the parallels drawn by Freud, a conscience, and that the

---

[31] *Etudes*, June 1950. The third party here is a priest.

psychical apparatus is not the soul, we can accept Freudian psychoanalysis *in toto*, whilst disagreeing with Freud about all attempts to introduce it into the domain of morality and religion.[32]

It appears that the terms 'analytic therapy' and 'Christian' are no longer contradictory. There is no longer any conflict between psychoanalysis and morality. The 'unconscious' will now inevitably be integrated into a complete human psychology. Whilst it is recognized to be the obscure source of most of our behaviour, the fact remains that it alone cannot resolve the entire problem of the human psyche. (ibid.)

We will not introduce any more quotations, as their main purpose was to demonstrate the links between the various arguments put forward by Catholics. Their frequency obviously varies, but these are the most common

Freud's philosophy is mechanistic and biologistic	30
It explains the higher in terms of the lower	15
The theory and the practice derived from it are dangerous	22
Psychological mechanisms have a material basis	21
The role of sexuality is exaggerated	35
Psychoanalysis is dangerous because of the emphasis it places on what is morbid and unhealthy	14
Its propagation leads to enslavement by the senses and to the liberation of unhealthy aspects of the personality	18
Christian principles are the foundation of everything	30
Their conception of man is complete	15
The Christian conception of man provides the only possible framework for a psychological theory (and therapy)	19
Psychoanalysis implies a metaphysics that exists on a different level	22
The affective and the unconscious are more than obscure forces	28
A limited degree of analytic therapy does not lead to conflict and does not necessarily undermine faith	25
The Church must adopt the concrete findings of psychoanalysis	22
Elementary determinisms are subordinate to the soul and the spirit	20
Spiritual advisers can work together with therapists (Christian psychoanalysts)	18

A list of the themes shows that in general it is statements of principle (line 1 across the five columns in figure 13.1), questions relating to affectivity, sexuality and psychological determinism (line 3) and warnings about the concrete implications of psychoanalysis (line 6) which are the

[32] *La Vie spirituelle*, no. 24 1953.

most frequent. The other themes tend to play a secondary role. A study of relations between themes demonstrates that the assertions in the first two columns (Freud's philosophy and Freudian theories) are equivalent to one another, but that they *have not been arranged into any hierarchy*. Their reciprocity and equivalence illustrates the use that is made of them: psychoanalysis and Freud's philosophy are mentioned only to the extent that they can be compared or contrasted with the Christian worldview, but no attempt is made at any point to identify a coherent body of doctrine.

The most frequent relations of equivalence to be established are between the mechanistic and biologistic aspects of Freud's philosophy on the one hand, and the material basis of psychological mechanisms on the other (18 out of 74 articles), followed by those between 'the dangers of the practice' and 'the liberation of unhealthy aspects of the personality' (15 articles out of 74). The contrast between the themes of the first two columns and those of the third can be specified as follows:

Line 1, columns 1 + 2 → line 1, column 3	22 times in 74 articles
Line 2, columns 1 + 2 → line 2, column 3	18 times in 74 articles
Line 6, columns 1 + 2 → line 6, column 3	20 times in 74 articles

The themes of the fourth and fifth columns (psychoanalysis without Freud's philosophy, and psychoanalysis compatible with religion) almost always appear together, and it is the equivalences between them that are the most frequently mentioned (22 times in 74 articles):

Psychoanalysis contains a metaphysics that exists on a different level	The Church must accept the concrete findings of psychoanalysis
The affective and the unconscious are more than obscure forces	Elementary determinisms are subordinate to spirit and soul
A limited degree of analytic therapy does not lead to conflict and does not necessarily undermine faith	Spiritual advisers can work with therapists (Christian psychoanalysts)

The interest of these quantitative findings is that they give us a better understanding of the structure of a schema whose formalism can blur the role each element plays in the whole. (In methodological terms, there does not appear to be any contradiction between the identification of these structures and their quantified expression.)

This formal level shows us that the Catholic press does not attempt to achieve a very satisfactory degree of coherence when it comes to describing and then rejecting Freud's philosophy and hypotheses. When things are rejected they are, so to speak, rejected at random. All the negative aspects of psychoanalysis are equivalent, in the same way that all cows are black in the Hegelian night. The model for the group is, in contrast, constructed as a hierarchical system in which the links of implication (and not reciprocity) between the assertions contained in the columns are a synthesis of compatible religious and psychoanalytic principles (columns 3, 4 and 5)

An exhaustive analysis of the positions adopted by the Church with respect to psychoanalysis cannot be made here. Our more modest goal is to identify, with some approximations, a coherent model which, when communicated by the Catholic press, succeeds in mediating between a discipline and the believers it has to orient. The primary function of propagation – the dominant form of communication in these newspapers and magazines – appears to be to organize and transform a theory into a whole which is compatible with the principles which establish the unity of the group. *Its second function is not to encourage a specific behaviour, but to prepare the group to behave in specific ways and to check that it does so, or to give it a meaning that it did not previously have.*

Invitations to act, either positively or negatively, with respect to psychoanalysis are the exception and not the rule in the Catholic press. The use of psychoanalysis is neither recommended nor forbidden. It is mentioned as a *possibility*. It is assumed from the outset that there are people who behave positively or negatively with respect to psychoanalysis. The former are asked to take into account the Church's principles because spiritual guides and psychoanalysts are not incompatible. On the contrary, it is recommended that they should work together. For a Christian, the fact that they can actually do so transforms the *meaning* of the recourse to psychoanalysis. The impression that there is a conflict between concrete behaviours and their meaning – given the widespread belief that psychoanalysis and the religious life are incompatible – is ruled out from the start. If the psychoanalyst is a Catholic, these seemingly contradictory poles can be harmonized and a behaviour that was once confined to worldly and 'secular' circles can take on affective and cognitive connotations that alter its substance. The instrumentality of propagation is, in short, defined both by the fact that it is capable of orienting members of a group, and by the fact that it can control their behaviour by giving it a meaning that is in keeping with the group's basic norms. This form of communication is implicit in all the group's activities.

By forming a system the Church has attempted to give it a satisfactory cohesion. The operation results in a theoretical whole whose cognitive characteristics are known, and a partial representation of what has been rejected. It is the different ways in which they deal with the positive and the negative that signals the difference between propagation and scientific or philosophical communications that are devoid of any hint of rhetoric. The 'negative' aspects of psychoanalysis (materialism, pansexualism and so on) are quickly dismissed, and the stereotypical use that is made of them plays a positive role. Indeed, making theoretical 'sacrifices' or subscribing to a few common prejudices is Catholic thinkers' and Catholic psychoanalysts' way of dissociating or distancing themselves from a psychoanalysis that is surrounded by an unsympathetic aura. As we have seen, Catholic fundamentalists are not willing to accept this compromise. At the affective level, this separation from a certain psychoanalysis has a reassuring effect; it makes it possible for priests to play a therapeutic role: the Church is present and vouches for them. That in itself means that the behaviour of believers can be controlled and guided. Whilst we cannot ignore the fact that such controls have a real effect in all systems of communication, their goals are not always the same. Whereas the goal of diffusion is not really behaviour as a whole, *the primary goal of propaganda is to get all members of the group to behave in the same way*. Propagation attempts on the one hand to control existing modes of behaviour by establishing stronger links between the group and members who are likely to adopt them, and to restructure the meaning of the sequence of elements on the other. Catholics are not calling for the extension of analytic therapy. They make repeated appeals for caution and consider the possibility of other therapies. Whereas diffusion always encourages the adoption of partial and 'atomizing' positions, we see here the appearance of an overall construct designed for the effective implementation of the regulation of cognitive, affective and behavioural processes concerning psychoanalysis. Or, to exploit the possibilities of ellipsis: whereas diffusion tends to encourage the development of *opinions* about specific problems, propagation constructs *attitudes* that can influence both representations and behaviours. Being more fully elaborated, more complex and more abstract, propagation addresses groups that already have a certain unity, a definite language and their own system of values, but also, in all probability, those sections of groups that have a high level of intellectual education. The print runs and roles of the Catholic press, and the make up of its editorial teams, mean that its role is not to address a mass of readers who can easily be reached by other media, such as sermons, parish newsletters, or those sections of the daily press that take their inspiration from religious circles.

The fact that the quality of the content that is communicated is dependent upon the extension of the readership to which it is addressed indicates a further difference between diffusion and propagation.

In the Catholic press, authority is embodied by priests and psychoanalysts who openly state the choices they have made and explain the religious reasons or principles that inspire them. Unlike *France-Soir* or *Guérir*, the Catholic press does not simply refer to an ill-defined but prestigious category of 'specialists'. The sender's degree of involvement is therefore obvious, and his dependency is above all a dependency upon principles and not readers. Non-involvement appears to be the rule in diffusion. Insofar as it is a form of communication, propagation is more like propaganda: there is the same use of systematic models, the same involvement and the same relationship with readers. Propaganda is, however, more concrete, and it is not content with giving a behaviour a new meaning: it tries to inspire or reinforce it. Its world is strictly dichotomous, and the situation that gives rise to it is different. Its stereotypes, which are widely used, define the affective world in a specific way. This is what we will now examine.

14

The Communist Party meets a Science that is very Popular and Non-Marxist

I Theoretical Perspectives

Propaganda has becomes one of the obsessions of the age, and we cannot speak of these obsessions unless we do so with passion and with the reverence we owe to the mighty. Even before certain scientific achievements filled the imagination with such terror as to make aphorisms about man's mastery of nature look archaic, the fear that individuals might lapse into dependency had long gathered around the notion of propaganda, the fiction of an alienation that is all the more complete in that it is internalized. The confidence in its efficacy has made propaganda a favourite instrument of communication so that rulers, social reformers, revolutionary parties and modern armies have elevated it to the height of an institution. Even though society misrecognizes or takes no interest in sciences that take man as their object, an impartial study would show that propaganda, which applies certain psychosociological principles to human behaviour, has mobilized human forces and economic resources on almost the same scale as those used to discover the structure of the atom or to build nuclear devices. Society cannot do without propaganda or atomic energy, since, at the stage of development it has now reached, they both correspond to a lifestyle whose content and finality are not always in keeping with our basic ethical aspirations. The immorality or morality of propaganda are obviously not society's own morality or immorality, but of the groups who use it and of the aims they set themselves.

In the following study, propaganda is viewed as a form of communication and action that is necessary in a specific social situation. By trying to distance ourselves from our own values, which is the affective precondition for an objectivity that is difficult to achieve, we will try to outline those of its characteristics that merit further scientific study. The general applicability of our observations will be limited by the fact that we are discussing propaganda published in the press and dealing with what is, after all, a very specific problem: psychoanalysis.

Lenin ([1902]1970) was the first modern theorist of this form of communication and he identified some basic features that have subsequently been ignored by scientific research. To be more specific, he saw propaganda as a means

(a) of shaping a group's worldview;
(b) of promoting an awareness of both that group's individuality and its integration into society;
(c) of complementing other modes of communication and social action.

Lenin's political writings abound in psychological insights and practical recommendations, but they do not give rise to any deeper conceptual systematization. American studies have tried to categorize and describe the techniques used by propaganda. They compare its symptomatology with more general phenomena, such as perception, conditioning and linguistic change, and make it possible to get beyond what was basically an inadequate conceptualization in some respects. Yet rather than studying these phenomena in direct relation to communication processes and analysing how they intervene within them and are modified by them, these studies simply try to generalize. To take one example. The study of language in propaganda was, quite rightly, regarded as being of fundamental importance. Language was, however, examined only insofar as it was a means, and no attempt was made to pay sufficient attention to its specific laws and their determinant function in communications. It was argued that stereotypical words are effective because they have an affective charge; this type of explanation and this use of linguistic knowledge mistake findings for givens, and look only at what can be included in an inventory – of inessentials – and provide a basis for further speculation. The authors forget to ask how and why the stereotype became a stereotype. In which context is it active? To what modalities of linguistic development does it correspond? Similar observations – about hasty generalizations and the partial nature of the aspects considered – can be made about theories based upon conditioning. It is only in recent years that an experimental current, which remains somewhat eclectic, has begun to make a specific study of the role such phenomena play in communications.

The presence of that current notwithstanding, it is surprising to see how little effort is made to discover objective laws. Various definitions of propaganda emphasize either the determinant intervention of an *intentionality* or that of a *behaviour*, rather as though there were no limits to the pure subjectivity of the propagandist, or as though the laws of psychology had only a minor effect on the techniques employed. There is always a suspicion that an element of Machiavellianism is involved, and the omnipotence of propaganda is exaggerated, even though we know that it often fails. Because they look only at findings influenced by behaviourist schemata – even if they are to some extent adapted to fit in with Freud's theories – most researchers lose sight of the fundamental hypothesis of any objective study in this domain: the situation and intergroup relations modulate all 'intentions', and psychological and linguistic laws determine 'behaviour'. This implies that not enough attention has been devoted to looking at what type of social relation gives rise to propaganda, and its function within the life and history of the group. As a result, it eventually comes to be seen as something that is *both arbitrary and artificial*. Because they are fascinated by instrumentality, most psychosociologists ignore the first and essential moment of all communication with others: expression.

Rules relating to the use of certain techniques with a view to achieving goals specific to propaganda have been outlined. Remnants of a psychology derived from the work of Pavlov, together with a few rapid and arbitrary remarks about instincts, provided the raw material for works that earned an incontestable noteriety. *The Rape of the Masses* (Chakutin 1946) is one example. References to scientific theories replace actual science. There are also methodological and ideological reasons why psychological problems are discussed without reference to the actual findings of psychology.

In methodological terms, the analysis is restricted to a description of the raw material, and no attempt is made to understand its causes. In ideological terms, the analysis of propaganda is transformed into a critique of propagandists. Because of the political character of most of the propaganda campaigns that have been studied (fascism, communism) and of the studies themselves, the methodological and scientific viewpoint is quietly but decisively abandoned in favour of a more polemical, essayist approach that reveals mainly the personal vision of the author. Although it does not affect all studies, this slippage takes us away from a central preoccupation with communication, and in the direction of a political anthropology whose interest – and interests – grows as the international tragedy in which we are involved unfolds.

Taken as a whole – and making due allowance for the positive features of the works to which they refer – these comments indicate that we have to clarify some of the central problems raised by the development of the communicational phenomena:

- Which psychological processes intervene in these phenomena?
- What are the objective preconditions for the production of communicational phenomena, and what are the elements that perpetuate or transform them?
- What are the links between psychological processes and those preconditions?

In this study of propaganda, I will attempt to provide what I consider to be answers to these questions; they are incomplete but can be further developed. The line of conduct adopted throughout this study can be summarized as follows:

- Existing studies have indeed identified a large number of the effects and properties – the symptomology – of propaganda: stereotyping, simplification, the effects of prestige, false identifications, etc.
- We begin the study of propaganda by tracing it from the moment of its emergence to its contemporary forms, and will not be satisfied with segments, moments or final states. Most publications suggest that the authors' perspective is that of the group on the *receiving* end of propaganda and not that of the propagandist group, leaving completely aside the interaction between the two perspectives.
- We will relate the various aspects of propaganda to better-known social and psychological processes, to the laws governing those processes, by examining how far this is actually possible;
- We will include linguistic processes, not considered solely as a bearer of content, or as a form whose laws do not have their *own* meaning. Whilst it is true that in communication language plays the role of a vehicle, it is a vehicle which has its specific laws, which are studied by linguistics, a science more advanced than our own, and which, therefore, may be able to shed light on psycho-sociological phenomena.

2 What can We expect to Read in a Communist or Progressive Publication?

The way in which the Communist press discusses psychoanalysis provides the opportunity for a deeper examination of all these questions and for some theoretical clarifications. Before we undertake that research, a more detailed description of the content that was analysed will allow us to familiarize ourselves with the material we will be looking at later. During this preliminary phase, we will describe the image of psychoanalysis that emerges from progressive newspapers and magazines, in order to bring out certain differences more clearly. We know that progressives and Communists coexist in harmony at the political level; we want to see if the same harmony is present in other domains.

The following Communist publications were analysed: *L'Humanité*, *L'Humanité-Dimanche*, *Les Cahiers du communisme*, *Démocratie nouvelle*, *Ce Soir*, *La Nouvelle Critique* and *Les Lettres françaises*. The progressive publications are *Europe*, *Action*, *La Tribune des nations*, *L'Ecran français* and *Libération*. A total of 192 articles about psychoanalysis published in the duration of the study were analysed in detail. The dailies, weeklies and magazines were divided into four groups:

(a) a 'central' group consisting of the publications of the Communist Party's Central Committee (*L'Humanité*, *L'Humanité-Dimanche*, *Les Cahiers du communisme*, *Démocratie nouvelle*, *Ce Soir*, *La Nouvelle Critique*);

(b) a 'political' group including *L'Humanité-Dimanche, Démocratie nouvelle* and *Ce Soir;*
(c) a 'cultural' group including, for example, *Les Lettres françaises;*
(d) a 'progressive' group (*Libération, La Pensée,* etc.).

The list is, like any other, open to debate. The articles were published in central (14 per cent), political (27 per cent), cultural (32 per cent) and progressive (27 per cent) papers. It will be noted that most of the texts on psychoanalysis appeared in the book and film pages of political and progressive papers. If we now look at the *space* taken up by articles on or allusions to psychoanalysis, we find that the central group accounts for 40 per cent of it, the political group for 20 per cent, whilst the cultural and progressive groups account for 15 per cent and 25 per cent respectively. The distribution of this space is testimony to the fact that it was the central Communist press that published most long articles on psychoanalysis; the articles published elsewhere are shorter and, as we shall see, part of the propaganda campaign against the United States. The headlines themselves are a good index. A distinction can be made between headlines that mention America (*American documents*), negative headlines that attack psychoanalysis (*The Road to Hell*), 'funny' headlines (*Go crazy if you want to be happy; The repression of an adventure*) and thematic headlines referring to youth, mental health or women (*Five Great Illnesses Still to be Defeated; Teenagers are not killers; Woman-as-object*).

The frequency with which the headlines appear varies, depending on the group to which the publication belongs (table 14.1). America is the point which attracts most attention in the *Communist* press, especially in the central and cultural publications. Negative titles use applications of psychoanalysis as a model that can be used to explain a film, place or character, and Communist journalists are critical of such applications. There is often an implicit reference to the United States, as most of the films discussed are American. The *progressive* press uses all these themes, but prefers comic headlines – a tried and tested distancing device – or investigative headlines dealing with specific problems. Even at the level of headlines, we can see one difference between the progressive press and Communist publications. Attitudes towards psychoanalysis are clearly in evidence: 100 per cent of articles appearing in central and political publications, and 88 per cent of those in cultural publications are hostile, whilst only 20 per cent of those in the progressive press are hostile; 53 per cent are sympathetic, and 27 per cent are ironic or express reservations.

A further division emerges if we look at what authority the authors have in the eyes of the group, and at references to an authority. The authority in question might be a journal (such as *La Nouvelle Critique*), a famous figure (Stalin, Maurice Thorez or Freud) or some basic principle (dialectical materialism). Principles act as authorities when they are not spelled out, but simply invoked as axioms that allow us to choose between

Table 14.1 Attitudes to psychoanalysis by group

	Central group (%)	Political group (%)	Cultural group (%)	Progressive group (%)
Headline with 'America' theme	40	24	31	11
Hostile	20	19	36	11
Comic	0	4	12	31
Young people, women, children	0	24	21	32
Mental health	20	19	0	10
No headline	20	10	0	5

Table 14.2 Source of authority by group

	Political/central groups (%)	Cultural group (%)	Progressive group (%)
Authority from Party Press[a]	27	0	0
Named authority[b]	27	53	70
Ideological authority of principles	44	47	30
No reference	2	0	0

[a] *La Nouvelle Critique, L'Humanité.*
[b] Marx, Freud, Stalin, Thorez.

different alternatives. Authorities *sign* more articles in central, political (27 per cent) and cultural (37per cent) publications than in progressive papers (11 per cent), where signed articles by less important figures are more common (63 per cent) than in the Communist press (40 per cent). Prestige in the eyes of the group plays a bigger role for communists. The same is true of references to an authority (table 14.2).

Appeals to authority, particularly to ideological authorities, are especially common in political and central publications. Cultural papers and magazines are more likely to personify ideological frames of reference by invoking the authorities – dead or alive – in whose name psychoanalysis is being criticized or rejected. Ideological principles are evoked less frequently in the progressive press, which follows the example of the press as a whole; authors who are mentioned by name are usually under attack. In progressive publications, authors with some psychoanalytic experience can be seen by the group as authorities; this is rarely (6 per cent) the case in the communist press.

What function do appeals to authority serve in the Communist press? Their primary function is to define the philosophical, scientific and political grounds on which psychoanalysis has to be refuted; they also have the secondary function of ensuring that the reader endorses the points of view that are expressed, or lending them the prestige of the individual who signs the article or the Party publication in which it appears. The combination of a named individual and the Party supplies a concrete context for a content which would otherwise look like no more than a discussion of principles.

Having looked in quantitative terms at the content of these articles on psychoanalysis and having demonstrated that a distinction should be made between communist and progressive publications, we can now survey a few texts. We will then examine them in statistical terms.

For Communist publications from the period between 1949 and 1953, psychoanalysis is a symptom of an American invasion at the national level, and of a bourgeois cultural invasion at the level of the class struggle. It is dangerous on both counts, and fighting it is the most urgent of all tasks. We can enumerate a number of themes and related expressions.

2.1 *The description of psychoanalysis*

(a) *Psychoanalysis is primarily an ideology.* 'As a whole, psychoanalysis looks in 1948 mainly like an ideology that is being used to penetrate the broadest possible social strata by using a great diversity of propagandist methods . . . progressive forces and the peace movement must express concern about this situation, and try to discover the extent to which a supposedly scientific activity is being used as a pretext to promote an ideology which implies more or less overtly conservative goals.'[1] 'An American psychosomatic medicine based upon the irrational concepts of psychoanalysis is being introduced at the same time, and it is aimed primarily at psychiatrists.'[2] 'Let me simply point out once more that the current medical fashion for psychoanalysis results from its obscurantist and irrational content, and from its apparatus of uncontrollable drives, which can be made to demand and say anything, and which is eminently suited to the "ideological rearmament" of American imperialism.'[3]

(b) *No heed should be taken of any of psychoanalysis's contributions, as it is no more than a semblance of a science.* 'This (war) propaganda would simply look ridiculous, if it were also not argued that it can be justified on supposedly scientific grounds.'[4] Before going on, it may be as well to pause and remember that the campaign against psychoanalysis was part of a larger campaign initiated in the Soviet Union by Zhadnov against bourgeois science and for proletarian science. Philosophers belonging to, or

---

[1] 'Autocritique. La Psychanalyse idéologie réactionnaire', *La Nouvelle Critique*, no. 7, June 1949, p. 57.

[2] 'Un Débat sur la cortisone', *La Nouvelle Critique*, 1952, p. 99.

[3] 'L'Avenir de la medicine', *La Pensée*, no. 37, 1951.

[4] 'Bilan de la psychanalyse', *La Nouvelle Critique*, no. 27, 1951.

favourable to, the Party emphasized its link to the revolution and the opposition between bourgeois and proletarian science. A few scientists, such as the great biologist Jacques Monod, left the Party. Others, including a group of well-known psychoanalysts, performed what was called their *autocritique*, self-criticism. 'We must not approach psychoanalysis on its own territory by delineating its contribution to psychiatry.'[5] 'There is no reason for us to decide what is valid and what is not valid about psychoanalysis.' 'There can be no question of attempting here to draw up a balance sheet of the positive contributions Freud and his heirs have made to our techniques or to our understanding of man.'

2.2 The action of psychoanalysis

(a) *Psychoanalysis is a tool used to make political interventions* 'The systematic exploitation of psychoanalysis, the direct interventions it is making into the arena of the class struggle, and the scale of the economic support it enjoys, pose the problem in political terms.'[6] 'Irrespective of what certain psychoanalysts may think, psychoanalysis cannot be dissociated from the political use that is being made of it. The development of psychoanalysis and even the contents of its doctrine and technique are intimately bound up with the history of social struggles.'[7]

(b) *Psychoanalysis deceives and paralyses men as they fight for a better future.* 'But, even though your survey included an almost unanimous protest over propaganda in favour of pentothal or lobotomies, the prattle about "psychoanalytic interventions", and "the rape of the personality" comes in the wake of "existentialist" or "psychoanalytic" propaganda, which is the ideal way to fuel the metaphysical anxieties of tortured minds, and to confuse the struggle for real liberation with the worsening of actual oppression.'[8] 'We can recognize the essential theme as an attempt to depoliticize individuals, and to convince them that vaguely psychoanalytic therapy is the only thing the world needs.'[9]

(c) *Psychoanalysis allays the fears of the middle class.* 'It was developed mainly in the 1920s and 1930s. Freud's pansexualism was used by a few groups of bourgeois surrealist intellectuals as a pretext for freeing themselves from the constraints of moral hypocrisy.'[10] 'It is spreading to wherever the ruling class needs . . . to calm the fears of social strata that have been declassed by a choice they could not avoid.'[11]

---

[5] 'Autocritique', *La Nouvelle Critique*, no. 7, June 1949.
[6] Ibid.
[7] Ibid.
[8] 'Lettre à Esprit', *La Nouvelle Critique*, no. 15, 1950.
[9] 'Documents américains', *La Nouvelle Critique*, no. 6, 1949, p. 92.
[10] 'Bilan de la psychanalyse', *La Nouvelle Critique*, no. 27, 1951.
[11] Ibid.

(d) *Psychoanalysis is an escapist and perverse technique.* 'Women's magazines promote bourgeois escapism. And psychoanalysis quite naturally comes to the rescue of that escapism.'[12] 'Light music programmes are escapist programmes. Mass broadcasting of works by the ideologues of reaction, the American jazz invasion, a "psychoanalytic" propaganda series by A.G.'[13] 'Those who produce the journal known as *Psyché* make psychoanalysis the direct servant of the capitalist masters, and take it upon themselves to tell this woman what her role should be: she can be either submissive or hostile to men.'[14]

(e) 'What was originally an ideological reflection of the discontents of a decadent bourgeoisie has now become an offensive weapon in the hands of the financial oligarchies and the American federal government.'[15] 'Psychoanalysis now reinforces the usual psycho-techniques used in police operations that serve the purposes of the bosses and the American occupiers who are trying to eliminate the rebellious and anyone who tries to resist them.'[16] 'Hitlerian medicine reintroduced astrology, magic and quacks. Truman's fashionable medicine is reintroducing *diabolic* possession and psychoanalysis.'[17]

2.3 The field of action of psychoanalysis

(a) *Psychoanalysis is penetrating every branch of knowledge.* 'Although it is described as an introductory book for the general public, this "encyclopedia" in fact mixes anatomical descriptions and physiological explanations with general remarks about psychology that are strongly influenced by psychoanalytic conceptions.'[18] '[G.G.'s idealism] is inspired by psychology, and especially the psychology that finds its classic expression in psychoanalysis.'[19]

(b) *Psychoanalysis has negative effects at the socio-political level.* 'Psychoanalysis is now being given the magical power to solve all problems: poverty and strikes, war and peace, educational problems, and criminology.'[20] 'In terms of social life, the main role of psychoanalytic propaganda in the mainstream press is that of a pimp.'[21]

---

[12] 'Les Trois K', *La Nouvelle Critique*, no. 27, 1951.
[13] *Les Cahiers du communisme*, 1957, p. 473.
[14] Ibid.
[15] 'Bilan de la psychanalyse', *La Nouvella Critique*, no. 27, 1951.
[16] 'De la psychotechnique à la sociologie policière', *La Nouvelle Critique*, no. 28.
[17] 'L'Avenir de la médicine', *La Pensée*, no. 37, 1951.
[18] *La Pensée*, no. 36.
[19] 'De la psychotechnique . . .', *La Nouvelle Critique*, no. 28.
[20] 'Bilan de la psychanalyse', *La Nouvelle Critique*, no. 27, 1951.
[21] Ibid.

These few pages have outlined the main features of the content and representation of psychoanalysis in the Communist press. The articles published in progressive newspapers and magazines are rather different. These are publications written for a 'bourgeois' and 'intellectual' audience whose views differ from those of the Communist Party in many respects. The publications in question try not to offend their readers, as that might compromise their vocation. Their vocation is to act as an intermediary between the Communist Party and other parties, and between a broad faction of the working class and a small faction of the middle classes. The ground on which they meet is primarily political. If it offended this middle-class minority, its values and its language when it talked about the problem of psychoanalysis or any other problem of the same nature, the progressive press would find it impossible to pursue its own goals, and would be identified with the Communist press. We might even go so far as to say that, if it is to achieve its goals, it must adapt itself to the middle class, and do all it can to understand its attitudes and values; if it can do that, its political content will be more easily accepted. These progressive papers and magazines were products of the wartime Resistance and are naturally left-leaning, in the same way that others have grown close to the centre and the political right. Their editorial teams are still relatively heterogeneous, and quite naturally have very different opinions. In the Communist press, every author and every article expresses the view of the Party, but that is far from being the case here. *Action*, *La Tribune des nations* and other papers portray psychoanalysis in quite positive terms. Claims that it is a form of therapy like any other are uncontroversial, and explanations derived from psychoanalytic conceptions are sometimes cited with as much fervour or as many reservations as in papers with very different politics. In an article by 'Y. de G.' entitled 'Five Main Illnesses Still to be Defeated' in *Action*, psychoanalysis is described as a scientific and serious way of treating 'madness'.[22] 'Psychosomatic medicine' is also discussed from a psychoanalytical point of view.[23] Drawing his readers' attention to the appearance of a new medical perspective, the author demonstrates that 'according to many doctors', the kernel of this medicine lies in its implicitly Freudian concept of anxiety and repressed conflicts, which are regarded as the basic causes of many organic or functional illnesses. He discusses Alexander and Wolf's work on gastro-intestinal ulcers, and the mechanics of therapeutic action are accurately described. Like all these dailies and weeklies, *Libération* takes the waistlines of its women readers very seriously, tells them that 'Madame can lose weight' and recommends that anyone lacking in will power should try analytic treatment.[24] The acquittal of the lay

---

[22] *Action*, 23 August 1951.
[23] Ibid., 28 March 1952.
[24] *Libération*, 4 September 1952.

analyst Mme C. is greeted with approval by *Libération* and described as 'A victory that will bring joy to the heart of anyone with a mentally deficient child who might benefit from psychoanalysis.'[25] 'And it is justified', concludes a four-column article on how beneficial analytic therapy can be for children. A professional medical association, which opposes any application of psychoanalysis by those not medically qualified, is criticized for its attacks on competent specialists.

It might be inferred from these examples that the therapeutic applications of psychoanalysis have been found acceptable. Freud's theories are sometimes used as universally applicable explanatory models. Their generalization is, however, conditional upon a further qualification: the social factor must be introduced to provide a more valid frame of reference. A translation of a book by Susan Isaacs received a glowing review in *Europe*.[26] Some reservations were expressed about the 'psychoanalytic jargon', but the only real criticism is that she provides solutions for the problem of relations between parents and children in a bourgeois milieu, and overlooks social factors. In a study of young people who commit suicide ('Why Do They Want to Die?'), the psychoanalytic explanation – assuming that it is correct – is described as incomplete because it does not tell us why there were more suicides in 1951 than in 1938.[27] In the author's view, the blame lies with the lack of social solidarity and the dislocation of families as a result of poverty and the absence of any ideals. Analytic hypotheses are not directly refuted, but their validity is not taken for granted. Without going into further detail, it should be emphasized that progressive publications are more willing than others to accept psychoanalytic schemata but attempt to integrate them into a 'broader' vision by giving priority to hypotheses of a sociological nature. We see here an element of mediation with both Marxism and a latent 'culturalism' that concurs with both the tradition of Durkheim and common-sense observations. Psychoanalysts do not appear to deny that social factors have an influence on suicides and delinquency, but they do not accord them the same importance as psychological factors and are tempted to invert the usual explanations when they do take them into account. Such issues raise quite of lot of theoretical difficulties, and the positions adopted are often contradictory. Precisely which factors are 'decisive' is still a matter for debate. Certain psychoanalysts adopt what might be described as an extreme point of view. As a result, the progressive press's 'social' prequisite looks very much like the golden mean that is so dear to any publication that addresses the middle classes in our society. Common sense, good sense and the golden mean merged into one another long ago in an attempt to discourage exaggerations, and they sustain a sheep-like

[25] *Libération*, 1 August 1952.
[26] *Europe*, February 1953.
[27] *Action*, April 1951.

conformity in the same way that savings sustain the wealth of the few and the mediocre lives of the many.

To be fair to the articles published in *Libération*, *Europe* and *Action*, they do not exploit this middle of the road position, even though doing so is a golden rule for part of the press. Even when the pansexualism and 'exaggerations' of psychoanalysis are mentioned, great discretion is used. The emphasis placed on social factors is justifiable and their relevance is demonstrated with great seriousness. Some of the complaints about psychoanalysis that we found in the Communist press can also be found in the columns of progressive papers. The 'object-woman' who is described as a parasitic preying mantis displaying both a predatory attitude and a desire to be submissive is, of course, the woman described by 'American psychoanalysis'.[28] Although the 'Freudian rhetoricians' he consulted were very inventive and imaginative, they leave the article's author dissatisfied. The situation he described seems to him to be mainly the product of an entire system, or of a whole (American) way of life that is based upon money. This 'object-woman' despises labour because she belongs to a class that despises it and because she cannot see beyond 'society' and her own 'set'. As society evolves, this type of woman will become extinct. In the meantime, psychoanalysis, America and the pejorative features of this type of woman are closely associated with one another because that allows them to 'compromise' each other.

Libération develops another theme that associates psychoanalysis with America, and justifies it on ethical grounds: the tyranny of subliminal advertising. Picking up news reports about the possibility of influencing purchasing behaviour by inserting adverts into a big film as it is being projected, J.H. writes:

> It was only to be expected: the Americans have discovered the unconscious, and are beginning to exploit it in that practical, profitable and commercial way of theirs. Until recently, the American unconscious only sold itself retail though psychoanalytic paths. It was an expensive luxury, and you had to have dollars to spare to have the right to an Oedipus complex.[29]

The headline 'Freud and the Eskimo, or Rape in the Cold' sums up the view, which we also encountered in the survey, that psychoanalysis works by 'breaking and entering'. As a rule, the application of psychoanalysis to activities that do not seem to be within its remit is condemned sternly and in very harsh terms, even though the tone is *lighter* than that of other papers. H.B.'s 'Psychoanalysis with Cream' informs *Libération*'s readers about how a dairymen's trade paper tried to use the teachings of

[28] *La Tribune des nations*, 4 April 1952.
[29] *Libération*, 18 June 1956.

psychoanalysis in a bid to boost sales; the effects were hilarious. The article provides an opportunity to remind readers of the paper's general attitude:

> Psychoanalysis is in fashion, and that is a fact. It is, of course, to be regretted that this panacea of a science has yet to penetrate all areas of activity, and especially those where its benefits might do most good. But on the whole – and amongst the middle classes – psychoanalysis continues to make startling inroads. It began by winning over the aesthetes, the artists and the fashionable women, and then the bourgeoisie, and it is not impossible that it will eventually come to the help of labourers who are sickening for a piece of steak . . . For the moment, let us simply note that the new science has made an interesting conquest: the French Dairy Corporation.[30]

The rest of the article is of no particular interest, but the first section contains three interesting assertions. The first, which concerns the fashion for psychoanalysis, is very general. The second, which is about whether or not psychoanalysis works, reveals the difference between progressive and Communist publications, whilst the third, with its talk of an expansion *aimed* mainly at 'labourers' coincides with the Communist claim that psychoanalysis is a tool for spreading propaganda based on a class ideology. The way the three themes are interwoven provides an amusing description of the pivotal role of this group of papers and magazines, which is to reconcile some very different conceptions, and especially those of the Communists and those of other social groups. If we wish to bring out more clearly the themes we have described, we must fall back on quantitative estimates. One interesting index is supplied by a periodical's degree of involvement with, or distance from, psychoanalysis. We can define its degree of involvement by estimating in comparative terms the extent to which the periodical or group is concerned with the theory, and the degree to which it regards it as part of its ideological world (table 14.3).

The findings are instructive. The table shows that the proportion of 'insider' articles in *Libération* is almost equal to the proportion of 'outsider' articles in *L'Humanité* and *Les Lettres françaises*. This corroborates our qualitative findings: the Communist press treats psychoanalysis like a foreign body or an enemy, whereas the progressive press regards it as a theory that it can accept, with some reservations. If I list the points that caught my attention, we can see that we have to make some fine distinctions between the various themes after simply describing their content. The most widely discussed theme is that of the harmful or useful, and honest or dishonest nature ('charlatanism') of psychoanalysis (*L'Humanité*: 38 per cent; *Les Lettres françaises* 36 per cent and *Libération* 35 per cent). It is *L'Humanité* and *Les Lettres françaises* that place most emphasis on its political function

---

[30] *Libération*, 17 February 1953.

Table 14.3 Is psychoanalysis part of the group's ideological world?

	L'Humanité (%)	Lettres françaises (%)	Libération (%)
Internal	27	15	65
External	73	85	35

(26 per cent and 17 per cent), whereas *Libération* almost never mentions it (3 per cent). *Les Lettres françaises* (20 per cent) and, to a lesser extent, *L'Humanité* (16 per cent) use the 'mythological' aspect of psychoanalysis as a means of devaluing it. Interpreting it as a product of the American way of life (20 per cent and 15 per cent respectively) is another way of compromising it. Paradoxically, it is *Libération* that makes the most frequent reference (15 per cent) to philosophical and ideological arguments about materialism and idealism. Only *Libération* enters into a more detailed discussion about the psychical apparatus and its relations with medicine, education and so on in the light of Freud's theories (32 per cent). The readers of these papers and magazines are asked to think about the harmful or beneficial effects of analytic concepts, and about the honesty or dishonesty of psychoanalysis.

Most communist texts remind their readers that psychoanalysis has to be seen as something whose existence is defined by such basic dichotomies as France/America, science/mythology or political/non-political. Progressive papers touch upon these polarities too, but they also look at family and psychological problems in the light of Freud's conceptions. These focal points outline the context in which groups of readers are encouraged to look at anything to do with this 'panacea of a science', and especially its role (table 14.4).

According to the Communist press, the primary role of psychoanalysis – the reactionary ideology of a decadent class – is heightened by the role it plays as an instrument of the bourgeoisie in the class struggle. References to policing and to the 'rape' of the conscious mind give these doctrinal constructs a brutal look. Once again, the progressive press has its own line, and recognizes that psychoanalysis does have a theoretical and therapeutic role to play. Because of its philosophical basis, its forms of action and its constitution, which demands that everything must be seen in terms of its actual or potential political implications, the Communist group assumes that the goals of psychoanalysis, which is the expression of a society it wishes to destroy, are adapted to its representation of that society.

Psychoanalysis is not just an ideology or pseudo-science. It is also used as an alibi, whose function and finality are one and the same, by a class and a country (the United States) which want to cover up the reality of social or scientific problems. The bourgeoisie generates pseudo-sciences, especially social pseudo-sciences, because its contradictions mean that it can

Table 14.4 Role of psychoanalysis, as defined by group

Role of psychoanalysis	Press			
	Central (%)	Political (%)	Cultural (%)	Progressive (%)
General ideological	60	70	47	4
Bourgeois weapon	20	8	20	6
Police technique	14	20	11	0
Mystification	6	2	8	0
Theoretical	0	0	8	54
Therapeutic	0	0	6	22
Theoretical and therapeutic	0	0	0	14

no longer resolve its own crises or adapt workers to the socio-economic structure it has constructed for its own benefit. Psychoanalysis is, first and foremost, an alibi, but it also represents an attempt to resolve the crises, worries and discontents of the middle classes (24 per cent). The themes of 'accepting the American lifestyle' (12 per cent) and 'stupefying the masses' (6 per cent) complete this instrumental picture of the doctrine. A small proportion (10 per cent) of articles in *Les Lettres françaises* concede that it has a theoretical and therapeutic goal; *Libération* mentions only its therapeutic goal (86 per cent), but also speaks of its profitable goal (14 per cent), which supplies the pretext for a lot of ironic allusions.

Psychoanalysis is an ideology, a social tool, a theory and a form of therapy, but it is also a form of action that is closely bound up with its goals (table 14.5). The Communist press emphasizes the way it justifies the existing social order, whilst the progressive press emphasizes the therapeutic and intellectual help it can provide. The *entire* progressive press sees mystification and deception as secondary considerations. The specialist nature of the publications concerned leads to specialization at the thematic level: political and central papers and magazines concentrate mainly on the doctrine's effects in the context of the ('cold') war, whilst the cultural weeklies have more to say about how French culture is being invaded and how morals are being corrupted. In both cases, it is conflict that determines the orientation of analytic activity: the drift towards war at the political level, and the debasement of French culture and national morale at the cultural level.

The themes that govern the Communist response to psychoanalysis are, in order, the superiority of the materialist conception for real social liberation (60 per cent), the need for cultural protectionism (24 per cent) and the existence of a Pavlovian scientific psychology (16 per cent). Progressive publications merely recommend the adoption of a cautious

Table 14.5 Effect of psychoanalysis, as defined by group

Effect of psychoanalysis	Press			
	Central (%)	Political (%)	Cultural (%)	Progressive (%)
Justifies existing society; masks real problems	36	28	37	0
Invades French society; justifies anomalies; esoterism	12	18	30	20
Weapon of war	28	13	0	0
Mystifies and deceives	24	41	33	28
Therapeutic help, intellectual effect	0	0	0	52

and circumspect attitude towards psychoanalysis (100 per cent). The fundamental difference between Communists and progressives resides, however, in the Communists' constant insistence on supplying themes that react to psychoanalytic theory (72 per cent),[31] whereas progressive papers do so only to a limited extent (22 per cent). If we now go on to make an analysis of the explicit intentions of their articles on psychoanalysis, we can understand the overall meaning and direction of the propaganda, for which it sometimes serves as a target and sometimes as a pretext. In general terms, the goal of articles published in the Communist press is to provide a critique of the theory, but they try above all to associate it with those groups that are Communism's permanent enemies: the United States – and especially American political power – and capitalism. Psychoanalysis, America and the capitalist class tend to infect one another, and each term can therefore be used to devalue the next (table 14.6). Examples illustrating this link have already given, and I will not go over them again.

A negative attitude towards Freud's doctrine and a negative attitude towards the United States can both help to produce the same behaviour and encourage the same rejection of psychoanalysis. The denunciations of the irrationalism of psychoanalysis simply reinforce the major theme. The adage 'We only destroy the things we can replace' proves to be particularly applicable to communications emanating from a group that has an overall vision of the world and of society. Catholics have replaced one psychoanalysis with another. When they banished psychoanalysis – especially from a 'cultural' press addressed to intellectuals – Communists also

---

[31] 'Themes that react' are defined as a publication's 'responses to propositions and actions attributed to psychoanalysis'.

Table 14.6 Goals of psychoanalysis, as defined by group

	Press			
Goal of article	Central (%)	Political (%)	Cultural (%)	Progressive (%)
Associate psychoanalysis with USA/capitalism	70	57	51	13
Denounce use; promote Pavlovian concepts	0	18	31	18
Denounce irrational aspects; promote healthy conceptions	30	25	18	0
Introduce psychoanalysis; stress its value	0	0	0	69

asserted the superiority of Pavlovian psychology. We might complete the adage by adding 'if need be'. A comparison of the percentages demonstrates that it is mainly intellectuals who feel the need for a psychological system that can provide a better answer to both the same problems and scientific epistemology. The central and political press have little to say about how Pavlov relates to Freud. It is the more specialist publications that compare the work of Pavlov and psychoanalysis. The need to provide a different frame of conceptual reference seems to have played a determinant role, especially when there is a justifiable emphasis on the major implications of research that has been ignored by even an educated Communist audience.

The progressive press and the Communist press use different representations of psychoanalysis. The latter adopts a systematically negative position, as is demonstrated by even a rapid content analysis. It is not, however, the fact that the Communist image of psychoanalysis is negative – this is not the only group to have such an image – that justifies the claim that it uses anti-psychoanalytic propaganda. We must now look at the other reasons why we can give our assertion a specific meaning, and those reasons are less superficial.

3 What Anti-psychoanalytic Propaganda are We Talking About?

The first question we have to ask is this: has the French Communist Party been waging a propaganda campaign against psychoanalysis?

We can answer this question by demonstrating that we find in articles dealing in one way or another with psychoanalysis a series of manifestations of this form of communication. Both psychosociologists and political writers have amply described them as being specific to propaganda. It must first be noted that Communist journalists assert the existence of propaganda designed to spread knowledge of psychoanalytic conceptions in France. Their own actions are therefore a form of *counter-propaganda*. At the level of a theoretical study, the meaning of the propaganda does little to alter the terms of the analysis. And it must be recognized that psychoanalysis has extended its field of activity since the end of the Second World War, partly as a result of American influence. We will have to return more than once to this point.

For the moment, let us look at some specific examples of this propaganda. The use of stereotypes is immediately obvious. These are the titles of articles on psychoanalytic themes:

> 'From Psychoanalysis to Sociology for Cops', [32] 'Public Barkers',[33] 'Truman Hunts Witches and Tames Lions',[34] 'The Children Who Were Turned into Monsters – The Guilty Men are not in the Dock',[35] 'Psychoanalysis, with its idealist methodology, is part of a family of ideologies based upon irrationalism, and that family includes Nazi ideology. Hitler did precisely the same thing by cultivating myths about race and blood, and they were the Nazi version of these irrational instincts.'[36]

Psychoanalysis is discredited by the contextual use of stereotypes with negative emotional and intellectual connotations of irrationality and Nazism.

At the same time, a second propaganda technique is used: disparate elements are put in a single category, either positive or negative. Thanks to its actual or imaginary properties, a single term is used to refer to things that seem, at first sight, to be dissimilar or unrelated. Their identification means that they are seen as so many expressions of the same category, or the same group of phenomena or doctrines. If the meaning of the identification is negative, it is possible to reach a dishonest compromise with the 'enemy'. The stated goal is not simply to justify the categorical unification of social diversity, but that operation certainly plays a primordial role in most propaganda campaigns. The impression of identity that the Communist press is trying to give has more to do with the ideological and American side of psychoanalysis than with its scientific side.

Psychoanalysis serves masters known as 'America', 'the police', 'the bosses' and 'fascism', and the assertion that they have something in common helps to discredit all of them. There is no need to repeat new arguments because what is true of one is true of all of them.

[32] *La Nouvelle Critique*, May 1951.
[33] *Les Lettres françaises*, 14 June 1951.
[34] Ibid., 28 June 1951.
[35] Ibid., 10 May 1951.
[36] 'Bilan de la psychanalyse', *La Nouvelle Critique*, no. 27, 1951.

Freud is perfectly at home in this portrait gallery of men whose activities appear harmful to science, especially as it is a priest who makes the comparison:

> According to (Father) Riquet, real science means the science of Heisenberg, with his uncertainty principle, Freud, Mendel and Weisman. There are some passing juicy quibbles about the Vatican Council and the science of Mr Huxley, who is such a jealous defender of the scientist's freedom of conscience, but why Heisenberg, Freud, Mendel and Weisman?

Coming at a time when he was criticizing the work of Lysenko and his school, the allusion to Julian Huxley is obviously intended to link psychoanalysis with the positivist theory of uncertainty and with Lysenko's enemies, who are led by the Church, or in other words an ideological and spiritual power whose behaviour is characterized by hostility towards Communism and ambiguity towards science.

A third technique known as 'appellation' consists in the use of favourable or pejorative adjectives that help to denounce or construct a social 'personality' along the desired lines. The expressions ' boudoir philosophy', 'mystifying doctrine', 'American psychoanalysis' and so on are used in place of 'psychoanalysis', a word which is rarely used without a pejorative qualification.

Distortions and simplifications have, finally, always been weapons in the propagandist's arsenal:

> 'Let me just point out once again that the current medical vogue for psychoanalysis results from its obscurantist content, and its apparatus of uncontrollable drives, which can be made to say and do anything and which are admirably suited to be American imperialism's ideological armature.'[37] 'Its productivity means that psychoanalysis is available to all. What progress! In the land of mass production, it now takes no longer to get rid of your worries than it does to manufacture a pair of nylon stockings. And it is no more complicated either.'[38]

Deciding whether or not a text is a distortion means deciding whether it is true or false, and we have already stated that we do not wish to do that. In the cases cited, however, the technique is so blatant that we cannot be criticized for giving an interpretation we are not supposed to be giving. The passage about analytic treatment can, for example, be regarded as a distortion because it takes no account, *at the expository level*, of the real possibility that analytic therapy can bring about a cure. This automatically eliminates other possibilities:

---

[37] *La Pensée*, no. 37, 1951.
[38] *La Nouvelle Critique*, no. 48, September–October 1953.

(a) There is no mention of the fact that it is the objective disappearance of the symptoms that indicates that the patient has been cured, and not only the reinforcement of beliefs.

(b) The relationship between analyst and patient is described as a purely verbal or ideological relationship, which overlooks the role attributed to the transference, which some Marxist authors belonging to the same party consider one of the positive contributions of psychoanalysis.

Having said that, we cannot rule out the possibility that a belief in the explanations supplied by psychoanalysis might be a therapeutic factor. We have spoken of distortions and simplifications, and not of falsifications. Is it not a simplification to say that its productivity means that psychoanalysis is now available to all, without looking more carefully, or in other words in greater depth, at the relationship between the doctrine advanced by Freud and its possible social implications?

To end this list of 'symptoms' of propaganda, it should be noted that 'pseudo-science' and 'scientific mystification' are the most common descriptions of psychoanalysis (36 per cent); 'American', 'perverted' and 'decadent' are used more rarely (30 per cent, 12 per cent and 8 per cent respectively).

We will not dwell on the meaning of these propagandist techniques for the moment. Although an extensive literature has been devoted to them, they are not in fact of any great interest. We are, it will be recalled, attempting to ascertain whether or not the French Communist Party uses antipsychoanalytic propaganda. The material we have looked at means that the question can be answered in the affirmative.

What circumstances led the Communist Party to wage a systematic propaganda campaign against psychoanalysis?

It has to be recalled that its hostility towards psychoanalysis is long-standing and that, even before the war, one of the reasons for the schism within the surrealist movement (Aragon, Sadoul) was its interest in some of the more striking aspects of Freud's work, such as dreams and sexuality (Nadeau 1948). Psychoanalysis and psycho-techniques were not practised in the Soviet Union. Some doctrinaire Communists, and especially Georges Politzer (1928), thought for a short time that the work of psychoanalysis could be the source of a concrete psychology, but then rejected it categorically. Yet, the Party's anti-psychoanalytic propaganda dates mainly from the period 1949–50. It is possible to provide a schematic sketch of the circumstances surrounding its emergence. After the Second World War, psychoanalytic notions penetrated *every social milieu* in France. They provided the basis for interpretations that were used in an attempt to understand – and resolve – a number of problems affecting individuals and society alike. The tensions of world conflict, the insecurity following the too brief respite between the end of the Second World War and the onset of the cold war, corollaries of a historical period in which the foundations of technology, science and politics were being transformed, all seemed to find a response in psychoanalysis. In its turn, psychoanalysis became the sign of such renewals and appeared as one of the twentieth century's great discoveries. At the same time, America's influence on our continent was growing, and the country was regarded not only as the symbol of technological efficiency, but also as the homeland of psychoanalysis and of the social sciences that were taking on different ideological and practical forms from those we were familiar with in Europe. The intellectual *milieu* was, because of its members' professional activities, the first to assimilate these trans-Atlantic doctrines. Through its intermediary, other social strata also became imbued with these new conceptions. Many scientific theories, as well as psychoanalysis and certain of the methods currently used in the human sciences, seemed to go against the principles of the Communist Party and the theories that prevailed in the Soviet Union. The membership of the French Communist Party included intellectuals and members of the bourgeoisie. Because of their actual or potential acceptance of psychoanalysis, and the possible use they might make of it in the scientific domain, there was a danger that these Party members might undermine the unity, representation and identity of the Communist group. The role played by psychoanalysis in the domains of education and pathology meant that every Communist had to take a stance on these everyday issues.

After the denunciation of governmental *tripartisme*, the launch of the Marshall Plan and the increase in the antagonism between the United States and the Soviet Union in the period 1948–49, the conflict between the political parties became sharper. The establishment of two military and political blocs divided the nations that had won the war. Citizens too were divided by their respective support of or hostility towards the Communist Party. In the context of these divisions, psychoanalysis, which was expanding in both the United States and France, became a sign of the outsider status of these various social groups. Support or silence about psychoanalysis became signs of the division between Communism and noncommunism *inside* the Communist Party. It was a source of conflict and posed a threat to its group identity. The existence of a multiplicity of explanations for interrelated phenomena at both the individual and collective levels threatened to disturb the unity of its social field and to destabilize the life of the Party. Increasingly intense conflicts – the course of this 'cold' war was punctuated by conflict in Korea and Indochina – led to the permanent mobilization of the Party's forces at a political level, and to its adoption of the doctrinal positions of the Soviet Union. Psychoanalysis was obviously no more than a pawn in this complex game, but it is psychoanalysis that concerns us here. Besides, when this propaganda campaign was launched, Communist spokesmen were right about its causes. They demonstrated that, before the war, psychoanalysis had been restricted to very limited circles. As they began to look at the situation, they noted that

'[Psychoanalysis] is now returning [from the United States] via the canal that supports the American way of life.'[39] 'The progressive forces and the peace movement ought to be worried about this situation, and must look at how the pretext of so-called scientific activity is being used to develop an ideology whose goals – overt or otherwise – are social conservatism or social regression.'[40]

The Party's external enemies were recognizable. The fact that the campaign began, in practical terms, with a self-criticism demonstrates the existence of actual or potential conflict within the Party. The self-criticism was entitled 'Psychoanalysis: A Reactionary Ideology', and it was signed by eight *psychoanalysts*.[41]

Our analysis demonstrates that propaganda campaigns begin when there is the existence of intergroup conflict, and when its object might pose a threat to the identity of the group and to the unity of its representation of the real.
We have advanced a hypothesis as to the nature of situations that can give rise to and characterize this form of communication. It can be tested by a historical study. It will be recalled, first of all, that whilst Communist thinkers had no great liking for psychoanalysis, it did not become the object of systematic propaganda until after 1949. If we look at the Communist press *before* the period when relations between the USSR and the United States, and between the French Communist Party and other parties, become openly antagonistic, we do not find any methodical critiques or refutations of psychoanalysis. In 1947, *L'Humanité* published ten articles alluding to psychoanalysis; five were film reviews and the other five merely used a few psychoanalytic terms. In 1948, the same paper published ten articles, four of them on films. Between July and December 1949, it published seven articles and, for the first time, three were polemical background articles. In 1947 and 1948 most mentions of psychoanalysis occurred in film reviews and used the terminology noted in our discussion of the cultural idiosyncrasies typical of its approach to psychoanalysis, the main one being the association between psychoanalysis, America and films. The terminology used by *L'Humanité* could have been used by any newspaper; crime, eroticism, psychoanalysis and Hollywood were often cited as characteristics of North American society.
Gaslight was reviewed in these terms

'A great film with a lot of qualities and a lot of flaws. A terrible semi-Freudian (the word is all the rage in Hollywood) tale of pathological insanity. This concentration on the sordid and the unhealthy marks the beginning of an

---

[39] *La Nouvelle Critique*, no 27, 1951.
[40] Ibid., June 1949.
[41] Ibid.

invasion.'[42] 'American films continue to wallow in a crude psychoanalysis, with its neuroses, its psychoses and its schizophrenia . . . it's all crammed in.'[43] 'Hollywood discovered psychoanalysis twenty years before the rest of the world did so. It is taking advantage of that fact to "update" its repertoire.'[44]

Greater indulgence is shown when the psychoanalytically inspired film is British. As the reviewer of *Mine Own Executioner* puts it:

> The Anglo-Saxons really do love psychoanalysis. Compared with American productions, in which psychoanalysis is no more than erotic or morbid icing, this British film has to be given credit for regarding it as an object worthy of serious study.[45]

As in the rest of the press, analytic concepts are sometimes used:

> 'Drug-taking, sexual repression and professional jealousy put him on the road that leads to murder.'[46] 'The character studies of both the obsessed actor and the repressed young widow sound the depths of pathology.'[47]

Until now the tone may have been unsympathetic, but it was restricted to a limited domain. In January 1949, it becomes virulent. *L'Humanité* ran the headline: 'Psychoanalysis: an ideology for police informers and spies'. The author described how psychoanalysis is 'flooding in' from America. It points out that it can be found in quite ordinary films, in *Confidences* and *Reader's Digest*, 'and now in *Le Monde*'. It is a pseudo-science which provides pseudo-explanations that mask problems and let the guilty walk free. Social conflicts are explained in terms of individual complexes. Psychoanalysis is a sociological phenomenon. It is reactionary and imperialist, and it uses 'wild *made in USA* imaginings' as an exercise in provocation. It is the duty of Marxists to denounce this 'latest expression of capitalist ideology'. 'It is the last hope of international reaction, which has no consistent theories.'[48] 'There are no two ways of looking at psychoanalysis: psychoanalysis means American-style psychoanalysis.' It is, on the other hand, seen as a valid form of therapy, and it is even hinted that it might be possible to use it to develop a rationalist individual psychology. The stance taken by the Communist Party's official daily inevitably

---

[42] *L'Humanité*, 5 January 1947.
[43] Ibid., 21 September 1947.
[44] Ibid., March 1948.
[45] Ibid., 3 July 1948.
[46] Ibid., 17 June 1948.
[47] Ibid., 26 March 1948.
[48] Ibid., 27 January 1949.

put pressure on psychoanalysts in the Party and, because of the situation it had created, forced them to clarify the relationship between Freud's doctrine and Marxism. The group's unified representation and its identity, or the very things that distinguished and established it as a distinctive group, were at stake. The purpose of the self-criticism was to eliminate all internal sources of conflict and ambiguity arising from the contradiction between the United States and the French capitalist class and its culture, which was the dominant culture in France. We have already had occasion to describe the content of this self-criticism. *L'Humanité* reproduced it in an article published in June 1949. The main lines of the argument are summarized, but the paper now *ruled out* the possibility of making a distinction between psychoanalytic theory and psychoanalytic therapy and of any rapprochement as to particular issues. Psychoanalysis is completely eliminated from the group's social field, and is now nothing but a *sign* of the conflict between it and other groups. Although it is not radical, there is a notable change between the articles of January and June 1949. The sequence of articles published between 1949 and 1953 adopts the same tone and sounds more propagandist. There are few references to psychoanalysis after 1953. If we look at the daily *Ce Soir* we can see the same pattern. In 1947, 1948 and 1949, psychoanalytic terms are used, and the comments on psychoanalysis are by no means unsympathetic and could have appeared in any paper:

> 'The atmosphere of the film is very Freudian, and one has the impression that every character's deepest motives are beyond their control and remain in the shadows.'[49] 'A text whose insights at times see into the very depths of the subconscious.'[50] 'Juvenile repressions, wild imaginings and unhealthy romanticism; all these psychological mysteries lead up to the murder of Alain.'[51]

In a survey of the wonders of medicine, psychoanalysis is mentioned as one of the techniques that can be used to cure mental illness:

> Ever since the Austrian doctor Freud expounded the famous technique he calls psychoanalysis, doctor-psychologists have accepted that the mind works on two levels.[52]

Narco-analysis is described as an 'accelerated psychoanalysis'. The same open judgements are repeated in an article on 'the truth serum', where narco-analysis, which is baptized 'chemical psychoanalysis', is defended against the usual criticisms ('breaking into the conscious mind',

[49] *Ce Soir*, July 1948.
[50] Ibid.
[51] Ibid., January 1948.
[52] Ibid., January 1949.

'police methods', etc.). As for Freudian doctrine in the strict sense of the terms, the author provides a quick outline and stresses its importance:

> Over the last few years, psychoanalysis has come to the fore as a way of diagnosing and treating neuroses.

After 1949, nothing more is said about the discipline. In March 1951, an initial attack is outlined in a review of *La Raison*, which is described as 'an interesting journal on mental illnesses'. France's late entry into the domain of psychopathology is deplored, but psychoanalysis is rejected in terms that have now become the norm – 'It mystifies the real problems', 'the American infatuation with psychoanalysis' – whilst the Pavlovian school's work on conditioned reflexes is regarded as a source that can breathe new life into psychology. *Ce Soir* continued to publish similar criticisms of Freudian conceptions and their indications until it ceased publication. An analysis of their historical development confirms the hypothesis that the form and content of these communications change when the social situation is tense and leads to serious conflict between political parties, groups of nations and social systems. In order to prove once and for all that there is a link between types of intergroup relations and propaganda, we now show that during the years of relative détente (after 1955), psychoanalysis was discussed in very different terms, even though this did not signal actual approval. The hope that the cold war was drawing to an end and the changes that followed the death of Stalin lowered the tension, and we see the appearance of critical comments that no longer use the techniques of the form of communications we are studying.

La Raison has these comments to make on an article by Politzer:

> In my opinion, Georges Politzer's polemical argument is mainly directed against Freudianism's *explanatory* conceptual apparatus – against its *extension* to sociology, history and philosophy – and against the *political* use that is made of psychoanalysis, and the way it is confused with Marxism. He challenges neither the importance of the facts discovered by Freud nor the seriousness of the problems that have been posed, and especially that of the social determination of the sexual . . .[53]

Other texts and articles reveal a desire for a debate with psychoanalysis:

> We would like to see analysts dealing with these questions one day. If we took realities we can all recognise as a starting point, we could find a common language, and improve clinical psychiatry, which is only valid if it practises psychotherapy, for the greater good of our patients.[54]

[53] *La Raison*, no. 17, September 1957.
[54] Ibid.

The centenary of Freud's birth provided some writers with an opportunity to reflect upon his work and influence. Past criticisms dating from the time when the propaganda campaign was at its height now appear in a very new light:

> This is Freud's centenary. Let us pay tribute to a brilliant and scrupulous researcher, a perspicacious and careful observer, a wise clinician, and a noble and generous man. But we should not see this centenary just as a pretext for sterile effusions. It provides us with the opportunity to draw up a balance sheet. Not a 'devastating revision' of our positions, but a serious consideration of the complex and contradictory phenomenon of psychoanalysis. It has conquered every domain. It exists in the equivocal heaven of ideas and on the unshakeable ground of clinical practice. It has won its scientific spurs; it is the only form of psychotherapy to have inspired a doctrine and to possess a technique.[55]

The circumstances surrounding the polemics of the past are also evoked:

> Given that any theoretical approach is part of an ideological tendency, and given that any ideology can justify or decide a policy, political considerations and circumstances can, by the same criterion, lead us to emphasize the political aspect of a theory. That is why the political use that could be made of psychoanalysis obliged us to denounce it as a tool used by the ruling classes to dominate and oppress us. It is therefore not our fault if scientific research loses its serenity and sometimes leads to polemics that shock the high-minded. It transpires that *political conditions* determined our criticisms. We could therefore be accused of being 'opportunists' and of allowing immediate political imperatives to influence our judgement. That would, however, be an error of judgement that is at once serious and ridiculous, as it attributes to us a way of thinking that is actually typical of our adversaries. The emphasis was in fact placed on the reactionary aspect of psychoanalysis at the time, not simply because of the political use that might be made of it, but mainly because its characteristically idealist vitalism meant that it would inevitably be used in that way, as Georges Politzer so brilliantly demonstrated. Even though we tried to denounce psychoanalysis in ideological terms, it seems that not everything has been resolved. Our day-to-day clinical practice and our thinking about psychopathology bring us into frequent contact with it. We are therefore naturally inclined to take an interest in the *other pole* of psychoanalytic research, in the *empirical approaches* that inspire it, and in the attempts at *partial* theorization they inspire.[56]

[55] Ibid.
[56] Ibid.

La Nouvelle Critique even published an article on Kafka, probably by a Czech author, in which the 'complex' comes back into its own:

> That this spectacle had destructive effects is not merely a hypothesis on my part; the 'Letter to my Father' contains three moving pages of this, and they clearly show that this experience warped Kafka's attitude towards his fellow men for ever, and that it gave him an acute 'social guilt' complex. This son of a well-off family discovered what it was like to be a wage-earning proletarian; and it was his father – God's representative here on earth – who taught him that lesson . . . We also find here, and especially here, a whole tangle of moral problems and scruples that led to a break for which neither Kafka nor Milena were responsible; precisely here, at the dawn of what should have been a liberating happiness, we see a feverish exacerbation of Kafka's Jewish complex . . . Many young people around us are now drawn to Kafka. I may be mistaken, but I think they will be disappointed when they have his books in their hands. It's often happened to me: someone begs me to lend them a book by Kafka, but once they have opened it, they give it back to me without having finished it, and say that they could not grasp or understand it. This sometimes gave me pleasure because knowing Kafka by heart implies having a particular sensibility that is by no means enviable. The reason why Kafka has become the favourite author of the many honest people who have nothing to do with intellectuals who hang around bars is that there is an anxiety complex in their countries.[57]

In the light of what has just been said, the reader can add his or her own commentary. Unless, having been ensnared by a style as essential and visionary as Kafka, he or she only observes 'metamorphoses' other than the one we are, provisionally, pursuing here. Thanks to its flashes of insight, prescience makes the heart intelligent and makes truth consubstantial with it. And no knowledge, no matter how correct, can deny it that virtue.

[57] *La Nouvelle Critique*, no. 93, February 1958.

15

A Psychosociological Analysis of Propaganda

1 The Functions of Propaganda

Although this analysis has been simplified in order to place more emphasis on the social situation that gave rise to a propaganda campaign, it does reveal the function of propaganda. It has a double function: regulation and organization.

(a) Its *regulatory* function takes the form of an assertion of the group's *identity* and an attempt to re-establish it by expressing its status as a subject that has been freed from contradictions that threatened its equilibrium and action. We have seen repeated references to the dangers that support for psychoanalytic notions poses for the 'peace movement', women or the proletariat. The Americans are trying to use them to subjugate the French people, and to prevent it from seeing what its problems really are. To the extent that the contradiction generated by psychoanalysis can be the work of Communists or an obstacle to their activity, any negation of what it represents is also a negation of the party, the group or French values. The goal of the regulation operated by propaganda is the elimination of the object that is causing the conflict, and it is determined by the fact that the *external* opposition and the *internal* contradiction are strictly dependent on one another. As the contradiction comes to be externalized, *the group comes to define itself in terms of the enemy*. The analysis in the last chapter demonstrated how the moment, and the tenor and tone of communications about psychoanalysis were conditioned by the antagonism between the Communist movement and other ideological or political movements. To put it more simply, it has often been said that propaganda tries to say 'white' because 'the other' says 'black'. Plekhanov (1947) noted long ago that contradiction plays a modulating role in the creation of a content that can emphasize the individuality of one class, as opposed to another. History is full of similar examples. Nazi scientists, for example, rejected the theory of relativity because its author was Jewish. Political parties or religious institutions have, at various times, attacked the groups *closest* to them in a bid to assert their identity. In the sixteenth and seventeenth centuries, the Christian churches invested more ardour – and cruelty – in fighting each other than in combating a rampant atheism. In defining psychoanalysis so clearly and criticizing all theories emanating from the United States or enjoying the support of other social classes, and replacing them with its own conceptions, the French Communist Party asserts its originality and identity as a group. Propaganda directed against psychoanalysis and 'bourgeois science' in general reinforces this self-assertion.

(b) The *organizational* function of propaganda implies an appropriate elaboration of the content of communications and a transformation of the social field – of its representation – within a given situation. Old relations are revised, and a new content relates them to various aspects of everyday life (Lenin [1902] 1970). The close association of psychoanalysis with the American way of life, of social exploitation with the exploitation of psychoanalysis, of psychoanalysis with the action of the police, and then the systematic integration of all these themes eventually give all of them a meaning they did not previously have. At the same time, the proximity of the threat posed by psychoanalysis becomes *tangible* and *concrete* when it is seen as a tool being used to lower the status of women, to fight the trade union movement and to subvert the peace movement. In the context of a propaganda campaign, the messages that are communicated are so organized as to construct a *representation* of the object that conforms to the demand for a unified social field and to Party activities. The formation of a representation is one of the basic techniques of propaganda. Effectively, if a group wishes to, or has to, act on the real, as a group or as a subject, it is desirable that it be represented as *its* real. The continued unity of the Communist Party's ideological world requires the construction of a representation of psychoanalysis that can justify and strengthen that unity. Thus, for example, since science was one of that world's basic values, psychoanalysis had to be completely eliminated from the family of the sciences. In these circumstances, Pavlovian psychology was the only possible alternative, providing an answer to all the questions to which psychoanalysis had been censored from giving any solution. This point-by-point contrast emphasizes the unity of the Party's own field, and demonstrates the futility of resorting to any contribution from outside. And yet, as we can see from the extracts cited, the articles we analysed do not, to use the same example, actually supply a theoretical demonstration of the superiority of Pavlov's psychology, or of the weaknesses of psychoanalysis. We see, rather, a collection of assertions that have probably been proven elsewhere, and of proposals for action, appeals and qualifications that form not a systematic critique of Freudian notions – rather like Politzer's earlier critique – but a wholesale reconstruction of an image of psychoanalysis that has a pre-ordained meaning. This is why we can say that propaganda constructs a representation.

Both functions – regulation and organization – become concrete activities *in a polarized situation defined by the type of conflict-ridden relations that we have outlined, and they appear to be eminently characteristic of this form of communication.* It was, perhaps, no coincidence that the Congregation for the Propagation of Faith should have been founded during the wars of religion, or that propaganda should have emerged in wartime, before taking the form of advertising in a competitive economy. The evolution of societies, their upheavals and their preservation require groups to assert themselves in explicit terms, and to assert their unity in terms of their opposition to other groups. Their mutual antagonism then stimulates reciprocity, reinforces their internal authority and encourages the emergence of specific modes of expression. Communications between groups, and within groups, are influenced and facilitated by a combination of antagonism and reciprocity. This presupposes the *interdependence* of coexisting opposites. Most theorists of propaganda have paid little attention to their radical interdependence in the communications system because they show little interest in looking closely at propaganda's objective basis. They see only a form that has been broken down into an action / reaction doublet, and regard it as something that is basically autonomous. If we examine the essential features of interdependence in such an uncluttered conflictual situation, we find a *polarity* of groups, constitutive of new poles whenever social objects appear in the social field. These poles are, in the domain that concerns us here, representations. We can see that a real principle of polarization is at work;[1] *in propaganda, the assertion of the group's identity requires opposition and it gives rise to the elaboration of a representation of the object that creates it.* The import of this principle will emerge more clearly below. It would require further research to look in greater detail at its meaning and to demonstrate its generality as the directional axis of propaganda. We would also have to look more closely at the differential structure of situations of conflict and situations of cooperation. So far, we have only considered the implications of such situations insofar as they are two different categories of the same type of relations, each with its distinctive sign. Taking his inspiration from the work of Sherif (1933), Avigdor (1953) has made an experimental study of the

---

[1] Asch (1952) stresses the importance of this polarity in his study of social psychology. An interpretation similar to my own can be found in Plekhanov ([1899–1912] 1963) who attempts to extend the antithesis principle to Darwin. Max Weber (1949) and Pavlov (1938) both emphasize the role played by contradiction in the definition of identity and social reality. The principle of polarization has, then, a very long history. It can also be seen as a generalization of the notion of *social distance*. Communicational polarity appears, then, to be a dynamic aspect of this family of concepts. The definitions of social distance given by Sherif and Sherif (1933) and Murphy (1953), and the concrete approach taken to it, are very similar to those outlined here.

nature of relations – cooperative or competitive – between groups. Certain tendencies emerge quite clearly:

> In cases of conflictual interaction between groups, stereotypes tend to be clearly defined and to display those characteristics that are most likely to induce behaviour that will exacerbate the conflict. In the case of cooperative or friendly relations between groups, the stereotypes are less clearly defined. Various positive features may be attributed to the other group, irrespective of whether or not they help to improve relations between the two. (Avigdor 1953: 167)

We have already discussed the same negative–positive dissymmetry in relation to attitudes. Subjects whose attitude towards psychoanalysis is unsympathetic have more clear-cut opinions and take more decisive decisions about how to behave. We have here the beginnings of an outline typology of the relations these forms of communication can establish. Particular attention should be paid to the extent to which propaganda comes into existence when intergroup relations are non-competitive, and to determining their differential features. *Within the limits of the present study, we can define propaganda as a mode of expression used by a group in a situation of conflict, and as the instrumental or action-oriented elaboration of that group's representation of the object of the conflict.*

Certain aspects of this definition require particular attention:

- Propaganda is defined both as 'manipulation' (instrumental use) and as an expression of the group.
- Current theories stress the controversial nature of the *object* or of the *problem* at issue, but it seems essential to me to place the same emphasis on the conflictual nature of the *relations* that make the expression and the representation of the object necessary.
- In emphasizing the fact that propaganda leads to the elaboration of representations, we are also describing the cognitive organization specific to this communications system; this specific organization *explains* the existence of many of the 'symptoms' and 'techniques' we have already noted; we will pursue this link later.
- It is, finally, generally recognized that the goal of propaganda is to incite a behaviour or an action.

2 Cognitive Aspects and Representation in Propaganda

An analysis of the organizational schemata of these themes and links allows us to arrive at an understanding of the cognitive processes involved, and of how they relate to the situation we examined earlier.

We are already familiar with the schema's content and quantitative dimensions (see figure 15.1, p. 318). It shows us that propaganda focuses mainly on class conflict, and on the antagonism between the Soviet Union and the United States in the political domain. The antagonism between Soviet psychology and bourgeois or American psychology also has a role to play. This model, like that of the Catholic press, is systematic. The obvious difference has to do with its simplicity and with the dichotomous nature of each group of themes. A comparison of the schemata identified in our study of two forms of communication – propaganda and propagation – allows us to note that, in propagation, themes and relations are organized at a relatively abstract level and give rise to a new conceptual system that is in keeping with the Catholic Church's foundational beliefs. The same is not true of propaganda: its assertions about psychoanalysis tend simply to put it in a specific context, and to give it meanings that can structure intellectual and emotional responses around certain concepts and concrete images of them. Talk of a mystificatory Nazi psychoanalysis and comparisons between the theory of instincts and Hitlerian or anti-Black racism that miss out some of the essential links in the chain of argument will not allow us to develop a conceptual system; they simply indicate the existence of such a system and then construct a representation of its doctrine. The same argument can be applied to any relationship constructed between psychoanalysis and the United States, the bourgeois class, the police and so on. There are some conceptual assertions and discussions, but the final outcome is the elaboration of an organized set of images and symbols with a representational potential. Its directional polarity reappears at the level of its thematic organization thanks to a *dichotomy* in which each class is, of course, the negation of its opposite. The antagonism finds expression in the exclusive nature of every term in the same column. The Soviet Union is, for instance, excluded from the world of the United States, and vice versa. Because it provides a basis for peace, the Marxist conception makes it unthinkable that any explanation could be based on a theory of aggressivity and so on.

The propositions are mutually exclusive to the extent that they belong to two groups, each of which is a direct negation of the other. We can see that, in our model, it is inconceivable that a judgement or even a term could be simultaneously found in both columns. The price that has to be paid for this dichotomy is reciprocity or complementarity because, given the way in which these visions are structured, each term's world is incomplete without its opposite. To say that the Soviet Union is the land of peace is to accept the existence of a country that is the land of war and so on. The model we are describing synthesizes the dichotomies we have listed. A further feature of all dichotomous divisions explains the mechanism that binds the themes together: anything that does not belong within one field must belong to the other. No theme can be a value shared by both because, if it were, the dichotomous division would disappear. Negation is therefore a natural feature of the cognitive structure of propaganda. To take an example: the Communist press initially saw psychoanalysis as something external to its vision of the real, but accepted the possibility of mediation at the therapeutic level. As the situation became more clearly defined and therefore more tense, everything that was not Communist, progressive or Soviet was, thanks to an immediate inversion, regarded as capitalist, reactionary and American. This led to the elaboration of a theory of bourgeois science and proletarian science which disappeared quite rapidly after the years when the cold war was at its height.

The use, the encouragement to use and the acceptance of such binary divisions facilitate the expression and choice of cultural orientations, as any negative proposition about the relationship between a term and a class can be immediately replaced by a positive proposition indicating the same term's relationship with a complementary class. The value-judgement 'psychoanalysis is not a science', which is part of the science/ideology dichotomy, can automatically be replaced with the value-judgement 'psychoanalysis is an ideology'.

Given that each column is the negation of the other, the role of the negation is *to provide a strict definition* of the meaning to be given to concepts, images and theories bound up with psychoanalysis. In doing so, it reinforces the group's self-affirmation, and uses the contrast to reassert its basic perspectives. The relationship between themes in the same column is one of strict inclusion; in propaganda, every term is univocally defined by its integration into a whole, and its meaning is defined by the dichotomy to which that whole belongs. Psychoanalysis, together with its theoretical and therapeutic extensions, is always included within the cognitive, political and practical space of the capitalist class, bourgeois psychology and the United States, and the function of that space is to negate the space of the Soviet Union or the working class.

In such a strictly delineated world, the link between one element in the dichotomy and any third term is an inversion of the relationship between the complementary element and the same term. If the link between Marxism and science is positive, that between psychoanalysis and science must be negative. We can now see how the polarized situation is reflected in a dichotomous schema that supposedly stabilizes the representation of the object of the conflict, and how its dichotomous nature explains the concrete aspects of propaganda. The very simple binary structure of representation leads to simplifications. Given that the goal of propaganda is to incite action, the simplicity of a representation of the real that offers only two solutions both stresses the relationship between the two poles it identifies and emphasizes the contrast between the two possible answers. In propaganda, the ruse of reason consists in presenting only one solution, one way out and one possible action, as the complementary pole exists only in order to reassert and reinforce the first.

An analysis of the organizational schema makes it easier to specify the link between the situation, the functions of this communications system and the form of the content that is being transmitted. The above remarks can be reiterated in terms that do justice to the existence – which is a philo-sophical and psychological given (Piaget 1949) – of the two levels of any representation: a logical level and a psychological level. At the logical level, a mere glance at the models allows us to grasp the importance of the use of pairs of concepts such as 'psychoanalysis/Pavlovianism', 'metaphysics/science' or 'no research into the possible validity of psy-choanalysis/study the contribution of Soviet psychology'. The *definitions* of the alternatives work differently. The alternative to the 'same' of the group is defined both positively and negatively. Pavlov's school is, for example, *both* 'the school of Pavlov' and the *negation* of psychoanalysis (A_1 = A_1 = Not A_2). The alternative to the 'other' is defined solely in privative or negative terms. Psychoanalysis is the *opposite* of science, the Pavlovian school or Soviet psychology. Even when the alternative is presented in positive terms, such as 'psychoanalysis is an ideology', it is identified with a category that has a negative value. We also note that the model is com-pleted by two poles that crystallize the opposition. The logical laws that appear to be at work here are those of *special identification* (Wallon 1945: 442), namely tautology and resorption.

In tautology, the application of successive operations to the same term adds nothing to it. And yet such operations do have an analytical function. Tautology makes it possible to distinguish between different manifesta-tions of unity, to 'lay them out' on the same level and to make them in some sense *equivalent* to one another. The unity that is psychoanalysis active in a given society is separated – ideological repercussions, the theory of instincts, aspects of therapy or metapsychological concepts – and all these terms are considered as equivalent and interchangeable, As the term itself indicates, resorption makes it possible to include these various aspects in a reconstructed unity. Each element in the model represents one aspect of psychoanalysis, as examined by Communist psychiatrists and philoso-phers, and all its elements can be gradually fitted together in such a way as to construct a representation of psychoanalysis as mystificatory science or weapon of war. The connection between the laws of special identity and representation has been demonstrated by Wallon: the tautological forms that intervene in a representation help to makes its relations with the outside world part of the object itself. He stresses that: 'In this case, [tau-tology] works in the opposite way to causality; it tends to dissolve objects into the actions and reactions they stimulate and respond to' (Wallon 1945: 442). Both the texts we have cited and figure 15.1 show the integration into the same representation of psychoanalysis of the different actions it sup-posedly promotes: it is a tool and an economic support of the bourgeoisie, and uses a derivative ideology to preserve the *existing* social structure.

A more specifically psychological analysis of representation stressed long ago that it has two characteristic features:

• the extension and transformation of the cognitive field;

PSYCHOLOGY

| BOURGEOIS PSYCHOLOGY | ≠ | SOVIET PSYCHOLOGY |

There is no reason to look into
what is valid in psychoanalysis

We must study the contributions
of Soviet psychology   ↔

↓   ↓

Critiques of psychoanalysis from
positions outside Freud's doctrines

Further pursue the work of
Pavlov's pupils

↓   ↓

Theory of instincts is
mythological

Theory of conditioned reflexes
(role of central nervous system)
is scientific

↓   ↓

Psychoanalytic concepts are
irrational and unfounded

Concepts have been verified
by lengthy research

↓   ↓

Psychoanalysis is a mere semblance
of a science (a pseudo-science)

Scientific and heuristic value

↓   ↓

Basis is metaphysical (idealist)

Basis is physiological and
materialist (dialectical)

↓   ↓

Psychoanalysis leads to a false
liberation and false cures

Allows guaranteed therapeutic
intervention

↓   ↓

Psychoanalysis is a mystifying
science

Pavlovianism is a truly
scientific theory

Figure 15.1 Schema 3

POLITICS

The USSR is a land of peace	≠	The US is a land of war and social exploitation ↔
↓		↓
Science cannot be dissociated from politics		Psychoanalytic ideology cannot be dissociated from a country's politics
↓		↓
Debate must be at the political level		Psychoanalysis is examined at the political level
↓		↓
Marxist conception is positive (basis for peace)		Irrational theory of aggressivity justifies war
↓		
Theory of the inevitable development of our society		Theory close to racist and and decadent conceptions
Unmasking threats of oppression is goal of Soviet policy		
↓		↓
Marxism is basis of soviet policy		Psychoanalysis is basis for US occupiers' psychological warfare
↓		↓
Allows true understanding of contemporary situation		Application to social problems is a mystification
↓		↓
Stalinist (Marxist) theory and Soviet conception are weapons of peace		Psychoanalysis re-imported from the US, weapon of war

Figure 15.1 (cont'd)

CLASS STRUGGLE

BOURGEOIS CLASS	≠	WORKING CLASS
↓		↓
Capitalist bourgeoisie uses (US) class weapons		Working class fights bourgeoisie by using Marxism
↓		↓
Psychoanalysis must be analysed in ideological terms		Marxism is doctrine of the working class
↓		↓
Justifies struggle against trade unionists, resistance and blacks		Marxism is a weapon in political, national and union struggles
↓		↓
Psychoanalysis is a pseudo-science supported by bourgeoisie		Real science developed in Communist Party
↓		↓
Describes as morbid behaviours aimed at transforming society		Marxism helps to show meaning of revolutionary action
↓		↓
Ignores realities of decadent capitalist society		Provides explanation of our society's problems
↓		↓
Class conflict seen as pathological (artificial liberation, escapism)		Marxism develops class consciousness; allows class to free itself from bourgeois ideology
↓		↓
Psychoanalysis an ideology (bourgeois and decadent)		Marxism forms basis of progressive proletarian science

Figure 15.1 (cont'd)

- the realization of an intention thanks to the transposition of a meaning from one level to another, and the subsequent creation of a duplicate of what is perceived to be the real.

The transposition may be direct, or may take various other forms such as distortion or simplification. It plays a central role in propaganda because it makes it possible to formulate, in all its clarity, the required dichotomy between the poles of communication. Its modus operandi is clearly shown by the figure. Dichotomous pairs appear in a domain whose unity is either given or assumed to exist, such as 'psychology' or 'the class struggle'. Alternatives are offered within each unity, initially in the form of a relationship of *difference*: bourgeois psychology / Soviet psychology and so on. The group that is organizing communications hopes to develop this difference on a plane other than the plane where the object is usually situated. It thus brings about a transposition. Psychoanalysis, for example, is considered from a viewpoint overlooking the conflict, and the group transfers its position and group identity to that viewpoint. It thus elaborates an image of psychoanalysis that is in keeping with its social field. Thanks to this transposition, the difference can be externalized, rather as though it were a real *opposition*. French Communist thinkers want to transpose psychoanalysis to a political level, refusing any dissociation between politics and science, and taking no heed of the transitions that allow them to move from one to the other or of the fact that a theory can have both positive and negative features. It is the completion of the transposition that provides the escape from the conflict. Indeed, unless the basic criterion by which all Freud's conceptions have to be judged were not political, it would be difficult to describe psychoanalysis as an ideological weapon or a pseudo-science. Had *several viewpoints* been adopted, it would have been difficult to dismiss Freud's concepts, as their negation is an expression of the differences between the Communist Party and other groups in the domain of psychoanalysis, psychosomatics and psychopathology. Communists are aware of this, as they demand the adoption of a clearly political position and refuse to look at the situation in any other light, because doing so would be an obstacle to the externalization of their hostility to psychoanalytic ideas and, therefore, American culture.

The two psychological preconditions for that representation have been met: a deliberate campaign against psychoanalysis and an intellectual construct designed to wage that campaign.

Once the Communist Party resolves to express itself, to free itself from the contradiction and to define the level – the political or the scientific – at which it can assert itself in relation to some other group – America, the bourgeoisie – its intentionality becomes meaningful and directional. It must then justify itself in intellectual terms by positioning the object in accordance with *a conclusion whose premise was formulated even before the links in the argument were established*. For the Party's spokesmen, the principle that 'psychoanalysis is not a science' – which means that it is an ideology – can be detected in any provisional inference. The intentional orientation is determined by objective socio-historical conditions, and the intellectual activity by the fact that its intention is to construct a representation and therefore obey the laws of special identity. The shaping of a representation transcends the real because the representation appears to be a duplicate of the real, but tends to lend it a certain permanence, to find something stable in a changing environment, and to find something constant in the initial fluidity of the links. When this process has been completed, we find ourselves in the presence of an almost closed and organized body of themes and links that supposedly exhausts the reality it reflects, even though what it reflects is distorted by the presence of the group's frame of reference. The conscious mind sees the representation as a unit, even though it has no immediate foundations and transcends the realm of the perceptible. It includes within a more stable system both what is present and what is absent, what exists and what is imagined to exist. Once this unified image has been established, it retroactively gives that same reality a meaning, and conditions the behaviours and attitudes of those who accept it.

The permanence or stability of the 'represented real' (psychoanalysis, in this case) is expressed quite clearly:

> A few groups of bourgeois surrealist intellectuals used psychoanalysis as an excuse to free themselves from the constraints of moral hypocrisy . . . In France at least, a small circle of initiates in the Société de Psychanalyse has an almost exclusive monopoly on psychoanalysis.[2]

It can thus be demonstrated that psychoanalysis has always been bourgeois, that it varies within certain narrow limits and that, being the offspring of certain mythical concepts, it has simply become what it always was: a class ideology. The permanence of the representation results from a reconstruction of the past, and it is associated with an image of the *constancy of the group's identity*. In its anti-psychoanalytic propaganda, the French Communist Party describes itself as a group whose every member rejects psychoanalysis, as a group that is a future ruler and one that has always had links with the healthy faction of the French population, with all honest citizens and with all scientific psychiatrists. Within this frame of reference, social 'space' and 'time' take on an *absolute* character. The constant keeps the variable in check, and current developments look like a repetition of past experiences. The combination of a constant representation and a group identity give rise to a tendency to make *universal assertions* that are *real* at certain moments in our collective history, and *illusory*

---

[2] *La Nouvelle Critique*, no. 27, 1951.

at others. Social psychologists stress the importance of the 'illusion of universality' which, without any good reason, denies the rational quality of what may be authentic behaviour. When it addresses the whole of society, symbolizes it and reveals its essential underlying features, a group or party can, without any illusions, regard itself as the 'we' or 'they' of that society. If an imperceptible objective shift produces discrepancies that are not directly expressed in images and communications, illusions begin to creep in. Such illusions can be forward-looking and full of future promise, and can therefore be communicational tools of mechanisms designed to produce a consensus. The Catholic Church was declared universal in medieval Europe. The Communist Party was universal in the modern world. Assertions of universality help to create, on the one hand, a belief in the irreversibility of the break or dichotomy between the generality of the group's representations and practices, and, on the other hand, the particularity of everything outside it. Because of the breaking of the symmetry between the two antinomic groups, the propaganda of the former, the Communist Party, is deeply polarized and negative. Does this way of communicating have an influence on those who make the propaganda and on the members of the group who receive it? This is still a question, because the obvious answer is not sure, and the non-obvious one not proven. Let us simply say that the pursuit of specific goals entails the use of a given system of communication. They result in a specific frame or structure of mind. The correspondence between the nature of the social situation and the communication tending to such a frame or structure of mind was my primary interest in the study.

The cognitive approaches we have just outlined do not exhaust all the possibilities opened up by message-schemata. We have concentrated on their essential features so as to shed light on the communication processes that generate them. The influence of this form of communication on the way of thinking of those who are on the receiving end and, in the long term, the propagandists themselves, has yet to be studied. Does a propagandist group, or a group which uses propaganda as a means of communicating with certain of its members, tend to 'think' along the lines of the principles we have outlined? Let us simply note that the pursuit of certain goals and the use of a given form of communication result in a particular structuration of the social field at the cognitive level because they obey laws specific to the psychological phenomena involved. The correspondence between them, the nature of the social situation and such communication was the first object of this study.

3 Representation as an Instrument for Action

Once it has been shaped and differentiated, the social model (the representation) is propagated by the dailies and weeklies of the political and cultural press, and establishes itself as a truth. At the same time, the group separates and consolidates itself as the *subject-group* in relation to a specific conflictual problem: psychoanalysis. At first, regulation and organization within a conflict-ridden relationship require the subject to express itself through its representation of the object; at a later stage, the representation, which has restructured the social field, incites the subject-group to act upon the reality it replicates (of which it is an image), and to *make its representation real*. That psychoanalysis is a representation is not enough, or no longer enough: for the members of the group, it must be as it is represented if they are to act on the basis of the identity they desire.

In this sequence, the representation, which was originally an *end* and the outcome of an image-expression of psychoanalysis that could eliminate contradictions, now becomes a *means*, takes its place as an intermediary between the subject-group and the reality-object, and is transformed into a tool the group can use when it acts. Summary claims that 'propaganda leads to action' or 'it creates collective attitudes' should be taken to mean *propaganda is an incitement to action, and it produces 'attitudes' by creating or modifying a representation of the real*. If we look at this more closely, we find that the goal of propaganda is not the same as that of other forms of communication: it strives to use a representation of the object to incite actual behaviour, and it underpins the participation in joint activity of individuals or groups who find themselves in an identical situation.[3] Lenin, for example, demonstrates that, if the workers are to be persuaded to join the revolutionary movement, the movement's propaganda must strive to give them not only a representation of the general features of society, but also one of the immediate realities of everyday life. The sole purpose of other forms of communication such as propagation is to produce attitudes, and to superimpose *symbolic* behaviours on real behaviours by exercising some *control* in order to do so. I have emphasized the meaning and limitations of that supervision. 'The objective of propaganda is action, not merely readiness to act. External rather than internal public opinion is sought. The learned attitude – the pre-action response – must affect behaviour. It must lead to what may be called an *action-response*' (Doob 1948: 397). Such behaviour follows, immediately and without any major fluctuations, the appearance of appropriate stimulating instructions; it presupposes intensive preparation and a precise 'localization' of the desired response. Psychological processes, either cognitive or affective, that can establish an immediate connection between the stimulus and the response, must result in the production of a stereotype.[4] This is not only because individuals immediately behave as they are required to, but

[3] The importance of the problem of participation in modern propaganda is underlined by Kris and Leites (1947).
[4] As Driencourt (1950: 21) observes: '[Propaganda] is also designed to stimulate immediate action. It does not have time to explain; the opinions and actions it is designed to provoke are always specific and extreme; all its energy goes into the adoption or

also because the situation is so designed as to offer *only* two possible solutions. This duality corresponds in part to the nature of a stereotype, which demands one of two responses: 'total support from the subject, or total rejection'. This allows Stoetzel (1943: 250) to state: 'in general, it can be said that propaganda leads to the creation of stereotypes'.

The above remarks allow us to describe how elements of a social representation can be oriented when they are transformed – in propaganda – into tools to be used by a group: (1) to promote greater social involvement; (2) to produce stereotypes; and (3) to indicate what behaviour or action is appropriate.

1   Members' participation in a social organization implies (a) that its frontiers have been differentiated; and (b) that a unanimous view is taken of a problem that is important to the organization, and to individuals belonging to it or gravitating in its orbit. Any 'distance' that might exist or any 'indifference' that the group or its members might display towards the problem at the heart of the conflict is completely abolished. This is not true of diffusion, where, as we have seen, the manipulation of 'distancing' or 'withdrawal' techniques (irony, objectivity, objections to specific points) is an essential precondition if the publication is to be adapted to its audience. Of the articles published in the Communist press, 35 per cent insist that indifference to psychoanalysis is impossible, that it is one of the capitalist class's most dangerous weapons, and that it is therefore important to pay great attention to it and to combat it. The tone of these appeals is not so familiar that we do not need to dwell on them. At this level, the Communist Party tries to make itself stand out as a working-class, trade union and national organization, and to define itself as an autonomous entity. In doing so, it destroys the unity of the public and of society by accentuating the lines that divide them. A total of 42 per cent of the articles emphasize the exceptional position of the Party and of those who agree with it, only those who accept the group's principles are in a position to refute or criticize the rejected doctrine on an informed basis. Individual authors or specialized groups do not have individual opinions about psychoanalysis; they are always described as expressing the views of the whole group. Eight psychoanalysts write:

> The progressive forces and the peace movement ought to be worried about this situation, and must look at how the pretext of so-called scientific activity is being used to develop an ideology whose goals – overt or otherwise – are social conservatism or social regression.[5]

---

realization of an idea or a concrete phenomenon that is limited and usually temporary. It must minimize the margin for unpredictability and hesitations, and not quantify in advance the negative results of individual reactions. It is therefore an orderly process, and uses cliché, concise formulae and stereotypes.'

[5] 'Autocritique', *La Nouvelle Critique*, no. 7, June 1949.

These psychoanalysts are writing as members of the 'progressive forces and the peace movement', and not as private individuals expressing private opinions. Another article speaks of the working class or the healthy faction of the French nation, and of the working class and honest intellectuals. The boundaries of the group are constantly redefined so as to get as many people as possible to identify with it, but they always centre on the Communist Party.

Elsewhere, the talk is of the 'Communist Party' and mothers who

> want to make a major contribution to the building of a better world in which there will be bread and roses for all, but in which there will be no psychoanalysis for the very good reason that those who need it to pervert minds will no longer be in power.[6]

The redefinition of the group's boundaries has several functions: it divides 'the public' along different lines, recalls, through repetition, the ties of solidarity that bind the group's members together, and focuses individuals' attention on the same representation, no matter what role they play in society. Progressives, mothers, women and trade unionists can all be affected by messages addressed to them; the Communist, who is not just a Party member but also a trade unionist, a woman, a mother or an intellectual who is being invited to adopt the Party's viewpoint in all situations in which she may be called upon to play a role that is not purely political. The attempt to broaden the Party's field of action results in a search for a *common* denominator, and strengthening its unity means polarizing its members, their tendency towards diversity notwithstanding. The propagandist theme of unity (which appears in 28 per cent of the articles) is stated either in a positive form (18 per cent) or as a reaction against splitting tactics (10 per cent): 'It [psychoanalysis] cannot be anything but a support for and an argument in the splitting tactics exemplified by you.'[7] This is the pivotal moment in a call for active involvement in the Party's anti-psychoanalytic actions. The representation of psychoanalysis is unlikely to inspire anyone to take any action at all if it remains an abstract figure that is confined to the heaven of ideas, or unless it is integrated into the immediately perceivable and imaginable field of the everyday experience of the individuals addressed by the content that is being communicated. The Communist press makes a conspicuous attempt to convince them of the imminent threat posed by Freud's doctrine in order to overcome the indifference of some of its readers. *L'Humanité*, for example, headlines a review of an issue of *La Raison* 'A harsh blow for psychoanalytic charlatans'.[8] The content of the article attempts to show that psychoanalysis has repressive and exploitative goals. Psychoanalysis, it is claimed, explains the workers'

[6] *La Nouvelle Critique*, no. 27, 1951.
[7] Ibid.
[8] February 1951.

desire to take militant action in terms of their 'aggressive instincts'. By demonstrating that psychoanalysis devalues the time, energy and security that workers sacrifice in order to defend their class interests, *L'Humanité* portrays the Freudian concept as the negation of an immediate and essential fact of everyday life. Once the Party activist sees it as one of many repressive practices, he can view it in concrete terms as another 'brainwashing' technique that is as dangerous as any other form of slavery.

One of the leitmotifs that the press discovers from time to time is the crisis affecting young people. It is as though the rise of new generations and the way they break with their elders could be conflict-free in a society haunted by the memory and spectre of war. This provides the opportunity to take part of humanity to task for its lack of experience and to contrast the wisdom, which is redefined to suit the circumstances, that comes with maturity and accession to social life with the obvious uncertainties of the young. All collectivities that wish to perpetuate themselves worry about the future and about how their children should be educated. The years 1950–1 produced a lot of moralizing literature and discussions, many of them cursory, about the discontents of young people. Psychoanalytic notions provide a frame of reference for articles on these subjects. An article by D.D. describes psychoanalysis as one of the sources that misrepresents the problems young people have to deal with today.[9] The article gives the reader the impression that psychoanalysis is helping to 'create' this generation's problems: those problems do not affect the majority of young people, who are perfectly healthy:

> Look at these young people (the unhinged minority), and then look at the thousands of young people who are fighting for peace and happiness. Look at Henri Martin and Raymonde Dien[10] – and there are a lot more like them. That is where the solution lies for all young people who are worried; that is the only positive doctrine on offer. All in all, the young people of France (or the young guard) are not in such a bad state, much to the dismay of all the pessimists who insist on seeing the so-called crisis as proof that nothing can ever change.

Psychoanalysis is an obstacle not only to the healthy orientation of young people, but also to the liberation of women, who are, in bourgeois society, either servants or playthings:

> It [psychoanalysis] is all the more dangerous in that it claims to liberate women. It attracts them to a domain 'beyond good and evil' that seduces

---

[9] *Démocratie nouvelle*, August 1951.

[10] Icons of the Communist campaign to end France's war in Indochina. In February 1950, Dien was arrested after lying on the tracks to block the departure of a train carrying military material for use in Indochina. Martin, an engine-room artificer in the navy, was arrested during a demonstration and charged with demoralizing the armed forces and sabotage. Both were given jail sentences [Translator].

them because they believe they are breaking with traditional prejudices. Eroticism is made to look like a scientific phenomenon, and abnormal and depraved morals are described 'in all objectivity'. We should not be surprised to see psychoanalysis being given a central role in the reactionary propaganda that is being directed at women . . . Existentialist heroines, like the heroines in the magazines and those of the psychoanalysts, are alone, have to deal with men who are their rivals (or masters), and are cursed by a double fate by society whose turpitude is described, even though no solution is offered, and by an essentialist gender (some speak of the soul, but it comes down to the same thing) about which nothing can be done.[11]

The turn of phrase, and the insistent denunciation of eroticism, revolt and the false liberation of women, appeal to the reader's vigilance and warn him or her not to be taken in by a few speculations with scientific pretensions, and to see the hidden dangers they represent. Activists, young people and women are warned that psychoanalysis is one of the ruses and misrepresentations of a parasitic and repressive class and a society that has no future. The warnings are adapted to their sector of activity, their aspirations and their deepest convictions. Psychoanalysis is everywhere: in women's magazines read by working women, in the psycho-technical examinations workers have to undergo, in the uproar caused by the rise of a new generation, in the self-proclaimed superiority of men and their disdain for the modest heroism of women, and in the events that go to make up everyday life. It is a sign of every possible crime or sin, and of all the lies and prejudices of a society in which workers feel that they are both citizens and foreigners. The propaganda directed against Freud's doctrine does not use subtle arguments to prove that it is incompatible with Marxism, and the conflict does not take place within the sphere of ideas. This is a struggle that sets class against class, party against party, and one bloc of countries against another. Every member of the group is invited to become involved in concrete and particular aspects of a universal conflict, and the weapons used are not what the Academicians like to call 'spiritual weapons'. The original specificity of psychoanalysis and its harmless theoretical and therapeutic concerns are no more than secondary aspects of an issue that affects millions of people, and they must all work together if it is to be resolved. In order to convince them that they must work together effectively, the propaganda inserts its representations of psychoanalysis into every nook and cranny of the hopes, desires and fears that punctuate lives made up of a dreary sequence of days and the expectation of a better future. As the role of propaganda is to make history and not to interpret it, it leaves the task of taking care of the general issues and redistributive justice to the future it is ushering in. Consolidating the unity of the group

[11] *La Nouvelle Critique*, no. 25, 1951.

and encouraging its members to participate in its approach are the immediate aims of a form of communication which realizes them by multiplying the points of concrete support for a cognitive form that has become a means and an instrument for action.

2   Once we begin to approach the problem of propaganda and manipulation, of its instrumental implications, and of the genesis of the process that initiates actions, we invariably turn to an examination of the phenomenon of *repetition*. Revitalizing links between the image of the object and the group and those of the concrete regions that have acquired an affective and intellectual meaning for the group leads to greater social involvement. Themes are stated and organized in such a way as to make them fit with other shared perspectives and experiences. It has often been noted that the role of repetition is frequently bound up with the processes of conditioning and memorization. There is no denying that it does play that role, but we have to shed enough light on it if we are to avoid facile formulae which, for many people, have a universal meaning. 'There is no magic in repetition. The connection between the propaganda stimulus and the related response is strengthened not because of the repetition as such but because each presentation in some way or other proves to be rewording and hence induces the propagandee to learn something new' (Doob 1948: 348). We do not know if we learn something new at every stage because we are receptive to propaganda, but it is true that repetition, which is a very widespread phenomenon in communications, takes a particular form in propaganda. It appears at several levels and fulfils various different functions, and it will help if we define them.

At the cognitive level, repetition is best analysed as a *homogenizing* factor. Tautology plays a major role here, as elements that have become equivalent in the model can be joined together to form an endless chain, and this makes it seem that they have a very similar meaning. Repetition, that is, crystallizes the representation Its structure is simplified and the links between its terms become more stable. Their homogeneity means that certain themes can be eliminated without any damage being done to the whole. Frequent associations determine the position of every proposition, and every new proposition finds a predetermined position. The conflict-ridden nature of relations between psychoanalysis and Communism is mentioned frequently (63 per cent), but the mode of expression can vary. This variation on the model's essential themes corresponds to the need to adapt the model to various domains, but it also gives it a particular liveliness or vivacity. Until 1949, the liveliness was provided by themes relating to Americanism (62 per cent). In 1949–50, it was provided by themes relating to irrationality and ideology (58 per cent), and after 1950 the emphasis was placed upon the 'false problems' with which psychoanalysis was associated (64 per cent). The way equivalent propositions are repeated in any given period is always determined by the model's main theme; the model may stress different things, but there is no overall change.

The *semiological assembly* of the representation of the object-theory is another aspect of repetition. Its intellectual content is closely bound up with a certain number of signs that can become interchangeable, and they reveal a substantial modification of that content. The system of signs is consolidated thanks to its frequent association with particular messages, and it actually transforms those messages. The phenomenon of iteration explains its genesis. It should first be noted that a certain sign becomes *necessarily* bound up with a signified, which transforms the arbitrary nature of the linguistic encounter into a normative necessity. The 'irrational' index can serve as an example. We know that psychoanalysis studies, amongst other things, processes that escape the conscious mind or which are transfigured in the course of their conscious expression. Their importance – which had long been recognized by philosophers – was reasserted by Freud with his usual vehemence. The theories he advanced were intended to introduce a degree of rationality – which may or may not be real, depending on one's point of view – into what most people saw as an irrational world. This is why psychoanalysis can be described as an irrational philosophy. Freud's conceptualization was, moreover, never rigorous or univocal, or at least followed neither the physiologically oriented line of classical psychiatry nor the Marxist line. This gives Communists a further two reasons to regard it as irrational. From a historical point of view, finally, psychoanalysis flourished at a time that was reacting against rationalism and therefore sympathetic to theories of this kind. Communists, who do not always make any distinction between these elements and the aura of irrationalism that surrounds Freud's doctrine, often (36 per cent) emphasize the link between the theory and its aura, and try to make it one of their most reliable indices: 'irrational psychoanalysis'. The same could be said of 'pseudo-science', 'ideology' and so on.

We also find that an index or symbol can either concern a part of a whole, or be a symbol precisely because it is a part of that whole. The social use made of psychoanalysis in the United States, or its theory of drives, are no more than parts of what is assumed to be the social reality of psychoanalysis. 'American psychoanalysis' can therefore be a sign that represents psychoanalysis as a whole. The repetition of that sign transforms it into a major index, and it can therefore define the direction taken by the representation. We must, however, do more than note that its direction is signalled in this way; the index tends to become consubstantial with what it indicates, just as the part comes to overlap with the whole. When it is being demonstrated that analytic theory and practice, the origins of the current spread of psychoanalysis and, in a word, all the characteristics attributed to psychoanalysis, are American, a *partial* index comes to represent the whole of psychoanalysis. The repeated link magnifies one part by likening it to others, and a part eventually becomes a totality: psychoanalysis becomes the symbol of the American way of life, just as American psychoanalysis becomes the symbol of psychoanalysis. They can be conflated because one is regarded as the latent content of the other. We can see here that the doctrine which initially was represented as *empty* of any content of its own has been transformed into a manifest sign, a *substitute* for a latent reality. The intentions of the group, and its main frame of reference, shape a latent content, and the object is no more than its appearance. Therapy, analytic theory and the way they have spread to France are no more than the *deceitful* appearances of a social and political structure, and psychoanalysis is its disguise and instrument. The existence of any specific content is denied or ignored by, for example, a refusal to discuss Freud's work. The schematic political explanation becomes the only backdrop, or the only context in which psychoanalysis ceases to have any meaning in its own right and becomes nothing more than the alienated symbolic form of a reality it serves but cannot master. Given the limits that have been assigned to it, the relationship that has been established between the manifest and the latent is a concrete expression of the group's *intention*. The constant reminders of the appearance of the object justifies a path which consists of perceiving all content as a sign. Anything that pertains to psychoanalysis is therefore no more than a sign of American bourgeois society.

Tautologization organizes and crystallizes the representation. The frequent iteration of a sign at the same time as a content transforms the sign into a schematic index of the whole. 'Synthesized' themes destroy the representation's original richness, and some succeed in 'containing' the whole. Hence the 'clichés'. At the level of propaganda, the fact that an entire content can be concentrated inside a system of indices maximizes the distance from other groups and homogenizes what is 'inside'. Repetition therefore tends to create an undivided unity in which there is no separation between the essential and the accidental, or between the method and the result. It shapes signs and associates them with one another to the extent that the model ceases to be present because of its content, and acts through the underlying network that has been established.

At another level, repetition takes the form of the quantitative iteration of the same sign; its function is the energetic mobilization of behaviour (at the motor or emotional level). This brings us closer to the mechanisms that generate behaviour.

Once 'Hitler' 'ideology' and 'psychoanalysis' have been inscribed in the same affective register, their iteration has a specific effect. In propaganda, this mobilization is often based upon a 'strategy of disequilibrium' that alternates between stimuli that threaten the integrity of the individual, their group and their values, and reassuring stimuli that trigger the desired response. The disturbing characteristics of psychoanalysis are signalled in 57 per cent of the articles, whereas 43 per cent immediately suggest 'remedies' that can ward them off. Repetition establishes a direct link between stimulus and response. The behaviour associated with the word 'ideology', for example, is rejection. 'Positive' words are paired with 'positive' behaviours, and 'negative' words with 'negative' behaviours.

These are obviously broader connections, as an association is established not only between a word and a response (or behaviour), but also between that response and a link. Anything relating to America is, for example, negative. If something is linked to that national group, it bears its hallmark, and the response it triggers is inevitably negative.

3   The absence of any distinction between the two forms of repetition – cognitive repetition and the repetition that results in stereotyping – stems largely from the fact that most studies of propaganda look at its terminal stage, at which point the representation is already shaped or ignored, whilst the iteration is seen only as a factor in stereotyping. If, however, the iteration is to be successful, tautological repetition must first 'install' the cognitive structure, and its ability to do so is dependent upon situational factors in the personal life of the receiver, or on the adequacy of the representation's elements for a certain existing reality. We can conclude that it is only because it is grounded in this way that quantitative iteration can succeed in making action possible. The success of propaganda does not, in other words, depend solely upon the repetition of a stereotype, but also upon the structuration of the content that makes the behaviour necessary. This is not always the case, and in practice short cuts are often taken. *The economy of propaganda in fact requires tautological repetition to be transformed into 'quantitative' iteration as quickly as possible, and it must therefore make use of representations that already exist.* Repetition facilitates the transition from the cognitive level to the emotional level, and creates a 'state of persuasion' which, at its paroxysm, is very like a 'state of passion' and, as we know, a state of passion is the ideological equivalent of an affective situation. Authors whose first concern is to elaborate an affective theory of propaganda see this simply as a conscious expression of basic drives, and fail to take into account the pressure exerted at the emotional level by the conscious or cognitive level. *They see propaganda simply as something that allows affects to express themselves, rather than as a way of organizing their expression.*

4 Language and Action

The transition from an expression-representation to an instrument-representation, which occurs thanks to the mediating function of both forms of repetition, also detaches cognitive processes from the material substance that acts as their support, namely language.

Language was until recently consubstantial with its reflexive content to the extent that it was a tool for communications and a framework for action – a system of verbal stimuli – but it has now begun to exist in its own right and to assert itself as a totality with features of its own. Repetition makes it autonomous, but it enjoys a very particular autonomy that transforms every word into the equivalent of a non-verbal sign. This is true in extreme cases. In propaganda, language [*langue*] retains the characteristics of an organized system of signs with meanings that are known to a group of speaking subjects. Linguistic communication is possible because words and sentences, in both their current form and throughout their evolution, are the fruit of experiences that have been fossilized in the course of the social life of people belonging to the same collectivity. As a result, the system of signs that a group encounters in a society is, by its very nature, *normative*. In propaganda, as in other forms of communication, the group attempts to transform this general language into a *particular* language. This particularization follows the same lines of polarization as those of the social representation and the overall position of the group within society.

The transformation occurs at the point where two languages meet. One (that of the group) is a *qualifying* language, and the other a *qualified* language (that of the object-theory around which the conflict develops; it will be used to resolve the conflict). The immediate effect of this transformation is a change in the meaning of words. An analysis of propaganda, as applied to psychoanalysis, allows us to observe the rules that appear to be followed when a specific language takes shape.

(a) *Rule of selection.* The representation the group is trying to shape determines the choice of the meaning the word acquires as it circulates. Different meanings are attached to the word 'psychoanalysis' (science, ideology, therapy, doctrine and so on), and Communists select 'ideology'. This rule is in fact merely an expression of the link that exists between representations and the structure of language. It reflects the process that gives a general term a *particular* meaning, and the particular the *form* of the general. The word 'psychoanalysis', for example, takes on the particular meaning of 'ideology'; as a result, it acquires a general import: psychoanalysis is an expression of a general form of American intellectual life and culture. Of all articles in the Communist press that mention psychoanalysis, 58 per cent use the term as a symbol for American life, art and science.

(b) *Rule of constraint.* The signifying word is reduced, and tends to merge with the one meaning given it by the specific way the context is organized. The word 'psychoanalysis', to take only that example, is, as we have already seen, accompanied by a context that has the effect of reinforcing the meaning given it by the Communist Party. If we look at Communist publications, we never come across associations such as 'psychoanalytic science', 'effective psychoanalytic therapy' or 'objectivity of psychoanalytic concepts', but we almost always find 'myth of psychoanalysis', 'American psychoanalysis' and 'bourgeois science'. The imposition of constraints that establish a particular content as the sole content of a general form makes the word transparent; its meaning ceases to be either general or particular, and becomes generic.[12]

---

[12] The word becomes a sort of 'title', in the sense that a book or film has a title that allows us to predict the multiple content it sums up.

(c) *Rule of hierarchy*. The group's hierarchy of values is reflected in the way significations are ranked. The underlying meanings of, for example, the word 'science' (materialist, Soviet, proletarian) are rated more highly than 'rationalist', 'American', 'bourgeois' and so on. Because of its constrictive and selective effects, propaganda reduces a word's range of meanings so as to eliminate the possibility of relativization or free interpretation on the part of its interlocutors.

The outcome of operations on the meaning of linguistic expressions is both the creation of a specific *langue* and the erection of a *semantic barrier*. The adoption of this language means that there can be no more peaceful exchanges with members outside the group. Ideas, some of them very simple, are put forward, on the basis of a partial analysis of social processes, as to the possibility of a social therapy based upon the semantic re-establishment of social communications. It has been suggested that most conflicts and difficulties result from linguistic dysfunctionality (Korzybski 1933; Wiener 1949). It is only a short step from this to believing that 'if we all spoke the same language', there would be nothing to prevent humanity from indulging its penchant for boundless happiness. And that step has been taken. It is, however, obvious that the affective, cognitive and social reasons for the distortions and barriers that are reflected in language are much more complex than that. It is only at that level that the real problems exist and that real reforms can take place. Communications and lexical signs are bound up with and are part of a system of behaviours (Lagache 1953). Provided that we do not forget that linguistic phenomena do have a degree of autonomy, scientific thought must take into account their insertion into a social whole, and the fact that they are elements of that whole.

The above 'rules' provide a convenient way of describing a few processes which had, in my view, to be differentiated: they underpin all semantic considerations. The constitution of this specific language goes hand in hand with the shaping of a representation. Once its formation is complete, assuming that it can be completed, once the adjacent vocabulary has been forged and once the words are in possession of meanings that are both specific and *justified*, the propaganda tool is ready for action. Repetition of the same elements formalizes thought. When the object acquires a permanent representational status, cognitive relations solidify and become embodied in a verbal system; words contract and are differentiated; thought becomes speech, and the parts are absorbed into various units that are ready for immediate use, whilst a replica of the real becomes its *hallmark*. Stereotyping makes the cognitive and linguistic tool meaningful and effective. This is apparent in the particular way the social 'stimuli' are organized. Because it has made the multiple facets of the discipline that is being represented equivalent to one another, a tautological homogenization drains them of their specific content, and at the same time stabilizes them and maintains a distinction between them. At times, that distinction becomes formal, because various iterations simply emphasize that these facets are interchangeable. Word-signs become attached to them: 'mystifying science', 'weapon of war' and 'ideology' can then be organized in relation to a particular experience, depending on the needs of the group and the domain of activity in question. The French Communist Party usually organizes signs relating to psychoanalysis around the United States, because its anti-psychoanalytic propaganda is essentially a *means* of waging war on what it terms American culture. When they speak of psychoanalysis, Communist journals signal the fact that it has been *re-imported* from the United States. It is described as being strongly influenced by Americanisms and they deny that, in its present form, it originates from anywhere else. The daily or weekly press always mentions 'American psychoanalysis', as though the most important sign, or even the hallmark, of psychoanalysis were the fact of its being American. A review of E.'s book on psychoanalysis notes:

> 'E. tries to be objective, but at no point does he discuss psychoanalysis' scientific pretensions. The apologist gets the upper hand over the critic. A lot more could be said about this commodity, which has been imported from America and not Austria.[13]

Psychoanalysis is, then, purely American. The other word-signs – 'bourgeois ideology', 'weapon of war', 'mystification' – are subordinated to and associated with the adjective 'American' in 48 per cent of cases.

The particular way in which the signs are organized also leads to stereotyping. They constitute what is known as a signalling system, and one sign – the signal – plays the dominant role. Propaganda uses the simplest system possible, as each sign tends to have *only one value*. The 'generalization' of stimuli-words such as 'psychoanalysis' is closely related to this organization. These words transgress their own domain and come to represent a whole series of other stimuli. The generalized term 'psychoanalysis' replaces many others, and synthesizes all things bourgeois, all things ideological, all things American and so on. When the American way of life is being discussed in relation to, say, a film, psychoanalysis is one of the most reliable of indices:

> The film looks like a very profound work and it has had considerable success in the United States. Everyday life is harsh, implacable and soul-destroying. Violence, corruption, warlike hysteria, fear of unemployment, racism, *unbridled psychoanalysis*, alcoholism and so on.[14]

[13] *Les Lettres françaises*, 18 June 1953.
[14] *L'Ecran français*, 27 August 1951.

The generalization of the signal-word and the discriminating effect it has inside a particular structure has both a linguistic and a psychological impact. This last point must be approached with great caution, as the theoretical hypotheses have not been tested through a study of communication phenomena. Insofar as they provide an insight into the relationship between the language used by propaganda and its role – inciting action – the value of these hypotheses is no more than analogical. We know that stereotyping is linked to the mechanisms that condition segmentary and strictly localized behaviours. We have only a limited understanding of the process that binds together verbal signs and the motor assembly of behaviours. We can, however, assume that it is because the stimulus-signal configuration is so simple that it is so easily generalized and learned, as the iteration allows the emergence of new behavioural patterns that associate behaviours with certain objects. As a result, it is also easier to generalize existing responses: an attempt can, for example, be made to produce the same response to 'psychoanalysis' as to anything American. Specialist studies scarcely touch upon the problem of the generalization of responses. In theory, it should be possible to establish a link between the generalization of a *stimulus* and the creation of *new* behaviours, and between the generalization of a *response* and resistance to the change of response that propaganda seeks to bring about. Stereotyping would, apparently, tend to make the two forms of generalization converge. The examples cited earlier clearly indicate that Communists want to identify 'American' with 'psychoanalysis' so as to provoke a new response – rejection – to 'psychoanalysis' and to strengthen resistance to any new behaviour with respect to the United States because such new behaviour might change the way they view Freud's doctrine. I describe these speculations, which do have some basis in the theory of learning, solely in order to demonstrate that there is a link between the goal of propaganda – action – and the linguistic transformations involved in the psychological mechanisms used to achieve the desired goal. These important aspects of communication should be studied both at the cognitive and linguistic level of the organization of the stimulus, and at the motor and emotional level of the constitution of the response, and not only at the latter level. When studied in that way, domains that are quite removed from psychology might prove to shed light on one another. It would not be very productive to go into greater detail, as we would stray far beyond the limited scope of a work that relates directly to our current understanding of propaganda.

As we have noted, the specific language of propaganda can be seen in two distinct perspectives: a semantic perspective, and a formalizing or signalling perspective. Because it is more closely linked to the latter perspective, stereotyping also shows that this language is an affective language. A lot of psychosociological research has been carried out on the action of stereotypes, and there is no need to rehearse its findings here.

That the words 'American' and 'police' have emotional connotations and that the point of using them is to transfer those connotations by giving psychoanalysis an affective aura is so obvious that we do not need to stress the point. In this case, the affective context of language is more important than the cognitive context, and *becomes* the essential context. A specific language slips out of its original context when representations give it a concrete form, bifurcates, and mutates into a system of signals on the one hand and an 'affective' language on the other. The two mutations complement one another. Stereotyping synthesizes and conceals this process. It must, however, be stressed that the expressions 'affective' and 'affective implications of a stereotype' are to be understood as referring to two kinds of effect: a 'categorical' effect and an 'assimilating' effect. When two words that once had very different meanings and very different affective 'charges' – such as 'myth' and 'psychoanalysis' or 'police' and 'psychoanalysis' – are used together in the same proposition, and with the same intent, their juxtaposition gives us a shock or a surprise. The combination 'explodes' the word 'psychoanalysis', so to speak, and gives it a new categorical life. When we frequently encounter the two words, or when they stabilize around a single meaning, their *assimilation* has, in contrast, a *reassuring* effect because it means that we can quickly find a sort of key, some security. Because they have been so often used in the same context, the words 'psychoanalysis', 'American' and 'bourgeois' eventually become interchangeable at the level of their affective resonances, and they leave no doubt as to how we are expected to respond to them. The two types of stereotype – the process that produces an affective *vocabulary*, and propaganda's trigger-words – are probably transformed into each other, with the rhythm of change being a function of their degree of repetition and acceptance. Readers who are familiar with research into linguistics will have noticed that these families of stereotypes are closely related to the two basic ways in which the grammatical structures of a language are modified, namely through attribution and analogy (Meillet 1904–5).

To go back, after this long digression, to the laws of special identity, which define the propagandist approach to cognition, we find that categorical stereotypes operate at the level of language in much the same way that tautology operates at the intellectual level, whereas assimilationist stereotypes prolong resorption. The former repeats the same sign, whilst the latter fuses two distinct signs. If we compare the linguistic effect of stereotyping with its cause and its general context – analogy – we can apply to it the conclusions drawn by linguists: analogy transforms grammatical forms as thought becomes standardized (Hermann 1951). Do we not see here one of the essential functions of propaganda, which is to establish the strictest possible unity at every level, that of language like that of thought, that of thought like that of action?

5 Final Remarks

The logics of representation, the processes that shape affective language, and the operations that 'assemble' behaviours complement and match one another. The same is true of expression and its instrument. The French Communist Party's propaganda, which we have been studying in this chapter, provides us with a very clear example: it is quite limited, and can therefore be clearly delineated, and its gradual development means that it can be analysed in a historical dimension.

What was our goal in this chapter?

First, we formulated a few criticisms of existing research into propaganda, and demonstrated the need to subject that phenomenon to an objective study that took into account both social conditions and the way they relate to its psychological and linguistic content.

Second, we suggested that propaganda should be defined as a process that shapes and instrumentalizes representation by demonstrating, following Brunswik, Piaget and Wallon, that the laws of logic and their psychological concomitants can be found in this form of communication. We also attempted to underline the link between dualistic social situations, the polarization of groups, and the functions of propaganda and its cognitive structuration.

Third, we emphasized the link between representation, its modalities of action and language. An examination of the role repetition plays in propaganda allowed us to demonstrate that equal attention should be paid to its cognitive and affective aspects. Far too little attention has been paid to the former in both social psychology and other domains. One form of repetition synthesizes the transformation of a representation into a set of linguistic signs, which raises the problem of special language and stereotyping. It was quite important to emphasize, at this stage in the argument, that theories which claim that the stereotype-word is unaffected by other developments remain at a superficial level, even though they do understand its instrumental aspect. This also has practical implications: the effectiveness of propaganda is not bound up with the stereotypical use of stereotypes, but with the *transformation* of representations into stereotypes. The doctrine of the all-powerful nature of propaganda is based upon a belief in the stereotypical use of stereotypes, but it overlooks the all-important problem of the representation's adequacy to a situation, and to intra- and intergroup relations. It is its adequacy that determines the development and effectiveness of this mode of communication.

Fourth, we stressed, like other authors, the importance of learning and conditioning processes, not in themselves but in relation to linguistic stereotyping. In the absence of any experimental research, we cannot get very far. But we are still entitled to assume that, given that the goal of propaganda is to produce behaviour, the mechanism of its production – learning – explains why it is that the language is so stripped down and why thought is simplified as a result of the generalization of signs. This provides, at least hypothetically, a link between the demands of social reality and those of psycho-physiological organization. But until such time as we arrive at a better understanding of these questions, we have to accept the hypothesis on a purely provisional basis.

Fifth, in our examination of affective language we attempted to demonstrate that, in this form of communication, cognitive organization corresponds to linguistic organization, and tried to outline their unity. In this context, we placed the emphasis on those linguistic signs that have only two values – positive and negative – as the poles of the social model and the representation.

The task we set ourselves was to discover the resultant unity that justifies the sequence of signs by comparing these phenomena with other and better known phenomena at every stage and at every level – situational, linguistic and psychological – of the analysis. It is to be feared that the inadequacy of our raw materials, our analysis and our general knowledge does not allow us to arrive at a flawless conceptualization of this process. We do, however, have here a line of investigation that could be pursued further.

Can the theory we have outlined be applied to all propaganda? Yes, because the example we have been studying is, despite its singularity, fairly typical. What is more, the phenomena that are usually associated with propaganda, as revealed by many studies, can be better understood once they have been reinterpreted. Phenomena such as stereotypes, prejudices and uniform behaviours converge, and support our hypotheses. No, because it would take further research[15] along the same lines into broader propaganda campaigns, and more specific experimentation on the formation of stereotypes, phenomena of repetition, and relations between signal-words and affective reactions. The most recent experimental research shows that the analysis presented here is necessary and may corroborate it.

Whether or not the arguments put forward by Communist thinkers are correct and whether or not their evaluation of the historical situation is valid are questions that can scarcely be dealt with here. The observer must recognize that some extensions of psychoanalysis have a social content of which they cannot approve. Their critique of psychoanalytic theory echoes other external and internal critiques of psychoanalysis that start out from very different positions. Freud himself does not appear to have understood

---

[15] It can be observed that we have not at any point taken into account 'Machiavellianism' or the 'conspiracies' of those who produce propaganda. In the first place this is because one does not find any 'Machiavellianism' in the case studied. Second, 'manipulation' and 'conspiracy' are forms of intention which need to be explained rather than providing explanations. The fact remains that they play a large role in propaganda.

or appreciated Marxism. He did not give a favourable welcome to social-
ism and Communism, and is said to have remarked that Communism and
psychoanalysis do not get along (Nelson 1957: 127). Yet it did seem to Freud
that some aspects of Marxism meant that it was part of his world of rational and scientific thought. This made him much more reluctant to condemn
Marxist theory than religion. His attitude towards the latter was usually
very clearly defined:

> It is not permissible to declare that science is one field of human mental activ-
> ity and that religion and philosophy are others, at least its equal in value, and
> that science has no business to interfere with the other two: that they all have
> an equal claim to be true and that everyone is at liberty to choose from which
> he will draw his convictions and in which he will place his belief. A view of
> this kind is regarded as particularly superior, tolerant, broad-minded and
> free from illiberal prejudices. Unfortunately it is not tenable and shares all the
> pernicious features of an entirely unscientific *Weltanschauung* and is equiva-
> lent to one in practice. It is simply a fact that the truth cannot be tolerant, that
> it admits of no compromises or limitations . . . Of the three powers which
> may dispute the basic position of science, religion alone is to be taken seri-
> ously as an enemy. (Freud 1933: 160)

Freud finds it inconceivable that the supremacy of science and reason
might be challenged. Whilst his attitude towards religion is quite confident, he finds Marxism disturbing for a number of reasons. First, it is one
of his adversaries: 'The other opposition has to be taken far more seriously,
and in this instance I feel the liveliest regret at the inadequacy of my information' (Freud 1933: 176). As a later passage shows, Freud did not in fact
try to understand Marx's work properly. He found it impossible to accept
that 'economic motives are the only ones that determine the behaviour
of human beings in society' (Freud 1933: 178). He found some aspects of
the Bolshevism disagreeable, but was not an implacable enemy of the
Soviet Union:

> At a time when the great nations announce that they expect salvation only
> from the maintenance of Christian piety, the revolution in Russia – in spite of
> all its disagreeable details – seems none the less like the message of a better
> future. Unluckily neither our scepticism nor the fanatical faith of the other
> side gives a hint as to how the experiment will turn out. The future will tell
> us; perhaps it will show that the experiment was undertaken prematurely,
> that a sweeping alteration of the social order has little prospect of success
> until new discoveries have increased our control over the forces of Nature
> and so made easier the satisfaction of our need. (Freud 1933: 181)

These pronouncements and these criticisms of Marxism insofar as it is the
official doctrine of a state clearly demonstrate that Freud, who was a man

with a very classical culture, had a relatively great confidence in the powers of Nature, and much less confidence in our ability to transform society. His attitude is based upon a combination of inadequate information, a lack of understanding and criticism. He is also convinced that only applied psychology can provide a scientific understanding of society. The way so many, though not all, psychoanalysts deny the importance of the social environment is inevitably the focus of criticisms from Marxists. The practical implications of their attitude have been noted, even (or especially) in the United States, where it can be argued that the worst thing about the Freudian revolution is the growing tendency to attribute any criticism of American society to individual 'illness'. A rebel is regarded as a neurotic rather than as someone who is making a valid protest. Orthodox Freudians have a tendency to support the status quo as though it were a natural order, and to blame individuals. Freud himself never made the same mistake, and no one could have convinced him that the Viennese society in which he lived was 'normal'.

Whilst the intellectual struggle, whatever form it may take, does not always resolve the problems it sets out to resolve, it does of necessity have truth as its ideal. We may stray from it at times, but we never abandon it.

We have not been able to measure the effects of Communist propaganda with any accuracy.[16] There is, however, no shortage of indirect evidence. The only social group to be really affected by this propaganda is made up of intellectuals. The other groups surveyed – workers, the middle classes and students in technical schools – do not accord it any great importance. The only themes to have a certain impact are those pertaining to the prioritization of social factors, as opposed to psychological factors, the dangerous nature of analytic therapy and its links with the United States. The American theme is very general: Communists insert it into a political context. The rejection of psychoanalysis is not, however, unanimous. It is accepted that it can have particular applications, such as criminology and education. Much of psychoanalytic *theory* is accepted. Neither its political character nor its application to the solution of social problems is rejected or accepted by significantly more Communists than other subjects from all the populations surveyed. If we accept that anti-psychoanalytic propaganda is in part anti-American propaganda, it seems that it has indeed been successful. The findings of the survey

---

[16] This question is a symptom of my naïveté at that time. Even though, given my experience, I should have known better, I was still convinced that the members of the French Communist Party had a higher level of knowledge of Marxism. In a recent book, Lucien Sève, who belonged to the leading group of the Party, showed that this was not the case. Marxism was spread outside the Party and rather ignored inside it. 'Thus the general landscape in relation to Marx tended progressively, no doubt to say it with some exaggeration, toward the dichotomy between a Party without a Marxist culture and a Marxist culture without a Party' (Sève [1969] 2004: 171).

demonstrate in detail the effects the campaign has had on the opinions of the people interviewed.

A detailed discussion of these different problems would take us a long way from our initial goal, which was to outline a theoretical analysis of propaganda that can be more widely applied. Perhaps the only thing that can either refute it or validate it is further research.

Fifteen Years Later

Three unanswered questions

Various parties asked me to update this chapter on the Communist Party's anti-psychoanalytic propaganda. I saw no reason to undertake that supplementary task, as it seemed to me that my analysis of the system of communication remains valid. I was told that the analysis had to be updated, given that the Communist Party's attitude towards psychoanalysis has changed. I bowed to that argument, but not without many hesitations. To update the analysis, things would have to be put into perspective, and some very serious questions would have to be answered. How was it that a Communist Party founded on the basis of a scientific doctrine rejected, at one time or another, most scientific innovations – from cybernetics to chemistry, from the Copenhagen version of quantum physics to psychoanalysis, – and accepted them only after a long delay? Why should people who, in the name of the Communist Party and Marxism, had acted as pitiless censors and exercised a sort of intellectual 'terrorism', either left the Party or adopted an intellectual attitude very similar to the one they once denounced so mercilessly and even pursued classic careers? We have only to look at the old collections of communist journals, and then at the censors' current publications, to see that this is indeed the case. When, as a student, I was working on my thesis, I had few contacts in so-called intellectual circles, and I imagined that the people who spoke in the name of the Communist Party, Marxism and the working class or who, in a word, spoke out against the bourgeoisie and 'bourgeois', 'American sciences', lived in close contact with that class and were only weakly integrated into the bourgeois class against which they had rebelled. The lingering images of Marx, Lenin, Politzer and even Nizan led me to think that a class position had a practical meaning as well as a theoretical meaning.

I can now see that the group of people who spoke in the name of the working class worked, on the one hand, alongside very Parisian psychoanalysts – with all that the word 'Parisian' implies – and, on the other, at the

Ecole Normale Supérieure, which, after all, represented the pinnacle of the university apparatus at that time, and perhaps even more than that. Of course they were members of the Communist Party and self-proclaimed Marxists. But when I read them, I could not help wondering, given their high degree of sociological integration whether, when they adopted a position with respect to this or that school of psychoanalysis, they really were challenging it from outside, or whether they were involved in quarrels within psychoanalysis in particular and bourgeois society in general. What, in other words, is the criterion that allows us and them to tell if they are expressing a class position? Are they speaking as 'proletarians' talking to 'bourgeois', or 'bourgeois' – or 'mandarins', as students now call them, speaking out against other 'bourgeois' or 'mandarins'? Hindsight means that we have to pay attention to these questions, which have more to do with a sociology of knowledge that has yet to come into being than with a social psychology of communications. I know that these are complex and embarrassing questions, but they are at the very heart of this real clarification and the requests that were addressed to me. Answering them would, however, mean writing a new book, and I have neither the inclination nor the time to do so. I have therefore simply collected some documents and briefly summarized them.

Documents on a development

The circumstances

The 1960s were a period of peaceful coexistence at the international level and of Gaullism in France. The working-class movement was denouncing the crimes and errors of the Stalinist period. Paradoxically these were also years of optimism. As the colonial empires had been overthrown on parts of Planet Earth, there was a belief that we had entered an age of abundance, consumerism, continuous growth and a planned improvement of standards of living. Memories of the hot war against Hitler and the cold war between the capitalist system and the socialist system were beginning to fade, and we were entering an era of phoney peace under the protection of nuclear weapons. At the intellectual level, structuralism was asserting its pre-eminence as we saw the publication of new 'readings' guided by its principles, whilst linguistics was becoming the dominant science and dethroning economics, history and even sociology. Everyone was turning away from empiricism, which had been the great post-war discovery, and towards rather formal theories.

What Lacan later called 'the structuralist tub' had in fact helped to bring about the unification of part of the human sciences and their theorists, from the Marxists to the psychoanalysts. The theorists were almost like De Gaulle: they had style, authority and charisma, and thought they had a universal intellectual stature. In the area that concerns us, they included Althusser and Lacan. Lévi-Strauss had made a scientific contribution that was unchallengeable but kept himself apart and devoted himself to purely anthropological work.

During these years, it was obvious that the diffusion of psychoanalysis in France had given it a dominant position that was unequalled in any other country, the United States included. All these circumstances had the effect of attenuating Communist hostility towards it and even of encouraging a rapprochement between Communists and psychoanalysts. Some saw this as a betrayal, as psychoanalysis, like linguistics and anthropology, was becoming a paradigmatic science at a time when there seemed to be a declining interest in the psychology of behaviour, sociology and even economics. The slogans called for a re-evaluation, from a Marxist point of view, of non-Marxist scientific advances, and for what has to be seen as a cultural *aggiornamento*.

The events

As far as psychoanalysis is concerned, an article published by Althusser (1964) crystallized a whole tendency and in some sense legitimized Marxist research in this area. The ostracism of the past had gone, together with the contempt in which it used to be held. Its ideological implications were, of course, still subject to criticism, but a new emphasis was also being placed on its theoretical and practical richness, and on its scientific character. Neither the methods nor the arguments used were new, and they do not merit a lengthy examination. What is more interesting is the fact that only one current within psychoanalysis was taken into consideration and judged to be compatible with Marxism: the structuralist-inspired Lacanian current. There was also a recognition that Communists had to adopt a more open attitude towards psychoanalytic works. But it was the development of the works themselves, from a systematic and theoretical point of view under the authority of Lacan, that made possible the new openness. Basically, two parallel developments made it possible for confrontation to give way to dialogue. Althusser's intervention was the first event, and the Communist Party's Argenteuil conference was the second. During the conference, researchers in the human sciences were encouraged to pursue their work, even if it led in different directions, provided that the Party's general line and historical materialism were respected. Marxist-inspired work on psychoanalysis flourished as a result. It also became legitimate, which had not been the case in the past. The Conference established the general line: a scientific psychoanalysis with its own object and its own laws had to be developed, and it had to be articulated with materialist science. Since then a great number of works have clarified and followed that line, and their content is of considerable interest.

Psychoanalysis: between science and ideology

Like any science born of capitalist society, psychoanalysis has a scientific kernel and an ideological shell. Marxist analysis makes it possible to extract the kernel from the shell, to integrate the kernel and to throw away the shell. As a science, psychoanalysis has a specific object: the unconscious. It is this that gives it its specificity and its interest. Everything it teaches us about the unconscious has to do with its object, and everything it tries to extrapolate into the social and the cultural has to do with the subjectivity of false class consciousness, and therefore ideology. Even though it is specific, psychoanalysis is therefore not exhaustive, and Marxists have the means to isolate its essential dimensions and to make it evolve. I quote:

> 'Psychoanalysis is specific but non-exhaustive.'[17] 'Psychoanalytic terrain is not and cannot be the main terrain for an understanding of concrete individuals.'[18] 'Psychoanalysis shows us how nature becomes culture within every individual, and how the corporeal becomes psychical . . . It teaches us that what makes human nature specific is the existence of the unconscious, of a psychical structure . . . based upon the internalization of the primordial relational experiences of early childhood.'[19] 'Although there is an element of ideological illusion about it, Freud's work does contain the discovery of a real object: the Freudian unconscious, and the science of that object is irreducible to any other existing science or to historical materialism.'[20]

This is why Lacan's research represents a turning point and merits our full attention:

> 'These Freudian concepts have been reformulated by Dr Lacan. Thanks to him psychoanalysis definitely looks like a science of the unconscious.'[21] 'This prompted a considerable amount of work which, under the slogan of a return to Freud, tried to discover in the light of the recent developments in linguistics and ethnology in particular what gave Freud's discovery its specificity by freeing it from all the weight of the dominant ideology, which had almost suffocated it.'[22]

Now that it had at last been set free, Marxists could take an interest in psychoanalysis. There was also another reason: its diffusion throughout society in general and the universities in particular:

> 'We are witnessing a mass diffusion of psychoanalysis, both amongst the general public and within the universities: as a result, the rumour begun by Freud's discovery of the unconscious is spreading and becoming both

---

[17] *La Nouvelle Critique*, no. 37, 1970.
[18] Ibid., no. 26, 1969.
[19] *L'Humanité*, 30 October 1970.
[20] *La Nouvelle Critique*, no. 39, 1970.
[21] *L'Humanité*, 24 February 1970.
[22] *France Nouvelle*, 9 January 1974.

persistent and powerful.'[23] 'Marxism cannot avoid these problems in that psychoanalysis is being diffused not only in the form of a therapeutic practice but also in the form of a theory of culture.'[24]

The facts are clear. First, there has been a return to Freud, and the terrain of psychoanalysis has been redefined around the unconscious. Second, this return and the rumours surrounding it have intensified both the social presence of psychoanalysis and the pressure it exerts on culture. Given this situation, Marxism and Marxists owe it to themselves to intervene, to check the data and to influence future developments. They must, in a word, define their attitude.

Clear-cut attitudes and ambivalent attitudes
The rejection of psychoanalysis is a hangover from the past, and is no longer tenable. How is the new attitude to be defined? This is the question that is being asked, and that Marxists are asking themselves. We can say that the new attitude is on the whole positive. It does not, God be praised, appear to be monolithic. Subtle indices allow two currents to be identified: one definitely positive, and the other more ambivalent. The first asserts the conviction that, given a few modifications, psychoanalysis stands up to a Marxist analysis:

> 'The psychoanalysis-Marxism antinomy, the choice between psychoanalysis and Marxism . . . This problematic, which we have been dragging behind us like a ball and chain for far too long, is in fact a false problem.'[25] 'Articulating psychoanalysis and Marxism raises considerable problems but also opens up many possibilities. What is at issue here is neither the essential problem of psychoanalytic therapy, nor of the insertion of that therapy into medical institutions, but only the implications of psychoanalysis in the field of research into the human sciences.'[26]

The second current, which is mainly illustrated by the work of Lucien Sève (1975), appears to be more ambivalent, as it both accepts psychoanalysis and rejects many of its concepts:

> Historical materialism, and historical materialism alone, makes it possible to construct the theory of a crucial object, because it is the foundation of the science of human relations. That object is the system of historically ordered social acts that determines the biography and personality of an individual. Those two objects are articulated together in all our lives.[27]

---

[23] *L'Humanité*, 24 April 1970.
[24] *La Nouvelle Critique*, no. 43, 1971.
[25] Ibid., no. 30, 1970.
[26] *L'Humanité*, 24 April 1970.
[27] *La Nouvelle Critique*, no. 39, 1971.

The issue at stake sheds light on the reasons for this ambivalence. What is that issue? At a methodological level: do we have to move from Marxism to psychoanalysis, or from psychoanalysis to Marxism? At the explanatory level: which is the crucial factor in development – labour or desire?

Whilst the first current avoids this issue or skirts around it, the second insists upon the absolute pre-eminence of Marxism and labour. Hence the implicit reservations about psychoanalysis and the dialogue with psychoanalysts:

> The problem is both that of historical materialism's assimilation of one of psychoanalysis's essential insights, and that of a recognition of its inability to ground a science of the adult personality in the system of social relations. The social dimension of labour has, of course, no status in psychoanalysis's conceptual system.[28]

As for the current dialogue, we are warned to make no attempt at reconciliation: the psychoanalysts have to make the first move:

> The renewed interest in psychoanalysis does not stem from purely external concerns about ideological ecumenism, but from the progress of our own research . . . And from the fact that many psychoanalysts appear to be taking an interest in Marxism.[29]

We are not in a position to say which of the two currents is the more important. Their existence seems to me to be plausible. The indices are, however, so fragile and so hidden that I do not see how the issue can be decided with any certainty without studying the question in greater depth. Regardless of which of the two is the more accurate expression of the Communist Party's attitude, both currents are attempting to remodel psychoanalysis in such a way as to make it compatible with the general principles of Marxism. Let us take a few examples.

Psychoanalysis in the light of Marxism
Before they can be assimilated, psychoanalytic concepts and psychoanalysis itself must be purified by a series of operations. The following quotations give some ideas as to their nature, and they do not require much commentary:
1   Science divorced from ideology:

> 'Psychoanalysis also has to be cleansed by the Marxist science of society of the sociological ideologies in which it is still trapped.'[30] 'Dialectical

---

[28] *La Nouvelle Critique*, no. 26, 1969.
[29] Ibid., no. 37, 1970.
[30] Ibid.

materialism needs to re-evaluate the psychoanalytic phenomenon, because its function is to prove a scientific re-evaluation of contemporary domains and ideologies.'[31]

2 Psychoanalytic method divorced from psychoanalytic theory:

'The main interest of the book [Chertok and Saussure 1973] is that it repositions psychoanalysis in its home territory – the clinical and the therapeutic – and allows it to retain its characteristic therapeutic empiricism, which makes it open to all theoretical reflections and approaches.'[32] 'I still insist that there is more to psychoanalysis than a scientific method, but it does comprise a scientific method with a therapeutic future.'[33] 'For a science, it is still too close to empiricism, with its vague and confused theorisation.'[34]

3 Children divorced from adults:

Psychoanalysis has a particular object and a particular domain, and historical materialism has a different object and domain. The object of psychoanalysis: the humanization of young children within the context of the family, and with the help of the Oedipal structure. Historical materialism is the science of social formations. It probably can generate a theory of the individual, and of individualization, but individualization and humanization are not the same thing.[35]

Hence too the condemnation of and the emphasis on the failure of psychoanalysis to recognize the specific determinations of the adult personality and the permanent temptation to discuss only the determinations of childhood.

The meaning of these divorces is obvious from the quotations. I will sum it up for the benefit of the reader. When they divorce psychoanalysis-as-science from psychoanalysis-as-ideology, these critics are happy to leave it to explore the unconscious and the neuroses, but reject the cultural, anthropological and historical theories and metatheories which, as we know, played such an important role in Freud's thought and the diffusion of psychoanalysis from *Totem and Taboo* to *Moses and Monotheism*. At the same time, it is asserted that Marxism alone is competent to theorize the cultural, anthropological and historical domains. The method–theory divorce, which is analogous to the divorce we found in the Catholic press, admits that psychoanalysis has undeniably accumulated a body of

---

[31] *L'Humanité*, 24 April 1970.
[32] *La Nouvelle Critique*, no. 70, 1974.
[33] Ibid., no. 44, 1971.
[34] Ibid., no. 30, 1970.
[35] Ibid., no. 37, 1970.

knowledge, and does not seek to change it. At the same time, it authorizes the intervention of Marxists who wish, and think it necessary, to give psychoanalytic theory the true scientificity that it has yet to acquire:

> 'There is no such thing as a Marxist conception; there are Marxist researchers who are trying to give psychoanalysis access to scientificity.'[36] 'The role of the Marxist researcher is to look at what is going on and to work towards a constructive critique on scientific grounds . . . Leaving psychoanalysis to the psychoanalysts would give social tranquilizers an even greater role.'[37]

What, finally, is the role of the concrete divorce between children and adults, and of the more verbal divorce between humanization and individualization? A lot could be said about this. But psychoanalysis is primarily interested in childhood and the family romance [*roman*], and if childhood came to be seen as the site of the essential determination of adult life and the historical novel [*roman*], it would be impossible to articulate it with Marxism. If, on the other hand, the world of maturity is divorced from the world of childhood, and the circle of society from the family circle, they can be quietly replaced by the relations of production and by the dynamics of history without any great difficulty. Provided, of course, that labour, rather than desire, has the leading role it deserves. Marxism's explanatory power can also be safeguarded. I quote once more:

> We do not criticize psychoanalysis for taking no interest in the productive forces or the relations of production. They are not its object. What does annoy us is that it claims to be able to explain cultural phenomena and social movements in terms of flows of instinctual energy, or in libidinal terms, which means that it inevitably fails to see the countless complex mediations that are required if we are to explain problems that exist at a specific level of human existence.[38]

Once all these things have been divorced, psychoanalysis becomes acceptable, so to speak. It is now possible to be both a Marxist and a psychoanalyst. But the two currents have not been synthesized in the true sense of the term. To date, Marxists have not been seen to make any specific contribution to the scientificity of psychoanalysis nor, conversely, has psychoanalysis made any contribution to Marxist analysis. That appears to be out of the question, for many reasons. It seems that these critics were preoccupied with resolving an inner-Party conflict over Freud's discoveries, and with transforming a cold war into peaceful coexistence at the scientific level. As these authors constantly remind us, the ideological

---

[36] Ibid., no. 30, 1970.
[37] *L'Humanité*, 24 April 1970.
[38] *La Nouvelle Critique*, no. 30, 1970.

struggle must go on, just as it did in the past. We will see in a moment how it goes on and who the enemy is.

This peaceful coexistence develops on the following basis. First, the practice of psychoanalysis. It is fully accepted: they would like to see it being democratized and made available to all 'on a public-service basis and in a context of democratic health protection'.[39] Once the financial barriers have been removed, democratization will begin to transform both the theory and the practice. Second, its integration into a scientific vision of society will give psychoanalysis access to a class-based critique and to progressive positions. Third, the model and assistance provided by the dialectical method will make it possible to discover and have confidence in its laws. This will preserve the value of Lacan's scientific victories, which have been misunderstood or badly received by the other schools of psychoanalysis, which are still paddling about in a pre-scientific and pre-Lacanian hell and squandering Freud's heritage. It is no exaggeration to say that there are Lacanian Marxists, or that they are the only ones to show their faces all the time, and take a clear-cut stance. And they are the authors of the most significant articles, or simply of most of the articles. They are involved in the interschool squabbles which, for the last twenty years, have been rocking French psychoanalytic associations, and in the academic wars they have started.

The absence of sex

It has to be said from the start that very little is being said about sexuality in all this. There is no end of talk about language, the unconscious, the Oedipus complex, epistemology and *jouissance*. Almost no one talks about libido. The reasons why are unclear. It has something to do with the evacuation of the biological. Here, they are following Jacques Lacan, and they give him the credit:

> Although he clearly indicates the place of the drive as a motor cause – the 'empty cauldron', as he puts it, 'from which psychical phenomena emerge', and gives it a specific materiality – he takes away its 'biological' insertion in the sense that there is no substance specifically dedicated to the workings of the unconscious.[40]

The question of the level at which sexuality has to be located is more embarrassing. I think that, whatever they may say, they are embarrassed about talking about sexuality in simple or concrete terms. A veil of abstraction periodically covers up anything to do with it. There is also more to it than this. In Freud's view, the libido has, as we have already seen, an

---

[39] Ibid., no. 52, 1972.
[40] Ibid., no. 37, 1970.

explanatory, and therefore essential, function. Marxists take a different view: labour and the relations of production are the factors that explain individual and collective history. They may accept that the libido plugs a gap in the reality envisaged by Marxist science, but not that it points to a gap in that science itself. The debate between psychoanalysis and Marxism revolves around an unanswered question that can be summarized as follows: is it sexuality and the economy that determines the evolution of man and society? There is nothing to prevent Marxists and psychoanalysis from reaching agreement about therapy, interpretation, desire and so on. But when this question is raised – and how can it be avoided? – there is open disagreement and the old contradictions reappear. How can this difficulty be avoided? By simply saying nothing about it and taking a scientific interest in psychoanalysis. Everyone knows that progress in the direction of scientificity has always meant the de-eroticization of the object, the de-sexualization of knowledge and the de-libidinalization of the subject, who loses all *libido sciendi*. In the name of the law, and for the greater good of the law.

On an infantile disorder
In the 1960s there was 1968, and in 1968 the month of May. One of its causes and effects was the birth and development of what is vaguely termed *gauchisme*. It is a well known fact that Communists have always fought against it on the grounds that it is an infantile disorder and that we grow out of it as we get older. The anarchists, the irregulars, the lumpenproletariat and the petty bourgeois are basically the scum of the earth; they carry germs that have to be isolated before they can infect the healthy sections of society and the proletariat. *Gauchisme*, however, is constantly being reborn and rises from the ashes like the phoenix; it is like a virus that, after a period of retreat, becomes resistant to antibiotics and spreads even more quickly than before. This time, its resistance was based on Freudo-Marxism, whose most famous thinker – I use the word loosely – is Reich. From the leftist point of view, the sexual revolution is part and parcel of the social revolution. This is the ground on which its Communist enemies gather to attack it in the language of the past, and with an intellectual and verbal violence that denounces, in the same terms, so-called liberation, the protests of some young people and, therefore, a certain psychoanalysis: a muddled psychoanalysis in, so to speak, jeans, and with long hair.
Here are a few samples. No commentary is required.

> The damaging effects of American-style psychoanalysis, which means mass psychological counselling for the bourgeois class, and of Freudo-Marxism, which is a leftist ideology made up of bits and pieces, have helped to widen the gulf between psychoanalysis and Marxism.[41]

[41] *L'Humanité*, 24 April 1970.

Worse than the anathemas of 1968? It's a rhetorical question. The important thing is that the ball is now in the other court – Reich's court.

> Trapped in the idealist problematic of Freudo-Marxism. On the one hand, the individual, motivated by drives emanating from what is basically a biological nature; on the other, society, which represses the drives so as to preserve the bourgeois order.[42]

Surprise, surprise, the materialism–idealism antagonism is back. It is used to determine the longitude of Reich, who has had an effect on the way young people behave and who has driven them to 'leftism' and not, for example, that of Lacan, who has had a purely discursive effect and who has reminded our youngsters of the name of the Father with a capital 'F' and of the presence of the Other with a capital 'O'.

Liberation? A class-bound fantasy:

> Psychoanalysis claims to be a doctrine of liberation, or even a revolutionary doctrine. This is a singularly naïve claim. It has a revolutionary impact at the level of sexuality, but to claim that the sexual revolution must precede, promote or aid the political revolution is yet another petty-bourgeois illusion.[43]

It is impossible to find out more about the author's sources of information or about the basis for his assertions. Yet we have seen in the course of some lengthy chapters that propaganda does not have to justify itself: it creates dichotomies in order to exclude, and stereotypes to incite action. I leave the last word to B. Muldworf, who once did so much to rebuild bridges between psychoanalysis and Marxism, and who now uses Professor Fougeyrollas's old weapons to denounce leftism and its Freudo-Marxist loyalties:

> Gauchisme is a clear expression of the individual's internal struggle to read a compromise, which is always being challenged, between the power of instinctual forces and the constraints of social life. It is understandable that, for both psychological and political reasons, it feeds on anti-communism. Political organization is seen as an 'alienating constraint' whilst bourgeois ideology finds made-to-measure victims amongst social strata that do not know where to turn.'[44]

> Those strata in fact experience their economic and social oppression as a sort of *existential repression*: hence the entire problematic relating to sexual

---

[42] Ibid., 1 July 1972.
[43] *La Nouvelle Critique*, no. 30, 1970.
[44] *L'Humanité*, 10 March 1972.

freedom and the demand for the right to 'inner experience' and individual creativity . . . The cult of spontaneity.[45]

And that, as we know, has nothing to do with science and the revolution. They come within the remit of specialists and have to be taken seriously, by responsible adults.

From propaganda to propagation

The content analysis looked at 84 articles, most of them published in *L'Humanité* (38), *France Nouvelle* (24) and *La Nouvelle Critique* (21). Madame Catherine Sender helped with the analysis, with great intelligence and kindness. Relations between the Communist Party and psychoanalysis should obviously be the object of a much wider and better documented study. If it were carried out by a courageous researcher who has been liberated – oh, yes! – from the taboos that people of my generation found it so difficult to overcome, such a study would shed an extraordinary light on the essential workings of the intellectual and ideological life of a political organization and a nation. In my own view, the findings are clear. The anti-psychoanalytic propaganda ceased towards the end of the 1950s and the early 1960s. We then saw the start of an era of propagation or of a form of communication that corresponded to the definition of an attitude and which allowed Communists to practise and discuss a science with a social value, and to draw inspiration from it. Everything that I wrote about the Catholic Church when I was working on my thesis could be said about the Communist Party as I write this book. This is a shocking comparison, and I am the first to be shocked by it. But how can it be avoided? It is the inescapable conclusion of my analysis of the system of communications in question and, to a certain extent, an expression of its truth. It is precisely because it is surprising that it is a valuable index of the fact that we have made a discovery, and that we must accept it.

The *rapprochement* between 'psychoanalysis' and Marxism has yet to take place. In my view, it is impossible. If it ever does come about, it will be thanks to the scientific hybrids that sometimes appear, and it will lead to major changes in both points of view and practices. Such hybrids are usually bred by creators and not commentators. The way that relativity was crossed with quantum theory in the work of Dirac which led to the discovery of the existence of anti-matter, for example. But even when conditions permit it, the *rapprochement* in question will have to go a long way down a road littered with memories of the past, and those memories are not going to fade in the near future.

[45] Ibid., 8 March 1972.

To close, I ask the reader to think about André Green's description of that path. It could, in all logic, have been my starting point:

Despite the reasons we may have to be satisfied with *La Nouvelle Critique*'s decision to initiate a discussion between Marxists and psychoanalysts, it seems to me difficult – it seems to me to be impossible – for it to begin without an account of a painful dispute between Marxists and psychoanalysts. As a psychoanalyst, I cannot forget the violent stance adopted by Marxists in the same journal, as they led to psychoanalysis being accused of being a reactionary ideology in 1948. It is true that we were in the very midst of the Stalinist era. Certain signs of change indicate a desire for openness, and this debate is one of them. I may be wrong, but I do not think that this is due to a change internal to the Marxist position; it is due to the major bridgeheads that psychoanalysis has established in intellectual circles since that date. It is therefore, I fear, a debate provoked by external circumstances. The 'truth' of psychoanalysis has finally been recognized. This summing up would be incomplete if we did not add that, for its part, psychoanalysis failed to see the contribution made by Marx, and that many psychoanalysts continue not only to take no interest in it, but doubt that there is anything to be gained by looking at it. It has to be said that, in reality, it is extremely difficult to establish the terrain on which the discussion might take place. Marxism, like psychoanalysis, has very high epistemological ambitions that stretch far beyond its specific field of application. At a time when we are witnessing the dismembering of totalitarian concepts, it might almost be said that only Marxism and psychoanalysis dare to claim to be general frames of reference, but their viewpoints are so different that it may seem rash to try to find a point where they can find common cause.[46]

[46] *La Nouvelle Critique*, no. 37, 1970.

16

A Hypothesis

Having distinguished and described separately each system of communication – propaganda, propagation and diffusion – we need to review them from a comparative perspective. The autonomy postulated for them is certainly not complete. Completion is not, however, everything. The distinctions we have made therefore remain valid, and we will not dwell on the issue.

The parallel between these forms of communication and certain aspects of social representations, namely those that are most closely bound up with the generation of behaviour – opinions, attitudes and stereotypes – allows us to bring our findings together. I do not claim that the correspondence we are looking for between communication and behaviour is any more than tentative. It is neither frivolous nor imaginary. Even if it were, formulating it would probably still be a meaningful exercise. A poet, a man who knew the value of a subjectivity whose emergence scientists are so often quick to cover with a heap of facts and the austere colour of laws, once said with great insight that 'the imagination is the most scientific of the faculties, because it alone understands the universal analogy'. A metaphor is a young analogy; when it is mature, it becomes a hypothesis.

An examination of the similarities and differences between diffusion, propagation and propaganda will help to establish the frame of reference we require. The nature of the ordered links between messages provides the first dividing line. The structure of diffusion is discontinuous and disorganized. In propaganda and propagation, in contrast, the organization of themes and principles can be described as *systematic*. The above analyses lead us to conclude that, in propaganda, the systematization is necessarily dichotomous.

In diffusion, the model – or in other words the set of themes and links – consists of elements that are relatively autonomous and mobile. The fact that they are combined so regularly binds them together, even though their contours are neither clearly defined nor explicitly delineated. The convergence of these elements, which is random, is due to the existence of a multiplicity of centres of reference – professional, religious, political and cultural – and of data that are, in qualitative terms, uneven. A direction, should there be one, is more an expression of an idiosyncrasy or a statistic-ally identified constant than a clearly stated intention. Propaganda, like propagation, presupposes that models are constructed in accordance with basic guidelines and by adequately informed individuals. The use that is made of them is usually explicit, and their normative demands are clearly formulated. The difference between the two forms of communication is one of degree. In the case of propaganda, explanations and reminders of basic orientations are continuous and iterative, but once the model of propagation has been established there is no constant reference to it. Catholics, for example, have elaborated a coherent vision of psychoanaly-sis; it exists but articles on psychoanalysis do not always refer to it. The same is not true of the Communist press: the Party's positions are often emphasized, if only by a proposition or a very brief expression. Explanation is authoritarian in propaganda, but, in part, persuasive in propagation.

The links between the source of communications, the sender-group and the receiver-group are univocal in the case of both propaganda and prop-agation. The existence of an institutional infrastructure that can control its members' behaviours and options supplies further proof that these sources are the expression of a specific group. The intentions and goals are present and obvious. The realization of the aims of communication is facilitated by the existence of a set of means of influence and collective rules, the sources themselves having a certain autonomy from and author-ity over the audience at which they are aimed. A Communist or Catholic publication has a leadership role, and its line of conduct is not dependent upon its readers' tastes or general interests. The group it represents has a unity, and its positions are devoid of ambiguity. The constant interference of instructions and information reveals that the function of propaganda and propagation is primarily instrumental.

Diffusion is inserted in a more mediated way into existing social insti-tutions. The audience it is aimed at is unstable, as can be seen from its varied interests and social and cultural loyalties. The need to adapt the paper or magazine to its readership raises the perennial problem of how to create reciprocal images that can control communication. It is almost impossible to construct other networks in order to determine the way the public behaves. Definitions of its behaviour fluctuate. The distance between the sender and the social object, the appearance or the reality of non-involvement leaves a margin of freedom within which there is a ten-dency to 'go to' the receiver. In the case of psychoanalysis, the instrumen-tal aspect of communications is not always obvious or necessary. Not that there is no authority or intention; they are concealed and discontinuous.

The objectives of propaganda are to ensure that the group acts rapidly and in specific ways, and intervenes in specific contexts. One of the

consequences desired by propagation is to control existing behaviour by
changing the context and the meanings attached to it. Diffusion tends to
create a potential for action to act; it presupposes nothing more than a possible alternative that does not have to be actualized. The incitement to
action is never imperative. One of the likely outcomes of this communication system is the absence of any practical effects that go beyond mere
'verbal behaviour'. Relations between communications and behaviour are
quite diversified: they are necessary and explicit in the case of propaganda,
necessary and implicit in that of propagation, and optional, fragmentary
and local in that of diffusion.

If we look at them in terms of the structure of their message, the elaboration of social models, the links between sender and receiver and the
behaviour they seek to incite, the three systems of communication are very
different. And it is precisely the difference between them that allows us to
compare, point by point, *diffusion, propagation* and *propaganda* with *opinions, attitudes* and *stereotypes*.

*If we could not distinguish in transmission distinct organizations of social
models that are expressed in definite acts, then the preparation of those acts would
no longer have to be related to their transmission. Any form of communication
would be able to give rise to any form of behaviour or, which comes down to
the same thing, communication as a whole would have a random effect on the
processes that generate behaviour.* The development of behaviour would, in
other words, be the same in the case of propaganda, propagation and diffusion. The very nature of this alternative obliges us to accept the hypothesis: *there is a correspondence between a system of communication and the
construction of behaviour.* The parallel between certain of their respective
structural properties makes the hypothesis more likely.

As we have seen, an opinion is an evaluative assertion about a controversial question. In his study of opinions, Stoetzel (1943) amply demonstrates that opinions are unstable, malleable and specific – or in other
words contradictory. An extensive experimental literature reveals the
random and distended relationship that exists between opinions and the
processes that generate behaviour. Diffusion, for its part, uses no unitary
or overall models; it uses themes with a low level of organization and
stresses one or another particular point without indicating or presuppos-
ing that any particular form of action is required. The concomitant thematic discontinuity and the contradictions and variations mean that the
stance adopted by a publication, and therefore its message, has a certain
instability. The fluidity of diffusion converges with that of opinions. The
link between various opinions, like that between the different articles that
are diffused, is not always obvious or necessary. If one modality of communication is necessary at a given moment as a source of opinions, diffusion is the obvious choice given their structural and dynamic kinship.

The correspondence between attitudes and propagation can be
described in a number of different ways. It will be recalled that an attitude

is a psychical organization with a negative or positive orientation with respect to an object. That orientation is revealed either by a general behaviour or by a series of actions with a common meaning. The concept of attitude is closely related to that of structure. An attitude is not a collection of specific and heteronymous opinions or responses, but an organized arrangement of all those opinions and responses. It has a regulatory function: it has a selective effect on everything the subject does or thinks. Behaviour is neither the immediate nor necessary outcome. The creation of an attitude is expressive of the subject's relationship with a socially pertinent object. The action that might ensue is only probable. But if it does take place, its context and value are preordained. There appear to be powerful affinities between the properties of propagation and those of attitude. They are, however, more obvious in the case of propaganda and stereotypes.

Stereotyping refers to the simplification of the dimensions of stimuli, and to the immediacy, and sometimes the rigidity, of responses. In terms of frequency levels, the notion of stereotyping expresses the degree of generality of an opinion or the acceptance or rejection of a representation by a group or individual. The function of the repetition of the associations that helps to establish stereotypes, and the polarized orientation that it generates, mean that a parallel has to be drawn with propaganda. Our description of the latter demonstrated the importance given to the rapid genesis of stable and unambiguous behaviours. The role of iteration, a mechanism that explains and stylizes the group's essential principles, and its conjunction with cognitive and linguistic transformations underline the major role of stereotypes. Many psychosociologists have emphasized the convergences between propaganda and stereotypes, and they are very easy to grasp. There is nothing fundamentally new to be added to that tradition.

The growing interest in communicational phenomena calls for an increasingly sophisticated examination of the role they play in the shaping of behaviours. Most studies attempt to establish the existence of a link between the content of what is communicated, and the content of a given audience's responses. A further look at this domain suggests substituting the recording of global effects with the analysis of specific interactions and processes, once they have been clearly identified.

When we know their consequences at the level of behaviour, our knowledge, and certainly our power, will be all the richer. Human beings must decide about the necessity for such a force and the use which will be made of it.

Afterword

The two parts of this book have, in their own way, allowed us to observe and understand how psychoanalysis came to penetrate French society, and what effect that has had. It has not always been possible to remain neutral as we studied this. That is a fact. The study of social representations, or some aspects of their study, throws us into the midst of major cultural and practical conflicts. If we try to avoid them what we discover will be of little importance. Being aware of this danger, I have not avoided taking political or religious attitudes into consideration, or passing judgement on them. I have tried to do so objectively. Degrees of objectivity are, by their very nature, open to discussion. That is why I emphasize the attempt rather than the outcome.

The analysis of social representations comes up against one major obstacle. It arises mainly because of the coexistence of a plurality of schools and interpretations within a science, and the reduction of this to any unity is an illusion. Given that it is impossible to rely upon a coherent frame of reference that is accepted by all competent people, not only is the researcher disoriented, but at the same time, he also gains the impression that the phenomenon he is supposed to study has eluded him.

Imagine that you wanted to state in unambiguous terms just what psychoanalysis is in order to trace the stages of how it has been transformed in society. The first obstacles you encounter are the specialists' reluctance to be specific and the diversity of the object. The specialists' hesitations are understandable, no matter whether we are talking about psychoanalysis or any other theory. Current opinion can confidently state that space has three dimensions: schools, perception and behaviour are all in agreement about that. A physicist would lay down many conditions before defining the nature of that same space. Even in domains that are considered to be 'exact', there are differences of opinion and the experts do not agree with one another. We become even more perplexed and puzzled when we turn to domains in which political, religious or immediate affective issues are at stake. In order to avoid these perplexities, we often prefer to turn to history and to a past where the actors are present only in a context which the person studying it must master. That is not really the best solution.

It is because we are involved with contemporary issues, and thanks to the interaction and clashes – sometimes regular and sometimes incoherent – between groups and ideas that we remain in contact with processes that can shed light on the past and give it a meaning. Psychosociology in fact has no choice. When we are dealing with behaviours, a strict methodological approach and adequate techniques can further the attempt to achieve greater objectivity and can challenge the discrepancies, should they become too great. The work of science is never done, and its virtues lie in its ability to begin again. It is folly to want to have an immediate key to all the difficulties. The difficulties are such that some people are reluctant to attempt an analysis of all the problems, and they then nibble away at the most superficial aspects instead of taking them on as a totality. It is an illusion to believe that this acquits us of our responsibilities. One day or another, we will have to go back to the totality, especially if we are studying it *in vivo*, and it is best to tackle it from the start, even if we do not really have the means to do so, and even in the midst of the uncertainties I am referring to.

Social psychology does not start at a very high level, and its knowledge is not excessive. Nevertheless, it does provide us with a few signposts that might allow us to go into these issues in greater depth. One might indicate first of all the necessity of a delimitation of the domains of social life and the exploration of their respective social representations as a function of a preliminary classification. Those representations must be strictly comparable, not because they can be related as descriptive contents, but because they are relevant to a shared conceptual vision. The purpose of a theoretical essay is to provide a basis that can be modified as required when we come to look at phenomena. Particular processes and aspects of the phenomena being studied must also be approached at a more localized level. Any detailed knowledge of their specific complexion is likely to have repercussions on our conception of the whole. Experimental observation and experiments allow us to specify the problems that we can only observe very indirectly. We can, for instance, trace the history of a new object of representation from its beginnings to its spread throughout a community whose contours can be clearly defined. If we use adequate techniques, the structuration of opinions can be compared with behaviour, and that can facilitate an examination of the respective roles played by fields of representation and attitudes in the genesis of behaviours. Despite all the research that has already been carried out, the entire domain of communications is there to be rediscovered if we concentrate more on its function and its mediators. The analysis of types of relation and of the nature of communication systems opens up a major field for experimental exploration. Those systems must, finally, be related to other psychosociological phenomena. Such contacts usually displace centres of gravity. If we displace our centre of gravity in this way, understanding their linguistic, cognitive and situational concomitants is more important than understanding the effects the content of the sender-source has on the receiver's reaction.

The social sciences are not technically equipped to solve all the problems I have listed or to give them a more adequate scientific formulation. But, because of the collective demands they must meet, it is impossible for them to restrict themselves to the realm of the possible. It is tempting for them to stray far beyond their initial vocation, using the methods we have in the hope that their wanderings and the need they express will lead to advances. When the gap between these methodological approaches and their theoretical aspirations narrows, the hypotheses will still have their importance, but they will be less widely applicable than they are here. That ideal can be attained if, in the future, society makes as much effort to discover the truth as it has made to conceal it.

I want to conclude this book by expressing two convictions. The first is that the grouping of the twin perspectives developed here concerning social representations and systems of communication is a question still to be solved. A question I kept asking myself while undertaking this study could be stated thus: how do people construct their social reality? While the actor sees the problem, the observer does not see the historical solution to the problem. Marx was aware of this dilemma when he wrote: 'Men make their own history, but they do not make it just as they please; they do not make it under circumstances chosen by themselves, but under circumstances directly encountered, given and transmitted from the past'(1968: 97). My second conviction is that the choice of psychoanalysis was the right one for opening a new field of research. Its novelty expressed in the strange answers given to familiar questions provided not only fresh knowledge but also a different orientation to everyday life. Neither intellectual praise nor scientific change guided this chance, but mainly the demand of the public, the conditions in which the members of the community were willing to expose themselves to its discovery during the ongoing conversations in French society.

One may apply the word 'revelation' to a striking or unexpected experience. In the present case, of course, the experience was that psychoanalysis, until then a movement chiefly restricted to intellectual and artistic circles, encountered the dominant religious expressions in France after the Second World War, i.e. the religion of the Roman Catholic tradition and the religion of revolutionary Marxism as the political doctrine of the Communist Party.

We are now informed about the circumstances in which this encounter took place, what was said and so passionately communicated about the dangers and shortcomings of psychoanalysis. It is probably an auspicious circumstance when a theory, instead of being able to get out of a field of tension, becomes a part of the culture in this tension, as also happened to the Darwinian theory of natural selection.

The usefulness, not to say the heuristic value of the theory of social representations, is, I think, that it suggests an approach to a metamorphosis of psychoanalysis in our contemporary culture and by this culture. I refer mainly to the relations between Freud's theory and practice, the talking cure and common sense, everyday language or the perceived experience of the public at large.

Since this study was completed we have witnessed the continuous recession of Catholicism and Marxism with communism disappearing into the background. Further, we have observed a growing individualism and the attention paid to private life, intersubjective relations, creating a public space in which psychological problems were more openly approached. At the same time psychological language was legitimized and widely used. We may disagree on the list of causes, but not on the trend and the outcome to be expected. Folk psychoanalysis is the creation and index of our age.

Appendix

The various samples are made up as follows: the 'representative' sample includes 402 subjects; a comparison with the Institut Français d'Opinion Publique's interviewees reveals a certain adequacy:

Table A.1 Comparison of representative sample with IFOP survey

Sample	Men (%)			Women (%)
IFOP	51			49
Survey	47			53

Sample	age 20–34 (%)	35–49 (%)	50–64 (%)	65+ (%)
IFOP	35.3	31	21.8	11.9
Survey	40	35	18	7

Sample	Wealthy classes (%)	Poor classes (%)	No information (%)
IFOP	30.6	61.8	7.6
Survey	31.7	63.4	4.9

- The 'middle-class' sample includes 335 subjects, of whom 40 per cent are office workers, 35 per cent housewives, and 25 per cent businessmen, industrialists and civil servants. In the 'middle-class A' sample, 49 per cent of subjects are women, and 51 per cent are men; 21 per cent, 41 per cent and 38 per cent have, respectively, a low, average and high level of education. In the 'middle-class B' sample, 62 per cent of those interviewed were women and 38 per cent were men; 43 per cent, 44 per cent and 13 per cent had, respectively, a low, average and high level of education.
- The 'liberal professions' sample includes 175 subjects, of whom 70 per cent are men and 30 per cent women; 24 per cent of these subjects

were doctors, 12 per cent were lawyers, 12 per cent were technicians, 9 per cent were priests and 43 per cent were primary or secondary schoolteachers.

- The 'student' sample included 140 subjects in the pilot study and 892 in the survey. Their specialities were as follows: sciences 22 per cent, medicine 18 per cent, arts 12 per cent, philosophy 20 per cent, law 16 per cent and other schools 16 per cent.
- The 'pupils at technical schools' sample included 101 subjects in the pilot survey and 200 in the survey; 44 per cent were male and 56 per cent were female.
- The 'working-class' sample included 426 subjects, 216 of whom had, as we have seen, no knowledge of psychoanalysis. Of the workers interviewed in Paris, 71 per cent were men and 29 per cent were women; 51 per cent were aged between 20 and 35, 33 per cent between 35 and 50 and 16 per cent were older.

Bibliography

Abelson, R.P. and Rosenberg, M.J. (1958), 'Symbolic Psycho-logic: A Model of Attitudinal Cognition', *Behavioural Science*, 3: 1–13.

Adorno, Theodor, W., Frenkel-Brunswik, Else, Lavinson, Daniel, J. and Sanford, R. Nevitt (1950), *The Authoritarian Personality*, New York: Harper and Brothers.

Althusser, Louis (1971), 'Freud and Lacan', in *Lenin and Philosophy and Other Essays*, tr. Ben Brewster, London: New Left Books, pp. 177–202, first published 1964.

Anzieu, Didier (1986), *Freud's Self-Analysis*, tr. Peter Graham, London: Hogarth, first published 1959.

Asch, S.E. (1940) 'Studies in the Principles of Judgments and Attitudes. II. Determination of Judgments by Group and Ego Standards', *Journal of Social Psychology*, 12: 433–65.

Asch, S.E. (1946) 'Forming Impressions of Personality', *Journal of Abnormal and Social Psychology*, 41: 258–90.

Asch, S.E. (1952), *Social Psychology*, New York: Prentice-Hall.

Asch, S.E. (1958), 'The Metaphor: A Psychological Inquiry', in R. Tagiuri and L. Petrullo (eds), *Perception and Interpersonal Behaviour*, Boston: Harvard University Press.

Avigdor, R. (1953), 'Etude expérimentale de la genèse des stéréotypes', *Cahiers internationaux de sociologie*, 14.

Bally, C. (1935), *Le Langage et la vie*, Zürich: Max Niehans.

Bartlett, F.C. (1932), *Remembering: A Study of Experimental and Social Psychology*, Cambridge: Cambridge University Press.

Bastide, Roger (1950), *Sociologie et psychanalyse*, Paris: Presses Universitaires de France.

Berelson, B. (1952), *Content Analysis in Communications Research*, Glencoe, Ill.: Free Press.

Berelson, B. (1965), 'What "Missing the Newspaper" Means', in W. Schramm (ed.), *The Process and Effects of Mass Communication*, Urbana: University of Illinois Press, pp. 37–47, first published in R.F. Lazarsfeld and F.N. Stanton (eds), *Communication Research 1948–1949*, New York: Harper & Row, 1949.

Berger, P.L. and Luckmann, T. (1967), *The Social Construction of Reality*, Harmondsworth: Penguin.

Blumer, H. (1951), 'Collective Behavior', in A.M. Lee, *New Outline of the Principles of Sociology*, New York: Barnes and Noble, pp. 166–222.

Bonnafé, Lucien (1948), 'Le Personnage du psychiatre: étude méthodologique', *L' Evolution psychiatrique*, fasc. III: 23–57.

Boulding, Kenneth Ewart (1956), *The Image*, Oxford: Oxford University Press.

Brierley, Margerie (1951), *Trends in Psychoanalysis*, London: Hogarth Press.

Brown, R.W. (1954), 'Mass Phenomena', in G. Lindzey, *Handbook of Social Psychology*, Cambridge, Mass.: Addison Wesley.

Bruner, J. (1957), 'Freud and the Image of Man', in B. Nelson (ed.), *Freud and the Twentieth Century*, New York: Meridian Books, pp. 277–85.

Burnstein, E. (1967), 'Sources of Cognitive Bias in the Representation of Simple Social Structures', *Journal of Personal and Social Psychology*, 7: 36–48.

Canguilhem, Georges (1986), *The Normal and the Pathological*, tr. Carolyn Fawcett in collaboration with Robert S. Cohen, Cambridge, Mass.: MIT Press, originally published in French 1966.

Cartwright, D. and Harary, F. (1956), 'Structural Balance: A Generalization of Heider's Theory', *Psychology Review*, 63: 277–93.

Cassirer, Ernst (1933), 'Le Langage et la construction du monde des objets', *Journal de psychologie*, 30.

Cavell, S. (1976), *Must We Mean What We Say?*, Cambridge: Cambridge University Press.

Chakutin, Serge (1946), *The Rape of the Masses*, New York: Fortean.

Chertok, Léon and Saussure, Raymond de (1973), *Naissance du psychanalyste de Mesmer à Freud*, Paris: Payot.

Cohen, A.R. (1961), 'Cognitive Tuning as a Factor Affecting Impression Formation', *Journal of Personality*, 28.

Dalbiez, Roland (1941), *Psychoanalytic Method and the Doctrine of Freud*, tr. T.F. Lindsay, 2 vols, London: Longmans, Green & Co, first published 1936.

David, M. (1966), *La Psicoanalisi nella cultura italiana*, Turin: Boringheri.

David, M. (1967), *Letteratura e psicoanalisi*, Milan: Mursia.

De Soto, C.B. (1961), 'The Predilection for Single Orderings', *Journal of Abnormal and Social Psychology*, 62: 16–23.

De Soto, C.B., London, M. and Handel, S. (1965), 'Social Reasoning and Spatial Paralogic', *Journal of Personal and Social Psychology*, 2: 513–21.

Doise, W. (1993), 'Debating Social Representations', in G. Breakwell and D. Canter (eds), *Empirical Approaches to Social Representations*, Oxford: Oxford University Press.

Doob, Leonard William (1948), *Public Opinion and Propaganda*, New York: Holt.

Driencourt, Jacques (1950), *La Propagande, nouvelle force politique*, Paris: Armand Colin.

Duhem, P. (1913), *Le Système du monde*, Paris: Hermann.

Durkheim, Emile (1982), *The Rules of Sociological Method*, tr. W.D. Hall, Basingstoke: Macmillan, originally published in French 1895.

Durkheim, Emile (1995), *The Elementary Forms of Religious Life*, tr. Karen E. Fields, New York: The Free Press, originally published in French 1912.

Durkheim, Emile and Mauss, Marcel (1963), *Primitive Classification*, tr. Rodney Needham, London: Cohen & West, originally published in French 1901–2.

Duveen, G. (2000), 'The Power of Ideas. Introduction', in S. Moscovici, *Social Representations: Explorations in Social Psychology*, ed. G. Duveen, Cambridge: Polity, pp. 1–17.

Evans-Pritchard, E.E. (1934), 'Lévy-Bruhl's Theory of Primitive Mentality', *Bulletin of the Faculty of Arts*, 2 (1), University of Egypt, Cairo.

Fauconnet, P. (1928), *La Responsabilité*, Paris: Alcan.

Fenichel, Otto (1946), *The Psychoanalytic Theory of Neurosis*, London: Routledge and Kegan Paul.

Foucault, Michel (1967), *Madness and Civilization: A History of Insanity in the Age of Reason*, tr. Richard Howard, London: Tavistock, originally published in French 1961.

Foucault, Michel (1989), *The Birth of the Clinic*, tr. A.M. Sheridan, London: Tavistock, originally published in French 1963.

Freud, Sigmund (1893), 'Some Points for a Comparative Study of Organic and Hysterical Motor Paralysis', *The Standard Edition of the Complete Psychological Works of Sigmund Freud* [*SE*], London: Hogarth Press and Institute of Psychoanalysis, 1953–73, 24 vols, vol I: 157–72.

Freud, Sigmund (1906), 'Psychoanalysis and the Establishment of Facts in Legal Proceedings', *SE*, vol. IX: 97–114.

Freud, Sigmund (1914), 'On the History of the Psychoanalytic Movement', *SE*, vol. XIV: 1–66.

Freud, Sigmund (1921), 'Group Psychology and the Analysis of the Ego', *SE*, vol. XVIII: 65–153.

Freud, Sigmund (1927), 'The Future of an Illusion', *SE*, vol. XXI: 1–56.

Freud, Sigmund (1933), *New Introductory Lectures on Psychoanalysis*, *SE*, vol. XXII.

Garfinkel, Harold (1967), *Studies in Ethnomethodology*, Englewood Cliffs, NJ: Prentice-Hall.

Gibson, J.J. (1960), 'Picture, Perspective and Perception', *Daedalus*, 89.

Giese, P. (1967), 'The Logic of Symbolic Psycho-Logic', *Behavioural Science*, 12: 391–5.

Glover, Edward (1940), *An Investigation of the Technique of Psychoanalysis*, London: Baillière.

Goblot, E. (1930), *La Barrière et le niveau*, Paris: Alcan.

Granet, Marcel (1950), *La Pensée chinoise*, Paris: Albin Michel.

Halbwachs, M. (1938), 'La Psychologie collective du raisonnement', *Zeitschrift für Sozialforschung*, 7.

Harvey, O.J., Hunt, D.E. and Schroder, H.M. (1961), *Conceptual Systems and Personality Organization*, New York: Wiley.

Heider, F. (1944), 'Social Perception and Phenomenal Causality', *Psychological Review*, 51: 358–74.

Heider, F. (1946), 'Attitudes and Cognitive Organization', *Journal of Psychology*, 21: 107–12.

Hermann, J. (1951), 'Le Changement analogique', *Acta Linguistica*, I: 118–69.

Hovland, C., Lumsdaine, A.A. and Sheffield, F.D. (1949), *Experiments in Mass Communication* (Studies in Social Psychology in World War II, vol. III), Princeton, NJ: Princeton University Press.

Hymes, D. (1968), 'Pidginization and Creolization of Languages: Their Social Contexts', *Item*, 22.

Isaacs, Susan (1930), *Intellectual Growth in Young Children*, London: Routledge & Kegan Paul.

Isaacs, Susan (1933), *Social Development in Young Children*, London: Routledge & Kegan Paul.

Jaspers, K. (1922), *Psychologie der Weltanschauungen*, Berlin: Springer.

Jung, Carl Gustav (1933), *Modern Man in Search of a Soul*, tr. W.S. Bell and Cary F. Barnes, London: Routledge and Kegan Paul.

Köhler, Wolfgang (1937), 'Psychological Remarks on some Questions of Anthropology', *American Journal of Psychology*, 50: 271–88.

Korzybski, A. (1933), *Science and Sanity*, Lancaster, Pa.: Science Press.

Koyré, A. (1950), 'The Significance of the Newtonian Synthesis', *Archives Internationales d'Histoire des Sciences*, 3: 291–311.

Koyré, A. (1978), *Galileo Studies*, Hassocks: Harvester Press, originally published in French 1939.

Kris, Ernst and Leites, Nathan (1965), 'Trends in Twentieth Century Propaganda', in Wilbur Schramm (ed.), *The Process and Effects of Mass Communication*, Urbana: University of Illinois Press, pp. 489–500, first published 1947.

Lagache, Daniel (1934), *Les Hallucinations verbales et la parole*, Paris: Alcan.

Lagache, Daniel (1953), 'Conduite et communication en psychanalyse', *Bulletin de psychologie*, 6: 354–7.

Lagache, Daniel (1954), 'La Doctrine freudienne et la théorie du transfert', *Acta psychotherapeutica*, VII.

Lagache, Daniel (1956), 'La Psychanalyse: évolution, tendances et problèmes actuels', *Cahier d'actualité et de synthèse de l'Encycopédie française*.

Lazarsfeld, P.F., Berelson, B. and Gaudet, H. (1944), *The People's Choice*, New York: Columbia University Press.

Lenin, Vladimir Ilich (1970), *What Is To Be Done?*, in *Selected Works In Three Volumes* I, Moscow: Progress Publishers, first published 1902.

Lévi-Strauss, Claude (1987), *Introduction to the Work of Marcel Mauss*, London: Routledge and Kegan Paul, originally published in French 1950.

Lundberg, G.A. (1926), 'The Newspaper and Public Opinion', *Social Forces*, 4: 709–15.

Martin, L. (1949), 'Psychologie de la pensée communiste', *La Revue socialiste*, 32: 464–87.

Marx, K. (1968), *The Eighteenth Brumaire of Louis Napoleon*, in K. Marx and F. Engels, *Selected Works*, London: Lawrence and Wishart, originally published in German 1852.

Maslow, A.H. (1963), 'The Need to Know and the Fear of Knowing', *Journal of General Psychology*, 68: 111–25.

McGuire, W.J. (1960a), 'A Syllogistic Analysis of Cognitive Relationships', in M. Rosenberg et al., *Attitudes, Organization and Change*, New Haven: Yale University Press.

McGuire, W.J. (1960b), 'Cognitive Consistency and Attitude Change', *Journal of Abnormal and Social Psychology*, 60: 345–53.

Mead, George Herbert (1934), *Mind, Self and Society: From the Standpoint of a Social Behaviourist*, Chicago: University of Chicago Press.

Meillet, A. (1904–5), 'Comment les mots changent de sens', *L'Année sociologique*, 1–38.

Mill, John Stuart (1970), *A System of Logic Ratiocinative and Deductive*, London: Longman, first published 1843.

Morgan, J.B. and Morton, J.T. (1944), 'The Distortion of Syllogistic Reasoning Produced by Personal Convictions', *Journal of Social Psychology*, 20.

Moscovici, Serge (1962), 'L'Attitude: Théories et recherches autour d'un concept et d'un phénomène', *Bulletin du CERP*, 11: 177–91, 247–67.

Moscovici, Serge (1963), 'Attitudes and Opinions', *Annual Review of Psychology*, 231–60.

Moscovici, Serge (1967), 'Communication Processes and the Properties of Language', *Advances in Experimental Social Psychology*, 3: 225–70.

Moscovici, Serge (1968) *Essai sur l'histoire humaine de la nature*, Paris: Flammarion.

Moscovici, Serge (1976), *Social Influence and Social Change*, tr. Carol Sherrard and Greta Heinz, London: Academic Press.

Moscovici, Serge (1993), *The Invention of Society*, Cambridge: Polity Press, originally published in French 1988.

Moscovici, Serge (2000), 'Ideas and their Development: A Dialogue Between Serge Moscovici and Ivana Markova', *Social Representations: Explorations in Social Psychology*, Cambridge: Polity, pp. 120–55.

Moscovici, Serge and Markova, Ivana (2006), *The Making of Modern Social Psychology*, Cambridge, Polity.

Moscovici, Serge and Zavalloni, M. (1968), 'The Group as a "Polarizer" of Attitudes', roneoed.

Moszkowski, Alexandre (1972), *Conversations with Einstein*, tr. Henry L. Brose, London: Sidgwick and Jackson.

Murphy, Gardner (1953), *In the Minds of Men: The Study of Human Behaviour and Social Tensions in India*, New York: Basic Books.

Nadeau, Maurice (1948), *Documents surréalistes*, Paris: Seuil.

Nelson, B. (1957), *Freud and the 20th Century*, New York: Meridian Books.

Nixon, R.B. (1948), 'Multiplication of the Decreasing Number of Competitive Newspapers', in Wilbur Schramm (ed.), *Communication in Modern Society*, Urbana: Illinois University Press.

Park, R.E. (1955), *Society*, Glencoe, Ill.: Free Press.

Parsons, A. (1955) *La Pénétration de la psychanalyse en France et aux Etats-Unis*, Paris: Faculté de Lettres (roneo).

Pavlov, I.P. (1938), 'Le Sentiment d'emprise et la phase ultraparadoxale', *Journal de psychologie*, 849–953.

Piaget, Jean (1928), 'Psychopédagogie et mentalité enfantine', *Journal de psychologie*, 25.

Piaget, Jean (1945), *La Formation du symbole chez l'enfant*, Neuchâtel and Paris: Delachaux & Niestlé.

Piaget, Jean (1949), *Traité de logique: essai de logique opératoire*, Paris: Armand Colin.

Piaget, Jean (1951), *Play, Dreams and Imitation*, London: Routledge and Kegan Paul, originally published in French 1945.

Piaget, Jean (1995), *Sociological Studies*, London: Routledge, originally published in French 1928.

Plekhanov, Georgi Valentinovich (1947), *In Defence of Materialism: The Development of the Monist View of History*, tr. A. Rothstein, London: Lawrence and Wishart.

Plekhanov, Georgi Valentinovich (1963), *Art and Social Life*, tr. A. Fineberg, London: Lawrence and Wishart, originally published as *L'Art et la vie sociale*, 1899–1912.

Politzer, Georges (1928), *Critique des fondements de la psychologie*, Paris: Rieder.

Pontalis, J.-B. (1965), *Après Freud*, Paris: Julliard.

Ramsey, C.V. and Seill, M. (1948), 'Attitudes and Opinions Concerning Mental Illness', *Psychiatric Quarterly*, 12: 428–44.

Rapaport, D. (1951), *Organization and Pathology of Thought*, New York: Columbia University Press.

Redlich, F.C. (1950), 'What the Citizen Knows about Psychiatry', *Mental Hygiene*, 34: 64–99.

Regis, Emmanuel and Hesnard, Angelo (1914), *La Psychanalyse des névroses et des psychoses*, Paris: Alcan.

Rokeach, M. (ed.) (1960), *The Open and Closed Mind*, New York: Basic Books.

Roqueplo, Philippe (1974), *Le Partage du savoir*, Paris: Seuil.

Rose, E. (1962), 'Uniformities in Culture', in N.F. Washburne (ed.), *Decisions, Values and Groups*, Oxford and New York: Pergamon Press.

Saussure, Ferdinand de (1974), *Course in General Linguistics*, tr. Wade Baskin, London: Fontana/Collins, originally published in French 1969.

Schramm, Wilbur (ed.) (1965), *The Process and Effects of Mass Communication*, Urbana: University of Illinois Press.

Segall, M.M., Campbell, D.T. and Herskovitz, M.J. (1966), *The Influence of Culture on Visual Perception*, Indianapolis: Bobbs-Merril.

Sève, Lucien (1975), *Marxism and the Theory of Human Personality*, tr. David Pavett, London: Lawrence and Wishart, originally published in French 1969.

Sherif, M. and Cantril, H. (1947), *The Psychology of Ego-Involvements*, New York: John Wiley and Sons.

Sherif, M. and Sherif, C. (1933), *Groups in Harmony and Tension*, New York: Harper & Row.

Stern, W. (1893), *Die Analogie im volkstümlichen Denken*, Berlin: R. Salinger.

Stoetzel, J. (1943), *La Théorie des opinions*, Paris: Presses Universitaires de France.

Tagiuri, R. and Petrullo, L. (1958), *Person Perception and Interpersonal Behavior*, Boston: Harvard University Press.

Tarde, Gabriel (1895), *La Logique sociale*, Paris: Alcan.

Thistlewaite, D. (1950), 'Attitudes, Structures as Factors in the Distortion of Reasoning', *Journal of Abnormal and Social Psychology*, 45: 442–58.

Wallon, Henri (1945), *Les Origines de la pensée chez l'enfant*, Paris: Presses Universitaires de France.

Weber, Max (1949), *The Methodology of the Social Sciences*, Glencoe, Ill.: Free Press.

Werner, H. (1948), *Comparative Psychology of Mental Development*, New York: Harper and Brothers.

Whorf, Benjamin Lee (1956), *Language, Thought and Reality*, New York: Wiley.

Wiener, Norbert (1949), *The Human Use of Human Beings: Cybernetics and Society*, London: Eyre and Spottiswoode.

Wittgenstein, L. (1953), *Philosophical Investigations*, Oxford: Blackwell.

Woodward, J.L. (1951), 'Changing Ideas on Mental Illness and its Treatment', *American Sociological Review*, 16: 443–54.

Zajonc, R.B. (1960), 'The Process of Cognitive Tuning in Communication', *Journal of Abnormal and Social Psychology*, 61: 159–67.

Zajonc, R.B. and Burnstein, E. (1965), 'Structural Balance, Reciprocity and Positivity as Sources of Cognitive Bias', *Journal of Personality*, 44: 570–83.

Index

sin 200; Catholic press 261, 262, 264, 272
sociability 47, 187–8; lack of 83
social change 45–6, 75–6, 150
social conflict 256, 306
social context 338; *see also* France, context
social contract 178
social controls 66, 68
social distance 313n
social factors, progressive press 294–5, 341
social influence, representation and xiv–xv
social organization and structures xxxii, 53, 250–1
social problems 26–7, 140–2, 182, 292, 341; *see also* delinquency
social psychology xxiii, xxix, xxx, 29; Moscovici's contribution xi–xvii; subjects for study 191, 193, 361–2; *see also* psychosociology
social relations 32, 106, 313; contribution of psychoanalysis to improvement of 115, 139–43; and diffusion 250–5; and propaganda 286; of psychoanalyst 92–7; *see also* groups; intergroup processes and relations
social representation(s) xxii–xxiii, xxix–xxxii, 160; basic processes 54 (*see also* anchoring process, objectification); difficulty of study 360–3; a dimension of social groups 22–9; factors determining production 163–6; and indirect knowledge 10–22; influence xiv–xv; Mosovici's theory assessed xi–xvii; natural thought 163; nature of concept 3–10; as process 29–32, 192; in propaganda 314–32; specificity of function 29–30
socialization 187–8; of knowledge xxix, 32, 34
sociology 29
Soviet psychology *see* Pavlovian psychology
Soviet Union 290, 303, 304, 305, 315, 319, 340
space, indirect knowledge 11

special identity 317, 322, 337
speech xxxii, 91, 152, 156–61; *see also* conversation; language
Spitz, René A. 268
spontaneity 354
spontaneous formalism, natural thought 168–70, 174, 193
Stalin, Joseph 288, 289
stereotypes 72, 83–4, 139, 356, 358, 359; in Catholic press 281; Communist press 301; natural thought 165, 170; propaganda xiv, 283, 285, 287, 301, 314, 324–5, 329–32, 334, 335, 336–7, 338, 339
Stoetzel, J. 325, 358
structuralism xxiii, 344, 345
subject, and representation 10–14, 20–2
subjectivity 91
suggestion 107, 109, 110, 111–12
surrealism 291, 303
survey xiv, xxxvii, 9, 233, 364–5; findings and propaganda 241–2; illustration of dimensions of social representation 23–8; notebook–questionnaire xxxiv–xxxv; populations interviewed xxxiii–xxxiv
symbolic behaviour 254, 324
symbolic level: classification and naturalization 56, 71, 72, 75, 185; explanatory theme in press 208; and language 155–6, 160–1; popularization and 49; propaganda and 315; and social representation 7, 9, 10, 21; transformation of theory into representation 62–6, 192

La Table Ronde 201
taboos xxxviii, 116, 146, 241, 264, 268; on communication 51–3, 104; transformation of theory to social representation 64, 65, 104
Tagiuri, R. 102n
Tarde, Gabriel 29, 172
tautology 317, 329, 331, 332, 334–5, 337
Témoignage Chrétien 201, 234n, 258, 260, 264, 266
Les Temps modernes 201, 203
thematic language *see* language